# The Deal From Hell

# THE DEAL FROM

# HELL

## HOW MOGULS AND WALL STREET PLUNDERED GREAT AMERICAN NEWSPAPERS

———

## JAMES O'SHEA

PublicAffairs
NEW YORK

Copyright © 2011 by James O'Shea.

Published in the United States by PublicAffairs™,
a Member of the Perseus Books Group

All rights reserved.

Printed in the United States of America.

No part of this book may be reproduced in any manner whatsoever without written permission except in the case of brief quotations embodied in critical articles and reviews. For information, address PublicAffairs, 250 West 57th Street, Suite 1321, New York, NY 10107.

PublicAffairs books are available at special discounts for bulk purchases in the U.S. by corporations, institutions, and other organizations. For more information, please contact the Special Markets Department at the Perseus Books Group, 2300 Chestnut Street, Suite 200, Philadelphia, PA 19103, call (800) 810-4145, ext. 5000, or e-mail special.markets@perseusbooks.com.

Book design and production by Eclipse Publishing Services

Library of Congress Cataloging-in-Publication Data

O'Shea, James (James E.)
 The deal from hell : how moguls and Wall Street plundered great American newspapers / James O'Shea. — 1st ed.
     p. cm.
 Includes bibliographical references and index.
 ISBN 978-1-58648-791-1 (hardcover) — ISBN 978-1-58648-865-9 (electronic)
 1. O'Shea, James (James E.) 2. Journalists—United States—Biography. 3. News-paper editors—United States—Biography. 4. Los Angeles times—History—21st century. 5. Newspaper publishing—California—Los Angeles—History—21st century. 6. American newspapers—Ownership. 7. Press monopolies—United States. I. Title.
 PN4874.O785A3 2011
 071'.3090511—dc22
                                    2011009204

First Edition

10 9 8 7 6 5 4 3 2 1

To the journalists who made
the *Chicago Tribune* and the *Los Angeles Times*
great newspapers

# CONTENTS

Preface                                       ix

Introduction: The Merger                        1
 1:  Beginnings: Des Moines                     15
 2:  Across the Street                          27
 3:  Otis Chandler's Legacy                     43
 4:  Twilight                                   55
 5:  The New Order                              69
 6:  The Cereal Killer                          85
 7:  His Seat on the Dais                      105
 8:  Inside the Merger                         123
 9:  Making News                               135
10:  A Changing Landscape                      149
11:  Market-Driven Journalism                  163
12:  Buy the Numbers                           181
13:  Count Kern                                201
14:  Civil War                                 219
15:  Up Against a Saint and a Dead Man         231

# Contents

16: Before the Fall  253

17: The Penguin Parable  269

18: Closing the Deal  293

19: Zell Hell  309

Epilogue  333

*Acknowledgments*  *349*

*Notes*  *351*

*Index*  *379*

# PREFACE

THIS IS NOT a book I wanted to write.

Soon after being fired as editor of the *Los Angeles Times* in early 2008, numerous friends called and told me I should write a book about my experiences over the years. I must confess that I had often thought about writing a book about the business I loved. I even kept a diary recording my experiences in Los Angeles in case I wanted to reconstruct some of the events for a book.

But I always thought my newspaper book would be a novel. In 2008, after several bruising years on the front lines of the newspaper wars, I had decided to put the whole thing behind me and try something else—maybe help with a political campaign or take various menial jobs to write a book about work in America. Or maybe resume my interest in photography or ride my bike from Belfast to Beirut.

Then I began thinking that no one had reported and written about the troubles confronting my craft from the perspective of a working journalist. And that's what this book is—a view of the media maelstrom from a journalist who worked in the trenches for more than three decades and loved every minute of it.

I make no apologies for my biases, and I make no excuses for the fact that I am first and foremost a reporter. As I began thinking about the disaster that has struck newspapers, I realized I really didn't know what had happened, even though I had a front-row seat running the newsrooms of two major American newspapers, the *Chicago Tribune* and the *Los Angeles Times*. If we really don't know how we got into this mess, I wondered if anyone could ever figure a way out. So I set out to report and write exactly what happened, without fear or favor.

It would be easy to condemn the people who caused this modern tragedy as venal and evil. Thousands of friends and colleagues the world over have lost jobs because of the way the industry has been managed. Some were venal, all right. But most of the people who led newspapers to this point in history were smart and thoughtful. They thought they were doing the right thing, and that's what makes the story of what happened so terrifying. It shows this disaster could happen to anyone in any industry.

■

Please visit thedealfromhell.com for pictures, videos, author interview, and more information about *The Deal From Hell*.

# The Merger

In April 1999, John Madigan walked decisively into the lobby of the Hotel del Coronado. Tall, imposing, and impeccably dressed, the Tribune Company CEO arrived at the red-turreted hotel as a star-studded guest list of some 1,200 publishers, consultants, and experts gathered for the national Newspaper Association of America (NAA) annual meeting. Seasonably cool temperatures chilled San Diego, as Madigan, head of the company that published the *Chicago Tribune*, bypassed the parlors and lobbies where publishers traded industry scuttlebutt about the story of the day, the evolving coverage of two Littleton, Colorado, students who had opened fire on classmates at Columbine High School. But the Tribune chief hadn't flown to San Diego merely to gossip or to hear luminaries like former President Gerald Ford, talk-radio host Dr. Laura Schlessinger, or Sergio Zyman, Coca-Cola's marketing guru, speak to newspaper publishers. Madigan had set up a private meeting with Mark Hinckley Willes, the CEO of the Times Mirror Company.

At six-foot-five, well groomed, and trim, Madigan has a chiseled face that could be on Mount Rushmore. A *Tribune* columnist once introduced him as a man "who has never had a bad hair day." Reared in Chicago, a town where even the choirboys are tough, Madigan arrived at Tribune in the 1970s from the world of investment banking. His goal was to whip the company into shape so its stock could be sold publicly. Reserved and sober, Madigan could be charming one moment and quite cold the next.

Madigan and his predecessor as CEO of the company, Charles Brumback, had created a corporate media powerhouse from the ashes of the old *Tribune*, a media icon made famous by the idiosyncratic Colonel Robert Rutherford McCormick, a colorful, rambunctious genius who had once tried to reinvent the English language to his eccentric taste. In the nineties, when Brumback was CEO, and Madigan the CFO, Wall Street and company insiders considered Brumback the visionary, and Madigan the financial market tactician. Brumback, a Korean War medal winner and accountant, was known for his combative personality. His embrace of new technology, and brutal, bottom-line mentality drew rave reviews from stock analysts. He overshadowed Madigan, a Marine Corps veteran who could be frank in private but highly insecure in public. After he seized the reins at Tribune, though, Madigan showed his true ambition and determination. He drove earnings into the stratosphere, cranking out a record 25 percent annual profit margin for the Tribune Company after only four years at the helm. Anyone who had bought 2,500 shares of Tribune stock in 1983 at the initial offering price of $26.75 had $1 million worth of stock in 1999. By the time Madigan entered the Hotel del Coronado, he was poised to make headlines that would shove Brumback and his legacy into the shadows. Just months before, he had challenged David Hiller, a lawyer turned newspaper executive in charge of the company's development arm, to come up with transformative ideas that would put the *Tribune* on the nation's major media map. He did not want one of those one-off TV station deals that had become standard fare at Tribune, but something big. Hiller's response: Buy Times Mirror.

Sitting upstairs in his room, above the din of the industry chatter, Willes had naïvely suspected nothing when he originally took the Tribune CEO's phone call and agreed to meet. With neatly groomed silver hair, an easy smile and melodious voice, Willes wore large wire-rimmed glasses and GQ attire. Evangelistic by nature and inclination, the devout Mormon brought to Times Mirror a mixture of William Randolph Hearst and Gordon Hinckley, Willes' uncle and the president and prophet who led the Mormon Church through a period of global expansion. Willes, who'd been recruited for the top job at Times Mirror by the legendary Chandler family in Los Angeles, could be both emotional and a tough corporate taskmaster.

Square, and proud of it, the Salt Lake City native had followed the stock market when he was in grade school and graduated from Columbia University with a PhD in economics while still in his twenties. At thirty-five, he'd been named president of the Federal Reserve Bank of Minneapolis, the youngest person the Fed governors had ever tapped to head a district bank. Willes spoke with ease and confidence to readers, newspaper executives, and Wall Street analysts alike. But he wasn't a newspaper careerist. After his tenure as a central banker at the Fed, Willes had spent 15 years at General Mills before landing his CEO job at Times Mirror. But Willes' lack of newspaper credentials meant little to the Chandlers; they had selected him to head the company founded by General Harrison Gray Otis for his ability to drive up the company's stock price. And he had delivered—fast.

As Willes and Madigan exchanged pleasantries in Willes' room and took the measure of one another, their respective companies were flourishing in an industry flush with cash. In response to competition from TV and radio, the industry had consolidated into huge corporate chains. The result? Thriving companies like Tribune and Times Mirror had far-flung operations comprising newspapers, television stations, and non-media assets that generated oodles of cash. In 1998, advertisers had pumped a record $44 billion into the coffers of American newspapers, adding muscle to the bottom lines of newspaper chains and the dwindling ranks of independently owned publishers. The gross numbers told only part of the story; newspapers posted profit margins of 20 percent and more, making them virtual cash machines that Wall Street investors coveted.

But the sky-high stock prices and fat returns that Madigan and Willes delivered for Wall Street obscured an alarming trend. Newspaper classified advertising was sinking in quicksand as publishers across the nation struggled to gain and retain readers. For their part, the journalists turned a blind eye to problems in their own industry, thanks at least in part to the time-honored wall erected between newsrooms and the business side of newspapers to maintain the integrity of the news.

The impending collapse of the classified ad franchise would strike at the heart of the industry: Of the $44 billion in industry ad revenue, classified represented nearly half, or $18 billion. A decade later, people would marvel at the speedy decline of newspapers, but even in 1999, some industry insiders warned that complacency, arrogance, and greed could cripple the business of journalism, particularly in companies with heavy investments in newspapers. Robert Cauthorn, director of new technologies at the *Arizona Daily Star*, warned publishers in San Diego: "We cling too long to a dream in which we can do things as they've always been done even as the world is rapidly changing us. Our fat profit margins have lulled us into a complacency that is very dangerous. Interestingly, the economy is retooling and transforming faster than we have retooled and transformed our industry. What happens if we step entirely out of cycle because the fundamental nature of the cycle has changed?"

Meanwhile, the news industry's flailing response to the emerging Internet threat exposed an unwarranted self-confidence. In the early 1990s, Brumback tried to interest big publishers in the New Century Network, a consortium of America's top-nine newspaper companies that would create a national news and information network online, for which customers would pay. In return, the customer would have access to a full-range of national newspaper content and services online. But industry leaders tried to ignore the Internet, fearing it would cause disproportionate damage to their existing business. Their internecine squabbles eventually destroyed the New Century initiative. Cindy Sease, a Sioux City classified ad director who also chaired the NAA's Classified Ad Federation, warned the publishers, "When we are up against huge software industry giants, we need to band together as an industry and stop worrying about knocking one another off."

As it happened, the threat posed to newspapers by software giants like Microsoft would pale in comparison to the one leveled by the little guy, a digital sniper working in an apartment, armed with little more than a dream and a computer. The industry's lock on lucrative classified ad markets allowed papers to charge $50 to $100 for a one-inch ad that would run once or twice a week. Even as Madigan and Willes sat down for what Willes thought would be a casual chat, a mere five hundred miles up the California coast, Craig Newmark, an ex-computer programmer from Charles Schwab & Co., filed papers to register craigslist as a small for-profit Internet company that would revolutionize classified advertising with free online ads.

Meanwhile, two young Stanford University graduate students an hour plane ride away had just finished solving an equation with 500 million variables and 3 billion terms. Using banks of computers, Sergey Brin and Larry Page created an algorithm called PageRank, which they housed in a start-up company they eventually called Google. Two months after Madigan and Willes met, Brin and Page announced initial public funding.

In a small Hollywood apartment, an untrained D student who worked in a gift shop at a CBS studio was gaining traction for a conservative news-aggregation site that would become a potent weapon in the cultural wars against the so-called mainstream media. Matt Drudge rooted through studio trash cans and collected gossip to cobble together a wide range of political and entertainment industry tidbits that he published on the Internet. He created the "Drudge Report," a gossipy, sloppy brand of journalism that would help undermine traditional journalistic standards and put organizations like the Tribune and Times Mirror at a disadvantage for their adherence to diligent reporting.

As Madigan and Willes sat down to talk, the Newmarks, Googles, and Drudges of the world were not even on their radar.

Willes was caught off guard by the proposal Madigan proceeded to lay out. From an investment banker's perspective, the proposed marriage of Tribune and Times Mirror made a lot of sense. By merging the two companies, Madigan envisioned a media powerhouse with a print and broadcast advertising scale and breadth that could reach eighteen of the nation's top-thirty markets, including TV stations, newspapers, and budding Internet sites in Los Angeles, New York, and Chicago. The combined company would be the nation's third-largest media company behind the Gannett and Knight Ridder companies. It would be a powerful brand that included America's best collection of quality newspapers, boasting a combined daily circulation of 3.6 million with television stations that reached an additional 38.4 million U.S. households. Madigan and others suggested that the new company would offer "national footprint, local reach," a showcase for the kind of *convergence* that media executives held out as their salvation. Willes listened politely as Madigan described a merger of two companies that had had distinct, yet similar histories.

■

Rising over Michigan Avenue, at the foot of a string of glittering shops, hotels, and restaurants called the "Magnificent Mile," the Tribune Company's neo-gothic headquarters symbolized the raw power, influence, and historic reach of the *Chicago Tribune*. For the design of the famous Tribune Tower, Colonel Robert R. McCormick, universally known as "the Colonel," had launched an international architecture competition in 1922. John Howell, a New York architect, and Raymond Hood, who would later design Rockefeller Center, had won the commission.

Perched in an office atop the "Symphony of Stone," which *New Yorker* press critic A. J. Liebling referred to as the Colonel's "atomic-bomb-proof eyrie," the globe-trotting Colonel lured thousands of tourists to his landmark by adding hundreds of stones and fragments from iconic buildings and sites to the Tower's walls. Among them were pieces from the Alamo, the Berlin Wall, the Taj Mahal, and even Abraham Lincoln's tomb. The Colonel and his successors had the building's facade engraved with the wit and wisdom of authors, politicians, jurists, and writers. Flannery O'Connor's incisive words, "The truth does not change according to our ability to stomach it," graced an inner wall. And the Colonel even had a couple of his favorite newspaper columns chiseled into the Tower walls.

At the top of page one of the paper, the Colonel immodestly anointed the *Tribune* "The World's Greatest Newspaper." The paper played a seminal role in the founding of the Republican Party, and candidates for offices of all stripes routinely trooped into the Tower to seek the blessing of the Colonel and the *Chicago Tribune*. By 1999, the paper had a daily circulation of about 650,000 and just over a million readers on Sunday.

The Tower's dominance at the foot of the city's premier shopping mecca symbolized the paper's outsized influence on the community and the Tribune Company's, on Wall Street. Over the years, the paper had its ups and downs, particularly when it printed the famous, erroneous 1948 banner headline "Dewey Defeats Truman." By the time Madigan sat down with Willes, though, the Colonel had died and *Tribune* journalists had reformed the paper, attaining grudging respect as worthy competitors of some of the biggest names in journalism. Within the past five years the paper had won two Pulitzer Prizes and had been a finalist seven times for the coveted award. It had cashed in on a relatively small investment Brumback had made in the then-fledging company America Online, which injected $1.2 billion in cash into the company's balance sheet. To a large degree, the *Tribune* set the financial standard by which newspapers would be judged, both by other publishers and by Wall Street analysts.

■

By the time the publishers met in San Diego, the *Los Angeles Times* had become a widely admired, powerful newspaper—the crown jewel of the Times Mirror Company empire. Headquartered in an art deco building in downtown Los Angeles, the paper symbolized the manifest destiny of its city and its state. With the help and the financial muscle of the *Times* and the Chandler family, Los Angeles had overtaken Chicago as America's second-largest metropolis and had become the capital of America's influential film industry. If the *Chicago Tribune* spoke for business and the Republican party in the conservative Midwest, the *Los Angeles Times* embodied the voice of the GOP on the West Coast. In its day, under the approving eye of the Chandler clan, the *Times'* blatantly Republican political columnist had literally created the political career of Richard Milhous Nixon. Like the *Tribune*, the *Times* could make or break local political candidates or power brokers, and it didn't hesitate to mix journalism and politics. In the 1960s, though, Otis Chandler, the reactionary family's prodigal son, assumed control of the paper and began purging its political bias, eventually building the *Times* into a nationally respected newspaper with the journalistic chops to make it a worthy competitor of the *New York Times*.

The nation's largest metropolitan daily newspaper, the *Los Angeles Times* had an institutional ego far bigger than the scrappier *Chicago Tribune*, and its journalists viewed themselves in a league of their own, superior to the bottom-line driven, hog butchers from Chicago. Under Chandler, the *Times* was a haven for writers pursuing quality journalism in long form. Journalists like Leo Wolinsky, a Los Angeles native, spent entire careers at the *Times*, developing pride in the paper, but also a fierce resistance to outsiders. The *Times* had won four Pulitzer Prizes in just five years and had been a finalist nine times. It boasted daily circulation of just over 1 million and 1.375 million on Sunday.

As Madigan spelled out the broad outlines of the proposed deal to Willes, he referred to it as a "merger." But, in reality, the Tribune Company planned to use its financial muscle to assume control of Times Mirror, eliminate its corporate staff, and run the show as it saw fit. The smaller paper with the financial chops would be taking over the larger, more prestigious *Los Angeles Times*. Though he didn't spell it out to Willes that day, Madigan's projected $200 million in cost savings would involve cuts to the editorial staff that would threaten the *Times'* esteemed foreign and national news bureaus, the bread and butter of the paper's journalistic reputation. Nor did Madigan discuss who would be chairman of the surviving company, although he probably had a pretty good idea.

Both men have different recollections of their reactions to the proposal that Madigan put on the table. "He [Willes] initially thought it was a great idea when I sketched out the positive aspects of a deal," Madigan later recalled. "He said it made a lot of sense. He thought the people in his management group were the best in the industry, and he didn't understand why they didn't come up with this. He was kind of kicking himself. So I felt quite good after the meeting."

But Willes said he told Madigan that he had no interest in selling Times Mirror:

> "It was a very informal meeting. We didn't have any charts or any data, just a conversation. I told him I wasn't interested in selling Times Mirror, but I'd be happy to look and see if it made sense to buy the *Tribune*. I think he was particularly interested in leveraging print and broadcast properties. And then I said, oh, by the way, the Chandler Trust would prohibit a sale, even if we wanted to. We went back and did a quick analysis and concluded it didn't make sense. I told the board, and John [Madigan], about that, and I thought that was the end of it."

Regardless of the different recollections, two things were clear. First, Willes didn't do a serious strategic review of the proposal. Second, he made the mistake a lot of people make when dealing with Madigan: he underestimated him.

■

As the *Chicago Tribune*'s deputy managing editor for news at the time, I supervised coverage of any big story about a major merger, whether in the media, manufacturing, or the medical industry. As much as the prospect of an acquisition by the bottom-line-driven *Tribune* scared journalists like Wolinsky at the *Los Angeles Times*, the idea intrigued those of us at the *Tribune*, raising hopes that our paper might finally get the recognition it deserved from its snooty rivals on the coasts. The largest newspaper between New York and Los Angeles, the *Tribune* never enjoyed the respect afforded papers like the *New York Times* or the *Los Angeles Times*, even though the paper routinely delivered outstanding journalism to its readers. One reason for the *Tribune's* junior-partner treatment was a simple fact of geography: A paper located in the middle of the country didn't get the attention bestowed on papers on the coasts. And it took a long time to live down the reputation of someone like the Colonel, whose jarring use of the paper to promote his personal and political agendas stained the *Tribune* for decades. The *Tribune's* efficiency, legendary under Brumback, also worked against it. When editors at other American papers clashed with management over budgetary issues, publishers, armed with data that major papers shared with each other, would ask their editors why they needed so many resources when the *Chicago Tribune* could get the job done with less—a reminder of the paper's nimbleness that didn't earn the paper any friends in the clubby world of journalism.

But the main reason for the dismissive treatment of the *Tribune* had to do with status and power. Although editors and reporters pay lip service to the quality of their journalism, the traditional pecking order measured big metro papers by the size of their staffs, the clout of their Washington operations, the reach of their foreign staffs, and the number of staff-written stories that filled their pages (as opposed to those filed by wire services, such as the Associated Press, the newspaper cooperative that services all member papers).

As an editor, I often used wires for routine pieces, freeing *Tribune* staff writers to craft stories I couldn't get on the wires or to bring enterprise and spark to the big stories of the day, a practice that benefited readers but denigrated the paper in the eyes of journalists who felt that every story should be staff written. Reporters appearing regularly on the network news talk shows and National Public Radio boosted a paper's status, too, but *Tribune* journalists, as stewards of the Midwest, were interviewed less frequently than their counterparts on the East and West coasts. When media critics wrote about news organizations that covered foreign and national news, many failed to mention the *Chicago Tribune*, even though the paper maintained two dozen prize-winning news bureaus throughout the United States and the world. I hoped that the *Tribune*, by acquiring the *Los Angeles Times*, would gain the power and stature necessary to give voice to the Midwest and create a platform to showcase our outstanding journalism.

■

After Willes and Madigan met, both returned to their respective head-quarters. Months would pass before their paths would cross again. Willes forgot about the proposal, but Madigan didn't. A backstabbing billion-dollar drama would play out in the city where drama is literally made.

No one has ever told the story of the biggest merger in the history of American journalism and its long-lasting implications. Embedded in the failure of the marriage of the Tribune Company with the Times Mirror Company is a far broader story of monumental egos, fallible souls, larger-than-life characters, and cultural clashes about the collapse of newspapers—the institutions that write the first, crucial draft of history and the only industry America's forefathers considered impor-tant enough to single out in the U.S. Constitution. The conventional wisdom is that newspapers—and by that I mean the credible, edited information they deliver, and not just the paper and ink—fell into a death spiral because of forces unleashed by declining circulations and the migration of readers to the Internet. But the Internet and declining circulations didn't kill newspapers, any more than long stories, skimpy attention spans, or arrogant journalists did. What is killing a system that brings reliably edited news and information to readers' doorsteps every morning for less than the cost of a cup of coffee is the way that the people who run the industry have *reacted* to those forces. The lack of investment, the greed, incompetence, corruption, hypocrisy, and downright arrogance of people who put their interests ahead of the public's are responsible for the state of the newspaper industry today. I saw it, both as a longtime reporter and as an editor at the *Chicago Tribune* and the *Los Angeles Times*.

In the fall of 2006, *Tribune* executives asked me to leave my job as managing editor running the *Chicago Tribune* newsroom to become editor of the *Los Angeles Times*. In normal circumstances, being named editor of a storied paper would have been a capstone to a successful career. But these were not normal times. If I took the job, I would become the paper's third editor in just over two years, preceded by editors who left after nasty, public fights with their financially pressed bosses back in Chicago over continual demands for budget cuts. The *Los Angeles Times* newsroom had become ground zero in a saga that pitted editors of newspapers against their owners and Wall Street patrons.

Each day, I had walked into the newsroom where I was determined to fight for the integrity of the news, no matter what. My passion for journalism and the interests of my staff had earned me respect in Chicago. But in Los Angeles, my long-standing ties to the Tribune Company would overshadow any of my accomplishments as an editor and journalist. "I don't care what you do here," one longtime friend and member of the *Times* staff told me. "You will always be viewed as a hatchet man from Chicago in this newsroom."

Many friends and acquaintances urged me to turn down the opportunity. The odds that I would fail were high, particularly given the mistrust and resentment in Los Angeles of anyone from Chicago. The Chandler family had lost faith in Tribune Company and created a poisoned atmosphere in the city and in the boardroom. A new editor would be greeted by attacks from readers angry about cuts in staff and space that the city fathers blamed on Chicago. A number of friends at the *Chicago Tribune* couldn't understand why I would go to rescue journalists who had treated us so disrespectfully. "Remember," one close friend said, "these are the people who refused to wear lanyards [securing their 2004 Democratic National Convention credentials around their necks] because they had the name *Tribune* on them." The prevailing view was that I would walk into an impossible situation.

But I had always followed my guts in a business where instincts rarely failed me, and my guts argued otherwise. As the son of an electrician and a housewife who had never finished high school, I had watched my parents overcome incredible obstacles. When I was a teenager, my dad died after a heroic battle with throat cancer. At age thirteen, I literally fought and conned my way into my first job, selling peanuts and hot dogs at Busch Stadium in St. Louis. I had survived military school, the notoriously tough Christian Brothers, the U.S. Army, and a grandmother whose husband called her the "War Department." I responded to challenges like Pavlov's dogs to a bell. I rejected the conventional wisdom, too. I would not be walking into an impossible situation.

Of course, I had doubts about entering such a poisonous atmosphere charged with raw emotions, wounded pride, and barely concealed contempt for anyone from Chicago. But my grandfather, a born storyteller nicknamed "Sawdust," had taught me early on the power of a good narrative to overcome adversity. I had a good story. I was first and foremost a journalist, someone who had represented other journalists well and who was not afraid to challenge authority. I was a newsman who would try to solve the huge problems that the *Times* faced without diminishing the quality or integrity of a great newspaper. I could not pass up the honor and challenge of being editor of the *Los Angeles Times*. So I took the job, hopelessly entwining my story and my fate with the narrative of a mega-merger that would go bad, one that would play a signature role in the collapse of an entire industry. For better or worse, I became eyewitness and participant in "the deal from hell."

# 1

## Beginnings: Des Moines

Gene Raffensperger swung around in the chair in front of the city desk and looked at his new reporter. I had shown up for my first day as a journalist on a daily newspaper wearing a wafer-thin, butter-colored safari jacket, tennis shoes, and bell-bottoms, which would have been fine were I in, say, Dallas. But I was in Des Moines, Iowa, a good two feet of snow covered the ground, the wind howled, the temperature hovered in the single digits, and the snow continued to fall. Scanning me skeptically from head to toe, Raffensperger, known in the newsroom simply as "Raff" finally asked, "You O'Shea?"

"Yes," I replied, somewhat sheepishly, wondering whether I should say anything about my clearly out-of-sync wardrobe. In my own defense, I had *planned* to buy a good winter coat in Columbia, Missouri—en route to Des Moines. It was in Columbia, at the University of Missouri School of Journalism, that I'd just earned my master's degree. But I was in my twenties, a carefree time of life when I opted for parties, pot, and pretty girls over a decent winter coat. "O'Shea," Raff said, scanning my face. "We've got one hell of a story on our hands." He explained that five high school kids on the east side of Des Moines had gone to a drive-in movie the previous night. They'd kept their car running to stay warm, but snow had fallen so hard it had blocked the car's tailpipe. Exhaust had seeped into the car, and all five kids had been asphyxiated. Raff's order to "go over there and talk to the parents," seemed unreal. I had never imagined that my first day as a reporter on a metro daily would involve talking to parents about their dead kids. "Get pictures from the high school yearbooks, ages, quotes, everything," Raff barked. "We want everything, *everything.*"

A tough editor in his forties who spit out questions like a Gatling gun, Raff wore horn-rimmed glasses and smoked a pipe. He could be funny at times and gruff at others, particularly when he was working with a rookie like me. Before I headed out the door on that cold winter day on my first assignment for the *Des Moines Register*, Raff rubbed his head and eyeballed me quizzically. "You ever done anything like this before?" he asked, his voice pitched with excitement. When I told him no, I hadn't, he sat me down at a nearby desk and stared straight into my eyes. His voice softened. "You probably think these parents are going to think, 'This guy's got a lot of nerve showing up here at a time like this,' right?" I didn't have to answer. "Look, O'Shea, just go there and you tell them, 'We know this is a bad time and you're in grief, but we want to get everything in the paper right. You may be upset at my coming here, but we know you would *really* be upset if we got something wrong.' Got that?" Raff demanded. I nodded and out the door I went, slipping and sliding in my old green Ford Maverick through the snowy, unfamiliar streets of east Des Moines, a working-class neighborhood.

Despite Raff's pep talk, I would rather have spent a night in jail than show up at the front door of a house full of mourning parents. When I finally found the house where they were assembled, I approached the front door, knocked, and watched with dread as it swung open and I looked at the stricken faces of grieving family members staring at an intruder with the unfathomable sadness of parents who had lost their children. I took a deep breath and, before I thought twice about it, gave my pitch. Raff was right; the families wanted to talk, and talk, and talk. Late that evening, I left with *everything* I could imagine that Raff would want. Now I had to write the story. After my first day as a daily newspaper reporter, the next morning's *Register* had a six-column banner headline story on page one, "By James O'Shea." Only the pros at the paper could spot the deft touch of an editor like Raff, who could write about tragedy as easily as most people could write a check.

I wish I could say that my first day in the newsroom of the *Des Moines Register* represented the culmination of a classic newspaper apprenticeship that started with a paper route, evolved to the editor's chair at the high school newspaper, and ended in a real newsroom. But my journey took a different path. I grew up in a working-class north St. Louis neighborhood so pronouncedly Catholic and Democrat that I felt sorry for the kid down the street whose dad was a banker and Republican. I had a paper route, but not for any dream of headlines and press passes. Guys in my neighborhood hustled newspapers to pick up spare change, but in my neck of the woods, the *real* reason they coveted a paper delivery job was because Fuzzy, the man who recruited us, would show us photographs of naked women once we'd signed on.

In St. Louis, I attended a military high school run by the Christian Brothers where the only thing I really learned was how to take a punch. I graduated third-lowest in my class, only because I rallied academically in my senior year. My older sister says she knew I was destined to be a newspaperman when, at the age of nine, I sold her diary to her boyfriend for five bucks.

By the time I got to the University of Missouri, most of my family expected I would be quickly tossed out, including my dad, who had told my mom that sending me to college was a waste of time. Thanks to my mom, the only person who believed in me at the time, I prevailed against all odds and graduated with a degree in English and philosophy, a Hemingway/Spinoza spin-off with zero idea what I was going to do with my life.

I got into the newspaper business in the army during the build-up to the Vietnam War. Instead of a tour in the steamy jungles of Southeast Asia, I ended up with an emergency assignment to Korea after some North Koreans shot at a bunch of GIs clearing brush in the demilitarized zone. The Pentagon, fearing an attack by a hostile North Korea, sent me and hundreds more to Korea during a frigid January so the North Koreans would be forced to stop and kill us before going south. We had rifles but no ammo. Bluffing North Koreans by running around with empty guns wasn't my idea of gallantry, so I started looking around for another opportunity and secured a spot on the 7th Infantry Division newspaper, *The Bayonet*. Long story short, I got into the newspaper business to get out of the infantry, not exactly an altruistic motive, but one that led me back to graduate school after the army and to the newsroom of the *Des Moines Register*.

I wasn't too sure I would like Des Moines. On my initial trip to the city on a job interview, a man told me Des Moines was a "pretty swinging place." Looking around, I just figured I had missed something. Then he added, "Of course, it's no Omaha." Walking back to my hotel, being whipped by Arctic winds, I kept thinking, "Jesus Christ, it's no Omaha?" But the optimism in me conquered the cynic, and in January 1971, I joined the staff of my first daily newspaper.

A statewide paper, the *Register* was a perfect place to start a career. In a glass case in front of the building that housed the paper's printing presses, a sign read: "There's only one paper in America that's won more Pulitzer Prizes for national news than the *Des Moines Register*. Our congratulations to the *New York Times*." Populated by would-be poets, editors, and reporters who knew Jim Beam as well as Jimmy Breslin, the newsroom looked like something out of *The Front Page*, Ben Hecht and Charles MacArthur's classic play about "yellow journalism" in Chicago during the 1920s. Stubbed-out cigarette butts littered the linoleum floors; big rolls of carbon copy paper hanging on wire hangers fed bulky Royal typewriters bolted to gray metal desks. Black dial and push-button phones rang incessantly as canisters stuffed with copy whizzed through pneumatic tubes to ink-stained printers and clanking Linotypes a floor below.

Fellow reporters looked at me facetiously when, during my first week, I asked about the location of my desk. An editor took me to a windowsill cluttered with stacks of old notebooks, zoning commission binders, and discarded hats and ties. Shoving the debris aside, he cleared a space and pronounced it my desk.

When things got too quiet, Raff would get up, run over to the pneumatic tube by the copy desk, flip open the hatch as if he were on a submarine, and yell: "Give me some steam, Mr. Green! I think we're gonna ram!" By far, the most memorable character in the newsroom was Jimmy Larson, the paper's page one news editor and headline impresario who fantasized about writing a banner headline that read: "Santa Found Dead in DM Alley." A brilliant journalist who invariably arrived at work with his shirttail out and a piece of toilet paper glued to his cheek from a careless turn of his razor, Larson dealt with slow news days by slapping huge headlines on an insignificant story—a move that effectively made news by stirring controversy and getting people talking. One of his most famous aggrandized headlines involved a story I had written when Des Moines barbers raised the price of a haircut to $3. Larson led the paper with the story under a huge banner headline that read: "DM Haircuts Go To $3.09. (He added the sales tax.)

Although no one knew it then, we journalists were living in the golden era of newspapers. At the time I walked into the offices of the Register and Tribune in 1971, nearly 80 percent of Americans reported that they had read a newspaper during the week. (The Register and Tribune was the parent company of the *Register* for which I worked, and which produced the morning paper and the *Tribune*, the evening paper.) Evening papers dominated the publishing world: 1,425 of them boasted daily circulation of 36.1 million compared to 339 morning papers like the *Register* with a total daily circulation of 26.1 million. In Des Moines, the *Register*, a statewide paper, had a larger daily circulation (about 240,000) than the *Tribune* (about 95,000), which circulated only in central Iowa, mainly Des Moines and its suburbs. The *Tribune* had most of the ads, but the *Register*, by virtue of its statewide reach, had the clout and stature. One wisecracking editor referred to the *Tribune* simply as "the practice paper." The *Register* also had a Sunday edition with a circulation of about 500,000.

Regardless of fate and circumstance, a journalist's first paper is like his or her first love; it will always occupy a special place in the heart. The *Register* was no different. I loved the kind of journalism I learned from the pros in Des Moines, but the paper also provided me with an added benefit. One day, I literally stopped typing when a small-town Iowa girl with hair as blonde as wheat and eyes as blue as the summer sky strolled past and sat down at the rewrite desk. I fell for Nancy Cruzen that day and married her a couple of years later, leading to a family with two wonderful children and giving her one of the great challenges of life: staying married to a newspaperman. Over the next several decades, she was the loyal partner at my side, a testimony to a woman of unparalleled integrity, grace, and charm. She deserves so much better.

On its masthead, the *Register* referred to itself as "The Newspaper that Iowa Depends Upon," and the paper and its reporters delivered on that pledge. Iowans loved or hated the paper, but they respected the *Register* for its independence, crusading nature, backbone, and integrity. The paper took on anyone and any cause, fearlessly. Most *Register* reporters and editors called Iowa home and had grown up reading the paper and hoping that they would one day join its ranks. As a result, they could write about Iowans and even poke fun at them because they knew where to draw the line. They taught outsiders like me how to see Iowans as they saw themselves. Iowans were a literate bunch with an excellent public school system, and they expected a newspaper that delivered.

Once, in Fort Dodge, Iowa, when I was having trouble nailing a story on a local police scandal, I stopped for lunch at a diner and thought about calling the city desk to tell my editors I had hit a brick wall. A man at the counter asked his friend if he'd heard about the police scandal. "I didn't see anything in the [Fort Dodge] *Messenger* this morning. I'll look at the *Register* tomorrow," the man replied, adding with certainty, "They'll have it." I finished my lunch, inspired by those words, and went out and got that story.

The *Register* was one of the last papers published by the family dynasties that dominated American journalism throughout much of the twentieth century. Prior to 1945, the newspaper industry was a vastly different landscape. Around the turn of the century, American businessmen like Iowan Gardner Cowles—an entrepreneur and skilled banker—started acquiring small, struggling daily papers, reversing their fortunes and ultimately merging them with other papers. By purchasing underachieving papers and helping them reach their potential, Cowles, and others like him, built local monopolies that evolved into publishing dynasties. In Chicago, it was the Medill, the McCormick, and the Field families; in Los Angeles, the Chandlers; in New York, the Ochs, the Sulzbergers and the Pattersons; and in Washington, the Meyers and, later, the Grahams. In Iowa, the Cowles family presided over a midwestern powerhouse that owned newspapers in Des Moines and Minneapolis and had founded *Look*, a national magazine that competed with *Life*, which pioneered photojournalism.

The owners believed in making money; in fact, most did and were quite wealthy. But they viewed themselves first and foremost as local *public service institutions*, part of a larger civic power structure that protected and guarded local standards and traditions. Of course, not all of the owners were angels. Some abused their powers and/or promoted particular political agendas. Some were downright scoundrels, and family ownership clearly had its pitfalls. But even the worst of family owners tried to build something that would endure and become the eyes and ears that reported community happenings and kept people informed. Within publishing dynasties, newspapers often were a point of pride—a vehicle established to serve citizens. Those who could afford to acquire newspapers did so under the assumption that they'd make a profit, but the bottom line was just part of the equation. They were interested in getting out the news and in maintaining a powerful seat in their respective communities. Newspaper publishers were often fixtures of local arts, culture, and charity boards. Their responsibilities were huge: At the end of the day, every newspaper is a production plant, one that must deliver a product to thousands of customers, come rain or come shine.

The pay was low and the hours long at the *Register*. I went to work for $170 a week, but that was because I had a master's degree, which was probably worth about $15 to $20 a week. In the 1970s, you didn't get into the newspaper business to make money. Fools, knaves, idealists, and dreamers went to work at the *Register* and many other newspapers across America because they liked to tell stories and they believed that providing people with information and crusading against abuses would make the world a better place. At the *Register*, I covered the news beats: courts, cops, and local politics (the crucial building blocks usually assigned to cub reporters), cutting my teeth on the basics and learning how to sift through facts, sources, and records for a story.

The Register and Tribune newsroom was like many in the metro dailies around the country. The city desk formed the nucleus around which the copy desks and news desks swirled, a world apart from the features, sports, or other desks around the room that dealt with specialized copy or less timely news. The staff was a motley crew comprising younger idealists and balding, "older" people like Raff. Reporters entered the building in the morning and headed for "the desk" to check a large leather folder that contained their names and any messages or notes from the overnight or early person—an editor who stuffed the folder with wire copy or announcements about any developments on their beat. Needless to say, there were few secrets. Reporters filed their stories with the desk, where they were edited for content and style before being passed to the copy desk, where seasoned editors double-checked everything and then wrote the headlines ordered by the news desk, where Larson and his editors figured out which stories were destined for which pages of the paper. With good cause, reporters prided themselves on landing on page one.

Often, a reporter would file a story with the desk and head next door to the Office Lounge, a newspaper bar, to wait for an editor's okay.

If the desk had a problem with the story, the editor simply called the Office, and Dorothy, the pretty proprietress, would chirp, "Jimmy, Raff's on the phone. He's got a problem with your lede." It was a little like having your mother call you at the local gin mill.

The *Register* had three deadlines in those days, starting at around 7 p.m. for the far reaches of the state and ending about 1:30 a.m. for local editions. We put much of the Sunday paper together on Friday, usually working six days a week about twelve to fourteen hours a day. *Officially* I worked 1 p.m. to 9 p.m. on weekdays, but in reality, I started off covering the courthouse, a prime beat, around 9 a.m. and left for the Office Lounge around 9 or 10 at night to join other editors and reporters ending the day with a drink and some war stories. On Saturdays, I had the dogwatch usually assigned to new reporters. From 6 p.m. to 2 a.m. early Sunday, I was pretty much it. The city editor was supposed to be there, but he would go off to dinner with his girlfriend and I rarely ever saw him again unless his wife called. It was a lousy shift, but I learned a lot, sometimes reporting a story by phone, writing it, sending it to the copy desk, and then dashing down to the floor below and editing it on a printer proof sheet so it would fit in the paper.

The *Register* was a well-edited paper. Larson rewrote banner headlines two dozen times until he got them right, and he could easily spot an error in a crossword puzzle. If you had a hole in your story, it usually got plugged by a sharp-eyed editor on the city or copy desks, home of the seasoned pros or "gray beards" who routinely whipped stubborn or arrogant young writers into shape. But the *Register's* real strength was its stable of aggressive, dogged reporters and talented writers. They were people like Nick Kotz, whose exposé of filthy conditions in meatpacking plants in Iowa won the *Register* a Pulitzer; George Anthan, whose coverage of food policy and politics was the best in America; James Risser, a two-time Pulitzer winner; or legendary Clark Mollenhoff, a fierce and fearless reporter and Pulitzer Prize winner who once hounded a local gangster so unfailingly that the exasperated man finally blurted out, "You ought to be thankful to me, Mollenhoff, I won you the Wurlitzer Prize." The writing could be tough but also humorous.

One of the funniest and most insightful columns in the nation graced the pages of the *Register*, written by Donald Kaul, a Michigan native who had immigrated to Iowa. Kaul had once lamented to his readers that he had missed the sexual revolution because it occurred in the sixties, a time that he was in Des Moines. The sixties didn't get to Des Moines until the seventies, Kaul explained, and by then he had left the state to work in the paper's Washington bureau.

The *Register* had a sophisticated but edgy tone and gave its readers the "Iowa angle" in any story remotely connected to the state. Reporters held governors, mayors, congressmen, county supervisors, city council, and local powers accountable for tax increases, public roads, legal loopholes, greed, trysts with strippers, and just plain stupidity. Local bylines enhanced everything from flaming exposés to features on life in Iowa, short and often funny "stupid neighbor" stories that Larson loved to run on the bottom of page one, yarns that gave the *Register* its unique feel. Jon Van, an Iowa native, who routinely dug out the most bizarre Iowa tales, wrote one about a farmer whose classified ad in his local paper sought donations of old bowling balls for his hogs so they could push them around with their snouts and have something to do ("they seem bored," he told Van). Another Van story started: "Persuading a mule to go down the basement stairs turns out to be about as hard as it seems."

But *Register* reporters and editors also had a special relationship with the public that infused the paper's journalism with a sense of public service and connection to readers that would be diluted in years to come. If some huckster or abusive state official tried to ride herd over state residents, Iowans alerted the *Register*, and the paper made sure it all played out in public, often far beyond the state's borders. When, in 1955, Millard Roberts, a Presbyterian minister with little knowledge of how to run a university, was recruited to head Parsons, a college in Fairfield, Iowa, he embarked on the so-called Parsons plan—aggressively recruiting students to beef up the student body. In his quest for numbers, meritocracy fell by the wayside, and a gaggle of wealthy kids who'd been rejected elsewhere, as well as kids who were trying to dodge the draft, arrived. All went well until James Flansburg got onto the story. His exposé drew national attention and prompted *Life* magazine to dub the place "Flunk Out U." (The college later became Maharishi University, a school for transcendental meditation.)

The *Register*, like any paper worth its weight, was interested in upholding the rights of the First Amendment. It wasn't easily cowed. If a government official tried to close a meeting, a *Register* reporter simply refused to leave and the paper's lawyer would threaten a lawsuit to ensure the public had access to the public's business.

The Cowles family had infused their newsrooms with a proud tradition of subordinating business considerations to the independence of their editorial department and their mission of public service. "Two avenues of popularity are open to the newspaper," explained Gardner (Mike) Cowles Jr., one of Gardner's three sons, who would play a key role in modernizing the company and making it a media powerhouse. "The first is to yield to flatter, to cajole. The second is to stand for the right things, unflinchingly and win respect. . . . A strong and fearless newspaper will have readers and a newspaper that has readers will have advertisements. That is the only newspaper formula worth working to. . . . After making all allowances, the only newspaper popularity that counts in the long run is bottomed on public respect."

About the same time I walked into the *Register* newsroom, David Kruidenier, one of Cowles' grandsons, became publisher of the paper and embarked on a long and determined effort to modernize the paper without diluting its editorial excellence and independence. Kruidenier beefed up the business operations of the papers, eliminating Linotypes and printers, saving the newspaper and its owners an enormous amount of money. Kruidenier also modernized the paper's design, an area in which the Cowles had long been innovators. When computers revolutionized the production and composition of newspapers, Kruidenier made sure the *Register* was ahead of the curve.

To continue its strong tradition of newsroom independence, he hired editor Michael Gartner from the *Wall Street Journal*. A spirited editor, Gartner added a touch of class, sophistication, and derring-do to the paper, reinforcing its crucial role in Iowa but also pushing Washington bureau investigative reports that soon landed the *Register* another Pulitzer. A creative and facile writer, Gartner effortlessly wrote the best headlines of any editor with whom I've worked. He made me the paper's business editor with the mandate to make the *Register*'s business coverage the best in the Midwest. Soon the aggressive brand of journalism we delivered prompted community business leaders to privately ask the publisher to muzzle us because we were "anti-business." Kruidenier retorted that a newspaper performs best not as a mouthpiece, but as a paper that reports on the community's strengths and weaknesses.

After five terrific years at the *Register*, I was offered a golden opportunity. When a desk opened up for the *Register*'s Washington news bureau, Gartner made me a correspondent, my dream job. I had thought it would take me a decade of working at the *Register* before I could set foot in Washington. In 1976, my family and I left Des Moines to join the best small-newspaper Washington bureau in America, a move that was a stepping-stone to other bureaus and jobs that would propel me to the top of my craft.

Unfortunately, the *Register* didn't fare as well. As the direct descendants of the patriarchs of the great newspaper families died off, they often left large, far-flung families with disparate interests. The Cowles were no exception. Seeing looming estate tax bills and the potential for far higher profits that reduced budgets could bring, some members of the Cowles family began to press for better financial returns or a sale to reap the unrealized value resting in the newspapers so carefully nurtured by their forefathers. They found an entire industry willing to help them with their problem.

# 2

## Across the Street

The morning I met him, Bill Jones sat at the oval table in his office, grease pencil in hand, scoring page proofs of the Sunday paper with bold red slashes. A top editor at the *Chicago Tribune*, Jones was a trim, blue-eyed ex-Marine with close-cropped hair and a tattoo, at a time when tattoos were not popular. He routinely worked in his stocking feet as he put out the newspaper on Saturday mornings. Jones' daring reporting symbolized the kind of audacious journalism that had lured me to the offices of the *Tribune*, a legendary paper with a bare-knuckled newsroom. At thirty-nine, and already a legend in Chicago, Jones had won acclaim a few years earlier as an undercover reporter posing as an ambulance attendant. His investigation exposed mismanagement, welfare fraud, sadism, and police payoffs in the city's corrupt ambulance industry, which he dubbed "misery merchants." Until Jones exposed them on the front pages of the *Tribune*, the racket had profited the ambulance companies at taxpayers' expense. (Eventually, the federal government picked up the tab for the fees they had collected through health insurance programs for the poor.)

When we met for the first time—a snowy day in March 1979—Jones and I hit it off. A few days later, he offered me a job. There was no doubt in my mind that I wanted to work for a big metro daily, and the *Tribune* seemed as good as any. It didn't have the stature of the *New York Times* or the *Washington Post*, but journalists across the country had crowned Chicago the undercover reporting capital of America in the 1970s, thanks to Jones and his iconoclastic colleagues. Chicago was an exciting place to work. Journalism there was as big, raw, and tough as the town itself. Over the past few decades, the newspaper industry had undergone a crushing wave of consolidation spawned by financial pressures and the competition of new technology: radio and television journalism. American cities that once had three, four, sometimes as many as ten newspapers competing for readers saw publishers discouraged by declining profits, high tax rates, and frustrated shareholders sell or fold publications. In the blink of an eye, publications with household names—*New York Evening World*, the *St. Louis Star*, or the *Cleveland News*—were closed. With newspapers around the country closing up shop, thousands of journalists and newspaper employees were out of work. When, in 1931, Roy Howard of the Scripps Howard chain folded the *New York Evening World*, he furloughed 2,867 journalists, printers, ad salesmen, and circulation men, some of whom went to their graves without ever working again. Critics mourned the loss of reportorial diversity as more papers increasingly fell into the clutches of a single owner. Of the 1,461 American cities that had papers by the 1960s, all but 61 were reduced to one-ownership towns. "A city with one newspaper, or with a morning and an evening paper under one owner," A. J. Liebling of the *New Yorker* wrote, "is like a man with one eye, and often the eye is glass."

Papers like the *Chicago Tribune* that survived the bloodbath emerged much stronger than they'd previously been—gaining monopoly control of circulation markets and lucrative advertising—particularly classified advertising of jobs, cars, and real estate that would become the financial backbone of the newspaper industry over the next two decades. By the late 1960s, editors flush with monopoly revenues sent reporters from big papers in Chicago, New York, and Los Angeles to cover the civil rights movements in the South. When America became entangled in Vietnam or idealistic Americans flooded the streets of Chicago to protest at the 1968 Democratic National Convention, newspapers like the *St. Louis Post Dispatch* and the *Los Angeles Times* sent their own correspondents and reporters to file fresh accounts to readers back home. Such fine-tuned coverage by national and regional papers changed the tone and impact of stories formerly the domain of local publishers and wire services, and transformed journalism from a notoriously low-paying job that relied on well-placed sources to something bordering on a profession. Trying to muscle in on the national advertising pie, television networks expanded their evening newscasts to thirty-minute segments, revolutionizing how Americans consumed the news. Explosive growth of suburban America prompted readers eager for cheap housing, new schools, and lower crime rates to move far away from the city center, vastly increasing the challenge of delivering a newspaper in the rush hour traffic that became synonymous with suburban sprawl. At the same time, an increasing number of women who once spent their daytime leisure hours reading the newspaper started entering the workplace, a factor that helped drive the last nail in the coffin of the most popular newspaper—the evening edition that landed on their doorstep in the afternoon. Traditional print editors who favored *objective* reporting had taken a hit too, after newsmen in the 1950s routinely repeated the unsubstantiated tirades of Senator Joseph McCarthy, the Wisconsin demagogue who ruined numerous lives and careers with his sensational anti-Communist harangues.

By the 1970s, the Colonel had died and publisher Stan Cook and editor Clayton Kirkpatrick had led the *Tribune* away from McCarthy-type tirades and slanted reporting championed by the Colonel and his successors into a new era of journalistic pride and prosperity, rejecting the reactionary politics that had stained the paper's reputation for decades. But journalism in Washington overshadowed anything happening in Chicago.

Two young police beat reporters from the *Washington Post*, Bob Woodward and Carl Bernstein, had toppled an American president by digging through records and mining sources further down the pecking order than those treasured by the nation's elite political journalists. Woodward and Bernstein broke an explosive story about a botched burglary at The Watergate Hotel that brought them fame, fortune, and a Pulitzer Prize. Soon newsrooms and journalism schools across America became magnets for a new generation of reporters eager to expose corrupt officials, social ills, and wrongdoing. Their long-form narrative and investigative journalism produced groans from old school newsmen who viewed themselves as craftsmen, "master plumbers," in the words of one old pro, not professionals minted by the Columbia Journalism School crowd.

Reacting with much the same suspicion and contempt with which mainstream journalists once viewed the emerging digital world, the old school of the sixties and seventies didn't exactly lay out the welcome mat for idealistic newsroom rookies. Jimmy Breslin, the iconic, hard-drinking New York columnist, once referred to the new breed as people who reject simple declarative sentences in favor of "these 52 word gems that moan, 'I went to college, I went to graduate school college, where do I put the period?'"

But this new host of reporters found a far more willing audience in a new generation of editors like Kirkpatrick who were searching for ways to distinguish their publications and generate circulation that would sustain their publisher's ad revenues. Investing in their morning and Sunday editions, editors added color photography, modern designs, better typography, broader coverage, and better-educated (and paid) reporters and editors. I was proud to be one of the new breed.

At the *Des Moines Register*, I had done the basics, covering police, courts, crime, and politics, and taking on investigative projects, before heading to the paper's Washington bureau. In the nation's capital, I relished covering the banking scandal surrounding Bert Lance, President Jimmy Carter's budget director, and carved out a new beat scrutinizing the impact of federal regulatory agencies on companies and citizens in Iowa. On the bus going home every night in Washington, I watched hundreds of chanting Iranian students in Lafayette Park across from the White House stage protests that eventually helped topple the Shah of Iran from power and led to the seizure of American hostages in Tehran. A severe recession loomed as President Carter appointed Paul Volcker head of the Federal Reserve, igniting the soaring interest rates and deep recession that would drive Carter out of office and install Ronald Reagan in the White House.

At the *Register*, we covered some of the big stories, but the paper Iowa depended on focused heavily on subjects of interest to Iowa, stories that the big papers ignored. Jim Risser, the paper's Washington bureau chief, won the second of his two Pulitzer Prizes covering the environmental damage done by American farmers who relied too heavily on chemical fertilizers. My *Register* reporting chops had evolved into a specialty many journalists shunned—business, economics, and finance, particularly the investigative variety. *Register* editors found Iowa coverage more compelling than what I wanted to do, and I decided it was time to move on to a bigger paper where I would get a crack at bigger stories. When a friend suggested I talk to Jones on a trip through Chicago, I agreed and a few months later showed up at work at the legendary Tribune Tower in May 1979.

The *Tribune*'s cavernous newsroom wasn't exactly a warm place. Jaded, seasoned journalists looked me over the first day, sizing me up as if I were a gunfighter new to the corral. The *Tribune*—which had intelligently managed to maintain its share in the market—published numerous editions around the clock, so someone was always "on deadline," the euphemism for "leave me the fuck alone." The language was coarse; the mood skeptical.

George de Lama, one of the paper's first Latino reporters, who would later become managing editor, recalled his first turn at the *Tribune*'s version of the dogwatch, the night city desk assignment usually handed to new reporters. He had hardly settled in when he got a call from City News, the storied local news service where famed writers like Kurt Vonnegut and Mike Royko got their starts. The City

News reporter asked de Lama what he knew about a barroom brawl between the *Tribune's* metro editor and Sean Toolen, a cantankerous reporter who spoke with an Irish brogue and got nasty when he drank. "I immediately called the cop shop to talk to Henry Wood [the *Tribune's* longtime police reporter]. I told Henry that City News called and said they had taken the metro editor to the 18th district [police station] and Toolen to Northwestern [Hospital] and could he make some calls to find out what was going on. Wood said, 'Who in the fuck died and left you in charge? Fuck you. You call the AP,' and he hung up," recalled de Lama.

■

*Tribune* veterans prided themselves on the sink-or-swim ethic that permeated the Tower; adapting to a big, tough newsroom was an initiation rite. Thanks to my roots in north St. Louis, I didn't find the atmosphere so intimidating. Although I didn't know it at the time, my first real job as a vendor selling concessions at Busch Stadium in St. Louis prepared me for the rough-and-tumble atmosphere that awaited me as a journalist.

As a kid of thirteen, I had hopped off a streetcar near Grand and Sullivan avenues in St. Louis to apply for a job at the ballpark. A long line of strapping African American men with families to support stretched down Sullivan Avenue. At four foot ten and about ninety pounds, I naïvely joined the throng, thinking I would simply wait my turn. When the door to the applications office opened, an orderly line devolved into a mob, shoving, kicking, punching, and jostling to get through the green door, a process that required getting past a small, wiry Italian guy named Tony who regulated the traffic by swinging a sawed-off baseball bat when he'd reached his quota. Those who didn't make it inside drifted back into line to await the next opportunity.

After my third attempt to pass Tony's threshold, I was farther back in the line than when I had started. I stalked off, walking down Grand Avenue with tears in my eyes, angry and humiliated that I had not fared better. Halfway down the block, I saw another door with an opaque window and a sign that read, "Missouri Sports Service, Charles Bailey." I knew that Bailey was the big boss of vendors, so I began pounding on the door's window. Soon, a tall man with thinning, silvery blond hair, wearing a blue suit and tie, yanked open the door and barked, "What do you want?" My Irish temper flaring, I shot back, "I want a job. I stood in that line over on Sullivan, but every time the door opened, a fight broke out and I couldn't get in. I want a job."

"How old are you," Bailey barked. "I'm sixteen," I lied. I was still thirteen and probably looked ten, but I had a fake ID. "Why should I hire you?" an exasperated Bailey retorted, never even looking at the fake birth certificate in my hand. I'll never know why I answered the way I did. I didn't know what to say, so I blurted out, "Because I turned the lights on in this place one time."

I don't think Bailey really knew what to think of this stupid, silly, scruffy kid standing before him, but my response piqued his interest, so he invited me into his office. I proceeded to tell him the story of how my dad, an electrician, had taken me to an afternoon Cardinals game on one of our rare outings. Late in the game, we paid a visit to a fellow electrician who worked at the electrical substation in the park, which had erected lights to illuminate the field in 1940. I gave Bailey all the details, telling him how the electrician in overalls, a T-shirt, and a Stetson hat took me into the substation as the afternoon sun faded. He put my small hand on a huge fork-shaped switch and said, "Flip it." As I pushed upward, power surged through the switch, sparks showered the floor, and banks of powerful lights over Busch Stadium surged to life. Fans roared in approval as robustly as they cheered a home run by Stan the Man Musial, a Cardinal home run hero. For some reason, I believed my turn at the switch entitled me to a job years later, and, as I told my story, Bailey smiled and soon led me down a long dark tunnel to the small room behind the green door. He told Tony with the bat and Leonard McNiff, the foreman of the vendor corps, to give me a uniform and a job. "He turned the lights on here," Bailey said.

McNiff introduced me to Slick, who ran the commissary. Slick gave me a stack of books about the Cardinals and told me I would earn a nickel for every one I sold. It was a double-header; I walked up and down the steps of the ballpark for eight hours. I made 15 cents. But I returned the next day, which, I suspect, was the real test, and sold picture packets of the Red Birds. I made $5.06, but I had learned two powerful lessons that I would apply for years in my career as a journalist: There's always more than one way through the green door, and never doubt the power of a good story. With the ballpark in my DNA, no newsroom would ever give me a rough start.

■

Although A. J. Liebling probably wouldn't have been satisfied with the situation that prevailed when I hit Chicago, the city still had two news-paper owners and numerous aggressive broadcast outlets engaging in a spirited competition that energized everyone's newsrooms. Reporters squared off against each other, fighting for the best story and going for the jugular, often in good ways, but sometimes in bad. My national editor once went out for dinner around 8 p.m. and came back with a black eye. Competing newspapers and television stations routinely dis-patched legmen to grab early editions of the big papers rolling off the presses and rush back to their respective newsrooms where reporters scanned the early-bird papers, picked up phones, called sources, and tried to steal competitors' stories. The rivalry created a great system of checks and balances. If, in making calls, anyone discovered *any* fault in your story, the slip-up would be emphasized and magnified in the com-petitor's account, making you look stupid in front of careful readers, sources, and colleagues.

To a newspaper reporter new to the city's streets, covering Chicago was like big-game hunting. From its gritty neighborhoods in the shadow of decaying steel mills on the South Side to the city's glittering shops along the Magnificent Mile, Chicago was the quintessential American melting pot. Saloons and churches marked neighborhoods as surely as the graffiti of street gangs. Signs scrawled in Polish, Spanish, Russian, or Chinese hung in windows of urban enclaves home to Serbs, Croats, Latinos, Japanese, Jews, Italian, Irish, or Africans. The newspapers vied for stories about cops on the take, City Hall and Statehouse corruption, street gangs, pin-striped patronage, mobsters, greed, and sex, the juicier the better. The racial divisions ran deep and raw. Douglas Frantz recalled the ubiquitous tenor of the bias from his days as a *Tribune* reporter covering the St. Patrick's Day parade on the South Side when Bernie Epton, a Jewish politician, was running for mayor against Harold Washington, the city's first black mayor. As Epton passed a group of parade watchers, Frantz said he heard one man yell, "Atta boy, Jew boy, go get that nigger." Sports divided the city as neatly as an alderman's ward map. Cubs fans lived on the north side; Sox fans on the south. If you lived on the same block as a big shot, your street got plowed in a snowstorm; if not, tough luck.

In better days, Chicago had eleven major daily newspapers, but by the time I came along, the city's journalism included a collection of urban, suburban, and ethnic papers dominated by the *Tribune*, owned by McCormick family members and others who had survived the Colonel, and the *Sun-Times*, the scrappier of the city papers edited by James Hoge and owned by Marshall Field, heir to the department store fortune. Each paper referred to the other as "across the street," owing to their nearby locations on either side of Michigan Avenue. Hoge delivered to his readers gutsy, quality, tabloid journalism with a sensational flair. Once, the *Sun-Times* bought an old bar, renamed it "The Mirage," and proceeded to document how many people and city officials they had to bribe to do business in Chicago. In another instance, the city went crazy when the paper splashed a story on page one saying that Chicago's Catholic prelate, Cardinal John Cody, had a *special relationship* with his housekeeper.

The *Tribune* reflected the views of its readership, too—the institutional Chicago of banks and brokers on LaSalle Street, the suburbanites, and the civic-minded leaders and families concerned about the health of the schools, city hall, and the parks. The *Sun-Times* often forced its more staid competitor to grapple with a saucy story. When Hoge published the Cody exposé, the *Tribune* desperately attempted to recover, at one point turning to its shrewd lawyer, Don Reuben, who also represented the Archdiocese. The paper ended up publishing a tear-jerking interview with the housekeeper that cast doubt on the *Sun-Times* scoop. By and large, the *Tribune* ran much more serious national and international news on its front page, often written by its larger Washington bureau or by its army of reporters who parachuted in to cover the big story. Jones ran exposés, but they tended to be on subjects such as car safety or civic-minded series on abusive tax assessments or corrupt police.

Advertisers turned up their noses at American tabloid papers like the *Sun-Times*, which had an editorial page that Democrats favored and a highly urban readership concentrated on the working-class and poor neighborhoods on the south and west sides, home to many black Chicagoans, a vestige of the city's divisive racial politics. After Rupert Murdoch bought the paper, star columnist Mike Royko walked "across the street" rather than work for the "alien," making the paper's problems worse as it vainly struggled to strengthen its finances amid a sea of economic uncertainty and ownership changes. At the *Tribune*, the story was quite different.

From the day I arrived at the paper in 1979, the staff talked of the *Tribune*'s founders with a mixture of respect for the paper they had created and relief that they were gone. The new generation of reporters and editors lured to the *Chicago Tribune* during the 1970s by its ambition and aggressive brand of journalism truly didn't appreciate what Joseph Medill, the paper's patriarch, and the Colonel had done for them.

The Medill and McCormick names now grace public spaces and institutions like the journalism school at Northwestern University; Medill is buried at Graceland Cemetery, and the Colonel at Cantigny, in the Chicago area. Both had notorious reputations as publishers and individuals. Medill was known for his firebrand politics; many people thought the Colonel loopy for good reason. In their day, though, both were giants who enabled the *Tribune* to evolve into a media giant.

Medill gave the paper its civic backbone and Republican Party footings by blending his political and editorial interests to benefit the paper. He once set aside his editor's hat to become mayor of Chicago, after reputedly penning the famous "Chicago Will Rise Again" editorial printed when a raging fire nearly destroyed the city in 1871. An arch foe of slavery, Medill helped found the Republican Party to support the presidential candidacy of Abraham Lincoln, then a young Illinois lawmaker seeking higher office. He advised Lincoln to "go in boldly, strike straight from the shoulder, hit below the belt as well as above and kick like thunder."

With his avid interest in politics, Medill forged the *Tribune*'s durable ties to the GOP, which became a substantial part of the paper's suburban Chicago readership base—one that would make advertisers covet its pages. In his will, he stipulated that the paper could only endorse a Republican for president. When Medill was Chicago's mayor, the paper's editorial board endorsed Horace Greeley, whose White House campaign was backed by Democrats, even though he ran for president from an offshoot of the GOP. When Medill returned to the *Tribune* at the end of his term, he fired the entire board. It wasn't until 2008, under new management, that the paper dared to endorse another Democratic presidential candidate: Barack Obama. Medill infused the paper with character and commitment to public service, but his pugnacious and controversial grandson, Colonel Robert Rutherford McCormick, made the paper world famous and built the financial foundation from which the Tribune Company grew.

Inventor, entrepreneur, commentator, politician, and self-promoting eccentric, the Colonel understood something that escaped most of his peers: readers embraced the personalities of the people who ran and wrote newspapers, if not the papers themselves. The Colonel stamped his enigmatic personality onto the pages of the *Tribune*, spawning some of the worst, most biased, unfair journalism in the nation's history and catapulting the number-three paper in Chicago to the most widely read and financially successful full-size daily newspaper in America.

Richard Norton Smith, the Colonel's biographer, listed his phobias and enemies, in no particular order, as the New Deal, Franklin Delano Roosevelt, Wall Street, the United Nations, Henry Luce, New York City, Herbert Hoover, Henry Ford, grand opera, Thomas E. Dewey, the East Coast, Walter Winchell, NATO, and Wisconsin, except for its firebrand Senator McCarthy, whom the Colonel tolerated because of his virulent anti-Communism. McCormick used the *Tribune* and later the radio station, WGN, which stood for "world's greatest newspaper," the monicker that the Colonel gave to his newspaper, to let the world know how he felt about things. He used both to castigate FDR, for whom he had particular political and personal hatred (something FDR attributed to his stealing a girlfriend from the Colonel when both were classmates at Groton). Once, when Eleanor Roosevelt had a minor traffic violation, the *Tribune* reported the story on its front page with a five-column headline that called for revoking the First Lady's license. A skilled horseman, handsome, muscular, six foot four inches tall, with a neatly trimmed mustache, the Colonel could be remote, cold, aloof, and aristocratic. He stole his two wives away from their husbands, men who happened to be his friends. He would stroll through the newsroom with a soldier's bearing, on occasion wearing an English officer's jacket, boots, and spurs, with his three German shepherds in tow.

The Colonel routinely used his newspaper to further his personal and political interests, tarnishing the paper's reputation for decades. *Tribune* editorial writers browbeat the Illinois legislature into dedicating public assets to help build Meigs Field, a small airport in downtown Chicago that the Colonel favored so he could fly his plane to work from Cantigny, his spacious, militaristic compound in Chicago's western suburbs, a base of the isolation he championed.

As interested as he was in pursuing his own agenda with the *Tribune*, the Colonel could display journalistic integrity. When a *Tribune* ad manager asked editors to downplay the divorce of a wealthy department store owner, the Colonel ordered the story *in* the paper and the ads *out*. Regarding some issues, the Colonel acted like a liberal. An avid defender of the First Amendment, he spent lavishly in a legal challenge to the so-called "Gag Law," convincing the U.S. Supreme Court in 1931 to overturn a ruling that suppressed a small, scurrilous Minnesota weekly local politicians attacked as a public nuisance. But on most issues, the

Colonel was conservative, reactionary, and insular. The Midwest was America, in his view; the East Coast was a collection of British sympathizers and Communists. Readers of today's comparatively bland newspapers would find the front-page headlines on the Colonel's papers jarring. He once launched a series of stories about the state of newspapers and magazines on the East Coast under the headline:

The Alien East: A Thing Apart From America
Its Millions Loyal to the Lands They Fled.

The Colonel embraced Medill's attempts at reforming the English language, spelling words like *though* as *tho* and *through* as *thru*, giving critics fodder for columns that portrayed him as more than slightly off plumb.

By today's standards, the Colonel's brand of journalism might sound downright offensive, but readers loved his paper for its readability, the entertainment value of comics like "Little Orphan Annie" and "Dick Tracy," and the tirades of the Colonel and his surrogates. The *Tribune* has employed some of journalism's most famous reporters: Ring Lardner, sports writer; gossip columnist Hedda Hopper; advice maven Ann Landers. Arch Ward, the paper's sports editor, created the idea of baseball's All-Star game in the pages of the *Tribune* by suggesting the best of the American and National League square off in a game; and the *Tribune* named the first female as a war correspondent. Years later the paper also promoted the first woman to be a police reporter. The *Tribune's* daily circulation rose to 1 million by 1942, and ad revenues flew off the chart.

For all of his odd ways, the Colonel also created a structure that *Tribune* executives would later exploit to build the multimedia company that would gobble up Times Mirror. Unlike many of his peers, the Colonel invested heavily in his company to maintain its independence, and he embraced change in the form of new technology. With revenues gushing from his paper in Chicago, the Colonel acquired an interest in the Mutual Broadcasting System and bought paper mills in Canada to ensure that his *Tribune* would always have an adequate, economical supply of newsprint. He pioneered the use of color and teletype transmission, and experimented with a crude version of what would become the fax machine. When commercial radio appeared on the scene early in the century, the Colonel acquired WGN in Chicago in 1924, in part because he saw its promise, in part so he could spread his message near and far. With WGN Radio in his portfolio, the Colonel started *Chicago Theater of the Air*. Every Saturday evening at 9 p.m., listeners could tune in to the Colonel's booming baritone lecturing on everything from military tactics and obscure Revolutionary War heroes to reports on his extensive world travels and idiosyncratic personal interests.

In 1948, he bought a television station, which he named WGN-TV. "I decided WGN must be a Chicago station," the Colonel said, making sure that his readers and audience understood that he was looking out for their interests. "A Chicago television station could not simply be the Midwest outlet of a New York network," he said. When federal regulators later prohibited cross-ownership of the major broadcast and print properties in major American cities, his acquisition proved prescient. Since the company already owned WGN, federal officials allowed Tribune Company to keep its station, grandfathering the ownership arrangement and giving Tribune executives a foundation to exploit and build a national media company years later.

As the *Tribune* grew, the Colonel enlisted his dysfunctional family to help oversee his expanding empire. He had earned his rank as an artillery officer years earlier on the battlefields of World War I, where he and his cousin, Captain Joseph Patterson, stationed near a French battlefield, planned to publish a "picture paper." At the war's end, Patterson, with capital from the *Tribune*, moved to New York to found the *New York Daily News*, a tabloid that would become the nation's largest circulation daily newspaper.

Another cousin, Eleanor "Cissy" Patterson, edited the *Washington Times Herald* and made it the top tabloid in the nation's capital before buying it from William Randolph Hearst in 1939. Her Auntie Mame antics, failed marriage to a penniless Polish count, and scandalous love affairs made her and the McCormick clan the talk of Washington. The Colonel eventually bought the paper and sold it in 1954 to Eugene Meyer and his son-in-law, Philip Graham, who folded it into what is now the *Washington Post*. Captain Patterson's daughter, Alicia, started *Newsday*, the tabloid that would become as successful on Long Island as the *Daily News* was in Manhattan.

Childless, and paternalistic toward employees, the Colonel grew increasingly remote when his health started to fail in the 1950s. By then, the *Tribune's* circulation had started to tail off; it had dropped 20 percent from 1946. The paper slowly started to change, initiating a new editorial department called "The Other Side" that exposed readers to different viewpoints and took the political edge off the *Tribune's* front-page cartoons.

When he died in 1955, the Colonel left behind an estate valued at $55 million, most of it in Tribune stock housed in the McCormick Tribune Trust. He had turned over management of the paper to three trusted executives, and the long process of change picked up speed, despite the best efforts of some of his trusted aides.

In 1974, just five years before I would meet Jones, the Cook-Kirkpatrick era began. Kirk, as he was known, vowed to change the news and opinion columns of the *Tribune* in ways that would have sent the Colonel on one of his famous tirades. "*Thru* is *through* and so is *tho*," Kirk declared.

The Colonel was buried in full uniform in an oversize coffin at his Cantigny estate, but his reputation and shadow lived long afterward at Tribune Tower. Even after working at the *Tribune* for two decades, I would get a feeling while walking down the halls of his famous Tower at night that somehow and somewhere, the Colonel was watching. One night I walked out of the rear door of the newsroom and took the freight elevator to the first floor to leave the building. As the elevator's doors closed, I looked back and noticed the label on the elevator door.

It read *Frate*.

# 3

## Otis Chandler's Legacy

Bleakwood Avenue runs through a barrio about eight miles due east of the *Los Angeles Times'* Globe Lobby, a marble art deco entry that features a massive globe, Hugo Ballin's murals of 1930s life in America, and bronze busts of General Harrison Gray Otis, Harry Chandler, and other members of the family whose name, in Southern California, is synonymous with wealth and power. For Leo Wolinsky, the distance between the newspaper where he would become a keeper of the journalistic flame and the downtrodden east Los Angeles neighborhood where he grew up might as well have been halfway to the moon.

A resourceful journalist with a twinkle in his brown eyes and a mischievous laugh that pervaded his speech, Wolinsky was a career newsman who knew the ins and outs of the newsroom better than most. In far-flung newsrooms, we shared a roughly parallel path—he at the *Los Angeles Times*, me at the *Tribune*. Products of working-class America, we both rose through the ranks to the pinnacle of journalistic power and decades later would play a role in each others' career that neither one of us could have imagined.

In the 1950s, S. J. Perelman called the *Los Angeles Times* "the most wretched fish wrap in America," second only to the *Chicago Tribune*. Much as the Colonel polluted the *Tribune's* journalistic reputation to make a fortune and further his eccentric political interests, General Otis and his entrepreneurial son-in-law, Harry Chandler, used the *Los Angeles Times* to build a financial and political empire that put Los Angeles on the map and made the Chandlers a California legend.

A jingoistic, anti-labor firebrand who called his newspaper headquarters "The Fortress," General Otis bought a quarter interest in the *Los Angeles Daily Times* in 1882 for $5,000. The paper had a circulation of 400, and Los Angeles' population totaled 12,500 restless souls surrounded by orange trees, wheat fields, and a handful of wineries. An Ohio native who, at age sixty-one, convinced his friend President William McKinley to pin a star on his epaulet for service in the short-lived Spanish American war, Otis used the pages of the *Times* to reward friends, punish enemies, and relentlessly promote Southern California. Otis, who weighed 250 pounds, was the walrus in the family. Harry Chandler was the fox, the sly man who married the general's daughter and started a family that eventually made the *Times* a powerful and financially successful civic institution that dominated the California Republican party as thoroughly as the Colonel's operation did in the Midwest. The way the Chandlers used the *Times* to enhance their financial interests made the Colonel look like a Boy Scout.

The classic film *Chinatown* was based on the story of Harry Chandler's secret purchase of huge tracts of land in a parched valley north of Los Angeles. He then ordered coverage and editorials in the *Times* to support construction of a canal to bring water from the Owens Valley (220 miles northwest of Los Angeles) to the San Fernando Valley. The massive project, financed by a public bond issue, vastly increased the value of Chandler's nearby real estate holdings and made Harry and a close circle of friends a fortune at the expense of the impoverished farmers who naïvely went along with the deal.

Like the right-wing *Tribune* of the Colonel's day, the *Times* promoted a staunch, conservative political playbook. In *The Powers That Be*,

David Halberstam related how Turner Catledge, then a young reporter for the *New York Times*, once asked Kyle Palmer, the *Los Angeles Times'* political reporter, for information about the Democratic gubernatorial campaign of Upton Sinclair, whom conservatives despised because of his Socialist ties. "Turner, forget it," quipped Palmer, who doubled as a charming schemer and political operative. "We don't go in for that kind of crap you have back in New York of being obliged to print both sides. We are going to beat this son-of-a-bitch Sinclair any way we can. We're going to kill him." And they did. Sinclair got 37 percent of the vote running on the EPIC (End Poverty in California) platform that advocated universal employment in the state. But Frank Merriam, the Republican candidate favored by the Chandlers, got 49 percent in a campaign that featured fake newsreels showing Russian Communists arriving in California to vote for Sinclair.

By the time Wolinsky joined the staff of the *Los Angeles Times* in 1977, much had changed, thanks to a gutsy, crafty woman who had married Norman Chandler, Harry Chandler's grandson. A strong-willed woman, Dorothy "Buff" Chandler knew how to get her way. After her husband became publisher of the *Times*, he staunchly supported Robert Taft as the Republican nominee for president in 1952. But Buff wanted Dwight Eisenhower to win the nomination. So she presented her husband with a proposition: If he ever wanted to have sex with her again, the *Times* would endorse Eisenhower. Ike got the paper's nod and the victory.

Buff had married Norman Chandler just after he'd graduated from Stanford University. Together they had Camilla and, two years later, Otis. Had Chandler family tradition prevailed, Philip Chandler, Norman's younger brother (who was allied with the more conservative wing of the family), would have assumed the publisher's chair in 1960 when Norman stepped down to become chairman of the Times Mirror Company, the newspaper's parent corporation. But Buff knew the paper had to abandon its old ways and adopt the new ethos of Southern California, which was becoming a more enlightened place full of people like her son, Otis, an adventurous, blond, blue-eyed Adonis.

45

After much arm-twisting, Buff persuaded Norman to name their son publisher of the *Times*.

On April 11, 1960, as flash bulbs popped, before an audience of 725 powerful Southern Californians, Norman stood at a podium at the Biltmore Hotel, a stately structure he had helped build in downtown Los Angeles, to name Otis the fourth publisher of the *Los Angeles Times* in its seventy-nine-year history. Otis, who maintained that he had no advance knowledge of his father's decision, stepped to the podium and uttered, "Wow." He was thirty-two years old.

Otis Chandler transformed the *Times* as thoroughly as Clayton Kirkpatrick transformed the *Tribune* in Chicago. Both men successfully reformed widely disparaged, discredited newspapers and made them remarkable journals and newspaper industry leaders. Otis Chandler was lucky. During his remarkable tenure, Los Angeles had equally remarkable explosive population and economic growth, anointing it as the capitol of the new American West and a magnet for immigrants from around the world. The city overtook Chicago to become America's second-largest city, and the *Times* under Otis' leadership, eclipsed the *Tribune* in stature and influence. Otis opened news bureaus in international capitals including Paris, London, and Jerusalem, putting the *Los Angeles Times* on a par with the *New York Times*. He beefed up the paper's Washington bureau, paid top dollar for writers and editors who would win the paper dozens of Pulitzer Prizes, and exercised the paper's journalistic muscle on subjects that had once been verboten.

Less than a year after he took over, Otis published a series of stories on Robert Welch and the John Birch Society, a right-wing political organization that portrayed Eisenhower as a Soviet dupe, the United Nations as a Communist front, and Earl Warren as a "red" Supreme Court justice. From a journalistic perspective, the series of five stories that exposed the organization's hypocrisy and deep roots in California were tame; they started in the opinion section, not on page one, and ran randomly on page two, or mostly in obscure spots inside the newspaper. But Otis' uncles, Philip and Harrison, and his aunt, Alberta, were Birch Society benefactors and staunch supporters of Welch.

Friends and neighbors took notice and started talking. Otis followed up by ordering a tough editorial in the Sunday *Times* that slammed Welch and the Birchers for their attacks on Roosevelt, Truman, Eisenhower, and the Dulles brothers.

"What is happening to us," the editorial asked, "when all loyal Americans are accused of being Communist dupes unless they subscribe to the radical and dictatorial direction of one self-chosen man? . . . The *Times* does not believe that the argument for conservatism can be won—and we believe it can be won—by smearing as enemies and traitors those with whom we sometimes disagree." Otis put the editorial at the top of page one and signed it himself. Readers in conservative enclaves like Pasadena were outraged, and the *Times* circulation immediately dropped by 15,000, a staggering sum. (Controversial stories of the era typically prompted a dozen or so folks to drop the paper.) Though it resulted in a loss of subscribers, the editorial represented the *Times'* declaration of independence from the past and made Otis an idol to generations of journalists like Wolinsky.

A new generation of young men and women was to carry Otis' torch into the future. In a sense, the journalists who fought to preserve the unique brand of journalism that Otis created and championed were the unsung heroes and villains of the *Los Angeles Times*. Fiercely loyal to Otis' standards, journalists like Wolinsky also treated the mere whiff of change as a dire threat to the man's legacy. Longtime *Los Angeles Times* editor John Arthur once told a magazine writer: "Otis is Zeus."

On the surface, Wolinsky was an odd keeper of Otis' high journalistic standards. Growing up in East Los Angeles, Wolinsky didn't read the *Times*. Like me, he was not one of those kids who started a neighborhood newspaper and became the editor of his high school newspaper. "My dad was an electronics developer at McDonnell Douglas. I'm not even sure what he really did. My mom was a housewife. We didn't take a daily paper. We couldn't afford it," he recalled. Wolinsky's neighborhood wasn't *Times* territory, either. A vast swath of barrios and industrial shops between the Los Angeles River and the city's eastern border, East Los Angeles, is a throwback. The once-dusty streets are now paved, and backyard chicken coops and citrus groves are rare. But the east side is the underbelly of a city better known for glitz and glamour.

By the time Wolinsky graduated from the University of Southern California, Otis had built the *Times* into one of the best and most prosperous papers on the globe by following the money. The paper's readers didn't live on streets like Bleakwood, or in barrios like Boyle Heights. They lived in Bel Air, Beverly Hills, Westwood, Culver City, the South Bay, or Malibu, alongside moguls and movie stars.

Given how large and diverse Los Angeles was, the *Times* needed people like Wolinsky, locals who understood the challenging nature of the vast metropolis the paper covered. Reporting on a large metropolitan area is no easy task for any newspaper. Under Otis, the *Times* circulation area grew to encompass some eighty-eight separate municipalities, ranging from Pasadena, the tony, tree-lined town that seems as midwestern as sweet corn, to Little Saigon, a vertical strip mall that rests on a flat sandy plain home to some 135,000 Vietnamese. Parts of Santa Ana in Orange County would be easy to mistake for a town in Mexico, while the neighborhoods around South Central and East Florence in Watts resemble the most hard-boiled ghettos in the Bronx. The northern reaches of the San Fernando Valley stretch to an urban desert, and the posh enclaves along the Pacific Coast Highway north of Santa Monica symbolize raw wealth and power. The *Los Angeles Times* circulates in an area about as large as the state of Ohio, but one that ultimately lacks a center of gravity. Despite years of development, downtown Los Angeles remains a drab urban landscape; its most enduring features are Frank Gehry's sweeping stainless-steel Walt Disney Concert Hall and a skid row that resembles a Palestinian refugee camp. (In one ten-square-block area, some 114 dialects are spoken.)

Though he grew up in a barrio, Wolinsky understood Los Angeles as well as did Otis, who had created several local editions of the *Times* to serve its diverse constituencies. One edition of the *Los Angeles Times* served the San Fernando Valley; one, Orange County. There was a paper for the San Gabriel Valley, and a paper for San Diego. "The way it was supposed to work," recalls Pete King, a longtime *Times* writer and editor who would one day recruit Wolinsky to run the a.m. city desk, "is that we would produce six different papers. . . . These papers had their own editors and in some cases, publishers. The talent level was so high that we could take the best of the stories for these papers and put them into one paper. We made a mega paper out of the six papers for people who wanted it. . . . The *LA Times* was important to a certain Los Angeles—the suburban, middle-class, upper-class Angelino. It was never a paper of East LA or the barrios." Over the years, the paper would be accused of having a bad case of penis envy of the *New York Times*, but King said the brand of journalism that Otis had created really wasn't about "knocking the *New York Times* off its perch."

"There was an *LA Times* way of doing journalism," King explained. "We didn't get plaudits for it. In fact, we were sometimes ridiculed by East Coast papers. But we were wildly successful. We had some excesses and we had some bad days. But on our good days, you wouldn't see anything like it in any other newspaper. . . . It was doing it our way. It fit the city. . . . It's not like we didn't do daily journalism. Like I'm city editor and Rodney King happened," said King in a reference to a police assault of the African American man that led to highly publicized riots in the 1990s. "It was not like we didn't cover the news. But we also did the narrative story. That was our 'A' game. I had a goofy theory. A story would jump [from one page to another] so many times, but the coverage was like LA, a city of sprawl. People didn't leave for work until 9 a.m. because of the traffic. So they had time to read."

It's easy to see why King, Wolinsky, and other journalists would go to extraordinary lengths over the years to protect Otis' legacy. Otis understood that the city he and his ancestors had built needed to be informed and entertained, and he capitalized on the power of his journalists and what they really cared about—their journalism—to provide that information and entertainment, elevating them to an almost mythical status in the newsroom and beyond. Reporters and editors at Otis' *Los Angeles Times* didn't live by the rules that applied to others. They were well paid, flew first-class on every trip over five hundred miles, and spared no expense on stories. And editors worked hard to make sure it stayed that way.

Nowhere was the ability of the *Los Angeles Times* to entertain on better display than in a celebrated feature that Wolinsky and other *Los Angeles Times* editors would fight to preserve for years: Column One—deeply reported, well-written stories. Through meticulous reporting and lucid writing, *Times* reporters and editors simply took their readers to places where other newspapers couldn't or wouldn't go. When editors needed an arresting profile on a controversial figure like Washington, D.C., mayor, Marion Barry, they called on a stable of gifted writers like Bella Stumbo who would capitalize on the paper's fat expense accounts to fill its generous news hole with deep reporting and copy that crackled. Stumbo and other *Los Angeles Times* writers simply spent more time, more money, and more and better words on a story, overwhelming would-be competitors.

The *Times* that Otis had inherited from his father was fat—full of ads bought by companies and merchandisers who coveted Otis' well-heeled readers. At the top of the front page on March 12, 1961, just after Otis became publisher, two numbers—21 and 430—competed for attention with the infamous signed editorial on the John Birch Society. That Sunday's *Times* had 21 sections and 430 pages to hold ads for everything from Liquid Snail Killers from the Cha Kent Company to a spread for the Dinah Shore Models Wardrobe at a local department store. Otis built upon that solid foundation to make the paper more lucrative so he could pay his journalists top dollar. He took the Golden Age of Journalism to Platinum. Ads created holes for copy written by those lucky enough to work at the *Times*.

To Wolinsky, the *Los Angeles Times* was more than a fat and happy place to work: "For me, it was a symbol. When you saw the people walking down the street with the *Los Angeles Times*, it was a symbol that they'd made it in society," he offered. The paper lured many star reporters westward from newspapers in the East and Midwest, but employed just as many Californians—journalists who'd labored at smaller papers to land a coveted job at the *Times*. Kathy Kristof grew up reading the *Los Angeles Times* and wanted to work there from the time that she decided to be a journalist. "I really didn't realize what we had until I started traveling and saw other papers. It was a unique paper. There was nothing like it in the country."

After graduating from USC, Wolinsky was bound and determined to "land a job at the *Los Angeles Times*." After five years of applying unsuccessfully for a roster of *Times* jobs, he got a break when he was a reporter for *The Breeze* covering Inglewood, a community in the South Bay, a collection of towns south of the city. The *Times* had a reporter in Inglewood but her husband was under investigation for a conflict of interest (he had a stake in Inglewood casinos), and Wolinsky applied for her job.

His moxie paid off. He soon became the South Bay reporter for the *Los Angeles Times*. "At first," Wolinsky recalled, with his trademark laugh, "I thought I had made a huge mistake. My editor was Hank Osborne. He'd assign these ridiculous stories. He once had someone cover the marathon and write stories about runners who would stop to defecate in the bushes. He'd have you go out and put a nickel, a dime, and a quarter on the sidewalk and when someone would stop and pick one up, you were supposed to interview them and write a story about what they picked up and why. I thought, 'This can't be the famous *LA Times*.'"

Even though most journalists native to Los Angeles coveted jobs at the *Times*, some balked at taking a job in a bureau such as the South Bay, one of several where reporters were referred to derisively as "zonies" by those lucky enough to hold jobs at the big newsroom on Second and Spring Streets. "The editors downtown were a little snooty about taking stories from the bureaus," said Kristof, who went to work at the *Times* as a college intern and would become one if its star financial columnists. "You were just not taken that seriously." Kristof said the zones were considered somewhat of a backwater at the *Times*. "They were fully staffed but they used to publish only three times a week. You could get your pants kicked off because you could write a story and it might not appear until three days later." Wolinsky was transferred from the South Bay to Orange County, which was considered another "zonie" bureau, but opportunity struck when the *Times* needed someone to help cover the sprawling Los Angeles County beat.

A highly regarded and respected Los Angeles journalist, Bill Boyarsky, who ran the City County Bureau, was everything that Wolinsky wanted to be. He recalled, "I met him at a journalism conference before I got to the *LA Times* in 1977. He was a smart writer, urbane and sophisticated, someone who had written books and won journalism prizes. He was my hero and my mentor." The *Times* had hired Boyarsky off an AP picket line, and his solid journalistic practices soon made him one of Otis' newsroom confidants, someone who appreciated and understood that the values Otis had embedded in the newsroom were not something to be taken for granted, but a legacy to be embraced and passed on to younger journalists who would listen to him. "Bill said if things worked out at the City County Bureau, I might be able to stay," remembered Wolinsky. So, in 1983 he started covering the board of supervisors for Los Angeles County.

The City County desk also represented a near-death experience for Wolinsky.

> There were a lot of people on vacation, so [they asked me to help edit] an investigative project by two reporters, one in LA and one in Sacramento. It was a story about . . . a lawyer who had used his connections with the administration of [former California Governor] Pat Brown to get some zoning changes for some property in which he had an interest. We worked on the story for a long time, and finally it ran on page one in the left-hand corner. I was so proud. And then I walked into the newsroom and saw one of the reporters in his editor's office. He looked ashen. I knew something was wrong.

As it turned out, many of the details in the 1985 story and the picture that ran in the paper were of the wrong person.

Parts of the story confused a law professor of the highest standing, who had the same name, with the craven wheeler-dealer. "I figured my career was over," said Wolinsky. "We did a page one correction the same size of the story. It was incredible. I don't think anyone ever saw anything like it. I think they paid him a settlement, too. All of the bigwigs went over the story. There were a lot of similarities; they had the same name; they were both lawyers; one worked for Pat Brown, the other for Jerry Brown; one reporter was in Sacramento and the other in LA; they never got together when writing it." Rather than fire him, the *Times* kept Wolinsky on, reckoning that his was an honest mistake, one any reporter could have made. This was, after all, Otis' paper— a deeply paternalistic operation that stood by its staff even when the waters were rough.

To make it to the top of a newspaper, you need more than talent and political skills. Timing is often everything, and Wolinsky had good timing. Soon after he was promoted to city editor in 1991, an amateur videographer filmed Los Angeles policemen beating Rodney King. Once television stations aired the footage, riots broke out throughout the city. At the *Los Angeles Times*, the newly minted city editor swung into action. He had to. His boss was on a cruise, and everyone else was on vacation. "It was just me there, and I had to react," Wolinsky recalled. "It was quite a moment for me. We won a Pulitzer for our coverage. But it also marked the start of five years of just incredible stories. There were riots, floods, the Michael Jackson pedophilia case. It ended with O. J. Simpson. It was just incredible."

Wolinsky attributed the success he would enjoy to being in the right place. The right place happened to be about eight miles west of Bleakwood Avenue, in a *Los Angeles Times* office with a picture on the wall of Otis Chandler.

# 4

## Twilight

I n 1984, Americans awoke to "Morning in America," the flag-waving advertising spectacle created to celebrate Ronald Reagan's successful drive for a second term as the nation's fortieth president. For the U.S. newspaper industry, though, it was twilight. Americans purchased 63.3 million newspapers in 1984, slightly over 1 percent higher than 1983 and a peak that would never again be achieved. Newspapers, the backbone of an industry that brought news to America's doorsteps for fifty to seventy-five cents, faced an erosion of circulation that major publishers would cover up until it turned into a landslide twenty years later.

On the surface, the nation's economy overshadowed potential problems. A boom triggered by President Reagan's tax cuts and massive budget deficits had begun: The economy was literally yanked from the depths of a recession that had driven the nation's unemployment rate to just under 10 percent. Anyone reading a newspaper or watching television wouldn't suspect any problems with the currency of news: Programs and articles were still rife with ads. In 1984, I was happily employed at the *Chicago Tribune*'s Washington bureau.

In 1982, Jim Squires, the *Tribune*'s editor, had strolled over to my desk in Chicago as I put the finishing touches on a series of stories I had written about the impact of the recession and a rising debt burden on the Illinois economy. "You know," Squires said in his signature southern drawl, "we need some goddamn investigative reporting in Washington. Go see [Doug] Kneeland and tell him you're going to replace de Lama." (De Lama was leaving Washington to become a *Tribune* foreign correspondent.) And that was that.

The exchange was vintage Squires, a forty-three-year-old Tennessee native known for his huge ego, tough talk, and impulsive style. A former *Tribune* Washington bureau chief, Squires had been named editor of the paper in 1981, when he immediately started the Squires shuffle—reassigning editors and reporters to different jobs in a staff shake-up that made everyone feel as if they'd been tossed into a blender. He once walked into the men's room and, while urinating, decided to reassign the reporter using a urinal next to him to the technology beat.

Squires' tenure didn't work out well for everyone; his ascension eclipsed Jones' career. But Squires put me right where I wanted to be: in the thick of the big stories of the day. Critics of American journalism like to pin the decline of U.S. newspaper circulation on content, particularly page one content. The indictment of editorial judgment cuts a wide swath: Papers don't publish enough *good* news; newspapers are *biased*; readers want sizzling, sensational stories on page one, not long, depressing accounts of starvation in Sudan; journalists edit their papers for other journalists, not *real* readers; blood and guts drive newspaper sales, not sober, serious news about the important issues of the day. Obviously, newspaper content affects sales, but most evidence suggests the impact is marginal. In the dozens of studies in which newspapers ask readers why they quit subscribing to a paper, anger over content pales in comparison to issues about paper delivery mishaps or missed papers. Indeed, what lies at the heart of the decline of newspaper journalism is not that simple.

As the "Morning in America" spectacle reached across the nation, newspapers were struggling with unprecedented social changes that would revolutionize media consumption habits, just as the great newspaper families began disintegrating and selling off their lucrative properties to corporations that subordinated journalism to that most natural instinct of capitalism: the desire to make cash machines out of cash registers. In the face of dwindling circulations and mounting debt, many newspaper owners began to focus more on making a profit and less on the civic duty and the moral imperative to cover the news on which their organizations were founded.

Sweeping demographic changes in the workplace triggered the jarring transition. Throughout the 1970s and early 1980s, a troubled economy prompted American women to get jobs in record numbers. Between 1970 and 1985, the number of women in the workforce jumped by 25 percent as inflation drove up living costs, and job growth stagnated, particularly during the recession that hit the economy in 1981. As U.S. families struggled to cope with sluggish wage growth, rising unemployment, and inflation, the number of homes with a working husband and wife soared 22 percent. By the mid-1980s, American men and women worked more and had less time to read the newspaper, particularly in the evenings when they returned from work. In the 1960s and early 1970s, television stations, eager to snatch ad dollars from newspapers, had started flexing their journalistic muscles, aggressively expanding their evening newscasts to half-hour segments. The result? Americans who came home from a hard day's work could luxuriate in a newscaster's summary of the day's stories, rather than plow through the newspaper.

The new workforce dynamic first hit the then-dominant form of newspaper—editions delivered in the afternoon that were typically read at dinnertime. In 1971, America had 1,425 evening newspapers like the *Des Moines Tribune*, and publishers sold some 36 million copies compared to only 338 morning papers like the *Des Moines Register*. Morning papers reported a total circulation of 26 million. Over the next three decades, Americans abandoned the evening paper in droves; by 2008, America had just 546 evening papers with a total circulation of only 5.8 million. One of those to die was the *Des Moines Tribune*, which published its last edition on Saturday, September 25, 1982, with the headline: "So Long, It's Been Good to Know You." The descendants of the Cowles family who owned the *Des Moines Register* reacted to the changing workforce as many publishers did; they folded the evening paper into the morning edition, consolidated staffs, and made the surviving paper stronger, essentially repeating a process that had periodically roiled the industry since its founding.

Between 1971, the year that I started at the *Register*, and 2003, the number of morning newspapers more than doubled to 787 titles with a combined circulation of 46.9 million, an increase of about 80 percent. Though the morning editions grew, they gained far less circulation than the afternoon papers lost. Between 1971 and 2003, morning papers sold 20.7 million more papers, but evening editions lost 27.9 million in circulation, a deficit of 7.2 million copies, just as overall morning circulation peaked. Moreover, the losses occurred as America's population grew substantially; by 2003, America had more than 80 million additional citizens, but they were not buying as many newspapers as their predecessors had. Nevertheless, Americans had come to rely on newspapers as a prime source of information on City Hall, the Congress, the workplace, school, even church. They formed a vital link to the kind of information citizens need to make democracy work and wrote the first draft of history—one that other media streams relied on. America didn't become more ignorant as the number of papers declined. Television news actually increased news literacy in America because viewers who turned on their TV sets around 5 or 6 p.m. had no choice but to watch the news.

For much of the 1960s and 1970s, only three networks manned the airwaves, and all of them simultaneously aired the evening news, partly because the broadcast licenses handed out by the federal government required some public service content, and partly out of pride. Broadcasters considered newscasts prestigious and wanted to have a better report than their competitors. The networks' news shows had a leveling effect. "The spread of [network] television across the country," noted Markus Prior, a Princeton professor of public affairs and expert on the media's impact on politics, "lowered the knowledge gap between the more and less educated segments of the population by increasing knowledge among the less educated while leaving it unchanged among the more educated."

With only three networks, one watched Walter Cronkite, Frank Reynolds, or Chet Huntley and David Brinkley. Once cable television emerged, things changed—dramatically. Suddenly, viewers could watch *I Love Lucy* reruns instead of tuning in to Cronkite. Between 1960 and 1984, cable subscribers soared from 650,000 Americans to 29 million, setting the cable industry on a path that would peak in the new millennium at around 65 million subscribers. As more Americans signed up for cable, newspaper circulation began to decline, and network news audiences plummeted by 50 percent from the peak in the 1980s.

The impact of these developments went way beyond the newspaper and network bottom lines. Prior's research suggests that American audiences fragmented according to their tastes and interests, a development that spawned the kind of political polarization now prevalent and one that carried ominous implications for America's collective intelligence. News literacy declined sharply among less educated Americans as they opted for the *I Love Lucy* reruns, while the educated class watched even more news as cable news shows proliferated. "Even if the level of political involvement in the population does not appear to drop," Prior suggested, "the growing inequality of this involvement, which is a direct consequence of greater media choice, poses serious problems for post-broadcast democracies." The arrival of cable television simultaneously increased the threats publishers faced. Educated readers were the prime audience for newspapers, and the time they spent watching news on cable ate into how much time they could devote to reading the daily newspaper, which typically carried more in-depth, objective news reports.

■

It's hard to believe that these momentous changes failed to generate panic in newspaper publishing circles. But they didn't. For one thing, growth in Sunday newspaper circulation offset some of the financial and civic damage; the number of papers publishing Sunday editions fat with ads jumped 55 percent between 1971 and 2003, pushing up Sunday circulation by about 8.8 million copies. With feature sections designed to lure advertising, Sunday papers not only gave readers a wider choice of content, but included an overview of the week's events in a tidy section. And thanks to a chance encounter between a Massachusetts newspaperman and a guy who made atomic bombs, Wall Street had arrived on the scene.

Critics characterize newspaper companies today as backward, sclerotic outfits, plagued by stagnant thinking and journalists trapped in the past. Actually, that's not quite true. Until recently, newspapers were pioneers in new technology, both in the newsroom and in the boardroom. Nowhere was this more evident than with Prescott Low, the publisher of the *Patriot Ledger* in Quincy, Massachusetts. In the early 1950s, Low, a progressive newsman whose paper had once published letters to the editor from John Quincy Adams, witnessed a new photocomposition process at a Boston demonstration organized by Vannevar Bush, a key scientist involved in the development of the atomic bomb. Invented by a Frenchman just after World War II, the photon, which Bush showed Low, used photocomposition to set type on film instead of the Linotype, a clanking, cumbersome contraption that had more than ten thousand moving parts and took four years for union operators to master. Low was astonished. The photon set type six times faster than the Linotype and had the potential to significantly lower labor costs. Low immediately ordered one and installed it in the *Ledger's* offices. With the photon, the *Patriot Ledger* no longer required $4-an-hour union operators to set type—off-the-street clerical workers could compose the paper with the new film process. Significantly, Low reinvested his savings into his editorial department, making his paper a prosperous and respected journal throughout New England. As word spread of Low's innovation and cost savings, other newspaper publishers embraced the new technology and started hard bargaining with their unions, leading to a couple of decades of labor strife and sweeping technological changes that would transform the industry.

Unfortunately for the newspaper families, the financial windfalls spurred by the new technology also drew the interest of the Internal Revenue Service. As newspapers converted to photocomposition, profits soared, prompting IRS appraisers to reassess the way they valued the assets, dramatically increasing potential estate taxes and offering newspaper families huge incentives to sell out to people like Paul Miller and Allen Neuharth, men who worked for a company that acquired newspapers like Imelda Marcos bought shoes.

Miller became the forerunner of what would become a fixture of American newsrooms—the respected working journalist who assumed a high-profile position in the corporation to give cover to corporate predators like Neuharth, whose second wife compared marital life with Al to "riding a roller coaster with a snake." Assuming control of a sedate group of twenty-five newspapers owned by Frank Gannett in upstate New York during the 1960s, Miller, as a figurehead chairman, and Neuharth, as his number two (though in reality Neuharth was the true power broker of the deal), converted the Gannett Newspaper Group into a journalistic juggernaut, acquiring other papers at a blistering pace in the 1960s and 1970s. In 1971, the year I started at the *Register*, Gannett averaged one newspaper acquisition every three weeks, and by the time I left the paper to join the staff of the *Chicago Tribune* in 1979, Gannett had acquired fifty-four newspapers, or an average of nearly seven papers a year, a pace that brought the total number of newspapers under the chain's umbrella to seventy-nine. Eventually, my first paper, the *Des Moines Register*, fell into the hands of Gannett, which Neuharth acquired for $200 million in 1985, ending a relationship between the Cowles family and Iowa that had lasted eighty-two years.

To increase its ability to acquire other papers, ease the bite of estate taxes, and fill the pockets of newspaper dynasty descendants, Gannett embarked on a trail blazed by Dow Jones, best known as the publisher of the *Wall Street Journal*, and became a publicly held company. Starting in the 1960s, newspaper companies big and small had become publicly held firms, a fact that enabled organizations like Gannett to use shares of stock instead of cash to build empires that would change the face of

American newspapers. By the 1970s, many major newspapers had gone public, including influential heavyweights such as the *New York Times*, the *Washington Post*, and Times Mirror, publisher of the *Los Angeles Times*. Some of the family dynasties benefited from public ownership but still maintained control of their fate by issuing two classes of stock, one for the family that carried more weight in matters of corporate governance and one for the public that didn't. But many families sold their papers outright to chains. By 1977, 170 newspaper groups owned two-thirds of America's 1,700 daily newspapers. By the time the Tribune Company acquired Times Mirror in 2000, a mere seventeen publicly held newspaper companies controlled nearly half of the daily and Sunday circulation in the nation. The *Chicago Tribune* went public in 1983, but the significance of the structural change was lost on the newsroom, which remained focused on journalism. By joining the ranks of stockholder-owned companies, Tribune executives and newspaper owners across America fell under the thumb of Wall Street. In the process, they agreed to be measured by different yardsticks, not just journalism prizes and civic pride but also profit, efficiency, shareholder value, cash flow, and the price of a share of stock. From 1983 on, the industry would answer not just to readers but also to shareholders with their eyes fixed on the bottom line and Wall Street analysts.

Unquestionably, the new order had a significant impact on the journalism practiced at papers owned by the public companies. "Going public forces management to tighten the belt, to come out of the ivory tower, to invest less in editorial," said one Wall Street analyst, whose views were typical of several surveyed by a group of University of Iowa researchers in the late 1990s. "Staffs are leaner and there is less investigative reporting. The quality of newspapers degraded, and part of that is due to going public."

Some critics suggest that the change in newspaper structure created a brand of corporate journalism that caused many of the problems plaguing the industry today, particularly the practice of targeting content to wealthier, elite audiences sought by advertisers, the source of more than 80 percent of the industry's revenue. There's some truth to that view; ownership of newspapers by a far-flung group of stock-holders unquestionably created pressures that led many newspapers down a perilous path that ended at the doors of bankruptcy court. But the death of journalism that those with a dark view of changing corporate structures predicted didn't really materialize. Despite the financial pressures and tighter budgets, editors working at newspapers owned by public corporations continued to produce outstanding journalism throughout the 1980s and into the new millennium; reporters continued to write stories that angered advertisers and their bosses. Newspapers controlled by public corporations were most often the recipients or finalists for Pulitzer Prizes, because creative and determined journalists still managed to get the appropriate resources to finance excellent journalism.

Far more significant to the decline of newspapers was a change in human dynamics and leadership spawned in newsrooms and news-paper offices across America. Tensions had always existed between editors responsible for writing and editing a paper and those respon-sible for making the money. Historically, many publishers thought of themselves as journalists first and business people second; they aban-doned their editorial perches reluctantly, referring to their editorial departments as "upstairs" and the business offices as "downstairs." James Schermerhorn, publisher of the long-gone *Detroit Times*, told an Associated Advertising Club audience in 1909: "Upstairs was the region celestial in a sense that three can keep a secret if two are dead, and upstairs and downstairs can keep the peace if there is no down-stairs. Then came the serpent in the form of the inevitable business expansion of an eager, glorious young nation. The alluring red apple of advertising, plucked from the tree of knowledge, caused the expulsion of the newspaper publisher from his editorial paradise."

To protect editorial departments from the undue influence of big advertisers who would become the industry's major source of revenue, publishers erected a philosophical wall between the editorial and busi-ness operations to discourage their biggest customers from using their financial muscle to get positive coverage. On one side of the wall were the editors who pursued the public service mission that made newspapers responsible for the *news*, defined by the Hutchins Commission on the Freedom of the Press in the 1940s as, "a truthful, comprehensive, and intelligent account of the days events in a context which gives them meaning." On the other side sat circulation, production, and advertising directors responsible for producing the paper, keeping and winning readers, and selling ads to people who were not always pleased with the headlines and stories journalists produced. Traditionally, the person with the authority to breach the wall was the publisher, who was responsible for the overall health of the paper.

Smart publishers kept their noses out of the news. If a big advertiser threatened to cancel his ads because he didn't like some aspect of the newspaper's coverage, a publisher could always throw up his hands and cite the paper's policy that prohibited anyone from tampering with the integrity of the public's business. Practically speaking, though, the business and editorial sides rarely functioned independently of each other. At their core, newspaper publishers run a manufacturing operation. Everyday, they make a complex new product that requires workers with clashing personalities to write and process hundreds of thousands of words that are packaged into a newspaper and delivered rain or shine for less than a dollar to the doorsteps of customers before they leave for work. For decades, the road to the top in the business office passed through the pressroom where editors and their counterparts on the production side got their hands dirty as they struggled to solve common problems, embracing processes and practices that built a mutual respect for each other and the jobs they had to do.

Stan Cook, the chief executive officer who took the Tribune Company public, recalled how he worked closely with editors like Clayton Kirkpatrick. "I met him doing mundane things," Cook said, relating a story about how he and Kirkpatrick stayed at work late one night fixing the color mix on a page one cartoon. "I looked to Kirk for his wisdom in what he thought about the paper because he was a reporter who dated back to 1940. He had fifteen years of experience and he was a city editor. . . . It was like a little university. If I had questions, I would go to Kirk." Similarly, when Kirkpatrick decided he wanted to reject the Colonel's brand of journalism and lead the *Tribune* in a new direction during the Watergate scandal, he sought help from Cook. Kirkpatrick knew he would be courting controversy with the *Tribune's* heavily Republican board of directors, and he knew he would need Cook's help for a campaign to reform the Colonel's *Tribune*.

Cook recalled:

> I had been working with Kirk, who is now editor of the paper, and Kirk said, "You know we are going to have to take a stand here on Nixon." What we talked about was a stand that he should resign. And I went up to see Hal Grumhaus, the chairman of the company. . . . I told him what we had decided to do and I think I had a draft of the editorial that Kirk had written . . . and I laid it in front of Hal Grumhaus and he looked at it and . . . he said, "You can't do this." He was very thoughtful about it; he realized it was a very important thing. I said, "Hal, we have to do it. Kirk and I are in total agreement on it and we have to do it." And he said, "We can't do this."

Cook and Kirkpatrick published the editorial anyway, making national headlines and taking heat from traditional *Tribune* readers, fellow Republicans, and members of the board. Many felt the repudiation of Nixon by a newspaper that was considered an arm of the Republican Party convinced the troubled president to step down. It unquestionably improved the *Tribune's* credibility among readers who had come to expect the paper to simply parrot the GOP line. In subsequent maneuvers that one editor compared to turning around an ocean liner, Cook and Kirkpatrick managed to not only make a profit but also turn the *Tribune* into one of America's best newspapers.

Over the coming decades in the newspaper business, though, the relationship between business and editorial would change. Many journalists pin the blame for the current decline of the newspaper business on the decision to go public, when publishers began worrying as much about the first quarter as the First Amendment. Publishers and ad men blame the trouble on newsrooms in denial populated by journalists who resist needed change. But nothing is that simple. It is hard to isolate one reason or event for the cause of the decline of powerful institutions that had weathered the challenges of time and turmoil. When you dig into the problems and peel off the anger, blame, lies, manipulation, and malice, the shortcomings and mistakes to which all parties plead guilty, the misfortune now plaguing newspapers traces to the severing of that bond of trust forged in pressrooms where editor and publisher alike got ink on their fingers. The next generation of leadership in Tribune Company and, with a few exceptions, in most of the rest of the industry experienced little common toil. Instead, mistrust, finger-pointing, and suspicion came to characterize the relationship between editors struggling to protect their newspapers and managers striving for the bottom line. Many newspapers and newspaper men and women simply lost their way, including Cook, a man who once pointed to the *Tribune's* newsroom and declared, "if anyone can solve our problems, they are out there, because they are the best that we've got."

When Cook named his successor, he didn't look toward the newsroom. The financial impresarios he had hired from the world of investment banking and accounting convinced him that the most important mission for Tribune Company, on the cusp of its Wall Street debut, was to improve its productivity. A new generation of leadership took over, people who had never struggled to meet a deadline, web a press, or register a photo. Editors worked *for* them, not *with* them. This new breed attacked the wall between editorial and business, saying that editors used it not only to protect the public interest, but also to protect fat payrolls, excessive editorial budgets, inefficient operations, and outdated technology. They subordinated the newspaper's public service mission to their goal of driving the returns of *Tribune* and other newspaper stocks into the stratosphere, making themselves and employees millionaires, developing close relationships with analysts and institutional investors who would come to own 70 percent of the stock of publicly held newspaper companies. They were doing what was *expected* of them, serving shareholders, journalism be damned. But the attacks simply increased resistance on both sides of the wall and generated the kind of misunderstandings that would become legion. Instead of developing strategies to produce the kind of content that would protect their most important asset—the public trust, they depreciated it like an aging Linotype. In early 1981, Cook anointed a plump, balding, tough guy from Toledo to succeed him. His name was Charles T. Brumback. He was an accountant—an expert on columns of numbers.

# 5

## The New Order

Charlie Brumback beamed with pride as members of the Great Lakes Naval Station band struck up the "Chicago Tribune March" on the steps of the massive new staircase he had built—at the cost of $250,000—to link "upstairs," the editorial department on the fourth floor of Tribune Tower, to "downstairs," the business offices below. Newsroom staffers wandered over to the huge, glass-enclosed, three-story passage to sample ice cream and listen to the tune commissioned in 1892 to memorialize the newspaper. Ninety-three years later, the tune was music to Brumback's ears for an altogether different reason. To complete the "Freedom Staircase," a massive hole had been jackhammered in the floor of the newsroom in a not-too-subtle hint to the journalists on the fourth floor to get with the program.

In Brumback's mind, the *Chicago Tribune* was a profit-churning business, not some highfalutin priesthood solely dedicated to truth, justice, and the First Amendment. If the paper didn't make profits, there would be no journalism. Profits required teamwork, a concept that, Brumback thought, was alien to most journalists with their hold-your-nose attitudes about how the company made a buck. To make his point, the *Tribune* chief, a Korean War veteran and military school disciplinarian, physically connected the newsroom to the business offices. When the moment arrived, as a gaggle of slack-jawed journalists looked on in disbelief, Brumback cut the ribbon draped across the staircase in a symbolic move that heralded the dawn of a new era in upstairs-downstairs relations. The dedication of the Freedom Staircase in 1985 was typical of Brumback, a blunt, tough, callous accountant who in 1981 had been drafted to run the *Tribune* from the *Orlando Sentinel*, a Tribune paper in Orlando, Florida.

As newspaper families sold off their inheritances, went public, and hired the bean counters of the world to deliver returns that would keep stock prices high and dividends flowing, professional managers—men trained as accountants or investment bankers—joined newspaper company staffs across America. Few of the new guard were as mean, intelligent, or hard charging as Brumback, though. Frugal, taciturn, and nearly bald, Brumback wore baggy blue suits and undistinguished brown shoes. In Florida, he had earned a reputation for turning off lights left burning after business hours. A Princeton graduate and native of Ohio, Brumback grew up in a comfortable suburb of Toledo. His bland demeanor and casual smile masked a quick, impatient mind. Dismissive and often harsh, Brumback would often cut subordinates off in midsentence; he once told *Tribune* employees doing page paste-ups that they were engaged in "idiot work"; he referred to a Tribune-owned tabloid in New York as "a paper for immigrants"; and warned another gathering of employees to take a good look at the person to the right and to the left, because by the end of the year, one of them would be gone.

Although he had graduated from one of the nation's best colleges, Brumback didn't tout his Princeton credentials. He attributed his success in business to the Culver Military Academy, the Indiana military high school he had attended. "Culver was more important to me than Princeton," Brumback said with pride. "The culture at Princeton was a little different. It was really training people for Wall Street, government service, and large corporations. Culver prepared me to take responsibility for my actions and [understand] what leadership [was] all about. I learned the importance of creating an environment where people work together as a team to accomplish something."

True to his military school roots, Brumback approached his new job at the *Tribune* like a general leading troops. On the whole, he considered the *Tribune* he took over in 1981 a flabby, undisciplined organization, one that was unable to capitalize on its considerable power because of poor leadership, backward technology, and a bloated payroll. Almost immediately, he forced the paper's editor, Max McCrohon, out of his job and replaced him with Jim Squires, a former *Chicago Tribune* Washington bureau chief and editor of the *Orlando Sentinel* under Brumback.

In addition to acquiring a militaristic attitude toward efficiently running organizations, Brumback had received a powerful lesson early in his career about how to effectively operate a newspaper.

> I had a friend who was a son of Jack Knight. The Knight family owned a newspaper in Akron, Ohio, near Toledo, where I was living. I went to high school with Frank Knight, who ... was my age and in my class. Before taking the job in Orlando, I went down and spent some time with Frank in Akron to get an understanding of the newspaper business. I told him that the newspaper business seemed to be very complicated and I wondered how in the world anyone could get a grasp of it.

He said, "Charlie, this is not a complicated business. All you got to do is step back and look at it as four separate, independent businesses working together under one roof. First you have the most important, which are the [editorial] content creators, the people who create the content of the newspaper that readers and subscribers will pay to read. These are the people advertisers want to reach. The quality of the content is extremely important. [But] these people are different. They are creative. They tend to be introverts. They are smart and they tend to stick together. You must realize they are different from others. If they are not different [from] your advertising people or your production people or your distribution people, you want to be careful."

And then he said, "Successful advertising folks are different from reporters and editors. They are outgoing extroverts. They wear a big handkerchief in their coat pocket that sticks out and they walk around patting everybody on the back. They are salesmen. They sell advertising. They are nice people; they are nice to everybody. You need people like this to sell advertising."

The third business under the roof—the production people, or those who actually manufacture the newspaper, "are not," Knight told Brumback, "like editorial and advertising folks. Most don't have college degrees. . . . Proofreaders, Linotype operators . . . paper handlers, mailroom and pressroom operators work with their hands and end most days with ink on their face, hands, and clothes. People who work in the production department are very important to the success of any newspaper."

Knight compared producing a newspaper to:

> the manufacture of 25,000 one-pound cakes of ice an hour. A printing press takes in raw material [large rolls of newsprint] in one end and puts out 25,000 one-pound products an hour from the other [during a ten-hour press run]. And you've got to get . . . 250,000 [of those] one-pound cakes of ice delivered to 250,000 different locations [every day] before they melt. Because once a certain amount of time goes by, the newspaper has very little value. The production process and the ability of your production people to create those 25,000 one-pound products an hour coming out of a press is extremely important.

Distribution was the fourth element in Knight's model. Because the news' relevance can melt like ice, Knight emphasized that the fourth business under the roof was important, despite its peripheral nature. Brumback recalled the way Knight had explained it. "You will find your distribution people are different," Knight told him. "They get up in the middle of the night in all weather. For most of them, it is a second job. They are the people that deliver your newspapers to your customers. You need to spend time with them and get to understand how they do their work." "This was the best advice I got before going to Orlando," Brumback admitted. "It helped me understand newspaper publishing. It is important to understand that each of the four functions is staffed with four different types of people with four different types of skills."

But there was one aspect of Knight's model that Brumback failed to buy into: the separation of the editorial and business operations, a necessary division that, early on, established a wall between *church and state* to protect the integrity of the news from powerful advertisers who would lean on publishers when they didn't like headlines.

Brumback hated the idea of a wall and dismissed it as a relic:

> Jack Knight [Frank's father] was a genius, a marvelous newspaperman [who would go on to build the Knight Ridder newspaper chain, at one time America's second largest]. But [Frank's] Uncle Jim was different. Jack was Mr. Outside. He moved around. He was a good newspaper publisher but Jim was Mr. Inside, . . . the one who handled the business affairs of he newspaper. . . . The dual-headed form of organization worked for Jack and Jim Knight because they were brothers and Jack enjoyed . . . news gathering and editorial work and Jim was a good businessman. They divided up their business into what some people today call the business side and the editorial side. [But] I felt there had to be one person responsible for the entire newspaper. While a dual-headed organization worked well for Jim and Jack Knight, when that organization is transmitted to subsequent non-family generations, it tends to create barriers between all functions responsible

for a successful operation. . . . I'm troubled when I hear someone talk about the "news side" and the "business side" of the newspaper. This divided organization is perpetuated mainly by editorial folks and, I think, it is taught in a lot of journalism schools. This model worked well for the Knight brothers during their lifetime, but it didn't work well for their successors.

When the Colonel built the Tribune Tower, the elevator carrying ad salesmen, delivery men, accountants, and the corporate brass to their offices had been rigged so it wouldn't even stop at the editorial department on the fourth floor. Even under the Colonel, who was a business-man to his core, editorial was considered the soul of the paper, a sanctuary where reporters and editors—though they might be subject to the Colonel's antics—labored free from the pressures of commercial operations. The editorial department's job was to create an audience by serving the public's need and desire for information; the business side existed to sell ads to that audience.

But Brumback, a notorious miser who scrutinized every penny spent at the Tower, turned that formula upside down, arguing that a paper that didn't make profits couldn't afford to cover the news. Brumback's attacks on the status quo didn't stop at the newsroom door. In one way or another, he assaulted each of the four businesses Knight had outlined as key in a successful paper, dragging *Tribune* employees kicking and screaming into the modern age, arming them with com-puters, jettisoning some *Tribune* loyalists and rewarding others, and instilling a rigorous sense of discipline throughout the organization. Once, Brumback ordered all of the blinds on the windows of Tribune Tower to be lowered to the same level and then walked around the out-side of the building to see who'd followed orders.

According to Brumback, he made clear to anyone who worked for him, including Squires, that regardless of title, they were executives whom he expected to be professional managers. "Editorial execu-tives don't like to be called managers," Brumback noted. "They would rather be called editors. This is a quaint distinction that appears be to universal in the newspaper business. But that didn't bother me. I looked on them—and they knew I looked on them—as managers and executives who had to manage their part of the business."

Squires understood how to play the game; in Florida, he had cut a deal with Brumback that would dramatically affect the *Orlando Sentinel* and later the *Tribune*, one that Squires in retrospect described as a Faustian bargain: "[He] let me decide what goes in the newspaper, what its editorial opinions will be, what time it goes to press, and how it presents itself in the community, and I promised to run the tightest ship in the business. It was a deal designed to deliver both prizes and profits."

Tribune Company had acquired the *Sentinel* from Martin Andersen, a high school dropout who lived large, enjoyed martinis, and idolized the Colonel. Brumback, who had been hired, fired, and rehired by Andersen, came along with the paper in what he described as a golden opportunity: "Orlando was a market in those days where our mistakes didn't show. It was growing so fast that even if we made a mistake or did something wrong, it generally would be covered up by the growth of the market. But overall the company was strong. We had good management. We had good people coming up in the ranks, and it was a very well run and successful newspaper."

During the four years Brumback and Squires ran the *Sentinel*, they increased the paper's operating profit margins from the mid-teens, the industry average, to the low twenties, among the industry's best. Budgets were set in order for profits to rise by 15 percent to 25 percent a year, and soon, Squires noted, the *Sentinel's* contribution to the bottom line was nearly as much as that of the *Tribune*, which was three-and-one-half times its size. As editor, Squires became much more involved in the marketing of the paper than many of his contemporaries thought acceptable, but he also used the money he got out of Brumback to engineer an about-face in the *Sentinel's* journalistic reputation. He was a pioneer in creating zones to target local news and advertising, and he redesigned the paper into clean, well-organized sections that delineated main news from local, business, sports, and features. True to his bargain with Brumback, Squires whacked the editorial department budget. At the time he assumed the helm, the editorial budget was 15 percent of the paper's overall revenue. It fell exactly 1 percent a year between 1976 and 1980.

The results turned heads in Chicago, where Cook was preparing to take Tribune Company public, and when, in 1981, he named Brumback CEO of the Chicago Tribune Company, the corporate arm of its flagship newspaper, Charlie decided to bring his editorial ace along. Brumback saw padded staff, retarded technology, and subpar revenues in Chicago, too. But, he also encountered unions—organizations that were decidedly hostile to his capitalistic instincts, and ones that he would eventually crush. The troubles that faced the *Chicago Tribune* in the early 1980s plagued many other big-city newspapers. The *Tribune* had substantial revenues, but they were not growing, particularly once inflation was factored in. Papers that tried to raise circulation or advertising rates to compensate for sluggish growth fueled counterattacks from new media—television, radio, free newspaper shoppers, and direct mail—all of which were growing, charged less for ads, or had greater audience reach. So, newspapers kept the prices low to prop up their circulation and the myth that they were a medium with a mass audience.

Meanwhile, costs at big-city newspapers had soared thanks to inflexible work rules, onerous labor contracts, and bloated payrolls. Brumback saw staffing levels as the root of most problems. Soon after arriving at the Tower, he started slashing jobs and taking on the newspaper's unions, arguing that the paper needed more efficient press runs and more flexibility in dealing with lifetime job guarantees, issues that rankled union leaders. Within a few years, the unions staged a strike, a dramatic miscalculation that the *Tribune*'s new general capitalized on with a ruthless counterattack that broke their backs. "We had temporary replacements for all of the work necessary to produce the newspaper [when the strike started]," Brumback recalled. To compound the effects of this ready workforce, the drivers' union, the Teamsters Union, didn't honor the picket lines. As a result, Brumback could still successfully deliver the paper. Eventually, the scabs that had come in as short-term hires were slotted into permanent positions when the strikers disregarded the call to return to work under the proposed conditions. Brumback said:

> The replacements came from some of the Tribune's other newspapers that were non-union. Others came from friends in the industry. . . . The out-of-town replacements were here up to a year. After a few weeks, we began to bring in young people right out of high school and college. We trained them to run the new technology equipment and within a few months we had a lot of well-trained workers. . . . Everybody that came in was told that this was a strike situation and it was temporary. . . . They were able to make extra money because they worked a lot of overtime. But then it became clear that the unions were not about to agree to our terms under any conditions. Finally we sent a registered letter to all of the strikers at their homes and told them that they had twenty-four to forty-eight hours to get back under the conditions that we proposed before they struck or they would be permanently replaced. They didn't come back. They were getting bad information from their union leadership who didn't want to acknowledge that they had lost the strike. . . . So we permanently replaced them.

Brumback also forced significant changes in the newspaper's inefficient distribution system in a convoluted agreement that forced him to spend about $45 million to regain control over routes that the paper technically owned—a payment he labeled a "disgrace." But the deal enabled the *Tribune* to create a system of independent delivery contractors that was more efficient, improved customer service, and, of course, cut costs.

Brumback was no entrepreneur. He was a manager, a hired gun, and an expert in numbers. Prizes and awards didn't impress him. But

Brumback and Squires both realized long before their peers that the computer and the technological advances it heralded would revolutionize the delivery of information. In Florida, Brumback had been deeply impressed with how The Walt Disney Company, owner of Disney World in Orlando, had used technology to enhance its entertainment business. He had also mastered the Apple computer at home and incentivized his managers to adopt the new technology by offering a free computer to anyone willing to teach himself how to use it on his own time. In 1981, when he made the same offer at the *Tribune* and no one bit, he lost no time in removing the paper's editor and ushering in Squires.

A gifted editor, Squires wanted to bring a more cosmopolitan approach to the *Chicago Tribune*'s news reports, whether it involved foreign, national, or even fashion coverage. "He thought big," remembered Lisa Anderson, a New York native and former reporter for *Women's Wear Daily*, whom Squires hired to write about fashion for the *Tribune*. "He told me he wanted to make the *Chicago Tribune* a world-class newspaper and to do that he needed sophisticated fashion coverage."

The *Tribune*'s journalistic reputation grew with Squires at the helm. The paper's parochial ways and tarnished reputation from the days of the Colonel and his successors were no more. As editor, Squires created the illusion of a paper with an expanding staff. For every two obscure middle-management editor positions he eliminated, Squires turned heads by hiring journalists with high-profile reputations, people like Douglas Kneeland, then the Chicago bureau chief for the *New York Times*, who then recruited fellow *Times* writer John Crewdson, a brilliant reporter from the paper's Houston bureau, and Nicholas Horrock, a combustible investigative reporter who had worked at the *Times* and *Newsweek* magazine. He changed the focus, purpose, and direction of the paper toward deeper reporting, more ambitious coverage, and a more sophisticated view of the world.

During Squires' initiative to beef up the Washington bureau, I landed my correspondent job in 1982. Meanwhile, he worked hard to open high-profile news bureaus in other cities across the nation and world. He folded the paper's suburban and local news inserts, replacing them with a zoning scheme that could provide local news and advertising more efficiently and give the paper a more refined feel. "Brumback's goal," as Squires explained in a book he wrote about his *Tribune* career, "was to make more profit than last year, not just a little more but the most possible. When these goals collided, our respective rank within the company decided the outcome. His always took precedence over mine, no matter what."

But Squires underestimated the difficulty of sustaining a journalistic shell game in which his high-profile hires and new bureaus obscured a squeeze on the newsroom budget. "I [became] a 'smoke and mirrors magician,'" he said, "juggling from the right hand to the left, robbing Peter to pay Paul, and lying to myself and my staff about how successful we were." To help finance his journalistic sleight of hand, Squires implemented policies that subordinated the interests of the reader to that of the advertiser, and focused his gun sights on the *Chicago Sun-Times*, the scrappy tabloid that was the *Tribune*'s only real competition.

Squires bragged:

> It was the last of the great newspaper wars on one of the greatest battlefields of them all. . . . It was an advertising driven contest in quest of the highest quality readers. We didn't hire more reporters, or include more news or print any more papers. We just shifted available resources to a day when circulation and advertising rates were the highest to generate more revenue. And the higher demographic profile of our readers combined with better reproduction of the advertiser's image by high-quality offset printing led to a better and more desirable response to advertising, tipping the balance to our side of Michigan Avenue once and for all.

Squires' strategy enabled Brumback to live up to his part of the bargain and more. "Productivity accelerated. Production costs decreased because we had fewer people," Brumback said. "The productivity per man hour skyrocketed, and within a couple of years, the *Tribune* became probably the most productive big-city newspaper in the country. And for several years, it was the most profitable newspaper in the country." Thanks to the higher ad rates, revenue jumped, too, because the paper could charge for an audience that had the kind of demographics that advertisers loved.

The *Tribune* wasn't the only paper with plunging production costs. Across America, newspaper productivity soared as professional managers replaced humans with machines. Squires noted:

> Between 1975 and 1990, newspaper production workforces would be cut by 50 percent or more. Presses that once required ten to twelve workers would now run with six or seven. Typesetting that used to demand huge departments, employing from thirty to three hundred skilled, unionized craftsmen, would disappear completely. Paper handling and loading, which once required waves of manual laborers, was replaced by computerized conveyer systems, robotic cranes, and remote-controlled flatcars. Human photoengravers would be replaced by laser beams, and film processors by computer processes.

The decline in the cost of production of the newspaper was not as dramatic as it seemed. Technology enabled managers to shift work that was once done on the floor of the printing plant to the newsroom, just as editorial budgets came under equally intense pressure to be cut. The burden of producing the newspaper fell more heavily on the shoulders of editors, but it also made them more indispensable to the operation. Meanwhile, those coveted cash flow margins at publicly held newspaper companies jumped to the 20 percent range by the mid-1980s. Nowhere was the trend more evident than at Tribune Company. Brumback continued his string of thirteen straight years of improving profits, tripling margins at the *Chicago Tribune* in just eight years from the 5 percent to 10 percent range to the mid-twenties. Buoyed by the profits at its flagship paper, Tribune Company's stock soared 23 percent a year, triple the average of the rest of the industry.

Although overall profits rose at a 23 percent clip in the five years after the company went public, revenues rose only 9 percent, putting pressure on Squires and others to squeeze their budgets to finance earnings growth. To Squires' credit, the situation didn't really affect me or most of my colleagues at the Washington bureau. When American sailors began escorting oil tankers threatened by Iranian missile attacks out of the Persian Gulf in the shadows of Iranian missile batteries along the Strait of Hormuz, I hopped on a plane bound for the Middle East to cover the "tanker war." When the paper needed investigative profiles of George Herbert Walker Bush or Senator Robert Dole's campaign for the White House, no expense was spared. With Washington as a base, I traveled America, writing stories about everything from the financial scandal that drove House Speaker Jim Wright from office to budget excesses in the Pentagon's Los Angeles–class attack submarine program. Those kinds of stories brought the *Chicago Tribune* high-profile journalistic accolades, particularly a series of stories I did on the savings and loan scandal.

Squires didn't fare as well, though. He faced incredible pressures to deliver budgetary miracles to meet a demand for higher and higher profits, pressures that would never cease. After he left the company, Squires blasted Tribune and the industry for its failure to reinvest in their newspapers to finance improvements that would have better served readers. "The profitability of newspapers," he wrote, "has come to depend on an economic formula that is ethically bankrupt and embarrassing for a business that has always claimed to rest on a public trust: the highest profitability comes from delivering advertising sold at the highest rates in a paper containing the fewest pages and sold for the highest possible retail price to the fewest high income customers necessary to justify the highest rates to advertisers." Zeroing in on the hypocrisy of newspaper publishers who ask for special legal and political rights on the ground that they exist to protect the people's right to know, Squires noted, "Nowhere does the Constitution define the 'people' as the predominantly white upper 30 percent of the population between twenty-five and fifty years of age who make $50,000 a year."

Yet manipulating newsroom resources to maximize advertising revenues is how Squires battled the *Sun-Times*. Like many before and after him, Squires allowed his bosses to capitalize on his reputation as a solid, professional journalist, essentially ushering in the policies he later described as bankrupt. To Squires' credit, he always pushed the staff to cover issues that affected the rich and poor—minority housing, Chicago's bankrupt schools, the plight of the underclass, and corruption at City Hall. When Cook decided to step down, the two contenders for his job were John Madigan, the investment banker brought in to take the company public, and Brumback. Charlie often frustrated Squires with his miserly ways, but Madigan was someone Squires thought was far worse. "Squires never liked Madigan," Brumback recalled. Squires said he openly campaigned against Madigan for the top job. Meanwhile, he made a speech to the board extolling Brumback's business acumen, his value as a mentor, and his wisdom in leaving editorial decisions to journalists. "I just made the case that Madigan had never run anything. Actually, Charlie was a pretty easy sell. None of them [company directors] liked Madigan," said Squires.

Instead of thanking Squires, Brumback reneged on a budgetary pledge he had made to his editor in order to post record profits. When he was named Cook's successor, Madigan was given Brumback's former job—Squires' nemesis was now his boss. "There was no way for someone who had fought Madigan's ascent to power as vigorously and openly as I had to remain a power at the newspaper," Squires said. "I lost the war. I knew I was dead."

Squires didn't help himself with his remarkably prescient report, "Project Prosperity," in which he urged Tribune to adopt new attitudes toward circulation and advertising, to invest its dollars in the company itself, and to abolish the industry's reliance on advertising rate increases justified by the Audit Bureau of Circulation, the industry-funded organization that certifies circulation totals.

After he wrote his report, one of Squires' friends in the corporate office said Squires' enemies, led by Madigan, used it to brand him a "dangerous heretic." At the time, he was not even fifty. Despite his ego and his faults, he was a fine editor and leader, a man who had a vision for the paper that was bigger than himself. He acknowledged that in his drive to adjust to a new "business paradigm and to excel at cost cutting and profit making in exchange for total control of editorial policy and news content, . . . I stayed too long and accepted too many bonuses to make a martyrs' list." Nonetheless, he gave journalists a powerful object lesson in grappling with the real power of the press as we struggled to save the journalism that we cherished.

On his last day at the *Tribune*, Squires visited Brumback, who informed him that his problem was that he didn't "talk like us." When told in retrospect that Brumback admitted Squires would probably have been the better choice to run the company than Madigan, Squires laughed: "Well, at least the old son of a bitch finally admitted it. All he ever did was add up the numbers and turn out the lights. All of the ideas of what to do were mine."

# 6

## The Cereal Killer

Leo Wolinsky stepped out of the elevator on the sixth floor of the *Los Angeles Times*, a maze of hallways and corridors that twist and turn like a pretzel before emptying into a large, bright atrium surrounded by the corporate offices of Times Mirror. The path from the cluttered, cramped newsroom with its frayed green carpet to the spacious corporate offices was so familiar to Wolinsky, he could have walked it blind. By 1996, he'd been at the *Times* for nearly two decades, had seen publishers and editors come and go, had survived putsches and coups, and had winnowed his way to the top as a managing editor in charge of the holy grail: page one. Steeped in the *Los Angeles Times* way of doing things, Wolinsky knew his way around the block. A natural newsroom politician, he was also a friend to many of the men and women who had toiled alongside him for years. Striving side by side to get the paper out everyday will teach you a thing or two about people, and Wolinsky was someone you could count on. Even more importantly, he had mastered a skill crucial in any newsroom: He knew the ins and outs of the production process; he was a pro who could get the paper out every day.

But in nearly twenty years at the *Times*, he'd never seen anyone quite like Mark Willes, who had summoned him to the sixth-floor meeting. In many respects, Willes was the *Los Angeles Times* equivalent of Brumback. Both were financial disciplinarians, and both had been recruited to their respective companies with the same mission: Cook had hired Brumback to improve productivity at Tribune Company; the Chandler family had brought in the evangelistic Willes from General Mills to be the CEO of Times Mirror and to do God's work on the *Los Angeles Times'* bottom line.

A meeting with the business side of the paper was nothing new; there'd been countless sessions with consultants over the years. But Willes and Kathryn Downing, the hopelessly challenged publisher, had engaged a new batch of consultants in a drive to increase the paper's circulation from about 1 million daily to 1.5 million or more. Publishers and journalists around the country mocked Willes' and Downing's well-publicized efforts. The golden era for newspapers was officially over: Most papers struggled mightily to maintain what circulation they had. Journalists and industry experts dismissed Willes' drive to grow circulation by 50 percent as ludicrous. Under Willes' and Downing's leadership, the venerable *Los Angeles Times* looked downright silly. Within the newsroom, Downing was known as "Calamity Kate," while CEO Willes was dubbed "Cap'n Crunch," a derisive reference to his legacy at General Mills.

But Wolinsky had a more nuanced view of the new numbers man. For one thing, Willes respected the power of print journalism. Wolinsky recalled, "I had mixed feelings about Mark. He was always calling in the consultants with all kinds of crazy ideas. But he was also smart and engaging; he really loved being in charge of the paper. He had a vision. It may have been nutty. But at least he had a vision. He really believed in the newspaper. He said our future was squarely in print. He ignored the Internet, thought it was just a fad. You had this great feeling that here was a guy who really believed in us."

On the hot morning Wolinsky was summoned to the so-called Salon, he was met with a scene worthy of a column all its own. A literal sniff test. As he later recalled,

I came into this room. There were a bunch of chairs. Michael [Parks, then editor of the *Times*] was there, a woman who ran HR [human resources], Kathryn, Mark was there. They were all sitting there looking at these canisters filled with shredded newspapers. They were clear, plexiglass, about a foot high, filled with shredded newsprint. One was the *New York Times*, one was, I think, the *Wall Street Journal*, and, of course, the *Los Angeles Times*. So the consultants told us to start *smelling* the newspapers, and you know what, lo and behold, the *Los Angeles Times* smelled the worst. That was our problem; that's why we couldn't sell newspapers. We didn't smell as good as the *New York Times* or the *Wall Street Journal*. Ours smelled worse because we had a higher percentage of recycled paper . . . it smelled like fish.

Wolinsky and his colleagues suppressed laughs as they listened to the consultants' take on the situation: Most Angelinos, sitting down for breakfast didn't want to pick up a newspaper that smelled like fish. But there was a solution, the consultants crowed: They could make the paper smell like Starbucks and coffee cake. And so it went.

Working for the former head of General Mills—a man mystified by the staff's reverence for Otis Chandler—anything could happen. Willes had been hired in May 1995, about a decade and a half after Otis had stepped down as publisher of the paper with a dazzling record that had earned him a well-deserved reputation as an icon of contemporary American journalism. Otis had left the publisher's office at the relatively young age of fifty-three, fed up with the backbiting ways of his hidebound conservative relatives. They were, in Otis' words, a "pain in the ass." He told his biographer, Dennis McDougal,

When I came into management, our pre-tax profit was somewhere around $2 to $3 million and I took it to $100 million. I took it [the company] to $1 billion in total revenues. That's one hell of a growth. And the non-Chandlers appreciated it. But I only got one compliment in all those years from the entire Chandler family. One of them said, "Thank God, cousin Otis, you worked so hard. We really appreciate what you did." They're just not that kind of people. It wasn't the editorial policy. They just couldn't bring themselves to give compliments. They're not built that way.

Wolinsky joined the staff of the *Los Angeles Times* three years before Otis stepped down as publisher. But Wolinsky didn't see Chandler often, and when in January 1981, Otis, a man who was always cool to the touch, became chairman of the board of Times Mirror, he withdrew into the newsroom shadows, deferring decisions involving his beloved paper to his successors. Eventually, a new generation of journalists arrived, clueless about the tensions that would surface in the imminent struggle at the paper. "Younger staff members took their editorial freedom for granted," McDougal observed in *Privileged Son*, a biography of Otis Chandler, "ascribing only token credit to the tall, fit and shy grandfather whom they occasionally ran into while waiting for the elevators or standing in line for the daily gourmet buffet in the executives' Picasso Room cafeteria."

A string of publishers and corporate politicians would follow Otis, only to get lost in his shadow. Tom Johnson, the affable Georgian Otis handpicked to succeed him as the first non-family publisher since 1882, came under immediate pressure from Robert Erburu, a lanky lawyer with Basque roots who would eventually play a hand in ousting Otis from the Times Mirror chairman's office a few years later. Doing the Chandler family's bidding, Erburu started to chip away at the wall Otis had erected to protect the newsroom from the pressures of the business. So skillfully had Erburu removed Johnson as publisher that some eleven years later, Johnson admitted to McDougal that he *still* didn't know, "why he was 'promoted' to the vacuous position of chairman of the Times Mirror Management Committee."

Johnson had named his own editor when Bill Thomas, the papers' longtime editor, retired in 1988. He was Shelby Coffey III, a handsome, glib young southerner from out East who ran marathons, pumped iron, and got credit for bringing a breezy wit to the *Washington Post*'s style section. "His deal was literary journalism," said Wolinsky. "Internally, he was seen as something of a dilettante. He quoted obscure poets, things like that. He loved Hollywood, and created literary teams. Column One really thrived while he was here." Under Coffey's tenure, the *Times* continued to excel, but hard-edged investigative reporting took a backseat to spot news coverage and the artful turn of phrase. Soon after he became editor, Times Mirror promoted another *Washington Post* refugee as publisher of the *Times*, David Laventhol, a highly regarded journalist who had run *Newsday* with a flourish. Coffey and Laventhol couldn't have been more different in appearance. Coffey was neat and preppy, while Laventhol was unkempt and always seemed to walk around with his shirttail out of his pants. Both generated controversy in the newsroom, too. Coffey, for a redesign that unfairly drew comparison with Gannett's *USA Today*, and Laventhol, for pulling back the *Times*' efforts to build circulation outside Los Angeles and eliminating first-class air travel for the staff.

"When Laventhol came in, it was the beginning of a slide in a way," Wolinsky said. "I stupidly offered to debate him on the first-class air travel. He started pulling circulation out of San Francisco and the Central Valley; he paved the way for the *New York Times*' national edition in California." Soon after they got their jobs, Laventhol and Coffey both confronted a poor economy that Erburu handled by imposing cutbacks, creating a drift in the paper's fortunes marked by relatively flat circulation and financial performance.

By 1992, Times Mirror reported its first net loss in a century: $66.6 million in red ink, a glaring number that was blamed on the recession that hammered California's defense industry and real estate markets and on costs incurred in a buyout. But the *real* reason for Times Mirror's fading fortune was the way in which Erburu and Laventhol ran the place. They opened the door for Willes.

Even though the ownership of the paper gave the Chandler family unprecedented power and influence in Southern California, the family had a hard time extracting cash from their controlling block of stock in Times Mirror. For years, they erroneously assumed that the trust created by Harry Chandler, which mandated that control of the *Los Angeles Times* would remain in Chandler hands, barred them from selling any of the stock they owned in Times Mirror. Dividends became particularly important to the Chandlers, since the payouts represented how family members could generate actual income from Times Mirror. As a result, the Chandlers closely monitored the company's dividend policies and made sure that anyone who ran the company understood the family's plight.

Initially, Erburu found it relatively easy to placate the Chandlers. Early in his tenure as CEO, Times Mirror paid about 39 cents in dividends for every dollar it earned, a policy that generated about $30 million in income for the Chandlers. But as the years passed, growth in Times Mirror dividends failed to keep pace with its corporate peers, and the company's earnings became erratic. By 1990, dividends consumed 77 percent of the company's earnings, generating $45.1 million in income for the Chandlers. By 1992, Times Mirror paid out $139 million in dividends, while it earned a mere $56.8 million before extraordinary expenses, a dividend deficit of $82.2 million. To cover the shortfall, Erburu, in concert with the Chandlers and the Times Mirror board, raised cash by getting rid of star reporters, shuttering editions of the paper, and selling about $1.7 billion in assets, a ploy that's like selling the family car to make your mortgage payments. Between 1980 and 1994, thanks largely to Times Mirror's dividends, the company racked up a cumulative cash flow deficit of $740 million. More critically, the ill-conceived policy diverted into dividends much of the cash the company needed to reinvest in its operations to keep its newspapers and television stations competitive in a rapidly changing media market.

In 1994, Laventhol announced he was stepping down as publisher because of debilitating Parkinson's disease. Richard T. Schlosberg III, a former air force pilot whom Erburu had brought to Los Angeles from Denver, replaced him. The health of Times Mirror fared no better on Wall Street. The company posted results that were so bad it faced the prospect of a dividend cut. Erburu, who was scheduled to retire after fifteen years at the helm of Times Mirror, rode to the rescue. To feed the beast, he and his management team suggested Times Mirror swap its sizable cable television division, which generated 36 percent of its operating income, for $2.3 billion in cash and stock, the largest asset sale in the company's history. Proceeds from the sale would generate an immediate cash infusion of $1.3 billion.

At first, Wall Street loved the idea. Times Mirror stock jumped nearly 12 percent to $35.75 a share on the news that Cox Enterprises of Atlanta, Georgia, was paying top dollar for the property. But not for long. Allan Sloan, then a reporter for *Newsday*, exposed the devil in the details: The company would not use the cash infusion to increase *everyone's* dividends, nor would the proceeds be passed along to investors. Erburu had structured the sale to create a special class of preferred stock carrying a payout that preserved and enhanced only the Chandlers' dividends. All other shareholders faced a dividend cut of as much as 80 percent to help the company generate the cash necessary to invest in technology to strengthen assets dedicated to news delivery. The Monday after Sloan's report ran in *Newsday*, Wall Street bid down the price of a share of Times Mirror to $32.75, as shareholders cried foul and stock analysts turned thumbs down on its proposed investments, which were the only element of the sale that made sense. The failure to invest in its future would continue to doom Times Mirror. Things only got worse after non-Chandler shareholders filed suit, alleging that the deal had been structured to benefit the Chandlers at their expense.

By early 1995, shares of Times Mirror were changing hands at about $18 a share, nearly half the value they'd held just after Erburu announced the sale. Embarrassed by reaction to the furor and public exposure of their greed, and forced to settle the suit with minority shareholders on less than generous terms, the Chandlers expanded the executive search to replace Erburu beyond the two internal candidates he had recommended.

In Minneapolis at General Mills, Willes had just discovered he would not be named CEO of the food maker when he heard about the Chandlers' search from a headhunter who asked if he might be interested in running a media company. "I think literally in about six weeks, we went from 'no, I don't want to even think about it' to being offered the job," Willes recalled. "What really intrigued me was the ability to play a role in helping the world be a better place."

After hearing of Willes' reputation as a financial disciplinarian who knew how to wield a budgetary axe, the Chandlers hired the buttoned-down industry outsider in May 1995, and he lost no time cleaning house at Times Mirror. Shortly after assuming his post, he earned the moniker "the cereal killer" when he made a trip to New York, to visit the offices of *New York Newsday*, which was headquartered in New York City and was the sister paper of Long Island-based *Newsday*. He listened to employees in Manhattan wearing "*Newsday* too smart to die" buttons and, with one day's notice, shuttered *New York Newsday*, a Laventhol pet project that had turned into a money pit. "We had a fiduciary duty to shareholders that was as important as our duty to readers," Willes said. "We had lost $100 million on *New York Newsday*. That seemed like a lot of money to me. To their credit, they really fought hard to keep it alive." But Willes said all he could see for *New York Newsday* was a future swimming in red ink, and he pulled the plug, leaving the New York metropolitan area with only one *Newsday*, the paper on Long Island.

He also stunned the *Times* newsroom by slashing journalist jobs in Los Angeles and, just as Brumback had in Chicago, launched an intense attack on the wall that separated the editorial and business operations of the *Times*, famously stating that he would use a "bazooka" if necessary to knock it down.

A practicing Mormon with an evangelistic streak, Willes meshed a strong commitment to family and the gospel with the ambition of a one-time B-minus student who climbed his way to the top of a major corporation. In the tradition of his church, he spent every Monday night with his family in something the Church of Jesus Christ of Latter-day Saints refers to as "Family Home Evening"—a time for families to come together as one to strengthen its bonds and to pray.

Willes speaks in a deep resonant voice like a preacher, resists the temptation to speak ill of others even if he feels victimized, and believes equally in "tearing down to build up." He approached the unpleasant side of running a big company as if he were an undertaker, for whom death is just another day's work. He bloodlessly delegated the dismissal of underlings who didn't share his view and quickly burned through the Times executive ranks. In Willes' first three years in the executive suite, nearly thirty executives were replaced or fled top management jobs at Times Mirror. In the past, the paper's masthead, a list of the top editors whose names appear on the editorial page, could go a decade or more without change. Under Willes, the staff began to see a number of alterations, prompting newsroom wags to nickname Willes' executive corps "The Flying Wallendas."

Willes skillfully played to the *Times* newsroom's sensibilities. "I really believe in the role of the newspaper," Willes said years later. "I believe in the fact that people having well-reported information is critical in having a civilized society. I believe if you don't know in some detail, not only what is happening in your neighborhood but also around the world, you can't have the kinds of conversations we need to have to make sensible political, economic, and education judgments." And, unlike many other news industry executives, Willes didn't treat readers as people you could take for granted because they had nowhere else to go. He mixed a message of consulting industry clichés ("We have to think out of the box") with a teary devotion to the apostles of print and ink. In his zeal to raise circulation, he cut the newsstand price of the *Los Angeles Times* from fifty to twenty-five cents, making the paper available to a broader segment of Los Angeles. He created new sections and editions designed to appeal to Latinos and targeted hyper local audiences. He sold off several lucrative properties, bolstering the Times Mirror's bottom line with one-shot surges of profit that he used to feed the Chandlers' voracious appetite for dividend income and the newsroom's equally gluttonous budget. Some of the most skeptical newsroom critics pinned their hopes on the new messiah in the making. At least he had the potential, many journalists hoped, to ensure their jobs.

When Willes arrived on the scene, Tim Rutten, an acerbic *Times* writer and critic, noted of the *Los Angeles Times*: "Not since the battle of the Somme have troops been so badly led as they have been led here in the past ten years. Now we have someone whose life every day has been a Darwinian struggle for shelf space. Maybe we're there, too. If he can bring his marketing skills in to save the newspaper, it will be a blessing to the whole industry."

And, indeed, Willes' initial results were good. Within months of his appointment, his opening moves had paid off. The price of a share of Times Mirror stock rose from $18 a share to $30, and then climbed to more than $70 a share. Dividends rose, a factor that appeased the Chandler clan, and operating income started to increase at a compound rate of 25 percent. *Business Week* named Willes one of its "Managers to Watch in 1996," and Wall Street brokers once again began recommending Times Mirror stock as a good investment. The newsroom watched with a mixture of fear and awe. At the same time that he was shaping up the paper's profitability, Willes was becoming somewhat of a star among the Hollywood stars. Newsroom stalwarts like Wolinsky noticed that Willes was really enjoying his job—maybe a little too much.

"I feel a little responsible for what happened to Mark," Wolinsky later admitted. "When he first got here, before he was publisher, he was looking for a place to take a vacation. I have a house up on the Central Coast and I told him he should go up there and visit Hearst Castle [at San Simeon]. He came back and told me he loved it. I think he decided he wanted to be William Randolph Hearst. He started acting like a dictator, like he was Idi Amin." Willes rarely applied the financial discipline he exhibited as a CEO to himself, or many of his executives, and soon he started to show the newsroom how to spend money.

Not long after Willes arrived, Wolinsky met with the new boss to tell him about a plan to revive the *Times'* Washington edition, which had been scrapped under Coffey. The new CEO listened to Wolinsky's idea and then told him he wanted to have a big party in Sacramento, and he wanted to meet the governor and legislators. Wolinsky recalled:

> I was supposed to set up the trip. So I got tickets on commercial airlines and lined up taxis to take us to the Statehouse bureau. But Mark had other plans. He rented a private Gulfstream [jet] and took us up there. It was Arnold Schwarzenegger's plane. We had limousines take us to the airport and pick us up in Sacramento. When we got to the bureau, first Dick Schlosberg [then publisher of the *Times*] got up to talk. He gave the troops a pep talk. He said he knew a lot of people were unhappy that we had to close the Washington edition, but that was the decision and we had to move on. Then Mark got up to talk. He said it wasn't a question of how to revive the Washington edition but a question of how quickly we could do it. He did it to stake his claim; he completely undermined his publisher. That's when I knew Dick's days were numbered.

Willes then hosted a splashy party in the lobby of the building that housed the *Times* Statehouse bureau, a grand space near the State Capitol where he could rub shoulders with senators, legislators, and the governor. Not long after, Schlosberg suddenly stepped down as publisher at the age of fifty-three, with the explanation that he wanted to spend more time with his family.

Although he had only been at the *Los Angeles Times* for a short period, Willes realized that being publisher of a big newspaper like the *Times* was a lot more fun than simply worrying about generating the earnings the company needed to pay the Chandlers' dividends. So, in September 1997, he replaced Schlosberg, adding to his CEO title the job of publisher of the *Los Angeles Times*, in a secret board meeting held while Otis, probably the only person who could have stopped him, was on an Alaska hunting trip. Soon Coffey stepped down, and Willes named his own editor—Michael Parks—an ace foreign correspondent at the *Times*, but someone who was not widely viewed as management timber. "I loved it," Willes recalled of his time as a publisher. "Even with all the criticism, I loved it, primarily because of the intellectual excitement of being able to talk to people who were really finding out about what was going on—from the people who were doing the gritty work in the courts in Los Angeles to the foreign correspondents. And the second thing I loved was making a difference."

Willes found some aspects of the newspaper publisher's job baffling: "The first thing that surprised me, and it shouldn't have, I just found it astounding that there was no such thing as a private meeting. So I'd have what I thought was a confidential conversation, and I'd read about it in someone's paper and I'd say, 'holy cow.' The second thing [was that] reporters were very bright people who understood that newspapers were a business and had to make a profit." But Willes found reporters reluctant to even discuss papers and profits in the same sentence. He said, "Well then, what are we missing in the idea that it's not possible to have a conversation about that without people assuming we've just broken down some sacrosanct separation between the journalism and the business side. What surprised me is that was a problem for journalists. I mean how can you report on the world and not be able to look at your own world realistically?"

The Chandlers who had brought Willes to the paper were not a small group in Pasadena that "meets at 'the club' on Sundays," pointed out Harry Chandler, Otis' son and one of the few members of the secretive family who talks publicly about his relatives. The extended family represents some 170 descendants, many of whom live outside Southern California. Most are not named Chandler; only eight of them sat on the board that appointed Willes; only seven (including Otis' son) worked for the *Los Angeles Times*; they are a fractured assembly. Yet they controlled Times Mirror through the family's considerable stock holdings and treated the company as their own. The family had hired Willes to be the CEO of Times Mirror, not the publisher of the *Times*. His decision to appoint himself publisher angered the family, particularly Otis. As CEO and publisher, Willes was his own boss, and there were no checks on the one man in charge of the day-to-day operations of the newspaper.

For editors like Wolinsky, Willes was a mixed blessing: "On the down side, Mark saw no reason that editorial should be treated any different than anyone else. I would argue that maintaining a wall between editorial and the business side was a matter of credibility. But he didn't accept that. In his experience, every department in a company should be going in the same direction. But he also saved the Washington edition with a flourish."

Few believed that the *Times* could achieve Willes' goal of increasing circulation by 50 percent to 100 percent. But circulation *did* increase under Willes, and he rewarded editors who went along with his ideas with the most important currency in the newsroom: people. "He had all of these ideas," Wolinsky recalled. "Some were great. Some of them worked. The zoned sections worked. He created a section for small businesses. He gave people stock options. He would sit down with editors and at the end of a meeting give them five or six more people. This was probably not sustainable. I suspect it would have eventually fallen apart. But for a while we had this great feeling that somebody really believed in us."

Willes launched the first brand advertising campaign in six years, increased weekend cultural coverage, published an eight-page bilingual section, purchased some smaller neighborhood papers in the market, created a "Reading by 9" program for kids, embarked on circulation-boosting campaigns with local non-English language papers like the *Korea Times*, did a bundling deal with the Spanish paper *La Opinión*, and shoved new sections in the paper covering subjects like health, transportation, and Southern California living. Under Willes, the *Times* recorded seven consecutive increases in circulation, although many gains involved adding gimmicks rather than readers. (The *Times* circulation jumped 17,000 thanks to its alliance with the *Korea Times* and about 90,000 when it was merely bundled with *La Opinión*.) Total gains fell far short of Willes' ambitious goals, but he increased total circulation by 150,000.

The newsroom watched Willes cautiously. Meanwhile, his relationship to the family that hired him deteriorated rapidly, largely due to the turmoil he created on the business side of the paper. "He didn't like the Chandlers," Wolinsky explained. "He couldn't understand why everybody thought Otis was such a god.... I think he was jealous of Otis." It's possible Willes might have thought the Chandler clan incredibly ungrateful.

In the first two and a half years of his tenure, Willes dramatically improved Times Mirror's financial performance. Between 1995 and 1997, the company paid out $2.1 billion in dividends and stock repurchases, compared to $417 million in the three years before he took over. He handed over all of the company's free cash flow to investors and the Chandlers, plus the proceeds of asset sales he engineered with a helping hand from Tom Unterman, the Chandler family financial sherpa. He sold off Harry N. Abrams, the nation's largest art and illustrated book publisher; the *National Journal*, a respected public affairs magazine; health science publisher Mosby, Inc.; and legal publisher Matthew Bender in a $2 billion plus deal that would later stick Tribune with capital gains taxes the Chandlers should have paid. Efrem (Skip) Zimbalist III, a former Times Mirror chief financial officer under Willes, explained:

> Mark was very direct. He was a visionary. He felt viscerally and emotionally very strongly about the newspaper industry. He liked our other businesses but loved newspapers. He really wanted the *Los Angeles Times* to succeed. But we operated in a complex market and he was struggling for ways to make it work. He put his heart into it and sold off certain parts of the company that he didn't think were

core . . . to raise cash to funnel to the Chandlers. Prior to Mark, we had a great mix of revenue with some assets that were not cyclical like the newspaper business. When the newspaper business was poor, the results were balanced by [non-core assets that] provided revenue. But Wall Street didn't like that. They wanted things to be real clear; they wanted clarity with nothing to confuse them. Mark started getting rid of [non-core assets] and that hurt our balance.

In Willes' tenure, Times Mirror, thanks to the genius of financial wizard Unterman, who had a legendary reputation for hatching tax avoidance schemes, reorganized its capital structure twice, rewarding the Chandlers with huge financial windfalls. The first of Unterman's efforts revived the dividends the Chandlers had sought, but failed to get in the 1994 sale of the cable business. In Unterman's second reorganization move, two trusts that he'd created entered into a complex deal with Times Mirror. The alliance generated regular cash disbursements plus tax-advantaged depreciation deductions to the Chandlers. In effect, the deal between the company and the trusts allowed the Chandlers to diversify their Times Mirror holdings without actually *selling* the stock. In one fell swoop, they circumvented the provisions of the trust saying they couldn't sell the stock, maintained control of Times Mirror, avoided any capital gains taxes, and got the dividends they so coveted.

Wolinsky watched the tension between Willes and the Chandler family bubble over when Otis retired from the Times Mirror board in March 1998: "They were going to have a going-away ceremony for Otis, and I went up there. I was kind of expecting him to make an inspiring speech about journalism." Instead, at the last minute, Willes combined Otis' final board meeting with a farewell party. "It was in the Chandler Auditorium," recalled Harry Chandler, referring to a large room on the sixth floor of Times Mirror, "and it was really awkward."

"Mark treated Otis like he was just another director retiring," Wolinsky remembered. Instead of a tribute to his fifty-five years of service to the company and newspaper, Wolinsky said, Otis was thrown a few dismissive remarks about how he liked to hunt, lift weights, and surf:

> Afterwards I went downstairs and I saw a couple of copy kids wheeling a cart down the hall with a bust of Otis that had been removed from the Globe Lobby. I stopped them and said, 'Hey, what are you doing? Where are you going with that?' And they said they had been told to take it down and put it in a closet. I asked them who told them to do that and they said Mark.

In his housecleaning effort, Willes was eager to wipe the slate clean—if not to erase Otis Chandler's legacy—to diminish his lingering presence, although he didn't recall removing Otis' bust.

Willes later acknowledged that his treatment of Otis was a mistake, particularly after Chandler left the board and grew more distant from the company: "In hindsight, because I'm not a politician and I don't know how to play politics, I don't even think that way and that would prove to be a mistake. I should have stayed closer to Otis because he became very critical. I honestly think to this day that, had I taken more time to fill him in, keep him informed, and get his reaction, we would have done better."

Despite Willes' best efforts, Times Mirror results started to lose their sizzle. By 1999, income from the company's operations totaled $248 million, up only $2 million from the year before. The massive increases in circulation failed to materialize.

Willes removed people with newspaper experience from the corporate suites and turned to executives from outside the industry, such as Steven Lee, an executive from PepsiCo, a consumer products company. He put Lee in charge of overseeing circulation and marketing the newspaper, a product he had never sold. When

Willes bowed to pressure to step down as publisher, he infuriated the Chandlers by tapping his number two, Kathryn Downing, a fellow Mormon and Stanford law graduate who had a long career in legal publishing but no experience in newspapers. He didn't even discuss his desire to promote Downing with the Chandlers, who expected to have a voice in naming a publisher of the family's flagship newspaper.

Willes' decision to batter the wall separating the editorial department from the business side was, not surprisingly, met with deep skepticism. He appointed mini-publishers to work directly with editors, blending the marketing of the paper with its news coverage. To him, the alliance made perfect sense. Ad salesmen could tip off editors about good stories, and reporters could alert salesmen to potential customers. People in the newsroom protested, arguing that the wall that had existed precisely because such nefarious alliances had damaged the industry's credibility in the past. But Willes ignored such cries and awarded editors who played ball.

"When I got there, I didn't completely appreciate what the term 'wall' meant to journalists," Willes said. He merely wanted journalists to think more about providing great reporting on subjects in which readers had an interest. "That is literally all I wanted to say. But I said it in the wrong way. I wanted to break down the wall but keep the line there. I never had any interest in having business influence the journalism."

Surprisingly, for someone interested in making a buck, Willes was not as interested in exploring new media as he was in building up the paper. Otis' son, Harry Chandler, had come to the company a few years before Willes to craft an Internet policy. He wanted Times Mirror to invest in a fledgling company named Yahoo! (Meanwhile, in Chicago, Brumback had made a small investment in an online start-up company called Quantum Computer Services, that would later be renamed America Online. The deal would pay off big.) But Willes didn't embrace the new media with the same zeal as other Internet advocates in the company, such as Unterman, at that time, his CFO. He slashed

Harry Chandler's new media division, angering and dispiriting one of the few people in the company with an eye on the future. Harry recalled:

> He [Willes] was a Luddite.... I've never told anybody this before. But there were three Chandlers still at the company then—me, Fred Williamson, and Susan Babcock. I was in new media and they worked in jobs on the business side. We were all pretty dismayed at what was happening at the *Los Angeles Times* and Times Mirror. About 30 or 40 percent of the business-side middle or upper management had left. So I made an appointment at Chandis Securities [the Chandler family holding company]. We met in a conference room in Pasadena above the accountants' office on Colorado Avenue and Orange Grove. We told them that we didn't know if they were aware of all the good people that were leaving, and we named many of them. We told them that we wanted to bring the situation to their attention. They listened and said thank you. Frankly I don't know if we had any impact. The only communication you ever get from the family is business. There are no family calls. That never happened. People on the board run everything. They are very secretive.

Wall Street meanwhile took a look at the predicament facing the Chandlers of the world and saw an opportunity to make a buck. Investment banks like Goldman Sachs and Merrill Lynch had used their elevated status as strategic advisers to the corporate elite to unleash a wave of consolidation. Soon deals like AOL's marriage to Times Warner Corporation would command headlines. In Wall Street's view, executives like Willes had a simple choice: to "buy or be bought." But the man who sanctioned sniff tests to ensure a better-smelling newspaper wasn't easily convinced.

From time to time, Willes had initiated strategic planning exercises to determine if Times Mirror would be better off merging with another media company or remaining independent. They were mock exercises, not actual proposals, and he didn't see any advantage to proposing a marriage of Times Mirror and Knight Ridder, or Tribune Company, or any other media company. "I felt we could take care of our shareholders just fine as an independent company," Willes recalled. Then he got a phone call from a fellow CEO from Chicago who wanted to get together for a chat at an upcoming Newspaper Association of America meeting in San Diego. "I didn't know John Madigan well, and thought it would be fun to get together, to get better acquainted," Willes recalled. "I thought it would simply be a conversation. Very naïvely, I thought that's all it would be, just a casual conversation. One of the things I have never been is politically astute."

# 7

## His Seat on the Dais

The white tour bus carrying John Madigan weaved through the streets of Havana. Once again, he and an entourage of Tribune Company executives had come to Cuba with the hope of interviewing Fidel Castro, and once again, Castro had stiffed them. Eric Ober, president of CBS News, had recently shown up in Havana with a group of network executives for a long, late-night session with Castro. So had many other lesser corporate luminaries. But for the second time in six years, the dictator gave the cold shoulder to the CEO of the Tribune Company, head of a widely admired Fortune 500 corporation and a group of executives who ran newspapers covering the world's largest diaspora of Cubans. As his bus passed bicycles and aging cars plying the frenetic streets of Havana, Madigan muttered to a colleague disconsolately, "We just aren't big enough."

Madigan wasn't the first *Chicago Tribune* loyalist to leave Cuba disappointed. Almost fifty years earlier to the day, Jules Dubois, the *Chicago Tribune*'s infamous Latin American correspondent, had been expelled from the island for his critical coverage of Castro, whom he had once portrayed as a young rebel commander and hero who ousted from power the cruel and corrupt dictator, Fulgencio Batista. On the surface, Madigan bore little resemblance to Dubois, a husky, blue-eyed correspondent who had braved pistol-whipping and violence to get his stories, once reputedly filed by carrier pigeon. But each man symbolized the ambition of the *Chicago Tribune* as more than just another local paper on the prairies of the Midwest. Dubois, a legendary correspondent, epitomized the *Tribune*'s commitment to foreign reporting by a free press in the 1950s and helped found the Inter American Press Association, an organization that the *Tribune* continued to support for decades. A half-century later, Madigan would assume his place in Tribune lore when he bet the future of the company on the largest newspaper merger in American history.

John Madigan was not the kind of man who wore his feelings on his sleeve. One got a clue to his thinking through a fleeting comment or a slip of the tongue similar to his "not big enough" comment on the bus. His cautious demeanor was no accident. Ever since he had been passed over for the CEO job in favor of Brumback, Madigan had labored in Brumback's shadow, a treacherous arena reserved for men with something to prove. And Brumback made sure that Madigan had his work cut out for him.

To anyone schooled in reading the tea leaves at Tribune, Brumback became the CEO in waiting late in 1988, when Cook named him president and COO of Tribune Company, a promotion that relegated Madigan to runner up. True to form, Brumback hit the ground running, seizing control of Tribune Company and shaking it to its core much as he had done with the company's flagship newspaper.

In his day, the Colonel had built a sizable and successful Canadian newsprint operation to ensure that his papers would always have an adequate, cheap supply of paper, a crucial commodity to a newspaper's future. But paper mills consumed a lot of capital and produced pulp, a commodity. As Brumback assumed his new duties with Tribune Company in early 1989, he concluded that the Tribune Company shouldn't be in the commodity business anymore. Canada's political system bothered the rock-ribbed Republican, too. Brumback believed

Canada's "socialist tendencies" challenged the possibility of earning a fair return. So, over the next five years, he spun off the newsprint operation, eventually selling the whole operation to Donahue Paper Corp. of Canada.

Even more daring, Brumback, fresh from his victory over unions in Chicago, stuck his thumb in the eye of organized labor at the *Daily News*, the New York tabloid that had been founded by the Colonel's cousin, Joseph Patterson, and had become a significant drain on the company's bottom line. At the time, the *Daily News* was run by James Hoge, the *Chicago Sun-Times* editor who had quit his job across the street when Rupert Murdoch bought the paper in 1983. Cook had quickly hired Hoge to run the *Daily News*, a paper that had long been at odds with its unions. Hoge devised a phased plan in which the company would make some long-term strategic investments the New York unions sought in return for union concessions the company wanted. When Brumback came along in 1989, though, he rejected the phased approach, preferring to take on the unions directly as he had successfully done in Chicago. Hoge, who had grown up in New York but had spent much of his career in Chicago, tried to warn Brumback about the stark differences between unions and politics in Chicago and New York, where the mafia had much deeper penetration of the unions with which he had to deal. But Brumback would have none of it. He soon hired Robert Ballow, a notorious union-busting lawyer from the King & Ballow law firm in Tennessee, and by 1990 the Tribune found itself embroiled in the longest newspaper strike in New York City's history.

Brumback's in-your-face tactics and naïveté about Big Apple politics led to a walkout marked by torched newsstands and even more tortured politics. At one point, Brumback's mandate to fix the *Daily News*, sell it, or "shut it down" had Mayor David Dinkins, Governor Mario Cuomo, and John Joseph Cardinal O'Connor in the streets backing a union boycott of the newspaper. After losing some $250 million over eleven years, Tribune paid British press lord Robert Maxwell $60 million to assume the paper's debts and take off its hands one of the nation's largest newspapers in one of America's greatest markets. Maxwell entered New York with much fanfare, but it soon became apparent he needed the $60 million badly; he was broke. Shortly thereafter, he fell off his yacht and drowned in an accident that many speculated was suicide, sending the financially strapped *Daily News* into the hands of Mort Zuckerman, the real estate developer.

When he picked his fight with the unions, Brumback didn't think he'd have to walk away from the *Daily News*, but at the end of the day, he emerged as the darling of Wall Street. Despite the problems caused by the strike and its embarrassing headlines, Brumback's decision to dump the *Daily News* extricated Tribune from a financial morass in New York, freeing the company to build a powerful multimedia corporation and sending its stock into the stratosphere. The company's stock price jumped 1 percent on the news of the *Daily News* sales and continued to rise. In August 1990, Brumback became CEO of Tribune Company. He was named Chairman in January 1993.

In Chicago, Madigan had won a crown jewel as a consolation prize for losing out to Brumback—CEO of Chicago Tribune Company and publisher of the *Chicago Tribune*, the job that ambitious executives had always used to catapult themselves into the CEO's chair. Tribune Company CEOs rarely had ever reached the top job without a tour in the *Tribune* publisher's office. But Madigan also faced a daunting challenge: He had to emerge from Brumback's shadow to demonstrate he had the competence, decisiveness, and ability to lead the parent company. Since everyone at Tribune Tower credited Brumback with turning the *Chicago Tribune* into a well-oiled cash register, Madigan had a hard act to follow, particularly after Brumback ordered the newly minted *Tribune* publisher to ship his top local talent to New York to help him fight the unions. Meanwhile, Brumback openly expressed doubts about Madigan's ability to succeed him. At one point late in his tenure, Brumback stunned *Chicago Tribune* media reporter Tim Jones, during an on-the-record interview, when he said he wouldn't completely relinquish his leadership role in Tribune Company because he wanted to see if Madigan had the chops to run the company.

But Madigan had three things going for him that many readers of the tea leaves didn't appreciate. One was his age. By the time he became CEO, Brumback was sixty; to appease Wall Street, Tribune Company had to start succession planning from the day he got the job. Secondly, Madigan's only credible rival, Jim Dowdle, was a television executive at Tribune, a newspaper company at heart and one that rarely went outside its ranks for top jobs. Finally, Madigan's biggest advantage was that he was a savvy corporate politician and knew how to play the game, far better, in fact, than almost anyone would suspect.

Taciturn, conservative, and aloof, Madigan grew up on Chicago's North Shore, a tony strip of land adjacent to Lake Michigan populated by country clubs, wide lawns, and stately homes that scream, "A Republican Lives Here." W. Clement Stone, the eccentric insurance tycoon who helped bankroll Richard Nixon, had a mansion on the lake. Donald Rumsfeld, the controversial U.S Defense Secretary, graduated from New Trier, the area's well-known high school, four years before Madigan.

The son of a corporate lawyer and big University of Michigan booster, Madigan towered over almost everyone in a room, but people tended to underestimate him, probably because of his meat-and-potatoes midwestern demeanor. His buttoned-down countenance obscured a huge ego and a fierce ambitious streak that rarely surfaced in public. Don Haider, a Northwestern University professor who grew up on the North Shore and was a friend of Madigan's sister, recalled how confident Madigan was, even as a teenager. "Griff Williams," Haider explained, "was a high-society band leader who had three beautiful daughters. They lived in a house on Forest Avenue [near Lake Michigan] with a broad, sprawling porch. You would always see boys on the front porch; everyone wanted to date the Williams girls, especially Holly." The competitors for Holly's hand didn't consider Madigan a big threat. "He was cautious, easy to underestimate," Haider said. A handsome, clean-cut young man, Madigan wore a plaid bow tie and a houndstooth jacket in his high school yearbook photo, but he was otherwise relatively undistinguished. When the time came for

Holly to make a choice, she picked Madigan. "He was either lucky or determined," Haider surmised.

After graduating from University of Michigan with an MBA, Madigan joined Duff & Phelps, a small, midwestern investment banking firm, where he learned the newspaper business basics helping Lee Enterprises, a minor newspaper chain, sell its stock to the public. Next was a tour at Arthur Andersen, at the time, a blue-chip accounting firm based in Chicago. But Madigan's real break came when he landed a job at the Chicago office of Salomon Brothers, led at the time by Ira Harris, a consummate wheeler-dealer whose struggles with an expansive waistline made as many headlines as his legendary deals. Harris knew Madigan from their days at the University of Michigan, and, although they hadn't been close friends, the flashy deal maker needed someone adept at corporate finance for the investment banking division he was building at Salomon. Madigan, he soon determined, was his man. Although Harris never grafted his pizzazz onto his new student, he gave Madigan an opportunity to see investment banking through the eyes of one of its masters, and Madigan took notes. When Tribune CEO Cook sought Harris' advice on the proper strategic direction for Tribune, a company then in private hands, Harris became a matchmaker of sorts. He put Madigan on the case to help determine whether Tribune should remain private or sell its stock to the public. Cook recalled:

> The problem with being a private company is if you wanted to grow, you almost become like [your own] banker. In those days, [Tribune stock] had become quite valuable. At one point, it was worth more than $100,000 a share.... To get those shares, either someone had to give them to you or you had to acquire them from someone who had been given the stock, and those of us who were high in the company had been given the stock.... As the [founding] family got bigger and old Joe had a son and then he had five sons and they started doling out these

shares, people started saying, "Why am I holding on to this stuff? I'd rather get the money," and you start playing bank [raising cash to buy or retire the stock].

After an exhaustive review of the company, Salomon determined that it was in Tribune Company's best interest to go public. During the evaluative process, Cook liked what he saw in the tall, presentable Madigan, and when Tribune needed a chief financial officer, Cook floated the idea by Harris. On the first day of the year in 1975, Madigan joined the Tribune as its new CFO. Madigan later recalled:

> We weren't ready to go public when I got here. Our margins were well below the industry average. We had Bob Salomon make a presentation to our management team about how we stacked up against public companies in the industry. It was one of the first times we opened up to ourselves, [to see] where we stood. Our margins were at the 5 percent level, and the *Los Angeles Times* was at 15 percent. I remember at the time I thought if we could ever get there it would be totally great.

He installed a system of procedures and accounts that allowed the company to accurately measure its results, dismantling antiquated financial yardsticks that fostered the gridlock, infighting, and misinformation that had plagued the company. Cook and Madigan shelved Kirkpatrick's journalistic expansion plans to make the Tribune a midwestern powerhouse and shifted the company's emphasis to improving productivity.

Companies convert to stockholder-owned institutions for lots of reasons. Over the years, Madigan would often talk about the importance of remaining an independent company, one controlled by local people rather than a faraway board of directors. Properly run, a newspaper is a strong instrument of local power, one that sets the agenda in a community, focuses public attention on crucial issues, and gives a community its voice. When owners know the local community and encounter the subjects of stories they publish at the local grocery store or bank, the newspaper shows it has a stake in the community and gains credibility. Cook and Madigan both felt strongly that going public would actually help Tribune remain locally controlled and independent. "Several of the private companies [had] imploded," Madigan noted, "when big shareholders wanted [to cash in their stock holdings] it would force sales like in Louisville," where descendants of the Bingham family sold the *Louisville Courier-Journal*, a respected state paper, to Allen Neuharth's Gannett Corporation. "We had [these] big shareholders around, the descendants of the original investors in the company [the Medills, the McCormicks, the Cowles family, the Lloyds of Chicago], and some of them wanted out. . . . We were afraid if we didn't provide them liquidity [or cash for their stock], they would force a sale," a posture that would inevitably mean a loss of independence and control by Cook and his team.

Becoming a publicly held company also creates stock certificates, stock options, and lucrative benefits for corporate officers and for underwriters like Salomon Brothers, who make a bundle helping a company ready itself for sale. In his days putting together deals, Madigan had learned how to make people like Cook, Brumback, and big shareholders, including him, incredibly wealthy. By the time Cook stepped down as chairman of the company in 1993, his reported stock holdings were worth about $47 million. Madigan's were worth about $25 million, and he had learned the game well by the time Cook moved him into the publisher's office at the *Chicago Tribune*.

One of the first things Madigan did as publisher was to get rid of people loyal to Jim Squires. A year into settling into the publisher's office, Madigan accepted Squires' offer to step down. In his place, he installed Jack Fuller, a Yale-educated lawyer, novelist, editorialist, and second-generation Tribune loyalist who couldn't have been more different from Squires.

Professorial in demeanor, Fuller wore a beret to work, spoke softly, and looked like he'd be more at home with a glass of sherry in a university club than with a shot at the Billy Goat, the Chicago news-papermen's watering hole. He quoted Voltaire when he talked to reporters. Madigan jokingly referred to Fuller as "the professor," and newsroom scuttlebutt painted Fuller as "too intellectual" or "brainy" to be editor of the brawny *Chicago Tribune*. But Fuller's professorial pedi-gree obscured his ambition and skill. Together, Fuller and Madigan formed a team that was to make the company that wasn't "big enough" much, much bigger.

Soon after he was named editor, Fuller brought me back to Chicago from Washington to run the paper's foreign and national news opera-tion, a great job that put me in charge of the main news section of the *Tribune*, which included most of the foreign and national news. I was thrilled. I'd had a great run in Washington where I'd won some honors and accolades, and where my coverage of the savings and loan scandal had landed me a book contract. I'd also had a couple of spats with my friend Nick Horrock, whom Squires had installed as the Washington bureau chief, and I decided it was time to move on. Putting me in charge of foreign and national news gave me a major voice in how the big news stories of the day would be played, a bigger staff, and more influence than the Washington bureau chief.

As head of the *Tribune*'s eighteen foreign and national news bureaus and more than forty correspondents, I presided over the highly visible network that Squires had built, one that had the potential to turn heads in the world of journalism, where stature was measured by heft. More important, I gained control of the news pages where stories from the bureaus would run, including those from Washington. It was a heady experience, until I learned the truth about my little empire.

Years later, as editor of the *Los Angeles Times*, I would see how a professional foreign and national news staff should be organized. Working within Tribune confines and Brumback's relentless push for the higher profits that the company promised Wall Street, Squires had built the bureaus but not the support system needed to service the growing cadre of foreign and national news reporters. If anything, he eliminated the infrastructure of supporting editors to finance the paper's expansion, creating a team of star hitters and pitchers, while skimping on hitting and pitching coaches. From an accountant's perspective, the staff looked incredibly productive, grinding out an admirable foreign and national news report with far fewer people or— as Brumback called them—FTEs (full-time equivalents) than papers like the *New York Times* or the *Los Angeles Times*. But in reality, the system wasn't really that productive. Instead of spending our time crafting a journalistic strategy to capitalize on an incredible stable of talent to distinguish *Tribune* content from other papers and wire services, overburdened editors scrambled to edit stories rolling in from correspondents who operated without adequate guidance and feedback from the editors closest to the readers. When journalists stationed in faraway places can't brainstorm with editors to develop customized stories, they fail to create journalistic value in their stories and fall victim to a sense of sameness. Although reporters may generate high story counts with staff bylines, economic downturns make them seem like luxuries that can be replaced by cheaper wire services (ones that pay their reporters less for stories on the same subjects).

Despite its limitations, the *Tribune's* foreign and national staff worked hard for me. But the anemic support system made everyone feel like copy processors instead of editors. We always had too much to do, and someone would inevitably come along and ask us to do more. Early in my tenure, Fuller summoned me to his office to ask me to stretch myself a little thinner, to "educate" Madigan about what journalists did. Instead of waiting for the economy to tank and allow the budget cutters to diminish expensive foreign and national staff, Fuller wisely made a preemptive move by building support with friends in high places and promoting the value of *Tribune* journalism.

My new student knew as much about the inner workings of my newsroom as I knew about the machinations of his boardroom. At one point, Squires had banned Madigan from even entering the fourth floor, arguing that his efforts to get obituaries written about friends and relatives and his contacts with correspondents stationed in countries he was about to visit amounted to interference in the editorial process, a penetration of the wall. "All he ever cared about was his seat on the dais," Squires later recalled. "He was always a power guy."

But I saw a complex, contradictory man, someone who seemed dreadfully risk adverse and seemed reliably predictable, until he did something totally out of character. Madigan could be amusing, blunt, and irreverent in private, but cautious and restrained in a crowd. He would complain about stories in the paper, but encourage editors to stand up to him because he knew editors were supposed to defend their reporters. Unlike Brumback, he rarely insulted subordinates in public; he delivered his harsh words behind closed doors with a silent, steely-eyed glare as cold as Lake Michigan. He seemed genuinely interested in what journalists did and liked the irreverent newsroom more than the reverential Tribune corporate offices. Eager to learn about the political, social, and economic issues that journalists encountered on the job, he nevertheless labored under an insecure, almost irrational fear of looking foolish in public. When consul generals representing foreign countries in Chicago would call on the new publisher to talk about issues, he would summon me, or one of my staff, to attend, with the understanding that we would intervene if the conversation wandered onto unfamiliar turf. When Madigan wanted a session to end, he would speak with his eyes, giving me that "get him out of here" look, and I would show the visitor the door.

Famed newspaper publishers like Joseph Pulitzer and William Randolph Hearst got their hands dirty using garish headlines, fake interviews, and lavish photo spreads to win readers in the fabled New York City newspaper wars known as "yellow journalism." But Madigan and most publishers of his era were as far removed from journalism as Chicago is from New York. The fine print that really interested Madigan and his contemporaries rested in a stock prospectus. The financial guys, lawyers and MBAs from the nation's elite business schools, didn't get ink on their fingers. The "journalism" they practiced wasn't yellow, it was green, the color of money.

Across America, most papers had been gobbled up by big media companies like Tribune Company. For better or worse, the industry had started another wave of consolidation. The conventional wisdom was to buy or be bought. Most papers had started to see their share of advertising (particularly classified advertising) slip as competitors penetrated their markets. Businesses, meanwhile, had discovered they could target their commercial messages much more effectively through direct mail. Newspaper subscriptions had for the most part held up, but single copies of the paper sold on newsstands had started a permanent decline in the 1990s. Meanwhile, the Internet had emerged on the scene as a threat, not only to the business side but also to editorial departments forced to compete with a new breed of news more concerned with speed and less interested in journalistic accuracy. Newspapers were becoming the medium of choice for older readers—a group that was largely anathema to advertisers. Far more so than their predecessors, executives like Madigan faced a new host of threats to the bread and butter of newspaper journalism.

A controlling person who insisted on punctuality, Madigan prized stability and discretion and, like Willes, actually seemed amazed that anyone would repeat something from a private business meeting to one of his reporters. Like the Colonel, he seemed to think he belonged to a privileged society that was exempt from the rules that govern the rest of us; he loathed waiting in line for anything, and he loved to travel the world, rubbing shoulders with world leaders, particularly if he was in the Tribune's Falcon jet. Madigan would come to know by name almost all of the seven hundred or so reporters in the newsroom, and he sympathized with their frustration at being the Rodney Dangerfields of journalism—toiling as they did at a paper that didn't get the respect bestowed on the newspapers on the coasts.

As they rose through the ranks, Fuller and Madigan acted as if they didn't care about the slights. When thinking about potentially controversial policies at the *Tribune*, Fuller would often half jokingly wonder how a move would play with "the gods of journalism," a reference to East Coast editors like Gene Roberts, the *Philadelphia Inquirer* editor famed for long-form investigative reporting. But in truth, we all resented the insolence toward our paper. When Madigan traveled to Washington to attend the fabled Gridiron dinner just after he'd been named publisher, he couldn't get over how journalists and dignitaries fawned over Arthur Sulzberger and Katharine Graham in the drawing-room parties that preceded the dinner. Riding the elevator together after the show, Madigan expressed his frustration to *Tribune* bureau chief Nick Horrock, wondering aloud why Sulzberger and Graham got so much attention while he got so little. "I explained to him that they came from famed newspaper families and were not just people who ran corporations. He took it pretty well," Horrock recalled. When asked about reasons for the shabby treatment years later, Madigan would say, "I think it's a coast issue. I think New York and Los Angeles look down on Chicago. We're not as good as they are. I think it is just a feeling of superiority."

But Wall Street, for one, was not giving Tribune the cold shoulder, not in the least. By the early 1990s, Brumback's pressure on publishers to increase their contributions to Tribune Company's bottom line had paid off with double-digit cash flow increases. The company's successful earnings allowed Tribune to capitalize on opportunities. Never mind the growth of the Internet, cable television had robustly expanded its reach, and the federal government had started relaxing regulations that governed who could own broadcast properties, igniting a public backlash that both the government and Tribune Company would dramatically underestimate. But Brumback, bolstered by his belief in technology, put the company squarely in the game. He started CLTV, Chicago's twenty-four-hour local news cable channel, acquired several local television stations across the country, and placed his $5 million bet on America Online. Brumback scaled back the Tribune's publishing division, divesting smaller newspaper properties so he could focus on his most profitable papers in Chicago and Florida.

He also started thinking about the future. Brumback realized before most other newspaper executives how the computer and its attendant technology would transform the newspaper industry. After the Tribune invested in America Online, in the early 1990s Brumback created Chicago Online, putting the Tribune Company at the vanguard of media and the Internet. He ordered *Chicago Tribune* content to be placed on the Internet and charged anyone for access to the stories unless they subscribed to the newspaper. He also tried to spread the gospel to the entire industry by promoting something called the New Century Network, or NCN, a consortium of the nine-largest newspaper groups in America, to pool their content so they could "monetize it," or make money.

Brumback had zeroed in on what would become a devastating problem for newspapers as the Internet began to thrive. "Charlie had a good idea but it wasn't the right answer," said James Cutie, a onetime head of online news for the *New York Times* and a NCN board member. "The group was too large. It was composed of nine newspaper companies all sitting around the table with the same skills. If someone had had the balls to charge for our digital copy, it would be a whole different ballgame today." Brumback later told me that he had also encountered opposition from the *Chicago Tribune's* circulation department, which viewed the new technology as a threat to its ability to attract print readers.

Within three years, the NCN folded, an entrepreneurial dream plagued by differing philosophies, internecine warfare, big companies, and even bigger egos. "Charlie was trying to get Silicon Valley to invest in it, and some guy from Kleiner Perkins [Caufield & Byers] wanted to invest $5 million," said Cutie. "Can you imagine getting all of that premium content for $5 million. We had this big meeting of all the major newspaper companies to vote on whether to go ahead. I think it was in Chicago because I thought it was like something out of the *Godfather* when the heads of all the crime families came there to vote about going into the drug business." The vote was five to four against joining Kleiner Perkins, a setback that not only killed the NCN but in retrospect was a blow to the industry.

Instead of charging customers to recoup their cost of creating content, newspaper companies put the content on line for free, hoping that a bigger audience would lure enough online ad dollars to pay their costs and boost profits. It was a bad bet. Some readers quit paying for their papers because they could get the content for free online. The technology allowed advertisers to see exactly how many people looked at their ads, intelligence that led them to bid down the price of all advertising, print and online. The result: a huge problem for the media grappling with a new generation of readers reared in the Internet age, one that expects fast, free content on computer screens, cellphones, and iPads.

Brumback had better luck when he started thinking about his successor. "He came before the board and told us that we didn't need to do a national search because we had two of the best people in the business already at the company—John Madigan and Jim Dowdle," said Newton Minow, a company director and former chairman of the Federal Communications Commission who had achieved fame when he described television as a vast wasteland in the 1960s. "He then gave us a presentation on both. At the end, half the board thought he wanted Madigan and the other half thought he wanted Dowdle," said Minow. After a year of due diligence in which he carefully sought out their respective visions of the company's future, Brumback decided on Madigan. "I thought Madigan was the best-equipped guy to do it because of his financial background. There were a lot of financial issues then, and broadcast was a minor part of the business. I talked to them. I asked each of them to write a report on what the newspaper would look like ten to twenty years from then. Madigan had the best vision. He's good at writing reports," Brumback recalled.

In 1994, the board promoted Madigan to president of the company and Fuller to publisher and president of the *Chicago Tribune*. A year later, Madigan got the CEO title and in 1996 became chairman, when Brumback retired. His rival, Dowdle, got the company's number-two job. Fuller became head of the company's publishing division, which oversaw the company's four newspapers.

Madigan and Fuller inherited Brumback's legacy as a bargain hunter. Because Tribune had acquired numerous television stations, Brumback did his best to get two for the price of one—one reporter who could file reports for both the newspaper *and* broadcast outlets.

Advocates of the idea like Howard Tyner, who had succeeded Fuller as editor of the *Chicago Tribune*, called the idea "synergy." Tyner and I never really saw the world through the same lens. I felt that asking a journalist to take still and moving pictures simultaneously would only produce bad still photos and bad video. But Tyner fiercely embraced the idea championed by his bosses. He had a television camera installed in the newsroom just outside the editor's office where *Tribune* print reporters would be interviewed for news shows on the company's much ballyhooed cable television station. CLTV stood for Chicagoland Cable Television, but the old hands at WGN, the company's more traditional station, called it Children Learning Television. The lone camera would eventually become a fully functioning television stage inside the newsroom where television anchors could interview print reporters about the stories they were covering. The studio was empty as much as it was occupied. Most television folks thought interviewing print reporters was simply bad TV.

Madigan and Fuller also sharply increased Tribune's earnings. In a shrewd move that reflected his financial market roots, Madigan had the company create a derivative, an arcane investment vehicle that allowed him to sell off Brumback's $5 million investment in America Online for $1.2 billion, a windfall that gave him so much cash that he went out shopping for something to buy.

■

Ambitious people always recognize the point in their careers when they need a change. I felt that way when I left a good future at the *Des Moines Register* and moved to the *Tribune*. In the mid-1990s, I got the itch to return to reporting and write a book about the consulting industry. I liked being in charge of major sections of the newspaper, but I was tired of working with far fewer resources than journalists at the *New York Times* or the *Washington Post*. Fuller had named Ann Marie Lipinski deputy managing editor for news, and we quickly became close friends and allies in a drive to make the *Tribune* a destination paper for investigative journalism. I confided in her that I had landed a book contract and that I was going to take a buyout to focus on writing my book. After Tyner hesitated to name Lipinski full managing editor, she was frustrated and understood my desire to make a change. About a half-hour before I was to discuss my plans with Joe Leonard, who ran the newsroom budget and headed up the buyout program, Lipinski came into my office. "You haven't talked to Leonard yet, have you?" she implored. When I told her no, she grinned, relieved. "Good!" she exclaimed. Tyner had reconsidered and was naming her full managing editor. "I need your help running this place." Lipinski declared. "You can't leave."

# 8

## Inside the Merger

In March 2000, Leo Wolinsky walked into the *Los Angeles Times* editorial recognition awards dinner filled with promise. Once a year, the paper's editors nominated and selected the paper's best work over the past twelve months. Over a lavish dinner, winning reporters and editors were rewarded with as much as $5,000. The *Times* paid its staff better than most American newspapers, but not many journalists ever got rich toiling in the trenches. The awards event was a good way to recognize a job well done with an offering of cash or stock to employees who weren't eligible for bonuses. (In Chicago, the *Tribune* carried out its own iteration at the Beck Awards, named after longtime managing editor Edward Scott Beck, who was managing editor from 1910 to 1937.)

Having left his Porsche with the valet at the Beverly Wilshire Hotel, Wolinsky entered the ballroom. Around nine hundred staff members and guests were expected. Well-dressed reporters, editors, and their guests mingled over cocktails, gossiping about newsroom politics and speculating on who would win the twenty-two awards that would be passed out that evening. Shortly before the program was to start, the *Los Angeles Times'* editor, Michael Parks, tapped Wolinsky on the shoulder and suggested they go for a short walk.

The day before the awards event, Wolinsky had sniffed around the business offices at the *Times* to investigate rumors buzzing in the newsroom of the company's sale to Tribune Company. "Everybody in financial said, 'No way it could happen.'" Wolinsky later recalled. "Everyone still thought the Chandler trusts wouldn't allow a sale of the *Los Angeles Times*. There were all kinds of investment bankers upstairs, and we started thinking maybe we, Times Mirror, were going to buy something." When Parks asked Wolinsky if he'd heard the rumors, as they strolled the grounds around the Beverly Wilshire, Wolinsky told him that he'd investigated them and they were patently untrue. Parks stopped in his tracks, looked Wolinsky in the eye, and said simply that he couldn't comment. "And that was it. The first thing I did was call David Shaw [the *Times* media writer] and told him he'd better start making some calls," Wolinsky later recalled.

Times Mirror insiders and outsiders bought the line that Wolinsky got from his friends in financial. Even Mark Willes firmly believed that the Chandler trust would ban the sale of the paper until the last Chandler heir died. Park's "no comment" stunned Wolinsky. He'd been at the *Los Angeles Times* for nearly twenty years, edited or worked on stories that had won fourteen Pulitzers, helped staff members through the things that hit all workplaces—nasty divorces, premature deaths, unfaithful spouses, drinking bouts, too much dope. The *Los Angeles Times* was his family. And now the very real possibility that the Chandlers would sell out to a bunch of people from Chicago who reputedly ran newspapers the way a butcher ran a meat market loomed large. Wolinsky realized the very real possibility of a buyout. "All of a sudden one of the premier establishments in LA was going to be owned by someone from Chicago. . . . It certainly was the end of an era," he said later.

Wolinsky's surprise at the news was nothing compared to Willes'. As the company's CEO, he should have known if his company were about to be sold, but he didn't have a clue. The last time Willes had even heard about the subject was following his meeting with Madigan in San Diego. He'd reported Madigan's approach to his board and did a quick analysis that concluded a deal didn't make economic sense. "I reported that to John and I thought that was the end of it. I mean I liked John, and I thought he was being entirely up front. It never occurred to me that he would do anything behind my back. I certainly underestimated him," Willes recalled.

Times Mirror was on a roll, with its stock price and earnings far higher than when Willes had taken over, and the Chandlers hadn't given him the slightest hint that they were unhappy. "Everything they had said to me," Willes said, "was 'thank God you're here. You are doing a wonderful job. We're so grateful.' I mean literally."

Soon after Wolinksy had taken his stroll with Parks, William Stinehart, a lean no-nonsense Chandler family lawyer, paid Willes an unexpected visit. "He walked into my office," Willes recalled, "and said that we'd reached an agreement to sell the company. I had no hint at all. I was so incredibly naïve. And I was so stunned and so angry. I think it's the first time and the only time in my life I refused to shake some-one's hand when they left my office. It was just incomprehensible after all we had done that they would do this for the sake of a short-term gain. To this day, it's incomprehensible. I felt totally betrayed."

It was also news to the non-Chandler directors on the company's board. Although the transaction was portrayed as a *merger* of Times Mirror and Tribune Company, it had all the earmarks of a hostile takeover by Tribune and the Chandlers. Skip Zimbalist, who had just become the Times Mirror CFO, said Willes came into his office looking white as a sheet: "He told me that Tribune wanted to buy it. He was visibly shaken; he looked totally shocked . . . like he'd been hit by a truck."

Although Willes had done the Chandler family bidding, the Chandlers didn't like the way he ran around acting like he owned the *Los Angeles Times*. The family owned the *Times*. As Zimbalist saw it, Willes had numbered his days when, without consulting the family, he named himself publisher and later appointed Downing publisher after he had been told he couldn't have both the publisher and CEO titles.

And then there was the Staples scandal. In the drive to eliminate the wall between the editorial and the business side of the paper, Downing had cut a partnership deal with the Staples Center, a $400 million sports and entertainment complex in downtown Los Angeles. To meet part of its commitment to the deal, the *Times* had agreed to publish a thick, 168-page Sunday magazine in October 1999, touting the center—an edition that lured $2 million worth of advertising. On the surface, there was nothing wrong with the Staples deal. Newspapers routinely run supplements full of puff pieces to lure ad dollars that support serious journalism elsewhere in the paper. But the Staples deal exposed Downing's inexperience as a publisher: As part of the deal, the *Times* had agreed to split $2 million of ad revenues with the Staples Center. Soon, the outraged staff at the *Los Angeles Times* denounced the deal publicly. "A fundamental premise of journalism is that a journalist should not be sharing revenue or have a business relationship with somebody he's writing a story about," Henry Weinstein, a highly regarded *Times* reporter told PBS. "Our own code of ethics for reporters specifically forbids this. What we saw in this deal was that the people who run the newspaper had done something that just flagrantly violated our own rules." The Staples faux pas became a huge story, one that deeply embarrassed the *Times* and, by implication, the Chandlers, to the rest of the publishing world.

Zimbalist noted:

> Staples could have happened to anyone. Kathryn had no publishing experience and she apologized and it was going to blow over until someone leaked it to the *New York Times*. The editorial department grew up under Otis and Tom Johnson and Shelby after him believing that their mission was to create the greatest newspaper in the world and be equal to the *New York Times*. Winning Pulitzers was important to them. Doing important journalistic

work and scooping everyone—nothing was better. Anything that infringed on their ability to do that was a cause for anger, alarm, and rebellion. When their brethren at the *New York Times* criticized them, they felt they had to uphold their honor and they got really mad.

In point of fact, the *Los Angeles Daily Business Journal* had broken the story, but in a flash, *everyone* started writing about it.

"You know I got blamed for Staples," Willes said, "and I had nothing to do with the Staples thing, they didn't ask me, they didn't consult me. I didn't know about it till after it become a problem." But Willes had made Downing the publisher, a move that he admits in retrospect was a mistake. She wasn't ready to become publisher, and the criticism fell upon the man who had put her in the job prematurely.

"Mark Willes is just a symbol—and perhaps even a victim—of the combination of fear and ambition that in recent years has led many managers of media enterprises to put stockholders ahead of readers or listeners," wrote Max Frankel, a former managing editor of the *New York Times*, in an op-ed piece that compared the Staples deal to a kickback scheme designed to generate positive coverage. "By giving priority to stock values and profit margins, they slighted their obligations to the public. Indeed they have shown themselves ignorant or even contemptuous of the ethical standards so long and painstakingly erected to protect the credibility of their news operations."

Even Otis Chandler broke his silence. From his retirement ranch north of Los Angeles, he released a statement that he had Bill Boyarsky read in the newsroom, calling the Staples deal "unbelievably stupid and unprofessional" and the Willes and Downing era "the single most devastating period in the history of this great newspaper." In an incredible instance of self-flagellation that could only be found in the newspaper business, the *Los Angeles Times* had media writer David Shaw write a thirty-thousand-word piece on Staples.

■

As the Staples scandal lingered in the collective journalistic memory, a short, stocky man with a winsome smile deplaned at O'Hare International Airport and made his way to downtown Chicago for a board meeting of Classified Ventures, a collaboration between Tribune and other major media companies dedicated to combating the threats that the Internet posed to the industry's lucrative classified advertising business. A native of Evanston, Illinois, Tom Unterman was about to leave his job as CFO of Times Mirror in 1999 to pursue his new career managing money, mainly for the Chandler family, but also some other clients. To those who knew him, Unterman was a "smart off the charts" lawyer and deal guy who had a reputation for cleverly avoiding taxes. Just before the board meeting, Jack Fuller, who by then had been promoted to head Tribune's publishing unit and a fellow Classified Ventures board member, pulled him aside: "I told Tom 'we are not going to give up on this. This is the smartest thing either of our companies could do,'" a not-so-veiled reference to the proposed Tribune–Times Mirror merger.

Unterman listened to Fuller and said nothing in reply, until a few months later at another board meeting when he told Fuller that "things were changing in Los Angeles and that he might be able to do something." The Chandlers, Unterman said, might be interested in a deal. Fuller then immediately informed Madigan and David Hiller, the original advocate of a Tribune–Times Mirror merger, and shortly thereafter Unterman had a meeting with Fuller and Hiller.

In Chicago a few weeks later, Fuller set up a meeting at Madigan's North Shore home to discuss possibilities. The Chandlers, Fuller learned, were far more embarrassed by the Staples scandal than anyone realized. "Tom said the Chandlers realized they couldn't get much more out of Times Mirror through cost cutting and were angry and embarrassed by Staples. They wanted to find new leadership [for Times Mirror]," Fuller recalled.

One of Unterman's clients had sent him a copy of *News Values*, a book Fuller had written in which he argued that newspapers had to maintain a strong ethical backbone despite the economic challenges the industry faced. Unterman had confidence in Fuller, and the Tribune publishing chief impressed the Chandlers, too. When Unterman began to work his magic, things moved quickly and quietly.

"We went there first, and then they [the Chandlers] came here to the Tower," Madigan recalled. A string of clandestine meetings unfolded at the Sidley Austin law offices and the California Club in downtown Los Angeles. Willes was deliberately left out of the loop. "They [the Chandlers] didn't tell Willes, and they didn't tell the other directors," Madigan explained. "They had all of this control [of Times Mirror], they had that high voting stock. They could just do this." Willes had made Unterman's job easier with his political naïveté. The steady stream of changes in his executive suite meant he had few longtime allies watching his back. Unterman, on the other hand, had solid ties to the family, a cunning mind, enough political smarts to fill the Grand Canyon, and good relations in his native Chicago.

Even in his days at Salomon Brothers, Madigan wasn't seen as a deal guy. His mentor, Ira Harris, considered him a strong corporate operations executive—someone good at imposing solid financial controls on a company, and a man who could maneuver easily in a boardroom. Putting together risky deals was not his forte.

Madigan and Fuller were hungry for a deal with Times Mirror though, and Merrill Lynch, Tribune's longtime investment banker, didn't pull down big fees sitting in the financial bleachers. The Tribune Company was known as a careful, plotting outfit that maintained a steady lumber, not a quick step. Madigan and Fuller were determined to reverse that image. As events played out after Thanksgiving in 1999 and into the new year, both sides moved quickly and secretly, lest anyone discover a deal was in the works.

In a move that surprised no one, the Chandlers had structured the terms of the merger to benefit their family, at the expense of minority shareholders. Overall, the Chandlers' holdings gave the family 28 percent of all Times Mirror shares, but the family could still control Times Mirror, because their stock enjoyed super-voting status. In effect, Chandler stock was worth ten votes per share, while regular stock received only 1 vote per share. The price Tribune was willing to pay turned heads. Madigan and Fuller's deal initially offered $92.50 per share to Times Mirror stockholders for shares then changing hands at about $47, a premium of nearly 100 percent. But, as Willes, Zimbalist, and non-Chandler directors soon learned, the family intended to exchange their Times Mirror stock for shares in Tribune, a move that would make the transaction tax-free to the Chandlers, while everyone else would get what was left of the stock pro rata, and the rest in cash.

The end result? Non-Chandler stockholders would be responsible for paying income taxes on their profits. By March 2000, Madigan and the Chandlers sprang the news on everyone. As Willes recalled, "John and his people came in to make a presentation to our board about why this was such a wonderful combination. They talked about their television ventures, you know, *Buffy the Vampire Slayer* and all that. I just sat there and thought, this can't be happening. I didn't know whether to sit there and cry or stomp out of the meeting. Fortunately I did neither."

Zimbalist explained:

> It was a pre-cooked deal. After the meeting with Mark, we had a board meeting, and the Chandler representatives confirmed it. We lined up a committee of the independent directors and hired Goldman Sachs to advise us. Our objective was to make a good deal and make sure all shareholders got as good a deal as the Chandlers. The Chandlers and the Tribune guys were trying to ram the deal down everyone's throat. The Tribune people were very directive and arrogant, telling us we had to do this and had to do that, . . . that by law and precedent, if the controlling shareholder wants to sell, the board can't stand in the way. They were friendly with the Chandler directors but hostile to everyone else. The independent directors were irate that the Chandlers hadn't told them about the deal. The deal also had a "no shop" clause

that said we couldn't seek other offers. That rubbed the independent directors the wrong way. Everybody had lawyers and investment bankers working on this.

Zimbalist and independent directors met in secret, too, to determine what to do: "We were trying to get some leverage, and we were looking at everything when all of a sudden this paralegal, a young woman, comes in with a big smile on her face. She found a clause in the charter of Times Mirror Corp. that said super-voting shares could not be voted as super-voting shares in a change of control. This meant they [the Chandlers] couldn't dictate the terms."

An atmosphere of smugness prevailed in the downtown Los Angeles offices of Sidley Austin when Zimbalist, a clean-cut, steel-gray-haired man, walked confidently into the conference room armed with his fresh intelligence about the company charter:

> We had an agenda and time table. Tom Unterman was there and a lot of other lawyers. I was a brand-new CFO. So I said, before we get to the normal agenda, I just want to say that we may have to slow down the process a little bit because we have to go out and see if we can get other bidders. . . . They all looked at me in this condescending way. They told me this is a "no shop" offer, kind of like this is the way things work in the real world, sonny. And I said, well, that doesn't take into account Article 16 or whatever it was in the charter because it says the super-voting shares go away in these circumstances. Everyone stopped and looked at Tom and then they asked for an adjournment. It was kind of a beautiful moment. We slowed it down, changed the terms, and we did shop it around to two or three companies. . . . We showed it to Newscorp, the New York Times Company. But no one else could move fast enough. The tax structures we had in place were complex. Tribune used the same audit firm that had sold us these

structures, so they were comfortable with them. We delayed things, but at least we felt we had tested the waters. We got the price up a little bit and we improved the terms.

On March 10, 2000, Tribune started "management interviews and due diligence," the proxy said, scrutinizing the details of the proposed deal and looking for problems, a process that should take months. On March 12, two days later, the Tribune and Times Mirror boards approved the deal. The Chandlers made quick work of Willes. Once the deal was agreed upon, Willes wandered the halls of the Times Mirror building. "He would cry very easily," Wolinsky remembered. "It was waterworks for the rest of the time he was there."

During Willes' tenure, the *Times* circulation rose, its operating profits soared at a compound rate of 25 percent, and earnings per share increased more than 50 percent. Some industry executives credited Willes with forcing a hidebound industry to face up to declining readership and a dubious outlook for long-term revenue. Willes raised some important issues, too. "Tom and everybody else were talking about putting our content online for free, and somehow make it up on the ad side. And I said, let me give you something to think about. If you are going to give away for free what you stand for, then what kind of message are you sending? It's a message I don't think you want to send," Willes noted.

But Unterman, who felt the Internet was the future, worried that Willes devoted too much effort and resources to increasing newspaper circulation, which would continue to fall regardless of what the industry did. In addition, Willes had sacked 2,000 people and presided over a revolving door in his executive suites. When he left Times Mirror—only after loading the last of the Diet Coke in his fridge into the back of his car—Willes walked away with a severance package worth $64.5 million. For his part, Unterman, who by then had formed Rustic Canyon Partners—a company that would manage the Chandler family wealth—earned an $8 million dollar fee for working both sides of the transaction behind Willes' back.

As word reached Chicago on the evening of March 12, 2000, that a group of high-level Tribune executives (including Hiller, the executive in charge of Tribune's development arm) were in Los Angeles, Lipinski and I headed into the Tribune Tower. Rumors had hardened enough for *Tribune* media writer Tim Jones to work up the story all weekend and prepare a draft. Lipinski and I began calling sources, trying to confirm the rumors and pry details from tight-lipped Tribune executives, whose reluctance to talk convinced us something was up. As we speculated on how the deal would work, John Puerner, publisher of the Tribune-owned *Orlando Sentinel*, took our call and heard us out. He was out in Los Angeles as part of the deal team, but said he couldn't talk. He promised to call back, though, and at about 10:30, Puerner phoned and told us we were good to go; we could publish our story.

The headlines the next morning stunned the industry. Tribune had acquired Times Mirror for $95 a share in cash and stock, a price that, in retrospect, would prove to be far too high. It was the largest deal in newspaper history, a combination of resources that made Tribune Company the third-largest media powerhouse in the country after Gannett Corporation and Knight Ridder. The difference was Tribune had hands down the best collection of quality newspapers in America: the *Chicago Tribune*, the *Los Angeles Times*, *Newsday*, the *Baltimore Sun*, the *Hartford Courant*, the *Orlando Sentinel*, the *South Florida Sun-Sentinel*, the *Morning Call* in Allentown, Pennsylvania, the *Newport News* in Virginia, and several small suburban papers just north of New York City that sold a combined 3.6 million newspapers every day. By then, Tribune Company had successfully acquired twenty-two television stations, making the broadcast wing of Tribune as large as a network with viewers in 38.4 million households in America, including stations in the nation's three largest markets, New York City, Los Angeles, and Chicago. "Frankly," Madigan wrote in a memo to employees that day, "the newspaper industry is consolidating, and the only way to survive and prosper in the face of this trend is to have greater size and scale." Madigan explained that Tribune wanted to blend Times Mirror's journalistic prowess with its broad media reach and realize synergies that would pay for the transaction: "A major portion of the value creation from this combination will be derived from faster revenue growth in our media businesses." He predicted that by 2005, revenue growth combined with expense savings would generate an additional $225 million in cash flow. The combined company's Internet audience would total 34 million, bigger than the websites of the *New York Times* and *USA Today* combined.

On March 13, Hiller stood before the glass-walled offices of Sidley Austin, looking at the grubby streets of downtown Los Angeles below. Madigan was on the phone with Chicago Mayor Richard Daley, personally briefing him on the merger. His picture would soon grace the cover of *BusinessWeek* magazine, and stories about Madigan and Fuller would fill pages of the *Wall Street Journal*, all because of an idea that Hiller had proposed the year before. Times Mirror stock had jumped 75 percent that day, rising almost $38 per share to close near $95 per share. Michael Costa, Tribune's investment banker at Merrill Lynch, walked over to Hiller, warily eyeing the minute-to-minute trading stock on his BlackBerry. "He looked up at me and said the market is having a little difficulty with our deal," Hiller later recalled. Tribune stock, which once had been valued at over $60 per share, had plunged to $27.75. As Hiller watched cars snake by on the streets below, Madigan approached and took in the underwhelming view. Glancing at Hiller, he looked at him and, without missing a beat, deadpanned, "Should we jump?"

# 9

## Making News

In early 1999, not long before David Hiller advised John Madigan to buy Times Mirror, an extraordinary series called "Trial and Error" ran on page one of the *Chicago Tribune*. The series blazed a trail of national coverage that would have historic consequences, even though it was news out of Chicago.

In 1997, just after I had been named deputy managing editor for news, which gave me responsibility for the *Tribune's* newsroom, legal affairs reporter Ken Armstrong stopped me as I strolled through the fourth floor of the Tower. He needed access to a LexisNexis database to research every death penalty case that had been appealed in the United States since 1963, and in Illinois since 1977. Database access would cost $18,000, a hefty price tag, given that Armstrong couldn't guarantee the outlay would lead to a story. But his sources in the legal community had told him that many capital cases had been overturned because of prosecutors' misconduct, and LexisNexis was the only way he could authoritatively document whether the tip was true. After a long discussion, I asked Armstrong to write me a memo outlining the proposed story, how he could take the coverage where no other paper had gone, why the *Tribune* should do it, and how the public and our readers would benefit from the coverage. Then I visited Joe Leonard, a high-powered *Tribune* editor, who controlled the newsroom budget with an iron fist, and got Armstrong the $18,000, which amounted to 30 percent of his salary that year.

Over the next eighteen months, Armstrong plowed through a mountain of data. One search produced 11,000 court opinions. He read every one, poring over the data to extract leads and sources. Robert Blau, the paper's projects editor, monitored Armstrong's progress and soon recruited Maurice Possley, a *Tribune* criminal justice reporter, to help. When their research hit journalistic pay dirt, Armstrong and Possley hit the road, spending hours in courthouses, jails, prisons, bars, and kitchens. They interviewed lawyers, judges, professors, police, con men, crooks, the condemned, and grieving relatives. Every two to three weeks, Blau, a demanding and exacting editor, summoned them to his office for progress reports. Finally, after two years of exhaustive research, "Trial and Error" ran in the paper, carefully documenting how appellate courts had reversed 381 homicide convictions because prosecutors withheld evidence favorable to defendants, allowed witnesses to lie, and engaged in deception designed to win their cases at any cost, even if it meant a death sentence for an impoverished, innocent person with a lousy lawyer.

Eight months later, Armstrong, Possley, and police reporter Steve Mills followed up "Trial and Error" with a series that mined the treasure trove of information generated by the data search. In four riveting parts, they published "The Failure of the Death Penalty in Illinois" and changed the parameters of the debate over capital punishment in America. Newly elected Illinois governor George Ryan put a moratorium on the death penalty in the state two months after the *Tribune* series ran. "A lot of people are like me. The death penalty was a fact of life," he explained to a *Chicago Tribune* reporter. "But as people become more and more aware of the unfairness, they become less enthusiastic. I question the entire system and the people connected with it."

The following year, Possley and Mills produced "Cops and Confessions," a series that exposed how Chicago police used forced, fabricated, and otherwise problematic confessions, often extracted through torture, to convict 247 people of murder in Cook County between 1991 and 2001. Not all readers appreciated the coverage. Some believed the freed defendants were guilty. But most readers expressed shock that the city's police department could operate with such impunity and disregard for the law they had pledged to enforce.

As an editor, I got the kind of rewards for the coverage that sends a tingle up your spine. On February 1, 2000, in Rome, Italy, the lights in the Coliseum burned for forty-eight hours to memorialize the death penalty moratorium Governor Ryan had imposed. Three years later, in January 2003, late on the day he was released from prison, Aaron Patterson, a thirty-eight-year-old black man who had spent seventeen years on death row for murder because of a coerced confession, walked into the newsroom of the *Chicago Tribune* to thank Mills for a story that had saved his life. Years later in a farewell message to her staff, Lipinski would cite that moment as one of the proudest in her years as the gifted and principled editor of the *Chicago Tribune*. "I will not forget him telling Steve, 'You're a real life saver, man.'"

By the time Tribune Company pulled the *Los Angeles Times* into its fold, the *Chicago Tribune* regularly produced groundbreaking journalism, the kind that generated a competition between the two papers that would become both healthy and troublesome. Even in the best of times, the *Tribune* never had a staff the size of its new sibling in Los Angeles. Brumback had infused into Tribune Company a phobia for seeking more staff. In my tenure as an editor, the *Tribune* editorial staff peaked at just over 700. When the company acquired the *Los Angeles Times*, its newsroom totaled nearly 1,200, a number that would become a highly divisive symbol of the tension that would flare between Chicago and Los Angeles.

As the editor in charge of the *Tribune*'s foreign and national news, I was accustomed to being outgunned by the bigger papers with more reporters and had adopted an editorial mission to align my ambitions to serve readers with the size of my staff. I saw a paper like the *New York Times*, which had a foreign and national news staff twice the size of mine, as a journalistic floodlight that illuminated the news landscape with expansive coverage. I used the *Tribune's* smaller foreign and national news staff of forty correspondents as a spotlight that focused on issues in the news, deploying my correspondents to write in-depth, enterprising stories that broke new ground or made sense of the day's events. Bringing the staff along on that mission wasn't easy. Journalists are highly competitive; they want their bylines on the big stories. But the strategy eventually sunk in, particularly after George de Lama, an excellent journalist, became my deputy and pushed me to bring enterprise to the news of the day, too. Eventually, the strategy evolved into a special brand of journalism.

I had formed an alliance with Lipinski when Fuller tapped her to run the metro desk, the heart of the newspaper where seasoned journalists break news and newcomers break in. Lipinski had hundreds of journalists on her staff, and she used them to flood the zone on a local story, overwhelming the competition by tossing more and better resources at a story than anyone else. She was a tough, aggressive, and smart editor who zealously protected her newsroom against outside interference or influence.

A newspaper has a range of editors that do a wide variety of jobs. But the overall responsibility is to sift through the vast array of stories and reports about events from throughout the world and pare them down to those that should go into the newspaper every day. On a slow news day, a story about the mayor in Chicago could be the page one headline. A day later, the same story might not even make it in the newspaper because a crush of significant news from elsewhere in the world could simply overwhelm it. The editor and managing editor oversee the process and also set the level of excellence the paper demands from its staff. Lipinski set the bar high:

> For better or worse, I tried to create a safe space in the newsroom where reporters could dream big. . . . I remember once President Clinton had taken a trip and broke some big news, and we didn't have our own story. This was

before we bought Times Mirror. When I asked why, someone told me the reporter knew we were having budget problems in the newsroom and had decided not to go on the trip to save money. That was the first time I saw budget challenges creeping into reporters' decision-making and it concerned me. I wanted my reporters to be coming to me with big ideas about the Human Genome Project, or investigating how people get sick and die on airplanes, and I couldn't have them not pitching ideas because they were caught up in worrying about budget cuts or a job that didn't get filled. It was their job to find those ideas and my job to figure out if or how to fund that ambition. Right or wrong, I didn't want my reporters worrying about that. That's what I got paid to do. They were supposed to worry about stories.

As the editor in charge of foreign and national news, I supervised the "A" section and the coveted space on page one and had far more travel money than anyone else. So Lipinski and I had formed a partnership: When I needed an extra reporter to cover a big story or when I wanted to hire someone, she would lend me a reporter or consider my job applicant for a spot on metro, where there were always far more job openings. When she needed travel money to send one of her reporters on a trip for a story, I'd free up some dollars from my budget and make space in the "A" section for the story, even if it meant holding a story written by one of the correspondents on the national or foreign staff. The deals led to a partnership of mutual trust and respect that would survive the incredible ordeals we would face as leaders in an industry in upheaval.

Luckily for us, in early 2000, the *Tribune* had as much financial as journalistic muscle. Thanks to revenues gushing in from its papers and broadcast properties, Tribune Company had ample resources when it acquired Times Mirror and remained in fairly good financial shape. The Chicago paper had always guarded its local markets from penetration from competitors, too, and had built a strong stream of non-newspaper revenues. Tribune Company made $650 million in profit on revenues of $5.3 billion the first year after the deal, a margin of only 12.3 percent, primarily because the adverse effects of September 11, 2001, hurt the bottom line. By 2002, Tribune Company resumed posting the 20 percent plus margins it had delivered every year since 1996. The *Los Angeles Times*, meanwhile, posted margins of 14 or 15 percent.

In the newsroom, we put that money to good work bringing *Tribune* readers signature coverage they couldn't get elsewhere from reporters like John Crewdson, who convinced Lipinski and me to let him investigate how more people die of illness on planes than in crashes. When we reacted skeptically to his pitch, Crewdson fought back, arguing that sketchy statistics from the airline industry and the Federal Aviation Administration (FAA) purposely diminished the problem; airlines didn't want anyone to know their planes lacked basic emergency medical equipment or that their staffs didn't have proper emergency medical training. The airlines, including Chicago-based United, were loath to even discuss the situation, a stance that made Crewdson more determined to unearth the story.

Once we gave the project a green light, Crewdson, a bear of a man and a brilliant reporter, traveled the country to report and write "Code Blue." He filed Freedom of Information Act requests that generated documents exposing widespread discrepancies between FAA records involving in-flight illness reports and those on the airlines' own computers or in FAA records on emergency landings. He scrutinized coroner reports from counties in which airports were located to show how airlines avoided reporting an in-flight death by getting the body off the plane so the medical examiner would pronounce the passenger dead in the airport or on the jet bridge.

Readers of means and advertisers occasionally pressured us to back off a story or remove a journalist they found overly aggressive. But we absorbed that pressure. Crewdson later proposed we investigate child charities, the kind that ask you to send a small amount of money to sponsor some doe-faced child in an impoverished country where a dollar is a dowry. He might as well have proposed a hit job on Bambi. Organizations like Save the Children Federation helped kids. They were considered good guys. Their boards were loaded with influential folks who wouldn't hesitate to use their muscle against some nosy reporter. But the organizations that Crewdson singled out had collected $850 million in donations over the prior four years, and Crewdson questioned whether the money really got to the kids or did any good. So we recruited Lisa Anderson, who had become a national correspondent, Michael Tackett, from the Washington Bureau, and several other *Tribune* reporters to sponsor twelve kids with four charities—Save the Children, Childreach, the Christian Children's Fund, and Children International. The reporters used their own names as sponsors and sent in contributions, usually about $20 a month, for two years, sponsoring kids in some of the world's most remote places. The charities sent our reporter-donors heart-tugging pictures of their children with feel-good narratives spelling out how so little out of their pockets did so much good.

In May 1997, the sponsoring journalists fanned out across the globe on a journey to unearth their sponsored kids in the series we later named "The Miracle Merchants." Searching for Anderson's sponsored child, Korotoumou Kone, Anderson, photographer José Moré, and *Tribune's* Africa correspondent Hugh Dellios creaked along in a battered Peugeot until a narrow ribbon of rutted, red clay no wider than a goat path turned into scrub as they traversed N'goufien, the rural Malian village Korotoumou called home. Korotoumou Kone, the reporters soon learned, had been struck by lightning four months after Anderson had started sending her money. She had been dead almost the *entire* time that Anderson had sponsored her through Save the Children.

We contacted the charity to get its side of the story. Of course, not all sponsored children were dead, and money from sponsors at all four charities did flow to impoverished villages, but our reporting documented significant examples of misuse and waste. Members of the charities' boards called pleading with me to "take it easy" on them. Dr. Bob Arnot, the physician who regularly appeared on national television and a member of Save the Children's board, demanded why I was persecuting the good guys. Tom Murphy, the head of Capital Cities Communications, which owned ABC News, flew to Chicago to complain about the investigation to *Tribune* publisher Scott Smith, who provided a sympathetic ear and also a sobering reaction, quoting the line from Flannery O'Connor that graced an inner wall of the Tribune Tower: "The truth does not change according to our ability to stomach it."

Our reporting exposed how charities received little independent scrutiny. Save the Children attacked our reporters as unethical and our story as slanted. One charity, Children International, not only refused to talk to us on the record, but also accused a *Tribune* reporter of bribing a source because he had bought a mattress for a child while he was visiting the village where the child lived. Eventually, Children International hired John Walsh, a high-powered New York attorney and expert at crafting threatening letters, including one he wrote to Madigan on the eve of the series, leveling accusations of misconduct against *Tribune* reporters and threatening a suit that would bring down Tribune Company. We published the series nonetheless, and Walsh never sued.

Though our colleagues on the East and West coasts may have overlooked our work, the *Tribune's* journalism had impact. The newspaper's criminal justice reporting literally transformed the debate over the death penalty and focused much attention on whether a poor black man in Chicago had a better chance of being executed than a poor white person who could afford a lawyer who didn't doze off during a trial. After Crewdson's airline coverage, President Clinton signed the Aviation Medical Assistance Act, which required some thirty domestic airlines to begin reporting passenger medical emergencies to the FAA, which now requires all U.S. airlines to carry defibrillators on airplanes. Years after Anderson told *Tribune* readers about Korotoumou Kone, a group of child sponsorship charities, including Save the Children, announced they would pursue and adopt meaningful certification standards to quell fears of funding abuses. In announcing the effort, officials from the charity world said the *Tribune* series jarred the industry into action. "The *Tribune* affair was a wake-up call for a lot of us," Jeffrey Brown, director of sponsorship programming for World Vision U.S., told the *Wall Street Journal*. "Even though we may be doing things the way they should be done, if others don't, it reflects poorly on us because people assume agencies are similar in their practices."

Some critics, including people in the *Tribune*'s newsroom, accused us of pursuing projects like "Trial and Error," "Code Blue," and "The Miracle Merchants" simply to impress other journalists by winning Pulitzers. I loved to see my reporters' work recognized by their peers for a job well done, but we didn't do any of those projects for a Pulitzer. We did them because we were the *Chicago Tribune*, and this was the kind of journalism that Lipinski's *Tribune* practiced, whether we were in Bamako or Barrington, South Africa or the South Side. We took on the criminal justice system, the airlines, and the charities because that's what journalists are supposed to do: Give voice to those without a megaphone, shine a light on society's darkest corners where injustice or corruption often lurks in the shadows.

Not everyone agreed with the mission. Newsrooms are complex places full of ego-driven people motivated by a lot more than money. True journalists become journalists because of their love of a story well told, and because they want to make a difference. The *Tribune*'s newsroom was home to reporters who resented Lipinski, me, and my trusted cadre of editors and reporters. They viewed editors like me as arrogant elitists who doled out opportunities to friends—"journalistas" clinging to a prudish, outdated model of newspapering that failed to appeal to readers who wanted to know about popular culture, not political strife. There's probably some truth to that, although I would have had more respect for newsroom critics had they confronted me face-to-face instead of in anonymous comments posted on the blogs that began to pollute the news atmosphere.

In creating a special place in the newsroom where reporters could dream big, we also created a cocoon that protected journalists from problems that would hurt our newspaper and industry. Right or wrong, Lipinski and I felt a newspaper had to be a community leader, a force that challenged its community to confront issues that probably wouldn't score high on some readership marketing survey. Our job was to tell stories as well and as thoroughly as we could, and if we succeeded, we would create the kind of audience that advertisers wanted to reach. As Fuller said in his book, the backbone of a newsroom had to be good journalistic values—ones that readers would respect even if the stories generated angered everyone.

The criminal justice, airline, and children's coverage never won a Pulitzer, but the brand of journalism these stories represented paid huge dividends in other ways. The *Tribune* developed a reputation that drew more high-quality journalists to its ranks, helping make up in quality what we lacked in quantity. One such writer was Paul Salopek, a one-of-a-kind individual who reported like a demon, wrote like a poet, and garnered the *Tribune* two Pulitzers for his well-reported stories.

Salopek was a rare breed. He took *Tribune* readers (and *Tribune* photographer José Moré) to rivers of blood in the war-torn Congo when the country was off-limits to journalists. He rode donkeys to get a story, piloted down the treacherous Congo River in a canoe. Nothing stopped him, not the Hindu Kush Mountains in Afghanistan, not death threats or a turn in an African prison. He walked, ran, crawled, and scraped to produce riveting journalism that rewarded *Tribune* readers with his incredible eye for detail that made stories spring to life, sometimes by poetic portrayals of death. In Hillah, Iraq, he filed a report on the victims of Saddam Hussein:

> The dead are rising up in Iraq. They are emerging from bald soccer fields as well as bleak prison yards. They are rising from innocent looking highway medians and jaunty carnival grounds. False teeth, clumps of women's black hair. The twig like rib cages of babies. The appearance of such heartbreaking relics represents the final, damning rebellion against Saddam Hussein's Iraq—an intifada of bones.

Salopek later explained:

> What I liked about the *Tribune* was that it was a big metro
> daily with a foreign staff and a respectably-sized national
> staff . . . where reporters seemed to be able to develop an
> individual voice, . . . not the kind of uniprose you find at
> so many other big papers. I was hired in metro as a general
> assignment reporter. I knew nothing about the Midwest.
> I had never been to Chicago. But I quickly discovered that
> editors on metro would give you lots of opportunities. You
> could go to them with four or five good ideas and they
> would say "yes" to them. It was an idea meritocracy. If you
> had a great idea, they were willing to give you a shot at
> making it real. And that was really unusual for someone
> coming from an international magazine [*National Geo-
> graphic*] that had such a rigorous process to get an idea
> approved because it was always so expensive. . . . The paper
> had an enterprise culture. It didn't have the resources of a
> lot of the bigger metro dailies, but it had this enterprise
> culture that I found so appealing.

I don't think Salopek would have survived, much less thrived at any
other newspaper, but the atmosphere at the *Tribune* was more level and
perhaps more entrepreneurial than most. We were willing to go out on
limbs for our writers. When Salopek requested a yearlong leave from
the paper to ride a donkey 2,000 miles from the Arizona border to a
small town in Mexico, we agreed.

Salopek converted his passion for storytelling into powerful journalism on subjects as complex as the Human Genome Project, or
dreaded diseases like Ebola, Africa's notoriously lethal virus.

Writers like Crewdson, Anderson, and Salopek found a home at
the *Tribune*. We encouraged our writers to fight for stories they
considered important, and we trusted them enough to send them on
missions at which other papers might well have scoffed. With a slimmer

staff, our physical resources were limited, but we believed in deep coverage when we landed on a story that sparked our collective interest. Importantly, we were not easily cowed.

Not every journalist at the *Chicago Tribune*, of course, was as principled, smart, or precise as Anderson, Crewdson, or Salopek. Journalists usually don't get into trouble trafficking in money, the currency that corrupts other businesses. The mistakes that embarrass journalists and their craft usually involve ego—a quest for fame or status. The journalists at the *Tribune* were no different from those at any other paper in that regard. In our quest for recognition or breaking the big story, we sometimes screwed up badly.

In one effort to beat the competition, we ran a story and headline that announced that Vito Marzullo, a notorious local gangster, had died. The next morning, his family informed us otherwise. Another time, in April 2005, Lipinski called me, sick about back-to-back errors that would embarrass the *Tribune* and cost it some money. A *Tribune* reader had recently opened up his paper to find his picture in a graphic entitled "Infrastructure of a Chicago Mob." The man was a legitimate Chicago businessman who happened to have the same name as the gangster who was in jail. The very next day, we ran a similarly erroneous report. The paper featured a photograph of Joey "The Clown" Lombardo, a hoodlum who had been the subject of a lengthy and unsuccessful FBI manhunt. In an effort to mock the FBI, the headline above the photo read, "Have You Seen This Clown?" The man pictured was *not* Lombardo.

Such outright mistakes make good stories today when reporters and editors gather over drinks. But they were decidedly unfunny at the time: Our sloppy journalism embarrassed the paper and cast in doubt the *Tribune's* credibility and reputation for getting things right. Eventually the paper reached financial settlements with the wronged parties.

Sometimes we made bad judgments—ones that were costly in other ways. In 2005, we started *Redeye*, a paper designed to appeal to younger readers. Almost everyone agreed that the standards by which we judged news for *Redeye* would be different than those we used to assess content for the *Chicago Tribune*'s older audience. We told editors to consider pushing the envelope for *Redeye* content. The change in philosophy affected the more staid *Tribune* too, to ill-effect.

Geoffrey Brown, the *Tribune* editor who oversaw Woman News, a *Tribune* section that ran midweek, authorized a front-page story of Woman News that examined the increasingly acceptable use of the word *cunt*. The section itself was controversial enough; many women felt the name Woman News was sexist. Complicating matters, I didn't get wind of the story until it had been printed. In a panic, I called a production editor who assured me that the section had not yet been inserted into the paper.

I will never forget Lipinski's reaction when I showed her the story. I thought she was going have a heart attack. As I stood there reassuring Lipinski that the section hadn't been added to the paper, an editor called to tell me I'd been misinformed. The paper was still at the Freedom Center printing plant, but the section had been stuffed into more than 600,000 copies of the *Tribune*.

Horrified at the predicament, Lipinski and I decided to organize a group of journalists and go to the paper's printing plant. Working from around four in the afternoon until well past midnight, we removed some 600,000 sections of Woman News from the next day's paper. Included in the paper was a note from the editors apologizing for the absence of the section. When I asked Brown what he had been thinking when he authorized the piece, he told me he had merely been pushing the envelope.

At the *Tribune*, we were fortunate not to have many scandals involving inappropriate personal conduct. Even minor transgressions involving little-known journalists will draw the same kind of publicity that newspapers devote to public officials. When a problem involves a popular and well-known columnist, the journalistic justice can be harsh.

Under Fuller and Tyner, Tribune Company had established a strong ethics policy that prohibited journalists from capitalizing on their positions to win favors of any sort. In the fall of 2002, I had just become managing editor of the *Tribune* when we got an anonymous complaint about Bob Greene, a popular, award-winning columnist at the paper. The complaint was registered by a woman who claimed that she and Greene had had an inappropriate personal relationship after she had visited the paper on a high school field trip and attended a talk by Greene. If the woman's allegations were true, Greene could have been fired. Over the next two days, Greene admitted to having had a relationship with the young woman, whom Lipinski and I tracked down and interviewed. Her complaint surfaced fourteen years after the relationship had occurred, but the incident had profoundly affected the woman's subsequent feelings about men. When I told Greene that he was suspended pending the outcome of the investigation, he replied that similar complaints against him would flood into the paper if the situation became known. We accepted Greene's resignation the next week.

Like any other profession, journalists are vulnerable to the temptations that come with celebrity. When the gaffes occur, journalists get a taste of their own medicine—a straightforward formula that always seemed just to me.

# 10

## A Changing Landscape

Several weeks after Tribune Company took over at Second and Spring Street, Leo Wolinsky drove down the Avenue of the Stars, past the complex of law offices, strip malls, high-end hotels, and liquor stores that comprise Century City—the midzone between downtown Los Angeles and sunny Santa Monica—and paid a visit to his lawyer, Larry Feldman. He was increasingly worried about his future at the paper. It hadn't taken Tribune Publishing president Jack Fuller long to replace editor Michael Parks with John S. Carroll, a tall, fair-haired journalist and former editor of the *Baltimore Sun*. Fuller defended his replacement as a matter of course—a person from a Times Mirror paper would be a better fit than a Chicago journalist—but that did little to quell the unease of people like Wolinsky. Under Parks, Wolinsky was made executive editor, the highest position under the paper's full editor. But Carroll, after he arrived, stayed to himself and made little contact with editors on the floor—including Wolinsky. When Wolinsky confided to his lawyer a message that Carroll had conveyed to the staff—that no one would be fired—Feldman reassured him that he could make a legal case to keep his job. Driving away from Century City, Wolinsky felt, if not relieved, a modicum of security from Feldman's counsel.

When outside forces descend on a storied local institution to impose a new order, it's not unusual for the collective pulse to rise by a beat or two. Tribune Company had not just picked off a huge paper reeling from the tumultuous reign of Willes and Downing; it had acquired a big paper with national ambitions. As editor of the *Baltimore Sun*, Carroll had traveled to Times Mirror headquarters for meetings, but he didn't know many Los Angeles journalists well nor they him. The conventional wisdom was that Tribune had acquired a paper in the throes of a crisis, but Carroll, who spent the first few days at his new post poring over the pages of the paper, found something quite different. "People were saying it had gone to hell. I think I had a more objective point of view than people who had been caught up in the storm. I felt it was an underedited paper. The people were very bright, but they didn't assert themselves to the degree I thought they should. It was just not part of the culture. I felt it needed more assertive editing," he said. In other words, it needed leadership.

The *Los Angeles Times* that Carroll inherited employed a number of excellent journalists who practiced world-class journalism despite the buyouts and layoffs ordered by his predecessors. About three weeks before Tribune announced its deal, the *Times* broke a story on page one detailing how the physician most closely involved with the government's approval of the controversial diabetes pill Rezulin had urged its withdrawal from the U.S. market because of mounting injuries and deaths attributed to the pill, which had generated $1.8 billion in sales for Warner-Lambert, the New Jersey–based manufacturer. David Willman, a quiet but determined investigative reporter in the *Times* Washington bureau and a native of Pasadena, had unearthed the story from records and sources at the U.S. Food and Drug Administration (FDA), one of numerous federal regulatory agencies that remained virtually uncovered by other major papers in the nation's capital.

A prize-winning, tenacious journalist, Willman had been sniffing around the FDA for a couple of years reporting on its permissive atmosphere, after Congress, under political pressure over the demand for AIDS drugs, told the FDA to work more closely with pharmaceutical firms to get new medicines to the market. The *Los Angeles Times* gave Willman's stories good play because he was an excellent reporter, not because an editor had decided that an obscure but important federal agency needed scrutiny.

"I told myself that it would take six months to a year to get people off the ceiling. The first week I was there I found myself feeling unexpectedly at home in the newsroom," Carroll later recalled. Before the *Sun*, Carroll had been editor of the *Lexington* (Kentucky) *Herald-Leader* and had worked at several others. He well knew that each newsroom had a peculiar brand of politics: "The *Times* newsroom was collegial; there were no games. Saturday night of the first week, someone asked me to go to the paper's book festival. I thought it would be half-dozen teachers in a basement. It turned out to be like the Academy Awards. We had drinks on a patio on one of those gorgeous, cool Los Angeles nights on the campus of UCLA. Here I was drinking wonderful wine with interesting people and I thought, 'I'm glad I took this job.'"

Fuller had phoned Carroll at the *Baltimore Sun* the morning that Tribune had announced its deal. At the time, Carroll was considering an offer from the Nieman Foundation at Harvard University to run the foundation's fellowship program for mid-career journalists. He had all but decided to go to Harvard when Fuller reached him: "Jack and I had been on the Pulitzer board together and we'd been friendly. I'd been at the *Sun* for nine years and eleven and a half at *Lexington*. I was getting bored. I was tinkering with a book and negotiating over the curator's job at Nieman. They had told me I would get an offer, and Jack urged me not to sign anything. I assumed he was talking about the *Los Angeles Times* editorship. It was the only logical thing from my point of view. Then he asked me to meet with John Puerner," whom Fuller had just named publisher of the Tribune's new Los Angeles property.

Carroll hit it off with Puerner when the two men met at the Willard Hotel in Washington, but Carroll's mind was made up. Or so he thought. He later recalled returning to his home in Baltimore and going out for a walk. "Just for the hell of it I started thinking about LA and what I would have done on the first day as editor, on my second day. Then I noticed I was walking with a lot more spirit in my step," he said. Back at his house, Carroll called Fuller to talk more about Los Angeles and made some calls about Tribune Company and its reputation for its single-minded devotion to the bottom line: "I knew there were risks. I talked with some people. Tribune had a reputation different than Times Mirror or Knight Ridder. I talked to Jack. I got no guarantees. But he said we'd be crazy to do something bad with that paper. This is the *Los Angeles Times*; we'd be crazy to screw it up." He decided to take the job.

Otis Chandler's larger-than-life personality had instilled in the *Los Angeles Times* staff an almost ravenous desire for a strong newsroom leader. All eyes fell upon the tall, lanky, unflappable southerner when Carroll wandered onto the third floor in the spring of 2000. Carroll soon heard the same song that anyone who occupied the editor's office in Los Angeles would hear from his editors: "I went in and spoke to each department head. One thing I kept hearing is that the newsroom was woefully understaffed. At that time, the head count was 1,163 people. That was triple what I had at the *Sun*." Willes and Downing had established a bifurcated staff with a huge stable of experienced veterans like Willman, and a smaller yet significant cadre of less experienced, lower-paid reporters to man "Our Times" editions, intensely local sections designed to serve readers and lure ad dollars from affluent neighborhoods like Santa Monica. "They had confused, to some extent, the identity of the paper," Carroll recalled. "It was like reading two papers: a small local weekly with certain editing standards that are necessary in papers of that size and then also a very sophisticated, big metro daily. The two clashed."

Wolinsky started to see a cadre of new faces walking the halls of Times Mirror:

> A lot of Tribune people started to show up here. People had mixed feelings. There was a lot of anger and frustration about Mark and Staples. One faction said well maybe this is a good thing because Tribune had a reputation as a

solid company and maybe that's what we need. Another faction was concerned. The *LA Times* had always been the number-one top dog in the company. . . . I had a lot of trepidation because the Chandlers were selling out. I know they were not always the best for us, but they did protect us and let us try to be the best paper in the country.

In the business offices of the *Times*, Puerner shook things up immediately. CFO Skip Zimbalist remembered:

It became clear that Tribune wanted to install their people and their operating systems into Times Mirror and they were not interested in hearing about why we did things the way we did. I don't think anyone was thrilled about getting a lot of money. Some longtime employees had accumulated a lot of options and never had dreamed that they would get $95 a share. But the senior management group had plans to take the company to the next level. They were saddened to see the company broken up. On the editorial side, there was a lot of respect for Fuller. There was some elation. Otis was happy about the change. On [the] business side, there was less enthusiasm once it became clear that Tribune ran things from the top. A few people at the top . . . told everyone what to do. I had good relations with the Tribune people. They asked me if I wanted to move to Chicago for a role with the company. I wished them well. I was familiar with the Los Angeles market. . . . We were operating at 14 to 18 percent margins and they were at 25. They wanted to apply the same techniques to LA as Chicago, and I didn't see it. I grew up in LA and knew the competitive landscape. It was a very complicated market and dominating it with one newspaper was a tough thing to do. The idea that you could get a lot more efficiency quickly and easily; I didn't see it.

In editorial, Wolinsky's fears accelerated when the quality of the workplace started, slowly but surely, to show signs of change: Employees' reserved parking spots, formerly denoted with their names, were replaced with parking space numbers; vending machines that had once dispensed aspirin for free were now coin-operated; a full-medical staff that had served the paper's employees was eliminated. Perhaps worst of all was the unshakable sense of resentment by *Tribune* staff for the perks that had become standard fare for their Los Angeles counterparts. Change was decidedly afoot.

Wolinsky felt the immediate threat of the new management when Carroll emerged from his office to convene a series of lunches and dinners with senior editors and reporters. Carroll thought he needed new editors to instill more discipline into the newsroom. "I wanted to hire them from the West," Carroll explained. "After looking around, I hired some people from the East. They had some excellent people on the staff, people like Rick Meyer, who was absolutely first-rate. But there was no discipline on story length. I felt kind of a bloatedness about everything. Story dopings [summaries] were too long. I ordered one-paragraph summaries of stories. I restricted the news meeting to a half hour. I had three managing editors and a slot for a fourth. I wanted one person." Carroll soon set his sights on a charismatic African American editor in his forties at the *New York Times* who had just turned down a job offer to become the editor of the *Miami Herald*.

Dean P. Baquet was an unconventional choice for someone as grounded in the clubby world of establishment journalism as Carroll, who was a card-carrying member of organizations such as the American Society of News Editors. You wouldn't find Baquet roaming the corridors of the American Society of Newspaper Editors or the Black Journalists Association conventions trolling for a job. A native of New Orleans, Baquet grew up in a working-class neighborhood where he helped clean his parents' Creole restaurant, Eddie's, one of those places with red-checkered tablecloths on the first floor and white linen on the second. The son of a mail carrier-turned-restaurant owner, Baquet lived in the rear of Eddie's with his parents and four brothers, until he left New Orleans in the 1970s to study English at Columbia University. But he dropped out of Columbia two years later, homesick for his native turf. During a summer internship at the *New Orleans States-Item*, he fell hard for journalism and returned as a reporter covering police, the courts, and city hall. He wrote hard-hitting stories for the paper, including one *Times-Picayune* article that prompted a local black political group to boycott Eddie's. One of his fondest New Orleans journalistic memories was of covering Governor Edwin Edwards, the infamous Louisiana politician who once told Baquet, "The only way I can lose this election is if I'm found in bed with either a dead girl or a live boy."

Baquet left New Orleans in 1984 when a former New Orleans colleague, Jack Davis, hired him to work at the *Chicago Tribune*. It was there, in 1988, that he would share a Pulitzer Prize with Ann Marie Lipinski for exposing the extent of corruption at the Chicago City Council. Two years later, he parlayed his success at the *Tribune* into a job as an investigative reporter at the *New York Times*. In 1995, he was tapped to be national editor, the job he held when he got a call "out of the blue" from Carroll. "I didn't know John and the conversation was a little vague, although I figured I knew what he was calling about," he said. "He'd already been named editor in Los Angeles. He said he was going to be in New York and wanted to know if we could have dinner."

Surrounded by lush green plants, dark wood, and nude paintings at the Café des Artistes just off Central Park, Carroll told Baquet he was looking for a managing editor. A week after their lunch, Carroll called Baquet to see if he'd like to come out to spend a little time with him and Puerner. After thinking it over, Baquet accepted. Upon his return to New York, Carroll offered him the job. "I thought this was a really strong paper, a great paper, that had just been bought by a company I had a lot of respect for. I knew Tribune," said Baquet. He also felt he could have a bigger impact in Los Angeles than he could in New York, so he, too, headed west.

Even though Baquet replaced him, Wolinsky readily admits that things got better the day that Baquet set foot in the *Times* newsroom:

> I felt like we had just been taken over by an occupying force with all of these nasty comments. . . . John [Carroll] felt cold. He can be great at times, but he could also be kind of aloof. . . . He would sometimes just get up and walk out of a meeting if the subject didn't interest him. . . . We got a little whiff of what might happen when Fuller came out and met with the masthead [editors]. It was a very unsatisfying meeting. He didn't talk about stories, or our journalism or anything. He just said, "You guys better get a hold of your budgets because if you don't, bad things will happen." We thought we had a hold of our budgets. . . . But Dean [Baquet] was different.

Wolinsky said that he didn't resent that Baquet had replaced him as managing editor, a position that made Baquet the next likely editor of the paper:

> I always felt that to be the editor of the *Los Angeles Times*, you had to be distinguished. I wasn't distinguished. But Dean Baquet was. . . . He had an immediate impact. I called Dean as soon as I found out he got the job. He was very good, and we talked about stories, and he reassured me. Once he got here, he started meeting with people left and right. He started to talk stories. He had a very positive attitude and viewpoint, and we all started to feel reassured, like we were back on track, like we wanted to be a great newspaper again. I started to feel more secure, too. I became part of his inner circle really fast.

Los Angeles has always been a great news town. Earthquakes, mudslides, urban wildfires, and riots routinely graced the headlines of the

*Los Angeles Times* in the so-called "biblical times" of the 1990s. The *Times* owned those stories, flooding them with more and better reporters than anyone. When two heavily armed gunmen wearing body armor wounded ten LA police officers during a North Hollywood bank robbery on March 1, 1997, the *Los Angeles Times* threw a dozen reporters and just as many editors and photographers on the story, covering every angle, from the fissures it exposed in national gun-control policies to the neighbors who cowered in fear as a shooting spree broke out in the neighborhoods surrounding the Bank of America office on Laurel Canyon and Victory boulevards. The next day, *Times* readers got eight stories on the shooting. The following year, Chuck Philips and Michael Hiltzik exposed corruption in the entertainment industry, including a charity scam sponsored by the National Academy of Recording Arts and Sciences, illegal detoxification for wealthy celebrities, and a resurgence of radio industry payola. As a newspaper, the *Times* had an impressive breadth and range, far greater, in fact, than the *Chicago Tribune*. It also had an editorial staff large enough to achieve those lofty ambitions.

Baquet knew he had inherited a great staff at a paper that lacked direction. Like Carroll, he saw the need for focus: "I thought the stories were too long. . . . It was cacophonous, not a cohesive, coherent paper," Baquet later recalled.

■

Much has been made over the years of the failures of the Tribune–Times Mirror merger and of the conflicts spawned by the shotgun marriage of these two storied newspaper companies. Both parties made mistakes. But the complaints and recriminations overshadowed one thing: Initially, the deal worked. It not only worked, it worked well, particularly when it came to the reformation that took place at the *Los Angeles Times* under Puerner, Carroll, and Baquet, three people put in their jobs by the dreaded Tribune Company.

"Overall, I had more time in the newsroom than any editor I know," Carroll recalled. "Puerner [a longtime *Tribune* veteran] supported my request to spend nearly all of my time on journalism, not in business-side or corporate meetings. He covered my back so I didn't have [to be on] patrol. That extra time in the newsroom made possible whatever journalistic success I had." To bolster the paper's features coverage, Carroll hired another *New York Times* veteran, John Montorio, an exceptionally talented editor who went to work upgrading the *Los Angeles Times* feature sections into some of the best in the country. To the consternation of many in Chicago, Fuller strongly supported the team he put in place in Los Angeles, despite carping from Chicago about the size of the *Los Angeles Times* staff, and the new editors and publisher delivered the results he wanted.

Tribune Company had figured the merger would generate $200 million in cost savings. By 2003, Puerner had cut the number of *Times* employees from 5,300 to 3,400. Although he shielded Carroll's newsroom from much of the carnage, he closed fourteen money-losing Our Times zoned editions, initiated $220 million in capital expenditures that boosted the *Times* color printing capacity, and built a new $50 million facility for preprinted ad inserts to offset the loss of classified advertising.

Tribune had rebounded from the damage inflicted by September 11, 2001, posting 2003 operating profits that were up by 70 percent. It used its online assets to take on Monster.com, an employment website juggernaut that had come out of nowhere to ravage the classified advertising business of the *Times* and other newspaper companies across the country. Capitalizing on its national scale, Tribune created CareerBuilder.com, an online jobs site that competed head on for classified job ads nationally with Monster.com. Hiller, the onetime head of Tribune's development arm who would become publisher in Chicago and later in Los Angeles, recalled:

> For years, the newspaper industry had been falling all over itself in these consortium efforts that went nowhere because the companies didn't want to give up autonomy or control. We used the scale of the new Tribune–Times

Mirror to break through that morass and go out on our own. . . . We invested heavily to create CareerBuilder. It was probably one of the most striking and successful new media stories . . . of a traditional company creating a successful online business. Everybody thought Monster had already killed the recruitment business, but we overtook Monster. We invested several hundred million in Career-Builder and invested a lot in marketing expense. . . . We did the unthinkable for a newspaper company and even invested in Super Bowl ads for CareerBuilder. We overtook Monster in revenue, traffic, and job listings.

Nowhere would the change be more dramatic than in the editorial department of the *Times*. Initially, Carroll and Baquet helped Puerner generate savings, slashing the paper's so-called news hole—the amount of space dedicated to content after advertising was in place. "When I got there, the *Los Angeles Times* probably had more news hole than any other paper in the country. It was huge," Baquet recalled. "We had editions in Orange County, Ventura, the Valley, they all had staffs and huge news holes." As the news holes shrunk, reporters and editors were either bought out or transferred to other sections of the paper, and the size of the staff started to fall, although it remained far larger than in Chicago. "We probably cut too much in Orange County and the Valley," Baquet said. "About 70 percent of what we cut was about right. We probably went 30 percent too far."

The managing editor at the *Times* had traditionally run page one meetings and didn't spend time ginning up stories with reporters. But Baquet changed that, switching Wolinsky's title to deputy managing editor and putting him in charge of page one so that Baquet could get his hands dirty working with stories and reporters. Carroll and Baquet refocused the *Times* to make it a national paper of the West, an alternative voice to the East Coast papers that dominate the news media, a strategy that made them vulnerable to charges that they short-changed local news. Like Baquet, Carroll helped set a new tone at the paper, revamping its editorial pages and, sometimes, personally editing big stories that were destined to be candidates for prize contests, such as the Pulitzers.

Much had been made over Carroll's zealous pursuit of Pulitzers. David Simon, a former *Baltimore Sun* reporter who went on to create the HBO hit series *The Wire*, purportedly modeled the ethically challenged, Pulitzer-obsessed editor in the show after Carroll, who had been Simon's editor at the *Sun*. There is nothing wrong with an editor coveting a Pulitzer Prize. At heart, that's just what the prize is for— stimulating, promoting, and recognizing outstanding journalism that serves the public good. The top editors of all the Times Mirror and Tribune papers pursued Pulitzers before they were owned by the same stockholders; the deal merely enhanced the competition and made managing editors like Baquet and myself more determined than ever to show each other up with great journalism, the best of which often didn't win Pulitzer prizes. Did our competitive instincts and zest for a better story spawn duplication and inefficiencies that would have made Brumback's skin crawl? Sure.

But so what if some nickel-and-dime corporate apparatchik could find instances of two reporters from Tribune family papers in the same town covering the same story. In reality, the duplication wasn't that extensive or expensive. And the superior journalism promoted intangible benefits to the bottom line. Readers respect newspapers that take on powerful interests, expose abuses of power, and illuminate the dark corners of privilege where secrecy thrives. Good, solid, spirited journalism provides an invaluable, credible public marketplace of ideas and debate for readers and advertisers alike.

Like the *Chicago Tribune's* best coverage, the *Los Angeles Times* journalism had impact. Willman's Pulitzer-winning coverage of Rezulin spawned three or four federal investigations of the FDA's policies. Few other papers had the drive, resources, and guts to take on Walmart as *Los Angeles Times* reporters did in a 2004 series that exposed how the low prices touted by the Arkansas chain came at the expense of the workers in exploited factories far from the American public's eye. In 2005, I was on the committee of journalists named to select finalists for the Pulitzer. Included in the three stories we selected as finalists was one that made me ache with envy and admiration for Baquet and his staff: a series of stories that documented how Martin Luther King, Jr./Drew Medical Center, a 233-bed hospital just south of the impoverished Watts neighborhood in South Los Angeles, had a long history of harming and, in the worst cases, killing the community members it was meant to serve.

In 2005, the *Los Angeles Times* won the Pulitzer Prize Gold Medal for public service for its King Drew hospital coverage, but more importantly, the paper focused attention on deadly medical problems and racial injustice at a major public health institution. Carroll was proud of the paper's work. So was Baquet. But there was one man in Chicago who thought journalists like Carroll and Baquet were more interested in pursuing Pulitzers than in winning readers and making profits. He was the first CEO of Tribune ever to come from the broadcasting side of the company and he didn't share the journalists' values.

# 11

## Market-Driven Journalism

In July 1982, a tall, athletic young man known for his crisp shirts and competitive streak had walked into Tribune Tower to start selling advertising for the company's Chicago broadcasting flagship, WGN-TV. Dennis Joseph FitzSimons had been recruited by Jim Dowdle, a burly white-haired ex-Marine who had started his career as an ad salesman for the *Chicago Tribune* but had left the paper in the 1950s to explore broadcast sales, where he'd worked himself ever upward through the ranks. Thirty years later, in 1981, Tribune rehired Dowdle, this time as president and CEO of Tribune Broadcasting. Tribune Broadcasting's main asset, WGN, had begun broadcasting via satellite, and had become a national superstation—picked up by many fledgling cable stations across the country.

In FitzSimons, Dowdle recognized what he needed to energize the underperforming ad operations at WGN. FitzSimons didn't have the midwestern pedigree common to many Tribune executives— he was a native of Jackson Heights, Queens. But he possessed the up-from-the-bootstraps, free-market mentality that the corporate brass

163

at the Tower championed. And he had the drive and determination needed to build a national broadcasting powerhouse.

Despite his New York roots, FitzSimons belonged in Chicago. Like Dowdle, he was Irish Catholic; he'd been educated by the Jesuits—first at Fordham Prep high school and later at Fordham University in the Bronx, where he graduated with a bachelor's degree in political science. The youngest of four sons of a beer delivery driver and stay-at-home mom, FitzSimons initially considered pursuing law but concluded after a tour in the army reserves that he needed a job more than another degree. He took a low-level job at a stock transfer company until he was laid off in a recession during the early 1970s, and then landed another job as a lowly assistant buyer at Grey Advertising in New York. When he learned that you made more money selling airtime than buying it, he jumped the fence to sales.

At his core, FitzSimons had a fierce competitive streak. He often challenged fellow employees to basketball shoot-outs at the company gym, and usually won. He stood just over six feet tall, with neatly-parted gray hair and a well-trimmed mustache. In a profile of FitzSimons, *Los Angeles Times* reporter Tom Mulligan had compared him to a boxer from the bare-knuckled era. But FitzSimons also was a careful, detail-oriented, and determined worker who learned to capitalize on the growing pool of market research data to hone his sales pitches. He rose rapidly as a marketing representative for several broadcast companies, including TeleRep, where he was group sales director in Chicago.

By 1981, at the tender age of thirty-one, FitzSimons accepted an offer to run the ad sales unit of Viacom International, where he developed a sharp eye for spotting TV shows with audiences that would appeal to the right advertiser. When economic commentator Louis Rukeyser developed *Wall $treet Week*, a popular stock advice show on public television, FitzSimons suggested that Viacom create a version for commercial television. When Rukeyser agreed to the deal, the road was paved for FitzSimons to sell American Express as the ad sponsor, a lucrative step for his career and his pocket. He was named director of sales and marketing at a Viacom station in Hartford,

Connecticut, a year later. By 1982, he'd accepted Dowdle's invitation to the Windy City.

When FitzSimons arrived at Tribune, newly elected Ronald Reagan had recently installed FCC commissioners with a friendly regulatory attitude toward companies that wanted to acquire and own lots of television stations. Television syndicators, meanwhile, had dreamed up alternatives to the big-three networks' national broadcast audiences by cutting barter contract deals. Instead of acquiring programming, or shows, for affiliate stations like television networks, syndicators bought talk shows and sitcoms and then swapped the programming with big independent television stations like WGN in return for designated commercial space that they could sell to advertisers.

Syndicators hoped to sign up enough independent stations to create a mass audience and sell advertising space to big national advertisers. Stations like WGN got cheap programming, against which they could sell local advertising and make a bundle. With experience in local and national advertising, FitzSimons offered a wealth of knowledge and was an ideal fit for barter markets, which would prove extremely lucrative for Tribune Company.

Within a year of arriving at Tribune, FitzSimons rejuvenated WGN's ad sales operations and boosted local ad revenue by 5 percent, a steep jump in a highly competitive business. In 1983, when Tribune acquired WGNO in New Orleans, Dowdle sent FitzSimons to run it, but he was soon back in Chicago, where he was made vice president of operations for Tribune Broadcasting, the number-two job in Tribune's television division. When Tribune bought Los Angeles station KTLA in 1985, FitzSimons coordinated the integration of the television station into the Tribune's existing television line-up. It was a game-changing acquisition for the company's broadcast division and one that reinforced its attractiveness to syndicators that could wrap up two big markets with one customer. Three years later, Dowdle selected FitzSimons to run WGN-TV, the Tribune's flagship station, a post that FitzSimons described as "the best job I ever had."

Unlike Dowdle and Madigan, said Jim Kirk, a former *Chicago Tribune* reporter who covered him, FitzSimons didn't rub shoulders with the North Shore blue-blood types who formed Chicago's corporate aristocracy. His friends were more likely to come from the world of broadcasting or advertising. An avid sports fan, he befriended Jerry Reinsdorf, the Chicago real estate developer and sports impresario who owned the Chicago Bulls basketball team and the Chicago White Sox (the rivals of Tribune-owned Chicago Cubs). Soon after he took over at WGN, FitzSimons also capitalized on his contacts and skills as a negotiator to demonstrate that he was as capable of high-wire acts as any North Shore hot shot.

WGN had been locked in a long feud with the National Basketball Association over who would control the televised basketball schedule of the Chicago Bulls. NBA Commissioner David Stern insisted that the NBA should control the schedule because WGN had a national audience. But WGN wanted control so it could dominate the local sports television market by televising the Bulls games, as well as games played by the Chicago White Sox and the Tribune's Cubs. Once FitzSimons entered the talks, the court squabbles ended, and Stern agreed on a twenty-five-game schedule, a huge boost to WGN's ability to attract national advertisers who coveted product association with Michael Jordan, the team's superstar. The deal made Tribune Broadcasting a fortune.

By the early 1990s, Dowdle had successfully turned the company's TV franchise into a money machine. Brumback, meanwhile, had started pressing everyone to come up with ways to leverage the company's print and broadcast talent and create "synergy" or "convergence," his inspired goal of getting the most out of every dime he spent on a journalist. Dowdle had convinced the company it needed more television stations. Together, Dowdle and FitzSimons led Tribune on a trail-blazing acquisition spree: In 1996 and 1997, it added ten stations to the six it already owned. Six of the new stations were added in one fell swoop when Tribune bought Renaissance Communications for $1.1 billion in cash, a staggering sum that many analysts thought excessive.

The combination of aggressive ad sales and cheap, rerun programming gave Tribune Broadcasting huge profit margins that overshadowed its poor cousins on the newspaper side of the company. But the broadcast business was in flux. Cable TV access broadened during the 1990s, and new, specialized stations emerged to bid for the same programs that syndicators had been offering to independent operators like Tribune. As cable and independent operators started bidding for the same programs, the prices they had to pay for TV shows jumped sharply upward. The result? Operating executives like FitzSimons had to squeeze costs out of stations to increase efficiency in order to afford new talk shows and sitcoms.

FitzSimons made a great right-hand man to Dowdle, the visionary leader and source of inspiration in the broadcasting ranks. While Dowdle dealt with investors and others trying to mine Tribune's broadcast strategy, FitzSimons, who'd become executive vice president of Tribune Broadcasting, effectively ran Tribune television stations and refused to be shoved around by the big boys. When TV syndication mogul Roger King of King World Productions feared that sensationalistic talk show hosts like Jerry Springer and the Tribune's Geraldo Rivera threatened his prized property, the *Oprah Winfrey Show*, he tried to drive Springer and Rivera off the air. FitzSimons not only resisted, but invited King to join in the national syndication of Rivera with WGN, setting the stage for a popular show and a new format. "Once the sniping was done," Rivera told the *Los Angeles Times*, "the show took off."

Thanks to a prime-time slate dominated by movies and sports, Tribune stations routinely posted enviably high profit margins. But Dowdle and FitzSimons knew the good times couldn't last. Cable stations that emerged in the mid-1990s could easily duplicate Tribune's successful formula. To stay on top, Tribune needed original programming. When Barry Meyer, then head of Warner Bros. TV operations, and Jamie Kellner, a recent refugee from Fox Broadcasting, approached Dowdle and FitzSimons to gauge Tribune's interest in a new network, they were all ears. Eventually, Dowdle convinced Tribune to acquire a

25 percent interest in what became known as the WB Network, an operation that he saw as the answer to the company's need for original televised content.

Investing in WB was a gutsy move that put Dowdle's and Fitz-Simons' careers on the line. The soaring profits that Tribune TV stations delivered had spotlighted both men as rising stars. But acquiring a share in WB in 1995 was a bet on an unknown entity with an uncertain future in a highly competitive industry. Dowdle and Fitz-Simons were convinced by Meyer and Kellner's pitch. WB would give Tribune stations less programming to sell ads against, but they figured they could probably squeeze more revenue from the shows because they would be first run. Instead of stale, old *I Love Lucy* reruns, subscribers could watch new programming like *Buffy the Vampire Slayer* on WB.

Brumback went along with the deal, but not with Dowdle. When the time came, he passed over Dowdle to anoint Madigan heir apparent. Although both men were stoic professionals, Dowdle was indisputably the visionary leader of the two, a man who thought more creatively than an investment banker adept at corporate politics and operating results. But Dowdle's misfortune elevated FitzSimons and gave him a shot at becoming the first broadcasting executive to run Tribune Company. When Dowdle decided to retire, FitzSimons stood at the helm of the company's most profitable division.

As the deputy managing editor for news at the *Chicago Tribune*, I didn't know FitzSimons, though, of course, I knew of him. Paralleling FitzSimons' rise through Tribune ranks was a phenomenon known as "market-driven journalism," which would lead to news shows that were more like tabloids than serious, sober news. Media scholars trace the roots of market-driven journalism to the late 1960s when television station owners discovered they could meet FCC public service requirements and attract advertising audiences by creating local newscasts with popular appeal rather than traditional journalistic fare. Enlisting help from media consultants or "show doctors," they fashioned newscasts that forced politicians to compete for headlines with the likes of pop-tarts like Britney Spears. And it worked. Market-driven journalism was more successful than anyone could have imagined. Not only did the news shows attract viewers, they could also be used as public service content to meet FCC requirements and round out the fare on stations of all types.

Although many print journalists scorned the trend as pandering, the new news had its fans in print: "Somewhere in the late 1960s, what I call the stuff-pot factor took over," noted John Walter, a managing editor of the *Atlanta Journal and Constitution* in the 1980s. "Stories lengthened. Attitudes toward stories changed. And we, the institution, became so convinced of our mission to save the world and comment soberly on it that we veered away from what we had. We'd been dulling newspapers up. Now we're returning to the 'I didn't know that' factor, where news is anything that will capture your interest and make you turn to the next page because you don't know what wonder and revelation will be cast upon you."

Unlike newspapers, which relied on circulation and advertising revenues, local television news relied more heavily on cash from advertising, giving television station managers a powerful incentive to promote sensational news reports that would attract viewers. Tribune stations racked up profit margins of 30 percent or more, drawing the attention of Wall Street and pressuring newspaper editors to embrace marketing strategies in an effort to stem the decline in circulation that had begun in the 1980s.

In one of the few studies ever done on the subject, John H. McManus, a California journalism professor and media critic, found evidence that local broadcasters usually subordinated journalism to "market logic" when the two forces conflicted: "Market selection logic is straightforward. . . . To maximize returns to investors, the newsroom should pick those issues and events that have the greatest ratio of expected appeal for demographically desirable audiences to the cost of news gathering. Further, stories should advance, or at least minimize harm to, the interests of advertisers and investors." Such values, of course, repulsed newspaper editors like me.

Madigan had put Fuller in charge of the publishing division, and Fuller in 1993 had named Howard Tyner, a former Tribune foreign correspondent, as editor of the *Chicago Tribune*. Tyner delegated the job of running the newsroom to his subordinates, people like F. Richard Ciccone, a seasoned managing editor and ace political reporter, Lipinski, and me. Tyner then focused on managing Fuller and creating the newsroom that Brumback wanted, one with a TV camera nearby.

As a person who spent his career as a print reporter, I didn't know many television journalists well. Although print reporters were a competitive lot who would sacrifice their firstborn to break a story, most dismissed local broadcast journalists as lightweights focused on anything that made good film, particularly crime and sensationalistic "watchdog" reports that newspaper editors would relegate to metro. As Tyner started pushing Brumback's "synergistic" journalism, I got to know more television reporters and editors, particularly through our Washington bureau.

Brumback had authorized millions of dollars to turn the *Chicago Tribune* Washington bureau into the Tribune Media Center that housed all Tribune Company papers as well as a television operation headed by Cissy Baker, a former CNN journalist whose father, Howard Baker, had been a senator and remained a big-wig in the Republican Party. A competent journalist with good political connections in a town where they counted, Baker proved easy to work with, but our instincts about what stories to chase were almost magnetically opposed. To help Baker in Washington, Tyner installed Jim Warren as the *Chicago Tribune* bureau chief. A rising star in Chicago, Warren was a first-rate journalist who happened to have fantastic television presence. But even Warren, a proponent of synergy, admitted that his discussions with Tribune station directors around the country made it clear they were not interested in the kind of substantial news stories that his print bosses demanded. The saying "If it bleeds, it leads" was, Warren told me, no exaggeration.

As editors in Washington and Chicago scrummed over how to work together, FitzSimons' ascension to Dowdle's former job created rampant speculation about who would succeed Madigan as CEO—Broadcasting's FitzSimons or Publishing's Fuller. Madigan didn't tip his hand for a while. He enjoyed basking in the glow of the CEO title. Though he had been overshadowed by Brumback, Madigan had great timing and did a great job running Tribune if one judged him by the yardstick most CEOs looked at—the company's market capitalization, or the price of a share of Tribune stock multiplied by the number of shares outstanding. When he took over at Tribune, the company's market capitalization was $4.3 billion. By the time he stepped down, it was a jaw-dropping $17 billion. But when Madigan, who knew that Wall Street needed a succession plan to maintain confidence in the company as a sound investment, promoted FitzSimons to executive vice president of Tribune Company in 2000, the die was cast.

As soon as it was apparent that FitzSimons would be the next CEO, Tyner summoned me to his office and asked me to help educate the new boss about what journalists do, just as I had with Madigan. FitzSimons, Tyner warned me, had sharp views about our craft, particularly regarding some of our columnists and the way we selected news for page one. I told him I understood, but largely, I naïvely viewed the opportunity of face time as a chance to shine the lights of Tribune Broadcasting's television cameras on the company's journalism.

My first meeting with FitzSimons, in which we discussed our respective backgrounds, was cordial. I floated the idea of a visit to the Washington bureau, Congress, or the White House press room, or to one of our international bureaus to see how we operated and to get a firsthand look at what journalists did every day. But FitzSimons seemed uninterested. Instead of taking me up on my invitation, he launched into an explanation of how things were done in the broadcast world. "I'm always being accused of looking at everything through the broadcast model," he said, "and I don't want to do that." Quickly, he turned the conversation toward David Greising, a business columnist he clearly disliked, and wondered aloud why we would have a business columnist with populist leanings—a ridiculous claim (I had hired Greising when he was Atlanta bureau chief for *Business Week* magazine, not exactly a hotbed of populism). Notably, Greising had angered local CEOs in his columns when he challenged them (sometimes relying on humor to make his point) about everything from slumping earnings to obsessive secrecy. But FitzSimons let me know that he didn't think Greising was funny. I left our meeting feeling that my work was cut out for me.

In naming FitzSimons the new CEO of Tribune, Madigan and the board had passed over Fuller, the highly regarded editorial writer, former *Chicago Tribune* editor and publisher, and Pulitzer winner. As he rose through the ranks at Tribune, FitzSimons had zealously championed the values of the broadcaster, and his ideals often clashed with editorial. With FitzSimons as the head of broadcasting, Tribune had continued its breathtaking acquisitions of television stations, and he was pushing the company to buy the Chris-Craft group of stations, the sole remaining block of independent stations that represented a competitive threat to Tribune. Instead, Madigan decided to buy Times Mirror, an initiative strongly backed by Fuller. Why, then, had Madigan anointed FitzSimons as the presumptive CEO?

Doubtless, because FitzSimons went over better on Wall Street than the so-called professor. And the company needed to recover from the curve ball Madigan had thrown at institutional investors when he acquired an old-line newspaper company that hardly fit in with the string of TV stations Tribune Company had recently added to its portfolio. "One of the issues that caused distress was that a lot of people who had bought into Tribune, you know, big institutions, thought Tribune was shifting into broadcasting," Hiller recalled, "and among that cadre of shareholders, there was a fair amount of indigestion about going heavily back towards newspapers, and some of them thought that it was an unsignaled bait-and-switch and they didn't like it." Putting a broadcast executive in charge of the company was an effective correction to appease people who played a big role in setting the price of Tribune stock. Besides, Madigan, like Cook, was always impressed with personal appearances, and FitzSimons truly looked like a CEO.

Soon after my meeting with FitzSimons, I made an appointment with Pat Mullen, the man he'd handpicked to succeed him to run

Tribune Broadcasting. I wanted to talk to him about launching the kind of synergy I was interested in—a local or national public service television show featuring *Tribune*'s team of talented journalists with big-name guests to discuss the most pressing issues of the day. When I described the show, Mullen seemed discombobulated. He failed to understand why anyone would tune in to that kind of show. He asked me if I had talked to any station managers. When I said I thought he, as the head of broadcast, was the one to make those sorts of inquiries, he informed me that he couldn't do anything until I had talked to them and won their support.

My meeting with Mullen simply confirmed my fears about broadcast executives: They seemed like dunces. In the months to come, I would learn that there were indeed smart and thoughtful individuals toiling in broadcast, but they usually kept their mouths shut for fear of being driven out for challenging FitzSimons' protocol. Like many Tribune executives, FitzSimons felt threatened by people who weren't of similar ilk. At heart, FitzSimons was a political conservative and staunch Catholic who was intolerant of a world with gay rights and labor unions. He preferred the more comfortable domain of a broadcaster, one dominated by market analysis and local news.

In 2001, just before September 11, Madigan announced that FitzSimons would become president and chief operating officer of Tribune Company, a step away from the CEO title he would get in 2003. And, by then, undoubtedly, FitzSimons would have the chops for the top job. Although Fuller had started cutting costs and integrating the temperamental Times Mirror papers into the Tribune fold, the process was as rugged as covering the war in Vietnam. FitzSimons simply had a better story.

By 2001, Tribune owned twenty-three television stations, including sixteen affiliated with the WB Network, which featured programming designed to appeal to the lucrative eighteen- to thirty-four-year-old demographic. When you combined its television stations with the more limited reach of its newspapers, the company could reach 34 percent of American households, which resembled the national TV networks.

The proportion of profits churned out by the broadcast division exceeded its contributions to revenue, too. FitzSimons's television properties accounted for about 28 percent of Tribune's revenues but 39 percent of its profits, a stellar performance that got him the top job. Now he faced the challenge of whipping the newspapers into shape to make them market-driven purveyors of local news, while making a profit like the TV stations.

My views of FitzSimons evolved the more I engaged with him, particularly once Lipinski elevated me to managing editor of the *Chicago Tribune*, a job that placed me in control of the paper's newsroom. As we interacted, I began to discover the depth of FitzSimons' conservative roots.

When I told FitzSimons that we should revive *Newsday*'s failed effort to publish an edition for New York City, he, to my surprise, agreed. A New York edition, he offered, would at least provide an alternative to the left-wing *New York Times*. When the *Chicago Tribune* featured a photograph of two men kissing after a Massachusetts court ruling approved of gay marriage, FitzSimons stopped me on the street to ask why the *Chicago Tribune* would ever run such an image on page one.

Although he was hardly as blunt or direct as the broadcasters McManus studied, FitzSimons clearly was in the "market-driven journalism" camp. I found him to be smart, hard working, honest, dedicated, determined, talented, and ambitious. But in my experience he could also be petty, mean-spirited, and almost obsessively single-minded. I think his tendency to be a meddling micro-manager also exposed his hostility to journalists. He said he didn't understand why a newspaper editor who presided over declines in circulation shouldn't be fired, just as a station manager with tepid ratings in broadcast would be.

Those of us in editorial countered that newspaper editors were not running popularity contests; if they were doing their jobs, they would routinely anger readers and vested interests in the community. But FitzSimons didn't completely buy it. He thought that journalists, like broadcasters, should use market research to give readers what they wanted, not news that some high priest of the news cycle deemed important.

Over the years, I'd seen many market surveys asking readers what they wanted in their news pages. If all we had to do was ask readers what they wanted and then give it to them, surely someone would have complied long ago and a winning formula would have been devised. FitzSimons correctly tried to get the journalists at the *Tribune* to focus on issues that no one wanted to confront, ones that questioned the value of stellar journalism if fewer people bought or read our newspaper. And the truth be told, editors like me did a poor job defending ourselves; we often retreated behind the wall separating the business and editorial sides and refused to take responsibility for declines in readership. But the problems weren't that simple, easy, or honest.

FitzSimons' drive to instill a marketing discipline into news soon created a surging tide of conflict at the company's newspapers. Just after he took over, FitzSimons ordered readership surveys for all Tribune papers, including some that compared how journalists regarded their papers with the views of readers. The results proved that readers and journalists were not always in sync.

FitzSimons and the like-minded publishers he began to appoint took aim at the journalism of papers like the *Tribune* and the *Los Angeles Times*, arguing that readers wanted local news, not long, complicated stories like one I had ordered up examining the struggle for the soul of Islam in the wake of September 11. If you just looked at the readership surveys, FitzSimons was right: The average reader in Southern California ranked his or her top news interests in order of relevance as local, Southern California, national, and news about the economy. But if you overlaid onto the charts the interests of the *Times* most dedicated readers, they reflected a different set of priorities: national, international, national government, politics, and arts and entertainment.

The discussions roiling the ranks at Tribune rarely grappled with the significant but subtle differences; the research was widely viewed as an assault on journalistic principles, with FitzSimons and his marketing hawks leading the charge. If someone challenged the results of his market surveys, FitzSimons doubled down to overwhelm them with the zeal of an evangelist smiting his opponents, particularly newspaper editors who, in his mind, were more interested in impressing their friends with Pulitzer Prizes than winning readers by giving them what they wanted.

"He [FitzSimons] wanted to edit the paper by referendum," Carroll recalled. "To him, news judgment and marketing were the same thing. I had this feeling from Dennis that we should judge what we put on page one based on marketing. He didn't want any complaints. My judgment was that we should get complaints. That is part of being a vibrant voice in the community."

FitzSimons didn't appreciate how fundamentally the newspaper operation that Fuller had built differed from his baby, the broadcast division. At the *Tribune*, Fuller picked people for leadership positions who sometimes disagreed with him, gutsy editors like Lipinski or Carroll. In Tribune Broadcasting, FitzSimons had selected his cronies—people like Mullen, a loyal soldier who towed the line.

Perhaps more shocking and disheartening to me even than FitzSimons' market-driven approach to news and his disregard for subjects he didn't agree with was his lack of curiosity. Once every three or four years, the *Chicago Tribune* convened a conference where national and foreign correspondents could get some face time with their bosses and discuss the stories that would be big news on their beats over the coming months and years. It was a great exercise that gave editors a chance to hear about upcoming news stories and reporters an opportunity to meet with fellow correspondents and the home office. Madigan had relished the conferences, often bringing his wife along, and offering editors seats on the company jet. Because the *Chicago Tribune* had fewer correspondents than the *Los Angeles Times* or other major papers, the *Tribune's* eleven foreign correspondents covered wide swaths of territory. Listening to their reports about their beats usually gave attendees an expansive view of developments that would be making global news headlines over the coming months. Many of the stories our foreign reporters were covering were destined to be the sorts of investigative journalism projects for which the *Tribune* was known.

In 2003, I saw our upcoming conference in Istanbul as an excellent opportunity for educating FitzSimons about journalism, and to my surprise he agreed to attend.

As the *Chicago Tribune* copy boy steered our car through Washington Park en route to Midway Airport on Chicago's South Side, Lipinski took a call on her cellphone from publisher Scott Smith, who was also traveling to Turkey. When she hung up she reported that we'd been delayed—FitzSimons didn't have his passport. I assumed that he'd simply neglected to pack it. I was wrong. FitzSimons didn't know he needed to carry his passport with him. Tim McNulty, the *Tribune's* foreign editor, had dutifully gotten FitzSimons a visa from the Turkish Consulate. FitzSimons had assumed that McNulty had taken care of everything and that he didn't have to carry a passport with him. "You guys are the world travelers," FitzSimons said sheepishly after we'd all arrived at the Signature Air offices at Midway. "I'm just a guy who goes to New York."

As we crossed the Atlantic, FitzSimons started talking about the war in Iraq, a subject of particular interest to me. I had decided to travel to Iraq after our foreign conference to learn firsthand about the dangers our correspondents faced covering the war, then in its early stages. As an editor who often put correspondents in harm's way, I believed that I should willingly go anywhere that I would send a reporter. I had traveled to many dicey places with *Tribune* correspondents, but this was a special case.

FitzSimons started to relax on the plane, chatting amiably with Lipinski, Smith, and me. When I told him I would be going to Iraq after Istanbul, he began questioning the thoroughness of the overall coverage of the conflict, using the same logic and language as Bush administration critics. I was ill at ease—especially with the knowledge that Donald Rumsfeld, then U.S. Secretary of Defense, had been a Tribune board member. By then I had heard most of the arguments: The media focused too heavily on the negative elements of the Iraq war and not on the positive actions of the American military (hospital-, school-, and road-building initiatives).

As editors, we deferred to reporters on the ground who were closest to the action to suggest stories, particularly in war zones. FitzSimons acted surprised that I would let a reporter decide what to cover. That wasn't the way things were done in broadcasting, where reporters received more direction from their bosses.

FitzSimons allayed my fears about any direct influence from Rumsfeld when he told me he based his opinions about the Iraq War coverage on discussions he had had with a journalist friend with firsthand experience of the war, who had told him that most news coverage of the conflict exaggerated the violence and gave a misleading portrayal of the U.S. efforts. The friend in question? Geraldo. I was stunned. Geraldo Rivera, then a Fox News reporter, had recently come under criticism in the press for his Afghanistan war coverage when he told his viewers that he had recited the Lord's Prayer over "hallowed ground" where "friendly fire took so many of our men and the mujahedeen." Rivera later acknowledged that he had never visited the site where the U.S. servicemen or mujahedeen had died, the "hallowed ground." I dropped the subject with FitzSimons.

Once we checked into our hotel in Istanbul, FitzSimons seemed to be enjoying himself. He shared a glass or two of wine with the correspondents and gave them an impressive briefing on the company's business prospects with a meticulously prepared PowerPoint presentation that left no one in doubt about his message: The Tribune Company would have to grow or be devoured by the giants of the media business.

Madigan had always encouraged us to use his rank and status to help line up interviews with powerful foreign leaders. Capitalizing on FitzSimons' presence, we had scheduled an interview with the recently elected Turkish Prime Minister Recep Tayyip Erdoğan, a charismatic former Istanbul mayor and moderate Islamic leader who had once been jailed by the Turkish military for reading a poem. The interview had been set for Friday, after the conference was scheduled to end. When FitzSimons was informed of the meeting, he told me he could not possibly attend. He had to be back in the United States by Thursday.

He expressed his regrets and told me he wasn't "like John in these things." I didn't ask what was important enough to stiff the prime minister of one of the few moderate Islamic countries that supported America at a time of war in the Middle East.

Later, the staff heard that one of the reasons FitzSimons had wanted to get back to the United States was to attend a baseball game between the Cincinnati Reds and the Chicago Cubs. When Erdoğan learned the Tribune CEO wouldn't attend the interview, he canceled. Cincinnati beat the Cubs nine to seven.

# 12

Buy the Numbers

In September 2000, just nine months after FitzSimons had been named Madigan's heir apparent, a letter from a street-smart lawyer landed at the home of Harold Foley, a computer programmer who had done some work for *Newsday*, the Long Island version of the tabloid newspaper that had thrived even though Willes had closed its sister paper in New York City.

"We are the attorneys for clients who have authorized us to investigate the possibility of commencing a Federal [racketeering] class action against *Newsday*, Inc., and *Hoy* LLC, growing out of a possible fraudulent inflation of *Newsday* and *Hoy* circulation records," read the letter. "At this stage of our inquiry we are concentrating on a computer program labeled 'Program—ID FUDGE ABC,' which we believe was designed by you."

At first, the letter generated little reaction, other than a threatening response from Randy M. Mastro, a lawyer for *Newsday* and *Hoy*, its Spanish language offshoot. Mastro, a New York lawyer from Gibson, Dunn & Crutcher, the same firm that has represented the Chandler family in Los Angeles, demanded that the author "cease and desist" making false statements about his clients and threatened him with repercussions.

Just six months before, Tribune had acquired Long Island–based *Newsday* as part of its merger with Times Mirror. Although the letter to Foley had arrived after the deal had closed, the allegations, if true, suggested that the Tribune Company had acquired some pretty serious circulation problems when it brought *Newsday* into its family of newspapers. But the company's accelerated due diligence hadn't detected anything was amiss at *Newsday*, which bragged about its consistent circulation gains despite trends to the contrary at almost every other paper in America measured by the Audit Bureau of Circulations, or ABC (the industry's auditing arm that verifies the circulation totals, the numbers newspapers use to set advertising rates, their major source of revenue).

Everyone at *Newsday* figured the problem outlined in the letter to Foley written by Joseph O. Giaimo, a dapper Queens lawyer, would just go away. But the problems didn't go away and neither did Giaimo. "You don't threaten me," Giaimo later told me, pumping his thumb toward his chest, "You don't threaten Joe Giaimo. I'm a street guy. You fuck around with Joe O. Giaimo. Bad idea. I'm a street guy."

Circulation departments have never been the choirboys of the newspaper industry. The Colonel's *Tribune* had hired the likes of Moe and Max Annenberg to bust heads, trash competitors' newsstands and even "toss a goon" down a *Tribune* elevator shaft in the rough-and-tumble circulation wars of the early twentieth century. When Brumback took on the unions at the Tribune-owned *New York Daily News* some eight decades later, union drivers torched kiosks, beat up replacement workers, and engaged in thuggery that prompted Tribune to pay someone $60 million to take the paper off its hands. The corrupt practices that would be unearthed at *Newsday* paled in comparison with the good old days, but news of the fake circulation on Long Island would reverberate through newspaper executive suites across America nonetheless.

Although the *Newsday* scandal first surfaced after Tribune had acquired the paper, the circulation games started years before the

Chicago company owned the tabloid that serves Long Island, the nation's most populous suburb, 1,400 square miles of woods, roads, and seashore that is home to both waterfront mansions in the Hamptons and gritty slums around Hempstead. Almost from the day that the Colonel's niece, Alicia Patterson, started *Newsday* in a Hempstead garage, the paper had made dizzying circulation gains. With an attractive tabloid format and a stable of smart writers, Patterson upended the conventions of suburban American journalism, much as her father had done with the *Daily News* in Manhattan. Within seven years, *Newsday* turned a profit, and by the time her husband, Harry Guggenheim, sold the paper to Times Mirror in the late 1960s, other American newspapers drooled at the way *Newsday* dominated its market.

*Newsday* was a showcase example of the pros and cons of a local monopoly. In its messages to advertisers, Tribune's only tabloid boasted the "highest household penetration in its circulation area of any major daily in the United States." In 2000, *Newsday* claimed that it reached 73 percent of adult readers in Suffolk and Nassau counties, far higher than the *Los Angeles Times* (37 percent) or the *Chicago Tribune* (41 percent). Year after year, *Newsday* carried more retail, automotive, real estate, and job recruitment ads than any newspaper in the New York market. It had three times more real estate advertising than the *Daily News* and four times more financial ads.

Nestled among the white-fenced, sprawling estates and low-rise office buildings in suburban Melville, *Newsday* wasn't one of those tabloid papers with lurid headlines like the *New York Post*; it used its enviable ad revenues to hire columnists like Jimmy Breslin, Pete Hamill, and Gail Collins; publishers like Bill Moyers; and editors like Tony Marro, a first-rate journalist who for years ran the paper that won nineteen Pulitzer Prizes and probably deserved more. But talent alone didn't bequeath *Newsday* the kind of dominance it enjoyed on Long Island; the paper needed muscle, too. It needed people like Louie Sito.

From all appearances, Sito didn't look like the Charles Atlas of the Long Island newspaper world. Slim and wiry, with a thick head of swept-back hair and a full gray mustache, Sito was a fast-talking Cuban with a sly smile who had emigrated to America in the 1960s when he was sixteen. After he landed a job on the loading docks of the *Chicago Sun-Times*, he began inching his way to a job in the American newspaper game, substituting guts, brains, and tough talk for the connections that usually spell success. Privately, Sito viewed the people who ran the newspapers where he worked as a bunch of privileged, country club snobs who had hired him because they didn't like to get their hands dirty. Generous with family and friends and suspicious of outsiders, Sito was hot tempered, but he had uncanny instincts for a good deal. And he wasn't above cutting a corner or two to get what he wanted.

Sito left the *Sun-Times* abruptly in 1964 and knocked around in a variety of jobs until 1990 when a friend from Chicago tipped him off about a job at *Newsday* where he could capitalize on his *Sun-Times* experience. Within two years, *Newsday* put Sito in charge of its distribution arm, and in 1994, when Ray Jansen became publisher, Sito was made vice president of circulation: the guy in charge of getting the paper out onto the streets. By 1999, Sito was vice president of sales, the number-two job in the company that put him in charge of *Newsday*'s and *Hoy*'s circulation, distribution, and advertising departments.

A federal prosecutor who investigated *Newsday* described the paper's business model as a curious mix of Stalinism and capitalism:

> If Stalin said you would produce 1,000 tractors, you would produce 1,000 tractors, whether or not they rolled off the production line. Even before Tribune, Jansen would not permit the circulation number to fall. It would simply not go down. He didn't want to hear it. Factor in that you then have the smartest guys from FitzSimons on down saying you have to hit your number and that we can always do more with less and you must meet your targets. If that's what the top people at Tribune are telling people, how do you expect them to meet these targets?

But what Sito discovered was that no one at the top asked him much about *how* he hit the numbers as long as he continued to hit them.

Sito's job at *Newsday* evolved into two broad responsibilities: solidifying the paper's local monopoly, and manipulating the circulation to make sure the numbers always rose. Sustaining the monopoly was pretty straightforward. If competing media entered *Newsday's* market, Sito showed up at the door with *Newsday's* checkbook to try to buy them out, regardless of whether it was a successful Pennysaver or Shopper or a struggling newspaper distributor. And usually he succeeded.

The second part of Sito's job was a bit more complex and risky. Anyone who has ever subscribed to a newspaper has heard the familiar "thump" a newspaper makes when it hits your door or doorstep in the morning. It is a simple and reassuring sound, something that starts many a day, almost like an alarm clock set off by carriers like those Sito controlled. But the process behind that thump is not so rudimentary. Newspaper delivery systems are complex, easy to manipulate, and instrumental to the rates advertisers pay and then pass on to consumers.

To make sure that *Newsday's* circulation increased, Sito and his team used—and abused—the three methods by which publishers placed newspapers into the hands of readers. In most cases, readers called the paper or responded to an ad and gave their mailing addresses and payment information, and *Newsday* would soon show up on their doorsteps. *Newsday* also sold the paper wholesale to independent agents who charged readers retail and covered delivery costs with the difference. Advertisers liked home-delivery circulation best because readers who ordered *Newsday* delivered to their homes were the most likely to read the paper and see their ads. Sito liked the independent sales agent approach because he could treat them just like Jansen and the Tribune bosses treated him: He told them what he wanted done and demanded that they deliver.

For those who preferred to buy the paper a day at a time, Sito sold *Newsday* wholesale to dealers who provided single copies of *Newsday* to readers who paid the cover price at coffee shops, delis, and grocery stores or to hawkers, down-on-their-luck souls who stood out on the street to sell papers to motorists stopped at red lights. If single-copy dealers had leftover papers they couldn't sell, they were supposed to return them to *Newsday* to receive credit for the unsold copies, which were not counted in the paper's circulation figures. Advertisers didn't like single-copy as much as home-delivery readers, but Sito did, particularly copies sold by hawkers.

Sito and his team also sold bulk subscriptions: a block of dozens of newspapers that businesses such as hotels could sell—usually at a discount that could reach 75 percent off the cover price—or pass out to customers as a sort of bonus for using their service. Advertisers didn't like bulk subscriptions because it was hard to know if the person getting the paper bothered to look at it. But many newspapers used bulk circulation to inflate their numbers. Sito and his operatives simply took the process to new levels.

Jansen and Sito's bosses at the Tribune pressured circulation chiefs to hit their numbers for all kinds of reasons, but the main incentive was that higher circulation generally translated into higher rates for advertising—the dominant engine of revenue at newspapers. Ad revenue at papers like *Newsday* typically accounted for 80 to 85 percent of the cash that flowed in from grocery stores, car dealers, employers, and department stores trying to lure Long Island consumers to their doors. In fact, for every dollar in circulation revenue that Tribune papers made, they typically got five to six dollars in ad revenue. So there was a huge incentive for Jansen, Sito, and the Tribune Company to put the best face on the numbers that reflected how many people bought and read their newspapers.

Although most people in the American newspaper industry don't like to admit it, lying about circulation is a time-honored tradition in publishers' suites. It's hard to say who started fudging the numbers, but one of the first times that the practice surfaced publicly was in 1876 when Victor Lawson took over the *Chicago Daily News* and said he would no longer conform to the industry's practice of treating circulation figures as trade secrets. With a fair amount of hubris, he announced that he would document his actual circulation numbers in the *Daily News* front-page streamers claiming to have the largest circulation of any evening paper in Chicago, astonishing his red-faced ad manager who convinced him to back off until the numbers actually reached the level the paper was privately touting to advertisers.

Circulation fraud was so prevalent at the time that the *patent medicine industry* urged American publishers to create a credible system to measure circulation. In 1914, newspaper publishers endorsed the creation of the ABC, a board composed of representatives from the industry and advertisers to set common standards by which newspapers could be reliably measured and to hire and train auditors to keep papers honest. Over the ensuing decades, the system had its ups and downs but seemed to work fairly well until circulation started declining, particularly after 1990, when it became clear that real circulation growth had gone the way of the Linotype. That's when newspapers like *Newsday* got creative.

At first, the industry simply changed the yardstick. Each household that receives a paper typically has more than one reader. So newspapers claimed the real number to look at was readership—a much squishier number calculated by research firms that made the industry look better. But ABC continued to publish the circulation results for the nation's largest newspapers and reporters covering the industry continued to focus on them, prompting industry leaders to criticize coverage for focusing on negative circulation results. For their part, reporters didn't begin to detect that the industry played with the numbers until scandals erupted publicly at papers like *Newsday*. Had papers like *Newsday* dedicated the imagination and creativity they used to inflate circulation to their real problems, I doubt they would be in such trouble today.

Most advertisers that commit ad dollars to newspapers focus on paid circulation, particularly home-delivery customers, but also those who buy single copies. They don't like copies handed out for free. In fact, under ABC rules, newspapers aren't supposed to count papers that publishers give out free or discount deeply. But Sito and his team devised ingenious ways to circumvent the rules. *Newsday* sponsored events like the popular hot-air balloon races on Long Island, a show that could draw tens of thousands of residents, most of whom needed a place to park their cars. Thinking fast, Sito's team helped line up parking for $2 and gave each driver a copy of *Newsday*, one of the benevolent sponsors of the races. Under ABC rules, free parking-lot papers couldn't be counted as paid circulation, but that didn't stop Sito. Anyone who looked closely at the tiny, fine print on the $2 parking ticket would discover that they had actually paid $1.25 to park and $.75 for *Newsday*. Under ABC rules, that was paid circulation.

The parking caper was one of *Newsday*'s more benign practices, and Sito and his team didn't game that particular element of the system as well as some other papers. The next time you check into a hotel, take a look at the cardboard sleeve that houses your plastic keycard. Chances are, there will be some fine print telling you that included in your room charge is $.75 for a copy of *USA Today*, whether you want it or not. If you ask the hotel what is going on, you're likely to get the same response as did Jay Schiller, a former ABC auditor who questioned both the Marriott and Hyatt hotel chains about the practice. A Marriott vice president told him the paper really was complimentary. Pete Sears, a Hyatt vice president, explained: "By including this verbiage . . . the newspaper companies are able to include our daily newspaper spend in their circulation count. In exchange for [a] very favorable 'subscription [rate],' we have agreed with our newspaper partners to refund any guest [the newsstand price] should he decline the paper. The cost of the paper in no way is added to the cost of your room." Gannett, publisher of *USA Today*, has cut deals with hotel chains across the country for such arrangements. Something that was referred to vaguely as "other paid single copy" circulation at one point totaled an astonishing 35 percent of *USA Today*'s paid circulation. If you add to the total the stacks of papers that sit in the lobby for the taking, the total comprised an even larger percentage of *USA Today*'s circulation.

At *Newsday*, Sito also engaged in far more sinister plots, arranging kickbacks for dealers who dumped unsold copies rather than return them to be counted against paid circulation. *Newsday* was delivered to homes that hadn't ordered the paper or to readers who were dead. Foley's FUDGE ABC software program was employed to create the illusion that the fake circulation was real. Ironically, Sito's house of cards wasn't exposed by his brazen disregard for the rules, but by the paper's desire to solidify its monopoly.

In March 1998, an arm of *Newsday* led by Sito acquired a Queens newspaper distribution company owned by Michael Pouchie and Anthony Orlacchio and folded it into United Media Distributions, Inc., which became the sole distributor of *Newsday* and *Hoy* in the greater New York metropolitan area. Pouchie knew the local newspaper distribution business cold from years of experience making sure readers on Long Island got their newspapers. And, as he would unabashedly reveal in an interview with me, back then he packed heat—in his case a .38 and a 9-millimeter. "I had a permit," he explained, matter of factly, sitting in his Queen's office with posters of news delivery boys in baseball caps on his wall.

A lawsuit filed by Joe Giaimo laid out the details of a scheme that would unfold over the next couple of years: After *Newsday* bought their company, Pouchie and Orlacchio said they ended up with 47 percent of United Media Distributions, while *Newsday*'s distribution arm, DSA, or Distribution Systems of America, owned 51 percent. As an independent agent, the suit said Pouchie had been distributing *Newsday* for years, and he knew what he was getting into—a few years earlier he'd begun meetings with people who worked for Sito to discuss the best ways to pad *Newsday*'s circulation. Giaimo's suit exposed the sophistication of the setup: Those involved in the scheme would receive alerts when ABC auditors were due to show up. Ed Smith, a *Newsday* and *Hoy* circulation consultant who would later plead guilty to fraudulent circulation practices, had entertained the auditors to gather intelligence for *Newsday* and conducted tutorials on how to lie to the ABC about paid circulation information.

At first, things seemed okay at United. But things took a turn when it began distributing *Hoy*, which was Sito's baby. Months before, Sito had noticed how *Newsday*'s penetration rate of 65 percent in several

Long Island communities started to plummet when Hispanic immigrants bypassed Manhattan for the suburbs. Sito had convinced Jansen he could turn adversity into opportunity with a Spanish language daily newspaper designed to capture this pocket of readers and recover some of the numbers lost on *Newsday's* end.

In November 1998, *Hoy* debuted with Sito, who had added the title of publisher of *Hoy* to his duties at *Newsday*. Judging from the spin, *Hoy* was an immediate hit. But it wasn't a hit with Pouchie, who distributed the paper, mainly to single-copy dealers, vending machines, and hawkers.

During the first week *Hoy* was on the market, United sold about 38,000 copies, or 7,600 copies for each of the five days the paper hit the streets. But Robert Garcia, *Hoy's* circulation director, who also would plead guilty to fraudulent circulation practices, ordered Pouchie to increase reported sales to 88,000 papers, or 17,600 copies a day for the reports that would form the basis of *Hoy's* ABC numbers. Those, in turn, were used to set ad rates. Giaimo's suit said the same thing happened the second week; United sold 40,000 papers, or 8,000 copies a day, but Garcia ordered up double that, or 16,000 copies daily. In week number three, Sito ordered Pouchie to rig the reports to show that United had sold 120,000 copies of *Hoy*, or 24,000 papers a day, when the legitimate daily sale really totaled only 8,000 papers. Giaimo said Pouchie refused. A week later at *Newsday's* Christmas party, Orlacchio got a message from Sito: "We'll screw you if Pouchie refuses to change the *Hoy* circulation volume." Pouchie resisted the muscle, though, and a week later, discovered that the locks on United Media Distributions' doors had been changed. He and Orlacchio had also been locked out of the company's computer system. In other words, they'd been fired, even though they still owned 47 percent of the company.

Not to be outdone, Pouchie and his partner formed a new distribution company and took one of Pouchie's old clients, a Puerto Rican newspaper called *El Vocero de Puerto Rico*, with him. *El Vocero* continued to be printed and delivered to Pouchie's old office at United, where he would pick them up and distribute them. But a couple of months after he'd been locked out, United refused to give Pouchie his papers and he went to the facility to demand them. "The cops told me a *Newsday* employee called them and said some mad man was inside waving a gun around," Pouchie said, adding that he had asked for his papers and when they said no, he started to leave: "When I got outside, there were like fourteen police cars with cops pointing guns at me. They told me to give up my guns and lay down on the concrete. I did and then they handcuffed me."

Elisabeth Vreeburg, a Queens lawyer, took the call from Pouchie, who she'd been representing in divorce proceedings. He was in a Queens jail, on a charge of trespassing, something about *Newsday*, fraud, guns, and his Puerto Rican paper. Two days later when Pouchie showed up at Vreeburg's office, she asked her partner Joe Giaimo, who had more experience as a litigator, to sit in. When Pouchie sat down, Giaimo recalled, "he wants to sue them for false arrest, and I hear his story about all of this circulation fraud, and I tell him, 'You got more than a false arrest suit here, brother.'" In truth, *Newsday* probably could have settled the whole controversy for $500,000 to $1 million at the time. "I'd probably have settled for a million," Giaimo later said, and none of the industry's shady practices would have been exposed in court.

But Sito said Jansen got his back up. After the dust-up over the Puerto Rican papers, in April 1999, *Newsday* had acquired Pouchie and Orlacchio's interests in United. When Sito later came to Jansen and told him that the duo, now represented by Giaimo, wanted some more money, Sito said Jansen told him, "Tell them we'll see 'em in court."

Sitting in his cluttered office across the street from a Chicken House restaurant near the Kew Gardens subway stop in Queens, Giaimo is as Queens as St. John's Law School, his alma mater. He once worked as legislative staff for New York City Mayor Robert F. Wager in Manhattan and as counsel to Moses "Mo" Weinstein, a legendary majority leader in Albany. Short, with thinning gray hair and a raspy voice, he walks fast and always seems to have misplaced something in the banker boxes stuffed with files scattered everywhere over the fraying blue carpet.

But Giaimo is always ready for a fight, and, within months, he'd lined up several companies that had advertised in the Long Island paper as clients and had a road map from Pouchie on the gritty details of the paper's circulation scam: "Look, they're dumping papers, they're dumping them everywhere and they want to threaten me? Ok. You want to be an animal," Giaimo said. "I'll be an animal. You want to be a prick, I'll be a prick." After Jansen and *Newsday* refused to engage him or his clients for the next few years, he finally filed suit in early 2004.

The charges of massive circulation fraud at *Newsday* caught Timothy Knight off guard. About a year earlier, Knight had dropped by to visit Jack Fuller at his rustic cabin in Michigan and learned that Long Island was in his future. A former Skadden & Arps corporate lawyer, Knight had joined Tribune in 1996 and had become one of Fuller's fair-haired boys, assuming a variety of jobs in the publishing group until Fuller told him to head east:

> There was an understanding that Ray [Jansen] would retire in the next two or three years when he was sixty-five. Jack had put a Tribune person in charge of all the other Times Mirror papers but nothing had been done at *Newsday*. . . . He said Ray really didn't want anyone from Tribune but that he would take me, or words to that effect. . . . Jack was pretty clear that it was unlikely I would be publisher but to go out there and learn another business unit and try to identify opportunities for *Newsday* to work with other parts of Tribune.

A boyish-looking man with a bright smile, freckles, and a receding hairline, Knight arrived at *Newsday* in March 2003 as the paper's general manager and went to work learning the paper and Long Island. Tribune had put Jansen in charge of all East Coast papers, and Knight soon discovered Jansen ran the place like a fiefdom. When Giaimo filed his suit, Jansen's folks told Knight not to worry: "It appeared at first it was some lawyer who was trying to gin up some clients because [someone] who supported the lawsuit . . . was an ex-employee or vendor who . . . had something that *Newsday* had taken over and the guy was unhappy; it was a disgruntled somebody, a vendor or distributor or something like that. They were small advertisers, out in the boroughs," Knight said. But Giaimo's suit got publicity, a lot of it, including stories in *Newsday* and other New York papers: "I'm in all the papers," said Giaimo. "I got former sales agents calling me, telling me stuff. I'm on CNN. Everywhere! I got people from all over the country calling me and saying they worked for papers and the same thing is going on in their city, Chicago, Milwaukee, Baltimore, Philly, you name it. From all over the country!"

The lawsuit got people's attention in Chicago. Fuller, who ran the publishing division of the company, told Knight they needed to get some answers—fast. Tribune had strong corporate and newspaper ethics policies that threatened employees with termination if the rules weren't followed. Tribune executives soon showed up at *Newsday*'s offices in Melville to help investigate the situation, along with lawyers from Sidley Austin, Tribune's outside lawyer, and auditors from ABC. Across the country, newspapers with dubious circulation practices watched the events at *Newsday* closely.

Knight didn't quite know what to make of the call from one *Newsday* reader—Elaine Banar, a hard-nosed federal prosecutor at the Eastern District of New York's office in Brooklyn. Banar recalled: "He [Knight] laughed at why we would even be investigating this. He said it was not that significant and why would we be wasting our time with subpoenas." By then, Sito had been promoted to head Tribune's Hispanic media efforts by Fuller, who faced diversity problems in his management ranks. Knight soon confronted Sito's handpicked successor at *Newsday*, Bob Brennan, about the allegations in Giaimo's lawsuit: "He said this was just a problem in one office in the boroughs. I hadn't seen enough data to form an opinion. And, you know, . . . you could argue that the lawyer [Giaimo] . . . was just trying to shake us down." As the internal investigation gathered steam, trouble surfaced in Chicago.

A Chicago edition of *Hoy* had been launched to replace *Exito*, the *Chicago Tribune's* Spanish language paper, and Fuller had selected Digby Solomon to launch it. Solomon recalled:

> I think it was a couple of weeks before the launch, and Louie stepped in with a bunch of people from New York, and they said they would take over distribution. He brought in Bob Brennan and Richie Czack. . . . As soon as Richie started, we couldn't get any numbers. We had sold [ads in *Hoy*] to national advertisers, but nobody could get any numbers [on how many papers had been sold]. I finally confronted Louie and asked why we couldn't get any numbers. He said *the* number is 10,000 but *our* number is 17,000. He put his finger up to his lips and said, 'don't tell anybody.' . . . Now if I'm going to accuse anybody of fudging numbers, I needed some evidence.

Solomon, also a Cuban native, headed out to the *Hoy* distribution warehouse the next afternoon:

> I got there and counted three skids full of papers, almost a full day's run of the paper that should have been delivered that morning, sitting on the loading dock. So I say to Richie, 'What's that?' Richie says, 'What's what?' And I said those skids, and he says, 'What skids?' and I say, 'Those skids.' That was enough. So I went in the next day figuring I may get canned, but this is wrong." Solomon reported his findings to his boss, David Hiller.

Meanwhile, back at *Newsday*, Knight and his investigative team got some disturbing news from Brennan, who had downplayed the seriousness of the problem months before. According to Knight:

He comes in and tells me that the story he told me is untrue. . . . I was shocked because he had essentially lied to my face a number of times. He never said why he did it. When I suspended him and told him you're off for the rest of the week, he thought I was overreacting. . . . We called the U.S. Attorney that night, and I called ABC because we had been putting forth a defense that had relied on Brennan and crew. We went to them as promptly as possible to say we are looking into it, but what we had told you clearly wasn't true. . . . It was probably one of the low points of my life because the guy lies to you and before then I was trying to support him, you know, let's get the facts before you convict somebody. . . . Ray [Jansen] was up at the U.S. Open in the Hamptons, and I called him and told him. . . . Okay, I've got a guy who has lied to me, our circulation director, his circulation director long before I was here. The story is breaking in the paper. You need to figure out what is going on with the government; they are trying to figure out what's going on, and what we'd told them is obviously not 100 percent correct because we had relied on Brennan and . . . they are not sympathetic, they are pissed. And the big issue is that Ray doesn't come back. . . . He stays in the Hamptons.

Although Knight felt that Tribune was doing everything it could to unearth the story, Banar and the feds didn't see things that way:

We were getting the same story from lower-level folks who told us about the pressure to deliver higher numbers. . . . We started to get a sense of a scheme. . . . The *Newsday* people will say that they convinced Brennan [to go to the Feds and] give it up, come forward. But Brennan had a different story and I tend to believe him. He said the pressure got to him. . . . The lawyer for *Newsday* also said the fraud was limited; that it was just one small department. He said they did an internal investigation and came back to us and said it was just one department."

She decided to expand her investigation to determine just who knew what in the upper reaches of the Tribune's corporate hierarchy. She wasn't alone.

As news of his lawsuit spread, Giaimo received a call from the U.S. Securities and Exchange Commission (SEC), and from a former agent and employee of *Newsday* who offered him an inside account of circulation fraud at the paper. He flew to Florida to meet with the insider and an SEC attorney from the agency's Miami office when his office called and told him to get in touch with Banar: "I called Banar from the airport to tell her I planned to travel to Miami to meet with the SEC. She immediately stopped me cold and told me that if there was a criminal investigation of the allegations in my complaint, it would be conducted through her office with the participation of the SEC and the Internal Revenue Service." Ditto for the calls from the U.S. Postal Service and the Nassau County Sheriff's Office. In other words, Banar pulled rank and took control of the investigation.

In mid-2004, Jansen stepped aside, and Fuller made Knight publisher, even though he had virtually no experience running a newspaper. Knight immediately hit the road trying to mollify advertisers angry at the circulation fraud revelations:

> In a perverse way, it was a great way to start off as publisher because I had to go speak to all of our advertisers. It was a bit of a mea culpa, and I discovered that *Newsday* had been extremely arrogant in dealing with advertisers. Over the past twenty years, we had pushed through rate increases not being customer service focused and not just treating people well with the viewpoint of, 'Well, where else are these guys going to advertise?' . . . It was good for me to hear it and set up a path on how we were going

to treat advertisers better. . . . The advertisers were angry but it was anger based upon twenty years of compounded bad behavior.

By now, though, the federal investigators were working their way up the corporate ladder, zeroing in on people in executive suites who had been applying all of the pressure for higher numbers. A federal subpoena from the SEC soon demanded "documents relating to or referring to communications concerning circulation figures or revenue or advertising fees or revenue between Dennis FitzSimons, Jack Fuller, Donald Grenesko, David Hiller, Raymond Jansen, Louis Sito, Robert Brennan, and Robert Garcia." Banar began to think that people at the top of the corporation knew what was going on: "They didn't want to be connected with it, but they knew. The internal auditors tried to figure it out, but people at the top kept things from them, too. . . . None of the internal audits ever got to the right questions."

As the *Newsday* investigation unfolded, two things became clear: the imagination of Sito's team worked overtime, and *Newsday* wasn't alone. When ABC auditors suspected that hawkers got copies of *Newsday* in preferential deals that allowed them to sell what they could and dump the rest in recycling bins, the auditors tried to clandestinely observe whether the sales actually occurred. But Sito's team got wind of the probe and dispatched *Newsday* employees to the hawker sites to buy up the papers.

■

The entire U.S. newspaper industry was watching the evolving investigation with bated breath. There was more than a grain of truth to the "everybody does it" defense that *Newsday* employees articulated. "I don't think people were doing stuff that was criminal," said Jack Klunder, the former director of circulation at the *Los Angeles Times*. "But a lot of people aggressively pushed the limits of the ABC rules." Circulation directors would convince the local Ford dealer to buy 1,000 to 50,000 papers at a discount to be donated to schools. The newspaper would publicly recognize the Ford dealer as a pillar of the community, school kids would get papers, and the newspaper got paid circulation because of the Newspaper In Education (NIE) program, which was permitted by ABC rules. What few knew was that the Ford dealer often got a discount on the ads purchased that was eerily similar to what he had paid for the papers: In effect, the papers often were free. As details leaked out of the secretive federal investigation on Long Island, other newspaper publishers looked within.

The potential scope of the problem the industry faced is buried in ABC audit reports, complex documents available to dues-paying members and full of granular data that newspaper publishers slice and dice to show advertisers how they can penetrate choice zip codes full of affluent readers. Even after *Newsday* cleaned up its act, its ABC audit for 2004, the year that Giaimo filed suit, reported that it sold an average of 482,182 papers a day. But if you add up the totals reported for home-delivery and single-copy sales, you get an average of only 354,215 papers sold each day, a gap of 127,967 papers that fall into a dubious category that includes bulk sales of papers provided at a discount to schools or hotels or parking lots for a balloon race. That's really "junk" circulation. Even if you assume that the ABC reports accurately on single-copy and home-delivery sales, 27 percent of the circulation that *Newsday* reported to the ABC fell into the junk category. And that's *after* the paper restated its circulation figures to remove bogus readership.

By 2005, when the scandal was unfolding, ABC audits revealed that many American newspapers had junk circulation profiles similar to *Newsday*'s, particularly large metro dailies where circulation decline was most acute. At the *Los Angeles Times*, junk accounted for 21 percent of its circulation; the *San Jose Mercury News*—23 percent; the *Houston Chronicle*—25 percent; the *Miami Herald*—23 percent; the *Atlanta Journal*—15 percent. A few papers like the *Chicago Tribune* showed only 5 percent, but many others had built up a sizable portfolio of junk circulation designed to inflate their numbers and support higher ad rates.

Banar summoned the Tribune brass one by one to a cavernous room in the spacious marble halls of the U.S. District Courthouse in Brooklyn. FitzSimons had made Hiller publisher of the *Chicago Tribune* and he soon found himself at the U.S. Court House in Brooklyn, under scrutiny by Banar and her team. Even whistle blowers like Digby Solomon were under suspicion:

> I had written a memo about what I knew and gave it to Crane [Kenney, the Tribune's general counsel] and then I got a call from this guy with the IRS. We had one meeting at the [courthouse in Brooklyn]. I thought I was going in as a friendly witness. I walk into this big room and here are all these people. One guy has a freaking 38 strapped to his bicep. It became obvious to me that Louie has spun the story well. They started asking me stuff like, 'Why didn't I tell Dennis FitzSimons to fire Ray Jansen?' Then I gave them a statement that contradicted one of their witnesses. And this guy [a prosecutor] says to me, why don't we take a break and you go out into the hall and discuss with your attorney the penalties for perjury.

The investigation that Banar started would last for years and have a huge impact in newspaper offices across the country. Circulation directors couldn't figure out where Banar and the Feds drew the line between pushing the limits on ABC rules and circulation fraud. Advertisers too began to question readership totals that included junk circulation. Soon publishers began quietly pruning junk circulation from their totals, accelerating the circulation declines in the numbers they reported to the ABC, and making a bad situation look worse.

The credibility of journalists took a hit too, even though most had no idea what was going on in their own business offices, a perverse effect of the wall that separated them from the business of journalism. Bloggers, politicians, press critics, and academics already had started attacking the credibility of journalists for things like failing to expose the Bush administration's faulty intelligence that led to the war in Iraq. Now they faced a more fundamental question: How can you trust news reports from people who don't even tell the truth about how many papers they've sold? Nowhere was the impact of the scandal felt more tangibly than at *Newsday*. Knight set up a huge room where the paper's employees began calculating the extent of the circulation fraud, and how much the paper owed advertisers who had paid ad rates based on the fake numbers. Knight concluded that *Newsday* had overstated its circulation by about 100,000 copies. When all was counted, the scandal cost *Newsday* $100 million in fines and ad rebates. And as for the man who started it all, Joseph O. Giaimo? His lawsuit is still pending.

# 13

## Count Kern

When the *Newsday* scandal broke, Fuller walked into FitzSimons' office to offer his resignation. Not only had Fuller promoted Sito, the man in large part directly responsible for the nightmarish circulation fudging, he had failed to rein in Sito's boss, Jansen, who had stubbornly resisted Tribune's efforts to place controls on *Newsday*.

I felt particularly bad about the fallout from *Newsday*. George de Lama, my top deputy, was Sito's cousin. De Lama is a man of unparalleled honesty and character. I rarely made a decision I didn't first discuss with him, and he saved me from myself more times than I can mention. I knew Sito and liked him, with the kind of affection you reserve for your most devious sources. Sito admitted circulation fraud in federal court, but he didn't invent it. Jansen insists that he knew nothing about Sito's "rogue" operation, but that was not true. Sito had openly disclosed bogus circulation numbers in a letter written to Jansen prior to the scandal. U.S. District Court Judge Jack Weinstein, who presided over the prosecution, didn't buy the rogue operation defense either. "In going over the papers and records of the case, I decided it was highly unlikely that all of this could have occurred without the knowledge of the publisher . . . who had a reputation of running the place with a strong hand, or higher-ups at Tribune. This was a fraud that totaled over $100 million. So I insisted the U.S. Attorney make further inquiries," the judge noted. In court, he publicly challenged prosecutors, demanding, "Why wasn't the publisher prosecuted along with the underlings?"

Fuller said that he didn't know about the fraud at *Newsday*, but admits he should have. Had he not promoted Jansen and Sito, the scandal probably would have been discovered much sooner. Rather than accept his offer to step down, FitzSimons placed Fuller in charge of the company's response to Banar's investigation, for which Fuller rightly felt responsible. As a former Justice Department lawyer, Fuller was up to the task. In short order, he started an internal investigation designed to bring the whole controversy to an end. But Banar was just getting started. She and her Brooklyn colleagues were highly suspicious when Fuller hired Tribune's long-term outside law firm, Sidley Austin, to conduct an in-house probe—particularly when the internal investigation contradicted Banar's witnesses, who had told her that the fraud was not limited to *one* small department. If Banar's witnesses were to be believed, Sito and Brennan, who'd been dismissed by Tribune, hadn't acted in isolation. And Banar didn't trust the auditors from ABC, which was financed by the newspaper industry: "The ABC guys were all paper folks." Banar noted. "There was no way they were going to blow the whistle. This was an industry regulating itself. They didn't want to do anything that would cause the fall of newspapers."

Federal prosecutors routinely cut plea and sentencing deals with cooperating witnesses in return for testimony, and once Banar corralled as cooperating witnesses the men who had been dismissed by Tribune, she saw a pattern emerge, not unlike the one that Giaimo outlined in his lawsuit: "From the lower-level folks, we started to get a sense of a scheme in which sales agents are pressured to inflate the numbers. That's when we really started to think there was something there." With encouragement from public statements of Judge Weinstein, Banar shifted her focus toward executives high up at Tribune—including

FitzSimons, Fuller, and Hiller. The Feds had concluded that Solomon was telling the truth when he said he'd alerted his superiors to the scheme. But prosecutors felt those same superiors had done their best to mask the extent of the problem.

For FitzSimons, Banar's investigation couldn't have come at a worse time. He had inherited the reins of a company that had consistently delivered strong financial results. Over time, Wall Street had come to expect high returns from Tribune. FitzSimons was under enormous pressure to cut costs while maintaining profitability north of 20 percent. The constant pressure to keep profits at a steady rate of increase invariably resulted in culture clashes—between Wall Street and Tribune's business operations; between the business side of the paper responsible for generating revenue and editorial; between TV journalists (whose already lean budgets had come under increased scrutiny) and newspaper journalists; between web journalists (who viewed their counterparts in print as dinosaurs) and print journalists; and, notably, between Fuller and FitzSimons.

Relations between Fuller and FitzSimons had never been smooth. Fuller had labored long and hard to educate the business side of the paper about the importance of editorial integrity, which he outlined in his book *News Values*. He had gone so far as to mandate mock page-one meetings for business executives to educate them about the thoughtful process editors went through to select top stories for page one. The sessions changed the way many business executives viewed journalists, but not FitzSimons. Fuller had given FitzSimons a copy of *News Values* when the company named him CEO. But FitzSimons, by Fuller's account, later told him he kept the book on his bedside table so he'd have something he could read—when he wanted to fall asleep. In 2004, when the Pulitzer board announced that Tribune papers had won five Pulitzers for news coverage in 2003, the awards provided Fuller a moment of respite from warding off critics and recent charges in the *Newsday* case. At a management meeting following the Pulitzer announcement, Fuller was incensed when FitzSimons dismissed the prizes as rigged, ego-driven rewards that journalists used to impress their friends in the business. The chasm between the president of Tribune publishing and its CEO was too great to sustain.

Fuller announced his resignation on October 28, 2004, six months after Giaimo had filed his lawsuit. For severance, Fuller received a "consulting fee" of $51,500 a month, for a year, plus office space in Tribune Tower. As an editor and journalist, I disagreed with Fuller on a number of things—chief among them, his libertarian politics and his lack of enthusiasm for investigative journalism. But I respected Fuller. He was someone who could embrace his critics, and he had the ability to truly inspire people. He promoted journalists with whom he routinely disagreed to positions of power and influence because he believed in the power of journalism. He knew a good newspaper editor needed independence as much as ink and paper.

On his last day at Tribune, Fuller dropped in on the *Chicago Tribune's* page-one meeting. He said he wanted to leave the building from the newsroom, his point of entry at a newspaper he had helped build into a respected institution of which he was justifiably proud.

Although his skeptics didn't believe him, Fuller said he didn't leave because of the circulation scandal at *Newsday*. And I believed him. He could have weathered a circulation scandal; he simply couldn't stand FitzSimons.

I felt the impact of Fuller's departure and the impending sea change almost immediately—the same way my Irish Setter used to duck under the porch before anyone knew a storm was brewing. FitzSimons replaced Fuller with Scott Smith, the publisher of the *Chicago Tribune* and a man I had come to respect despite his waspy North Shore pedigree and soulless belief that doing more with less was one of the Ten Commandments. Hiller, the lawyer who had been in charge of due diligence on the Times Mirror deal, was named the publisher of the *Tribune*. My gut told me that things had changed more fundamentally than these new appointments might suggest, and as a reporter I had learned to trust my gut. At meetings with business colleagues, I felt a cool shift. I detected a sense of empowerment in the irreverent questions that flourished about why editors put depressing news of the Iraq war on page one instead of "what readers wanted"—frivolous celebrity gossip and less serious news. The business side of the paper began to look at editorial differently, with less respect and with less intimidation. It was painfully clear that we no longer had a powerful advocate in the upper reaches of the Tower.

Following Fuller's departure, the culture clashes that had begun to brew only intensified. It was notably apparent at the *Los Angeles Times*, the company's largest source of revenue, which had a staff nearly double the size of the *Chicago Tribune*. The *Times* newsroom resented the Chandlers' sale of the paper to Chicago, even though Willes and the Staples incident had smeared the paper's reputation to the rest of the publishing world.

Lipinski had been promoted to editor of the *Tribune* after her boss, Howard Tyner, had been given a high-level job in the publishing group to help devise ways that the newspaper, television, and Internet operations could work together. During Tyner's first editors' meeting at Tribune Tower, which included editors from all the Tribune papers, *Los Angeles Times* editor John Carroll made it clear that he could care less about *synergy*, the buzzword that everyone used to describe collaboration among Tribune business units. Carroll was paticularly caustic on the subject and made remarks that *Chicago Tribune* editors considered insulting, comparing *Chicago Tribune* stories to advertorials. Commenting upon the *Los Angeles Times'* tendency to run long stories that often "jumped" (continued to different pages of the paper), *Newsday* editor, Tony Marro, whose tabloid was known for much shorter stories, quipped: "If I wanted to run *Los Angeles Times* stories in *Newsday*, I'd have to jump them into the *Hartford Courant*."

■

I had always envied the sheer size of the *Times* editorial staff. In Chicago, my staff and I fantasized about what a difference it would make in our ability to compete in the marketplace if Fuller would take just a hundred jobs from the *Times* and give them to the *Tribune*. But I knew cooperation between the papers was no game-changing strategy and that it had its limits. Tyner had not been given any real authority to make people cooperate. So he relentlessly tried to jawbone the papers into working with each other, although none of the champions of synergy could really articulate exactly how cooperation would help with anything other than to lower costs.

Tribune's headquarters in Chicago was known as "synergy city," but in truth the idea of working together had never really worked. We had created newsrooms in television studios and broadcast outlets in newsrooms, but most television journalists privately thought interviewing a print reporter on air was simply bad TV. Some newspaper reporters willingly participated in interviews, but many balked. Most KTLA broadcast journalists castigated the *Los Angeles Times* on air as arrogant because the paper looked down its nose at KTLA's celebrated morning news show, which Baquet described to me as "the gong show."

The company's effort to place correspondents and reporters from various Tribune papers near each other also backfired. The *Chicago Tribune* probably had more in common with *Newsday* than with the *Los Angeles Times*. But synergy with *Newsday* didn't work either.

To save on rent, we had moved the *Chicago Tribune's* four New York correspondents into 2 Park Avenue in New York, where *Newsday* and the *Los Angeles Times* also had bureaus. But Jansen soon engineered a renovation in New York, erecting a wall that made it physically impossible for *Tribune* correspondents to go to the bathroom unless they exited the bureau space, walked down a hall, and reentered the bureau through another door. When New York–based *Tribune* reporters had chance encounters on the elevator with journalists from *Los Angeles Times*, they were often ignored. When the *Times* sent a platoon of reporters to New York to help out with coverage of the terrorist attacks on September 11, 2001, Lisa Anderson, the *Tribune's* New York bureau chief, couldn't help but notice that the *Los Angeles Times* bureau catered meals from Eli Zabar's lavish Madison Avenue deli.

No one really had the guts to say what synergy was really about until Tribune Company promoted an ambitious corporate aide who would expose the whole scheme for what it really was: the desire to cut staff as much as possible without readers catching on. Gerould W. Kern came to the *Chicago Tribune* in 1991 as a deputy editor on the metro desk. Unlike many *Tribune* editors, Kern had never worked as a correspondent, covered a war, or distinguished himself as an investigative reporter. Prior to the *Chicago Tribune*, the biggest job he'd ever had was as managing editor of the Arlington Heights *Daily Herald*, a suburban Chicago newspaper where he helped drive up the circulation by strengthening the paper's zoned local news and mimicking the more sophisticated coverage of the *Chicago Tribune*. The *Tribune* hired him in a drive to improve its zoned coverage: local news sections targeted to a narrower audience of readers and advertisers.

Although I rose to lofty positions at the *Chicago Tribune*, I looked at my job as more than a job. I was well paid; I made more money at the *Tribune* than I ever thought I would as a journalist. But I would walk out before I'd do something that would compromise my journalistic principles. To me, journalism was a calling, something I did because I loved to chase a story, to report, to tell readers what people in power didn't want them to know.

When he worked in the newsroom as an editor in charge of the features department, Kern viewed what he did as a job that needed doing. When I ran the news operations, he would arrive in my office agonizing over why Lipinski didn't seem to view us as equals. He desperately wanted to become the editor at a Tribune paper because, he would say, "These are such wonderful jobs." Kern was an adept manager; he helped the *Chicago Tribune* refine its zoning strategy for local news, and Blair Kamin, the *Tribune's* architecture critic, won a Pulitzer Prize while Kern ran the features department. But Kern was crushed in 2000 when Lipinski passed him over to make me the managing editor of the *Chicago Tribune*. He seemed to think Lipinski had chosen me not because I was a better journalist, but because she, for some inexplicable reason, didn't like him. He thought you needed to be much more than a strong journalist to effectively manage a newsroom. When the *Chicago Tribune* didn't promote him, he landed a job in the Tribune corporate offices.

First as the associate editor and later as editorial director of Tribune Publishing, Gerry became known to me as Count Kern. He started counting: how many journalists Tribune papers used to cover Hurricane Katrina, how many reporters *Tribune* had in its Washington bureau, how many *Chicago Tribune* stories ran in the *Los Angeles Times*. Kern wrote up elaborate reports full of color-coded pie and bar charts that championed what would become a creeping centralization of editorial decision making in Chicago. He distributed them to Smith and FitzSimons, spoon-feeding the most ardent critics of the journalists in the company with the kind of "research" that FitzSimons loved. Kern noted how one journalist from each of Tribune's largest papers would be sent to cover a major event instead of "working together" and relying on just one paper to cover a story. Eventually, Kern advocated for key centralized desks to be responsible for the lion's share of news content—which they'd drop into pages and distribute to smaller Tribune papers around the nation. In effect, everyone would be reading the same news story, whether you lived in Los Angeles, or Orlando. Kern was careful to couch his reports with language about not wanting to diminish Tribune Company journalism. But the broader message being championed by terms like co-location, shared content, duplication of content, family paper content, "news that readers value" (local), and nondifferentiating content (foreign) was synergy. Synergy was the Trojan horse with which FitzSimons and Kern attacked the values of journalists, cut costs, and set their focus on local news because it was often cheaper to produce.

Kern raised a legitimate question about whether the Tribune Company really needed such an extensive network of correspondents stationed around the nation and world. Did the *Chicago Tribune* and the *Los Angeles Times* each have to send a correspondent to cover the same event, as sometimes happened? Couldn't one reporter do a story for both papers, saving half the costs?

The answer, of course, is yes in some cases but no in others. At the *Los Angeles Times*, John Carroll argued that every story in the *Times* should originate with an editor based in Los Angeles where he or she is closest to the reader and the needs of the paper. An editor in New York, Chicago, or Washington might not have the same tastes or make the same judgments as one in Los Angeles, the city the *Times* is supposed to serve. But there is an even more fundamental justification for news organizations such as the *Times* and the *Chicago Tribune* to maintain expensive foreign and national news staffs. At its core, a news organization with journalistic values exists to cover the news for its readers and provide insightful, meaningful journalism, the kind that educates and gives citizens the kind of information that empowers them, facilitates good decisions about the public's business, and scrutinizes the political and civic institutions crucial to a democracy.

When news breaks, you can always get the story of what happened from the Associated Press or some other wire service. That's what you currently get on most of the Internet sites that aggregate the news. But the Associated Press exists to give customers a quick and superficial story. If an editor in Chicago or Los Angeles who is conversant with the needs of the local community wants a writer to dig deeper, explain, investigate, or tell the reader of the wider implications of a breaking story, he or she can't simply pick up the phone and ask for a better story from the AP. You get what you get and not much more.

If, on the other hand, an editor has a correspondent nearby, the journalist can develop the sources and information to provide readers with a better, deeper, or more insightful report. In my own experience, people around the country in the 1980s knew when the federal government swept in and closed their local savings bank. The AP reported the closure. Left unanswered was the question why? Was the bank simply poorly run or were deeper, more systematic problems afoot, ones that could jeopardize the nation's financial system and cost the government agency that backed its deposits a bundle? As a reporter in the *Chicago Tribune*'s Washington bureau, I dug into those problems and discovered that hundreds of savings banks across the country were failing, not because dozens of bank examiners simultaneously discovered they were poorly run but because deregulation of the industry had spawned corruption, mismanagement, self-dealing, and sloppy banking practices that would eventually threaten the nation's financial system and cost taxpayers billions in a bailout needed to prevent the system from collapsing. The *Chicago Tribune* exposed the scandal *before* it made headlines elsewhere and helped create public pressure for federal officials to take action. Two decades later, history would repeat itself in the subprime mortgage scandal, but few papers reported on the extent of the debacle until *after* the damage, which plunged the nation into a recession that has thrown millions of Americans out of work and will cost taxpayers billions. The industry simply didn't have as many journalists watching what was underway.

The examples of excellent reporting from correspondents at the *Chicago Tribune, Los Angeles Times, Baltimore Sun, Newsday, Orlando Sentinel, Sun Sentinel* in Southern Florida and most other Tribune newspapers would make an extensive list. Was there duplication of effort on certain occasions? Yes. But was the price of that duplication worth it if it resulted in superior journalism that these papers routinely gave their readers? Yes again, particularly since the cost of duplication was relatively little. Puerner noted that the *Times'* entire foreign and national news budget didn't equal what Tribune Company, which owned the Chicago Cubs, paid Sammy Sosa to swing a baseball bat. It really comes down to values. What, in your soul, are you as an editor and the newspaper company that employs you trying to do—report the news needed to sustain a democracy or make and save money? If the latter is more important, then you have an identity crisis. And if you can no longer afford to cover the news because of mismanagement or a social and technological revolution, then the problem doesn't stop at the door of Tribune or any other company around the country. The community has a problem, and so does America.

The intense scrutiny that Kern and FitzSimons began leveling on the newsroom in their desire to expose duplication wasted a lot of time for editors throughout Tribune Company. While the entire industry was facing an impending revenue crisis, I—and editors like me—spent the better parts of our weeks writing reports to FitzSimons to prove that we had taken audience research into consideration when deciding which stories to place on page one, and attending Kern's endless meetings to discuss how we could work together. The whole enterprise was a waste of time and money. When I ran into Kern at a party, after he'd been moved over to Tribune publishing, I noticed that he'd assumed the same disparaging tone that business executives used to address us lowly editors. The clash of cultures had arrived and the *Los Angeles Times* was ground zero.

Wolinsky started to worry when he heard rumors of tension surfacing between people in Chicago and *Times* editor Carroll and managing editor Baquet. Then Kern showed up in Los Angeles and began counting the paper's editors, several of whom overheard the phone call he made to Chicago in which he caustically reported the outrageous levels of staff at the *Times*, which faced far more difficult deadline and delivery problems than the *Chicago Tribune*. Wolinsky recalled:

> There was all this talk about synergy, about doing these sections to serve all of the papers, mainly in the business section area. John [Carroll] didn't want to do it, Dean didn't want to do it. I kept saying, "Look, these guys want to do this, so let's jump on the idea and own it." But they didn't want to. . . . Then I started getting reports that Carroll was arrogant in meetings with Tribune people, that he would go to meetings and sit there reading something while others talked. He would be totally disengaged, then get up and walk out. I knew this was the way John did things. . . . But he seemed to have John Puerner's support, and Puerner was a great Tribune guy, and I figured he was okay. But then Puerner left.

Puerner, who had gone to work for Tribune Company fresh out of college, saw the decline in revenues that had decimated classified advertising start to infect display ads—the kind that the Hollywood studios in the *Times'* backyard ran to trumpet their latest films and the kind that big department stores ran. To prosper, he thought the *Times* had to generate unique content to justify a higher newspaper cover price and a fee for Internet access, a method known in the industry as paid content. Puerner didn't think the *Los Angeles Times* could succeed by providing better local news coverage than the *Long Beach Telegram*: "There was just no way that you could out Long Beach, Long Beach. I looked, and in every market where we tried to do that, we were number two. . . . You had to look at the big topic areas—public safety, health care, the huge issues the *Times* was uniquely positioned to cover."

But investing editorial resources to provide superior coverage meant building up the expensive foreign, national, and business news staffs, a strategy that the Kerns and FitzSimons of the world strongly opposed. They knew cutting prestigious foreign and national news staffs set editors' teeth on edge, but they were counting on the reductions to generate costs savings. "Jack [Fuller] and I didn't agree. We had long, honest conversations about this. But he was the buffer," Puerner said, "he was a big buffer. When he left, there was increased corporate presence in Los Angeles. Frankly it made things more difficult for us to manage. . . . It became clear that our philosophy collided with the need in Chicago to cut costs . . . and that these two differences in philosophies were irreconcilable." Puerner left the *Times* in May 2005, and Jeffrey Johnson, another Tribune veteran and smart executive who had earned his stripes reducing the cost of the *Times'* backward production process, filled the publisher's seat. FitzSimons had effectively placed people with little publishing experience at the helm in Los Angeles, Chicago, and New York, his three largest properties and the source of more than half of the company's revenues. And then there was a whiff of a rumor—this time about the *Times'* circulation numbers.

*Newsday* had gotten newspaper executives around the country to take stock of the risks involved in lying about the numbers. In July 2002, Congress added to the industry's woes by passing the Sarbanes-Oxley Act, which mandated that top corporate officers sign off on the accuracy of all internal reports. Congress also had passed legislation creating a "do not call" list, which hurt newspapers' phone circulation sales. And then there was the Internet—a fabulous, fast, free alternative to delivering news and advertising to hordes of willing readers.

As newspapers began to look inward, the *Dallas Morning News* and the *Chicago Sun-Times* preempted the Banars of the world by publicly announcing they had discovered bogus circulation—announcements that triggered internal investigations, scrutiny by ABC, and more headlines. Many of the industry's circulation chiefs started to squirm. Newspapers had to figure out how to prune any questionable circulation from their ABC books without making a bad situation look worse.

Even industry stalwarts like Brumback, a former chairman of the Newspaper Association of America, admitted that the numbers in ABC audits left a lot to be desired: "They aren't worth a damn," Brumback later noted, "You just give them [ABC auditors] the numbers you want and they put them in a nice, fancy little booklet." But even a cursory look at some audits shows that newspapers, particularly major metro dailies like the *Los Angeles Times*, used the ABC's flimsy rules to obscure the extent of dubious numbers. Just after he took over, Puerner decided to scrap much of the circulation Willes had added through joint distribution deals with Spanish language papers and the local news sections called "Our Times." He saw the Internet as the answer. "We were discounting deeply, and I wanted to get down to a number we could justify to advertisers," he said. "I wanted to go the other way and start a paid content strategy; start creating value for online content and get away from relying on those huge numbers." In other words, he wanted to create the kind of journalism that would justify a higher price for the paper, in print and online.

After Puerner's first year in the publisher's office, the daily circulation of the paper fell by 4.46 per cent, or 48,772 papers. In 2002, the *Times'* circulation dropped an additional 66,451 papers, or 6.36 percent, as Puerner jettisoned circulation Willes had taken on. Sunday circulation remained pretty steady, and the numbers seemed to settle down by 2005, the year Puerner left. Under Steven Lee, the marketing executive who had been hired from PepsiCo, the *Times* had launched a promotional program to reverse the slide called "Ten for Ten": ten weeks of the *Times* for only $10. Klunder, who had resigned as the head of circulation under Willes and taken a job at the Los Angeles Newspaper Group, which published the *Daily News*, could see what was happening from afar. To encourage salespeople to sell the "Ten for Ten" program, the company set a commission high enough that a salesperson could get a name from the phone book, pay for the subscription out of her or his own pocket, collect a commission high enough to still make a profit, and hope that the new "subscriber" would like it enough to continue the subscription when someone reached him ten weeks later.

Klunder had run the *Los Angeles Times* circulation department and his father had run it before him. He felt a sense of loyalty to the paper, even though he didn't work there anymore, and he didn't want to see the paper take a wrong turn. So he called the ABC with a tip that all was not right in the *Los Angeles Times* circulation department. ABC auditors descended on the company and went to work helping it fix a problem that would make the industry look even worse if the public got wind of yet another circulation scandal.

Aside from the rare editors like Wolinsky who maintained good contacts with the business-side operations of the paper, few in the *Times* editorial department knew about the circulation problems. Had any industry covered by *Times* or *Tribune* journalists had such cozy relations with its regulators, we would have been all over the story. Granted, a few reporters did investigate the circulation problems plaguing our industry—at *Newsday* James Madore and Robert E. Kessler had dug in, and Chris Twarowski of the *Long Island Press* did an excellent job detailing the scheme on Long Island. But it's likely that their stories would never have seen the light of day had it not been for Giaimo and Banar. Most media reporters across the country slavishly repeated ABC numbers that glossed over the depth of the industry's problems. In newsrooms, we accepted those numbers like the gospel. Carroll claimed that he knew nothing about the *Times* circulation problems. But then again, he had other things on his mind.

■

In early 2005, Carroll got word that the *Los Angeles Times* had won five Pulitzers for stories that had run in the paper the previous year, an extraordinary achievement. But he got no congratulations from people in the higher ranks of Tribune Company; instead he learned that Tribune would impose another round of budget cuts, which would mandate cuts in the *Times* news hole and eliminate sixty-two news-room jobs.

In mid-2005, Carroll attended a management forum in Chicago where the attitude toward the *Los Angeles Times* was decidedly hostile: "I remember one guy from broadcasting standing up and saying the next time we acquire something, we will do it our way from *day one*," said Carroll. With Fuller and Puerner out of the way or on their way out, FitzSimons solidified control in Chicago, including control of all of the newspaper's Internet operations. Thanks to his refusal to use stories written by the Tribune's correspondents in the *Los Angeles Times*, Carroll had few allies in Chicago, even among journalists who worked at the *Chicago Tribune*.

Carroll paid a visit to Norm Pearlstine, who was head of editorial operations at Time Inc., but had been based in Los Angeles years earlier when he'd covered the West Coast for the *Wall Street Journal*. Pearlstine knew the Los Angeles business community well, and he knew Eli Broad, the real estate billionaire and Los Angeles civic booster. He helped set up a meeting between Carroll and Broad. "I had no illu-sion that this was a disloyal act. I was doing something out of line for Tribune," Carroll recalled. "I went there on a Saturday morning. I didn't ask him to do anything. I asked his advice if there was anything I could do to get the paper in local hands. He started talking about getting several nonprofits to combine and buy it."

Broad wasn't the only one interested in buying the *Times*. David Geffen, who had made billions in Hollywood, also made it known he was interested in the *Times* and that he, unlike FitzSimons, would actually invest money in the paper. Rumors swirled that Geffen had offered FitzSimons $1 billion for the *Los Angeles Times* and that FitzSimons had rebuffed Geffen, whom he didn't like. Wolinsky took it upon himself to find out what was going on.

"I went to see him [Geffen] at Jack Warner's old estate in Beverly Hills. The place was full of paintings," Wolinsky recalled. "It was unbelievable. I hardly said anything. It was a two-hour diatribe about Tom King [a former *Wall Street Journal* writer who had written a book about Geffen that he didn't like] . . . all of the people he didn't like, including a lot of people at the *Los Angeles Times*." Wolinsky left not knowing much more than when he'd arrived. In the following weeks, neither Broad nor Geffen made a move.

Carroll started thinking about his future, too. He had talked of resigning, but his wife urged him to stay on: "I thought that I'd probably be fired and that if I was fired, it would be a big disruption and if they did that, they probably wouldn't name my deputy, Dean, to succeed me. Dean and I talked about this. . . . I felt that Dean could last longer, perhaps until there was a change in CEOs. There was always the possibility of change from above."

In July 2005, *Times* publisher Jeff Johnson assembled the staff to announce a change in newsroom command. Carroll, an editor who had won thirteen Pulitzers in five years and had revived the *Times* from the depths of the Staples scandal, was stepping down and would be replaced by Baquet. The staff gave Carroll a standing ovation when he and Baquet embraced. "I'm taking over one of the best newspapers in America at the top of its game, in a city I care about, succeeding somebody who's a close friend," Baquet announced. "While every newspaper now is under budget pressure, I wouldn't be doing this if I didn't think I could still make the paper better."

In the barrage of publicity surrounding Carroll's departure, one writer happened to note that Carroll's tenure in the editor's office represented a puzzling, even disturbing, case study in journalistic excellence accompanied by declining circulation. Carroll didn't think that the paper's editorial content had anything to do with the circulation decline. Instead he cited the problems spawned by the *Newsday* scandal, the do-not-call list, the cuts in promotional and marketing budgets, and increased competition for readers' time.

Behind the scenes, the circulation department at the *Times* was working furiously to make sure that no one could discover that Carroll's sentiments were more accurate than anyone knew, including Carroll. By the time ABC auditors acted on Klunder's tip and swept into the *Times*, circulation boosting programs like "Ten for Ten" had helped inflate home delivery circulation by about 100,000 copies, which was about the extent of fake circulation at *Newsday*. Johnson said everyone was scrambling to avoid being placed on an ABC list that alerted advertisers across the land to newspapers where ABC audits exposed a disparity of greater than 2 percent between the numbers verified by auditors and those the newspaper had claimed on its publisher's statement, the basis of ABC's reports to the public.

Lee, who had recently received a coveted Tribune Company corporate achievement award, was now under the gun. The former PepsiCo executive in charge of marketing and circulation at the *Times*, said "Ten for Ten" was just one of the programs that contributed to the problem. "There was all kind of pressure to get the numbers up at the same time they were cutting costs. Tribune always had the feeling that the *Los Angeles Times* was this huge operation that sucked up costs. I think the Tribune guys put all of their chips on the table with a merger that was questionable on economic grounds and they wanted to justify it by slashing costs. Then you had all of these ABC rules that were kind of screwy and everyone was trying to push the limits."

The outside vendors the company had hired to sell papers through "Ten for Ten" and the other programs were cheating "and we didn't have out best people on checks and balances to watch them." Lee said it was like the old sport's cliche that "if you're not cheating, you're not trying." He said "everyone was focused on getting the number up and getting around the rules and when the auditors came in and caught them, I was the head marketing guy and circulation came under marketing.

It was not my area of expertise but at the end of the day, I was the head of the department and I took responsibility for it."

The *Times* successfully stayed off the dreaded 2 percent list, Johnson said, thanks to someone in the circulation department who came up with a technicality that satisfied ABC. The paper also used its junk circulation to obscure the extent of the circulation decline that made its way into public reports. Once auditors removed dubious circulation from the *Times* books, the newspaper's home delivery number dropped by 123,738 papers over a two-year stretch that ended in 2005. Simultaneously, the *Times* had sharply increased its junk circulation, the kind allowed under ABC rules. Indeed, between 2003 and 2005, the paper had added 116,000 copies in junk circulation to its totals. Without the junk circulation, the *Times* would have reported a 17 percent decline during that period instead of the 3.1 percent recorded in ABC audits.

Lee resigned and moved on. "It was clear that I didn't have a future with the company," he said. And Johnson turned around and hired a seasoned circulation pro to replace him—Jack Klunder.

# 14

## Civil War

Anybody watching the Weather Channel in the summer of 2005 knew that New Orleans would be hit by Hurricane Katrina. Nobody guessed how bad it would be, though. My son, who lives forty miles west of the Crescent City, called me from Houston, Texas, to tell me his flight home had been canceled. He'd rented a car to try to drive home, with the hopes of beating the storm. I protested to no avail and grew increasingly worried as reports of the storm's unyielding force flowed into the *Chicago Tribune* newsroom.

Covering a natural disaster like Katrina challenges any newsroom: It's a scramble to find reporters and photographers hotel rooms, communications in ferocious weather are strained at best, and the general tone of a city under environmental siege is one of unease. Katrina was a special case, though, and not just because I feared my son had wandered into the eye of the storm. The fallout from the disaster exposed a persistent vein of racism that shocked many Americans, scattered the poor to points near and far, and shattered the nerves of an already stressed and corrupt police force in New Orleans.

Big newspapers across the country reacted quickly to get the most out of the story. At the *Chicago Tribune*, we immediately dispatched Howard Witt from our Houston bureau and Lisa Anderson, who had become New York bureau chief and a seasoned natural disaster reporter. Working in tandem, Witt and Anderson secured necessities like maps, headlamps, and waders, set up an emergency newsroom, booked cars, established cellphone reception, located supplies, and found a house we could rent temporarily, all the while filing stories and briefing editors back home on the lay of the land. *Tribune* editors in Baltimore, New York, Orlando, and Los Angeles reacted similarly as the casualty toll mounted. Everybody, including Gerry Kern high up in his Tribune Tower office, swung into action. In New Orleans, Kern saw a tremendous opportunity.

Over the next couple of months, Tribune journalists would share scarce rooms, eat meals at their laptops, work sixteen-hour days, and spend weeks away from their families, as Kern began compiling the raw material for "Hurricanes Katrina and Rita," his 2005 report about "Tribune's coverage of the big storms and the implications for future national coverage." It was an impressive document that in twenty-two richly colored pages detailed how many stories each Tribune paper ran on Katrina and Rita, what percentage of those stories were written by staff, and what percentage by writers from papers in the Tribune family. Kern examined what percentage of papers covered common themes, and counted stories by topic (there were ninety-nine stories covering hurricane evacuation and shelters but only ten on pets, zoos, and aquariums). An appendix detailed that the *Los Angeles Times* received 97 percent of its stories from its staff at the site of the disaster, while the *Orlando Sentinel* got 30 percent of its stories from staff in the disaster zone. Kern gave his Tribune bosses a report card that told them what they wanted to hear: While coverage from Tribune reporters was good, there was a need to "leverage [Tribune's] scale and talent." The media would later be criticized for exaggerating the Katrina debacle. With their own reporters on the scene, papers like the *Chicago Tribune* had questioned the accuracy of those reports from wire services and other sources. But Kern focused his report on the duplication of effort, and not on the content of reporters at the scene.

■

Baquet had settled in as editor of the *Times*, and we had joined forces in an effort to deal with some of the legitimate issues that Kern raised. We all understood we could save the company money with common-sense steps like collaborating to limit the number of people each paper sent to cover a story. But we also knew that cooperation had its limits and, despite what Kern thought, could compromise the quality of our news reports. Our main goal was to limit the centralization of news coverage championed by Kern and others at Tribune Publishing. We didn't want to hurt smaller papers with foreign and national news staffs like *Newsday* and the *Baltimore Sun*. But this was every newspaper for itself, and Baquet and I came up with a plan to cut the foreign and national staff 20 percent by phasing out numerous foreign and national bureaus at the smaller papers, forcing them to rely on the *Los Angeles Times* and *Chicago Tribune* for coverage. This was not fun, but all Tribune papers faced enormous challenges as revenue started to dry up and the company's stock price sunk. We understood that the mission at hand was to maintain the integrity of our newspapers.

In Los Angeles, Baquet was sitting on a powder keg. He was a charismatic man who was popular with his staff, but there was a lingering sourness over how Carroll had been forced out of the organization, despite his claim, upon stepping down, that he was doing so to spend more time with his family. *Times* employees had had it, and in a survey conducted by an outside research firm, they let the *Times* editors know just how disheartened they were. Although the *Los Angeles Times* newsroom viewed itself as the lone voice of journalistic dissent, the Tribune Company policies also angered *Chicago Tribune* journalists, but the anger was not as public as in Los Angeles, where Kevin Roderick, a former *Los Angeles Times* reporter who had started the blog *LA Observed*, had a pipeline into the newsroom.

In the fall of 2005, for the first time in decades, I had to lay off a handful of employees at the *Tribune*. I started losing highly regarded reporters, like Jeff Zeleny, a brilliant young political writer whom I had hired from the *Des Moines Register* who left for the *New York Times*, and Jan Crawford, for my money the nation's best legal affairs reporter, who went to a national network television job. Baquet and I fought cuts and knew that keeping star reporters would be much harder without a robust foreign and national news staff. But the problems that we faced paled in comparison to the bad news that started to engulf FitzSimons.

The first dose came courtesy of the due diligence in the Times Mirror deal led by Hiller and Tribune's general counsel, Crane Kenney. The proxy on the deal suggests it had lasted only two days. As noted earlier, Times Mirror had sold the Matthew Bender & Company, a legal publishing subsidiary, and health science publisher Mosby, Inc., for more than $2 billion. Times Mirror had structured the convoluted sale as a tax-free deal that allowed the company, then controlled by the Chandlers, to avoid federal income taxes. But the IRS had challenged Times Mirror's handiwork, and Tribune inherited the dispute when it bought the company. Tribune knew what it was getting into and could have paid the tax and applied for a refund, thereby avoiding the IRS' substantial interest and penalties. Unterman said he told Tribune Company that that was the strategy that Times Mirror had planned to follow. But given the optimistic revenue projections that underpinned the deal, Tribune considered the Bender case an acceptable risk. Bad bet. In September 2005, the Tax Court ruled that Tribune owed the government *$1 billion* in unpaid taxes, interest, and penalties. Chagrined, FitzSimons said the company would pay the $1 billion and appeal. Wall Street pounded Tribune's already depressed stock price. (Eventually the case was settled with Tribune paying about $650 million in taxes and penalties.) But the Bender case was just the start.

At first, relations between the Chandlers and the management in Chicago had seemed cordial. Soon after Tribune purchased Times Mirror, three Chandlers and Unterman took seats on the Tribune board. However, about a year after the deal was closed, Madigan kicked Unterman off the board because Tribune needed more people with CEO pedigrees. From day one, Unterman, a Jewish Democrat, thought the Tribune board, which was packed with Madigan's friends, was insular and suspicious of anyone who wasn't white, Irish, Catholic, and Republican. It soon became clear that Tribune board members were determined to keep control of the company in Chicago at all costs. Unterman warned Madigan that he might one day need someone on the board that had a good relationship with the Chandlers. But Unterman said Madigan ignored the advice.

The Chandlers became concerned with the slide in newspaper stock prices in mid-2005. To diversify the family's investment in Tribune, the Chandlers wanted to carefully unwind two trusts that had been established earlier to increase their dividends and avoid taxes. They had a lot riding on the timing of the transaction and the financial valuations that would be placed on the assets in the trusts, which included real estate headquarters for most of the Times Mirror papers and some Tribune preferred and common stock.

The Chandlers' negotiations with Tribune about how their trusts could be skillfully handled involved a range of proposals. But they soon found themselves locked in a disagreement with FitzSimons that turned bitter. FitzSimons said the Chandlers wanted to place valuations on the assets in the trusts and time their dissolutions in a way that would minimize the family's taxes at the expense of Tribune shareholders. Smarting from the $1 billion welt the company had suffered in the Bender tax case, the non-Chandler Tribune board members said no way.

The dispute came to a head in May 2006 when FitzSimons and the Tribune board authorized a "leveraged recapitalization" or "Dutch auction" in which the company would buy back up to 25 percent of its stock from shareholders for up to $32.50 a share. Managers typically engineer buybacks to goose a company's reported earnings by retiring stock so profits can be spread across fewer shares. It is a tactic largely viewed as an alternative for weak managers who, in the words of one Tribune executive, "are not looking out for our tomorrow."

But the move infuriated the Chandlers, who thought the recapitalization was a bad idea and a move that would jeopardize the value of the assets in their trusts. "It was like giving the Chandlers the finger," Unterman said. So the Chandlers trotted out the family lawyer, William Stinehart, who publicly filed a blistering eleven-page critique of the company, its management, its board, and its lack of strategy that, in effect, put the company up for sale. "It's the beginning of the end game," Edward Atorino, a stock analyst at the Benchmark Company, told reporters.

In the spring of 2006, *Newsday* hit the news again when Sito, Brennan, Czack, Smith, Garcia, and four others pleaded guilty in the U.S. District Court to a range of fraudulent circulation practices. Judge Weinstein didn't sentence anyone, though, because they had begun cooperating with Banar's investigation as she continued to scrutinize the upper reaches of the company, particularly after the judge raised questions about how such a substantial fraud could take place without the knowledge and culpability of higher authorities at Tribune.

Even journalists accustomed to a heavy diet of news had a hard time digesting the developments at Tribune Company and keeping their focus on their jobs. In August, Kern convened a meeting with Baquet, myself, Earl Maucker, the editor of the Tribune-owned *Sun Sentinel* in Fort Lauderdale, and a couple of others to discuss—you guessed it—"working together." Kern held the meeting at Maucker's paper in Fort Lauderdale.

A native of Alton, Illinois, Maucker, the *Sun Sentinel's* longtime editor, was a go-along kind of man who lived in a huge, gorgeous house. He took us to dinner in his yacht, *The Final Edition*, which docked at a pier in his backyard. The paper he ran did some excellent investigative reporting, but Maucker bought FitzSimons' line of mixing marketing and local news with a heavy emphasis on parochial stories. After dinner, we cruised the canals around Fort Lauderdale, smoked cigars, and had drinks on a delightfully pleasant night. We were there to discuss foreign and national news collaboration (otherwise known as budget cuts), but most of the discussion revolved around the turmoil engulfing Tribune, as we swapped rumors about who in the upper reaches of Tribune would survive and who wouldn't.

Baquet and I had arrived early to have dinner in Miami the night before and to talk strategy to ward off the centralization that Kern was championing with the support of Scott Smith, who had succeeded Fuller as head of the publishing group. "If I tell Scott that I won't make any more cuts, do you think he will fire me?" Baquet asked. (Smith's philosophy was to push managers until they reached their limits.) "No," I reassured him. "He will just keep pressing you to agree to cuts and will quit when he thinks he got as much as he can get."

Later I asked Baquet if he had indeed resisted Smith's pressure for more cuts when he had returned to Los Angeles. "I did," he replied. "I felt pretty good about it, although I don't think Scott did. I told him I wasn't going to cut anymore. I then got up, walked over to him, shook his hand, and said, 'You have to do what you have to do, and I have to do what I have to do.' I then walked away and he just kind of sat there and slumped in his chair."

Meanwhile, FitzSimons discovered that his problems weren't limited to the breakdown in the talks with the Chandlers. In the midst of his fight with the family, he learned he had prostate cancer and had to check into a hospital to deal with his health. Once FitzSimons had recovered from his surgery, private talks with the Chandlers resumed as the family started proposing scenarios in which the company would either be broken up in tax-free spinoffs or sold at a premium at a time when buyers of newspapers were about as plentiful as Dead Sea Scrolls. The Tribune had said it would find another $200 million in budget cuts to help repay the $2 billion it had borrowed to buy back stock, and Smith started seeking plans to implement the cuts when another bomb dropped.

The headline in the *New York Times* of September 15, 2006, said it all: "*Los Angeles Times* Editor Openly Defies Owner's Call for Job Cuts." The day before, Baquet had gone public with his opposition to more budget cuts in a *Los Angeles Times* story, and his publisher, Jeff Johnson, had backed him up. "Newspapers," Johnson said in a quote that infuriated Smith and FitzSimons, "can't cut their way to the future." Gambling that the Tribune Company wouldn't fire him, Baquet reiterated that he was not opposed to cuts. "But you can go too far," he said, "and I don't plan to do that." The simmering tensions between Tribune and its largest paper had reached a tipping point. I called Baquet to voice support but also to warn him that taking the controversy public placed him in uncharted waters. Smith and FitzSimons summoned Johnson to Chicago, berated him for his comments, and offered him an opportunity to back down. Johnson declined the offer and headed back to Los Angeles. He had, in the words of the *Times* columnist Steve Lopez, "drunk Baquet's Kool-Aid."

A week later as the Tribune board met to hear about FitzSimons' compromise plan to deal with the Chandlers, the *New York Times* ran a September 21, 2006, story entitled: "At *Los Angeles Times*, a Civil Executive Rebellion." With that headline, the *Los Angeles Times* newspaper and boardroom became a national stage in a fight between editors and owners of newspapers: "Would Mr. FitzSimons fire Mr. Johnson and Mr. Baquet and risk a full-scale revolt at Tribune's largest property?" the *Times* story asked. "Or will he try to smooth things over and thereby risk undermining his authority with other Tribune editors and publishers?" The fight was on.

A group of twenty Los Angeles civic leaders had written a letter to the Tribune voicing concerns about budget cuts and calling on the beleaguered company to invest more money in the paper or sell it to someone who would. Baquet clearly wanted to rally support for the paper during a time of intense pressures, not only in Los Angeles but across the country. The *Washington Post*, the *New York Times*, papers in Dallas and Akron, Ohio, all had announced layoffs and buyouts as they struggled with the demands of Wall Street investors and the changing habits of readers and advertisers on Main Street. As prospective buyers like Broad and Geffen circled the *Times*, the newsroom circulated petitions voicing solid support for Baquet. Most of the editorial department signed them. The staff commissioned Baquet T-shirts, and rumors emerged of a "suicide pact" between Baquet's top three aides, managing editor Doug Frantz, features editor John Montorio, and managing editor for readership and production Leo Wolinsky, all of whom had reputedly agreed to resign if Baquet were replaced.

On November 9, 2006, the *New York Times* ran yet another story, one that carried ominous implications for Wolinsky: "David Geffen spends more time schmoozing with an elite cadre of journalists than just about any other mogul in Hollywood," the *Times* article read. "The billionaire often invites them to his sprawling estate in the heart of Beverly Hills, where De Koonings and Pollocks hang on the walls. In September, his guest was Leo Wolinsky, a managing editor of the *Los Angeles Times*, and they approached the delicate question of whether Mr. Geffen might try to buy the struggling newspaper."

FitzSimons had already expressed his disregard for Wolinsky. When he'd arrived, Baquet had wanted Frantz to be his managing editor for news and had moved Wolinsky aside, putting him in charge of the things that Baquet didn't have time for or didn't like to do—the mechanics of producing the paper. He had asked Wolinsky to investigate the papers' slide in readership and what it would take to reverse it. Having someone in place to tackle readership issues pleased FitzSimons, and he told Wolinsky to call Kern to have him line up several readership experts to interview. "I didn't need Gerry Kern to make phone calls for me. I could do that myself," Wolinsky recalled. "I actually called every one of the people that Dennis mentioned, but when he asked Kern if I had called him, Kern said no." In point of fact, Wolinsky did a thorough report on the *Times* readership and circulation problems, which he presented in writing. And he organized a one-day off-site meeting for top *Times* editors at his house to discuss the issue. But no one made FitzSimons aware of the effort. He thought Wolinsky had ignored him—something akin to mortal sin. "That's when I got on his bad side," Wolinsky recalled. The *New York Times* article simply hardened FitzSimons' views about the *Los Angeles Times* and Wolinsky.

In October, I wandered into the *Tribune* on the early side and sat down as usual in Lipinski's office to discuss the morning paper and any potential problems looming on the horizon. "They're going to ask you to go to LA," she said abruptly. I told her there was no way I would do that, and she responded that it was up to one of the two of us to go. Lipinski said there were two big papers in the company and each of us would have to run one of them. Hiller had asked her to go to LA, but she felt that would create change and stress in both newsrooms. "I suggested it was better to let me continue on in Chicago while you went to LA," she said. The situation in LA was considered *impossible* in many newsrooms across the country because of the public nature and intensity of the dispute between Baquet and Johnson and their bosses back in Chicago. I remember thinking, nothing is *impossible*, and felt a stirring inside me that responded to daunting challenges. But the situation was complicated. Dean Baquet was a friend of Ann Marie's and mine and neither of us wanted to do anything to undermine him. When Lipinski asked if I would just have breakfast with Hiller, then publisher of the *Chicago Tribune*, I agreed but only to discuss the situation (not my possible transfer) and give him my opinion about what was happening in LA.

The next day, a cloudy October morning, we sat down together at Chicago's Intercontinental Hotel. We got right down to business. Hiller told me the Tribune planned to replace both Johnson and Baquet and that he would soon be leaving to become publisher of the *Los Angeles Times*. Everyone, he said, including FitzSimons agreed that I should replace Baquet. He then asked if I would agree to be an "acting editor" of the *Times*. I let him know in no uncertain terms that I would not talk about Baquet's job behind his back—he needed to deal with Baquet, not me. And second, if he and Smith were looking for someone to go out to Los Angeles to cut the staff, they should get someone else, because I would not do it.

Hiller then asked me if I would consider joining him if he and Baquet couldn't work out their problems. I reiterated that I would consider it only after he dealt with Baquet. I agreed to meet with Smith on Monday and give him my perspective and to provide Hiller with an objective, written critique of the strengths and weaknesses of the *Los Angeles Times* from a journalistic perspective, regardless of who was the paper's editor. Before the breakfast ended, Hiller gave me his word that he would try to work with Baquet if I would agree to consider the job should the two men fail to see eye to eye about the paper's future.

On Monday, I advised Smith to back off on plans to fire Johnson and Baquet. I thought it would be a public relations disaster. I offered to go to Los Angeles and iron out a compromise plan to smooth things over. "Do they both have to go?" I asked. Smith replied: "Jeff has to go. Dean doesn't, but Jeff for sure." He and FitzSimons felt that Johnson's refusal to issue a statement rescinding his hostile position sealed his fate. But it was clear to me that Smith was thinking of replacing Baquet. Referring to a tolerance for budget cuts, Smith said, "We all reach our limits." When that happens, Smith firmly believed that a change in leadership was needed. He told me the company needed someone with strong journalistic credentials to settle down a rebellious newsroom. He allowed that Kern had suggested he become the editor, but Smith had told him he would be "toxic" in the *Los Angeles Times* newsroom. "We're depending on you to do this, Jim," Smith said. But in the next breath, he said he would give Hiller a shot at working with Baquet.

I left the meeting and called Baquet, who asked if I had any intelligence on what was going on in Chicago. I put my cards on the table: "Something's going on, my friend. They just offered me your job, and I'm going to tell you what I told them. I told them I wouldn't talk about your job behind your back. Jeff is out. Hiller is going to replace him. I think you should work with them because your paper is not going to be better off if you leave." Baquet, rather generously, said he would support my appointment as editor in Los Angeles if that's what it came to, but that he would try to work with Hiller in the meantime, even though he doubted it would work out. "If I were you," he said, "I'd get my beach shorts ready."

Hiller had already left for Los Angeles to attend a black-tie celebration of the *Times'* 125th anniversary. The next day, he replaced
highly regarded Johnson as publisher, just as Johnson learned that his
wife had been diagnosed with breast cancer. Hiller and Baquet met for
breakfast. When the waitress asked them what they wanted to drink,
Baquet jokingly said Hiller would have some Kool-Aid. Both men
laughed. Back in Chicago, FitzSimons summoned me to his office and
pulled out the lengthy critique of the *Times* that I had written for
Hiller. Again, I said that I wouldn't talk about Baquet's job behind his
back, but it was clear that he was interviewing me for the editor's job.
"Tell me," he asked, "what do you think of Leo Wolinsky?"

# 15

## Up Against a Saint and a Dead Man

Baquet stood before the audience of editors at the Associated Press Managing Editors convention in New Orleans in 2006. He had just pushed back when his budget-cutting bosses in Chicago said "cut," and he'd survived to fight another day. FitzSimons and Smith may have fired Johnson for his intemperate remarks about cuts, but Hiller had lived up to his word and tried to work with Baquet. Although Baquet didn't cover any new ground in his New Orleans speech, this time he spoke not simply as an editor, but as a newspaper industry hero. His battle cry for other editors to stand up and fight produced rousing, rebellious cheers (and headlines) from a largely sympathetic and admiring audience. In Los Angeles, Hiller was far from pleased.

I took a call from Hiller at my home just after the first story about Baquet's speech got traction. I knew that any agreements between Baquet and Hiller were tenuous, but I hoped they could work through their differences. Even though the impossible challenge in Los Angeles had stirred the Don Quixote in me, I refused to undermine a friend for a mere opportunity. And for personal reasons, I was eager to stay in Chicago: I wanted to convince Lipinski that a roving correspondent's job based in Rome would be a fitting reward for my service to the paper.

Hiller, who seemed stunned at Baquet's remarks, asked me what I made of them. I told him he had to consider them in the context of the moment and of the news industry writ large, but Baquet's stance had clearly rattled Hiller. He said he didn't know if he could work with Baquet and said that I should make sure "my boots were ready." Once Baquet returned to Los Angeles, he and Hiller had dinner and agreed that theirs was not a match made in Hollywood. Hiller said they should "sleep on it," but the next day he notified Baquet that he wanted a new editor. For better or worse, I was LA bound.

The honor that accompanies the editor title at a famous newspaper evaded me during the next few days. With Baquet's support, I accepted the job in Los Angeles and said my goodbyes in Chicago to a newsroom that I had helped build over the past fifteen years. I also had to deal with a surge of news coverage about the change of command. Every editor and journalist should become the focus of a hot news story. I was shocked at the sloppy and shabby reporting, particularly on the Internet, where reporters and bloggers picked up stories on me and repeated them without bothering to phone or verify the facts. Of the hundreds of stories written by fellow journalists, only a handful of reporters—from Tribune papers; the *New York Times*; and one blogger, the notorious Nikki Finke of Deadline Hollywood—bothered to call and confirm details in reports riddled with errors. Many of my friends thought I was crazy for agreeing to go to Los Angeles, and one asked how I could go help "those people" after the way the journalists in Los Angeles had disparaged colleagues in Chicago.

But I had made up my mind to accept the job if Hiller and Baquet couldn't work things out. And I actually felt that I could make a contribution. I left my newsroom for another one 1,000 miles west, determined to stay in Los Angeles as long it took to help a newsroom in turmoil and a company that had been good to me. Once I arrived in Los Angeles, the impact of what had happened hit me as I was driving out of LAX and Wolinsky called to ask me how I wanted my name to appear on the masthead.

I pulled my car over and just sat there absorbing the moment. "Just use James O'Shea," I told Wolinsky, "no middle initial." I was alone in a rental car with no one to help celebrate a battlefield promotion. (My wife had wisely decided to remain in her job at the Field Museum in Chicago.) After thirty-five years in the newspaper business, my name would appear on the November 13, 2006, edition of the *Los Angeles Times* as editor of one of journalism's crown jewels, the largest metropolitan daily newspaper in the county and a major force in news around the globe. As I maneuvered onto the freeway and headed for my hotel in downtown Los Angeles, I started to think about the one thing greater than the esteem that accompanied the title: the challenge I faced as a newly minted editor in the eye of a journalistic storm that was shaking the news business to its core.

I had barely checked into my hotel when Hiller called and suggested we have dinner. He seemed thrilled to see me. His first few weeks on the job had been rough, addressing a hostile newsroom after engineering the exit of two popular leaders. Unhappy newsrooms were nothing new. But entering the *Times* at that moment was a little like being tossed into a pot of boiling oil: Most of the newsroom hated the paper's new publisher. Hiller admitted to me that he'd never experienced anything like the hostility he encountered with Baquet's departure. He hadn't helped himself when he wrote an op-ed for the *Los Angeles Times* about his racquetball games with Donald Rumsfeld, the infamous Republican Defense Secretary who had just stepped down after maneuvering the United States into an unpopular war.

The next day I walked into the *Times'* historic Globe Lobby as editor for the first time. Three floors above, the staff had plastered the newsroom with pictures of Baquet and Otis Chandler. The building pass I had received from the security guard in the lobby said it all: It was good for one day. I was the paper's third editor in two years. Entering the newsroom and taking in the images of Baquet and the beloved, late Chandler legacy, I thought: "Okay, I'm up against a saint and a dead man." The situation was decidedly tense, but it was also thrilling. Across the nation, anyone interested in the future of journalism had their eyes glued to the situation in Los Angeles. Journalists lived for great stories, and I had a doozy. "No matter what you do," Doug Frantz, the paper's managing editor, told me, "you will always be viewed as a hatchet man from Chicago in this newsroom."

Most of the paper's journalists sat on the second and third floors of the *Times*' sprawling six-story, art deco building. The news department on the third floor was a seedy affair with a threadbare green carpet, yellowish lighting that made everyone look pallid, and crowded, grimy cubicles. The remodeled features department on the floor below created a reverse upstairs-downstairs effect. In contrast to many newsrooms with large, open city rooms, the *Los Angeles Times*' resembled a maze with reporters and editors crammed into small, crowded spaces surrounded by the traditional newsroom flotsam: discarded zoning commission binders; books and once vital notebooks, outdated City Council agendas; Jimmy Carter political campaign credentials; and long-forgotten, discarded personal effects.

Some of the journalists I would meet in the coming days—who well knew that the newsroom was often its own worst enemy—told me about colleagues who had perfected the art of laziness and had limited their output to one measly story a year. Most of the staff had blithely read about the elimination of hundreds of thousands of jobs in California's airline and defense industries but treated a relative handful of job cuts in the *Times* newsroom as a threat to the First Amendment. Journalists across America were in denial, but nowhere was that more glaring and public than at the *Los Angeles Times*.

Although I didn't have experience as the editor of a paper, I had run a big newsroom as a managing editor of the *Chicago Tribune* and had strong journalistic and leadership credentials. The staff was properly suspicious of my *Tribune* pedigree, but I was determined to do something about that. Journalists are creative people who can't be ordered to write good stories or great headlines. But if they respect you, they will follow you anywhere, because good journalists traffic in fairness. With that knowledge in the forefront of my mind, I climbed onto a desk in the *Los Angeles Times* newsroom on November 13, 2006, looked the assembled staff square in the eye, and declared that the new editor was above all a journalist and a seasoned newsman who would make tough calls but would also be fair. "I will make decisions that won't be popular," I told the assembled staffers, "but I will also make decisions that won't be popular in Tribune Tower, just as I did in a variety of jobs in Chicago over the years." All I asked from the newsroom was an opportunity to earn its respect. Managing editor Frantz told me afterward that he thought my remarks had gone over well. *Times* reporters videotaped my speech and my Q&A to put it on the web (for the record).

Fortunately for me, Baquet's endorsement helped me immensely. Key editors like Frantz, Montorio, and Wolinsky rejected rumors of the suicide pact that had buzzed at the news of Baquet's replacement. But it didn't take long for me to determine that the culture wars between Los Angeles and Chicago had taken a severe toll.

From the outside, the *Times* appeared to be an army of journalists united in defense of its defrocked editor and in opposition of the marauding horde in Chicago. In reality, the staff resembled a pack of quarreling tribes. Tribune-mandated budget cuts had ignited intense internecine warfare as editors scrambled to lock in their share of diminishing resources instead of confronting the huge challenges on the horizon. When I met with department heads, metro's head complained to me about how the national and foreign departments had somehow bypassed cuts. Ditto in business, sports, and features. The budget scrum was really no different than what was happening in Chicago; it was just more intense and more public. The truth was, everything you did in Los Angeles was public; news would be leaked almost immediately to Roderick at *LA Observed*. When I wrote a memo, I was aware that it was only a matter of hours before it would become public fodder.

As I settled into the newsroom at the *Times*, I sympathized with Baquet. He hated the budget and management part of the job (he'd delegated that to Wolinsky), and he'd focused the lion's share of his time and talent on journalism: talking to reporters about their stories, editors about their sections, and everyone about their jobs. By 2006, though, he had started spending an increasing amount of time fighting budget cuts. Over dinner during my first week on the job, Baquet told me he had deferred many hard decisions with the hope that he would eventually prevail and would fix them later. I soon discovered I faced a dysfunctional online operation, an abortive redesign of the paper, chronic misallocation of resources, and a raft of special deals that elevated the status of some reporters at the paper. The *Times* had three people in each of its Denver, Seattle, and Atlanta bureaus, but only one staffer was covering the San Fernando Valley, home to 1.8 million people starved for news about their community. Janet Clayton, who ran metro, stunned me when she admitted that she had not replaced the overnight police reporter (a footnote in the slew of cutbacks), leaving a paper covering Los Angeles without anyone reporting on the police beat at night. To me, it was unthinkable.

A lunch with California Governor Arnold Schwarzenegger telegraphed the rocky road ahead. When I asked him what he liked and disliked about the *Los Angeles Times*, I expected him to mention a story that had angered him or his wife, Maria Shriver (like the *Times'* infamous election eve story about his tendency to grope women). Instead, he replied that he hated the font of the headlines on page one. I thought: "If the headline font is so garish I have Arnold Schwarzenegger talking about it, I'm in serious trouble."

On arrival in Los Angeles, I had immediately taken Wolinsky out to lunch and asked him what the hell he'd been thinking about when he decided to meet with Geffen. Wolinsky told me he had been criticized in the Staples affair for not knowing what had been going on, and he'd wanted to have an upper hand on the news this time. He apologized profusely, and I decided that, although he'd clearly stepped out of line, it wasn't a firing offense. And besides, I needed someone with Wolinsky's knowledge of producing a massive, complex newspaper in a city I didn't know. F. Richard Ciccone, a former managing editor at the *Chicago Tribune*, once pointed out to me that if I got hit by a truck on my way to work, the paper would still come out on time the next day. But if editors like Wolinsky—who knew the production process cold—got hit, the paper might not come out. Wolinsky had the kind of vital knowledge that was crucial to a new editor. I could always move Wolinsky if I wanted to, after I had more time in the editor's office. During the first couple of months, there were some surprises, but things generally developed as I had expected, except for one challenge I hadn't anticipated.

Even under the best of circumstances, stress defines the relationship between a publisher and editor. Smart publishers usually delegate dead-line duties to their editors and focus on the business side of the paper for good reason. A publisher's intervention in a story can easily trigger a conflict or signal favoritism—at best an embarrassment, at worst a threat to the paper's editorial integrity. "When people complained, I always told them there's nothing I can do about it," Madigan once confided in me, "because it's the news." The publisher's office is the *one* place in a newspaper where the line between editorial and the business side can be most easily breached. For whatever reason, that line was not sacred to Hiller.

In a perfect world, I don't think Hiller, FitzSimons, or Smith would have selected me to be editor of the *Los Angeles Times*. I had clashed with each of them many times, just not as publicly as Baquet had. I was simply too independent for people who valued team players above all else. I had worked often with Hiller when he was publisher at the *Chicago Tribune*, but our relationship changed when I arrived in Los Angeles. In Chicago, I had Lipinski, the formidable editor of the *Tribune*, as a buffer to separate me from Hiller. In Los Angeles, it was just the two of us.

To many locals, Hiller seemed a curious choice for publisher of the *Los Angeles Times*, particularly given the lasting legacy of Otis Chandler. Otis had worked his way up through the newsroom and resembled a Greek god who could toss a spear across the Pacific. He was muscular and handsome, a motorcycle-riding sportsman who rebelled against his family. Hiller, by contrast, had never worked as a journalist. Slender and well groomed, with wavy gray hair and a relaxed sense of humor, he was a Harvard-educated lawyer from Park Ridge, Illinois. He had joined Tribune Company as general counsel before working in the company's development arm putting together and sealing deals. Prior to becoming publisher of the *Chicago Tribune*, he had run the newspaper company's Internet operation. A single man in his fifties, he lived in a Santa Monica apartment in a building that he was fond of telling people had once been home to Lawrence Welk.

Although Hiller had limited publisher experience in Chicago, his political roots and loyal nature appealed to FitzSimons. A self-described member of the political right, Hiller had served as an assistant attorney general in the Reagan Justice Department but also as a law clerk to Associate Justice to the Supreme Court, Potter Stewart, a judge with liberal leanings. He had also worked at the Tribune's law firm, Sidley Austin. He communicated his political leanings with the halting, lawyerly questions he used to make a point.

Many Tribune employees back in Chicago liked Hiller, and for good reason. He was friendly, intelligent, funny, and perhaps most importantly, he was the consummate team player. He came off as a kind man, someone who wanted desperately to be liked. The kind of guy who ran for class president. And he loved to sing. In the midst of a crisis, I'd get the feeling Hiller was about to jump up and sing, "Everything's Coming Up Roses." As publisher of both the *Tribune* and the *Times*, he successfully lobbied the Chicago Cubs and the Los Angeles Dodgers to let him sing the national anthem in Wrigley Field and in Dodger Stadium. At a staff party celebrating the paper's 125th anniversary, Hiller grabbed a microphone and started crooning show tunes.

Being the editor of a paper is like few other jobs in America; it's like owning a baseball team—a business that at heart belongs to the public it serves. If you breach the public's faith in your product, you fail. I viewed my job as a custodian of a public trust—a role that involved a lot more than collecting a big salary. I had to protect the integrity of the institution I ran and by extension the news at all costs.

As I assumed the responsibility of editing the *Los Angeles Times*, maintaining that public trust had become increasingly difficult. The industry faced an unprecedented assault by everyone from bloggers and blowhards on the political right and left to critics of the so-called mainstream media. Editors of papers large and small struggled with newsrooms in denial and owners under the gun to maintain solid financial returns to their shareholders.

In Baltimore, a wealthy hedge-fund investor had just forced the Knight Ridder chain to put itself on the auction block, and in June 2006, the Sacramento McClatchy publishing chain had stepped up and bought much of the company. McClatchy promptly began selling off papers it didn't want, including the *Minneapolis Star Tribune*, which sold the following year for $530 million, a staggering $670 million less than McClatchy had paid for the paper just nine years earlier. The sale shocked an industry where papers had routinely commanded far higher prices.

In my quest to deal with problems that could no longer be deferred another day, I worried most about diminishing the newspaper. The *Los Angeles Times* put out an excellent newspaper with 1,200 journalists in the newsroom, and I felt I could produce an equally excellent paper with just over 900. But I searched my soul asking at what point the cuts, bureau closings, and newsprint savings would fundamentally dilute the quality of the newspaper. Readers in Los Angeles complained about cuts in the paper far more than they did in Chicago. I told myself that I would not dare leave until I improved the paper that I'd inherited.

I had barely settled in Los Angeles when my worst fears were realized. Almost immediately, the Tribune Company pressured me for a staff cut. My experience in shaving budgets taught me that the Tribune numbers game was a road to nowhere. The corporate staff assessed the needs of the company, engaged in the give and take that public companies routinely practice with Wall Street analysts, and figured out how much excess cash the business needed to prop up the stock price and deliver 20 percent plus returns.

Once the finance guys set a target, each paper had to submit budgets that hit the magic number measured by cash flow. If Tribune needed $100 million in cash flow to keep Wall Street happy (and fund management bonuses) and the *Los Angeles Times* contribution was $50 million, then the paper would have to move heaven and earth to reach the goal, readers be damned. It was a lazy process in which accountants did the math and ordered cuts to reach a budget goal. The exercise put a premium on cost cutting and devalued the kind of enterprise or editorial risk taking that could actually generate revenues. The unstated understanding was that the newspaper could always be cut, because not that many readers noticed, and most didn't have an alternative source of news.

I had not entered Los Angeles with a budget or job-cut target. Smith and Hiller had asked me to commit to a reduced staff level, but I told them I couldn't say how many people I would need to run the *Los Angeles Times* since I had never worked in that newsroom. "I'm a reporter," I told Smith, "and a pretty damned good one. If I go out there, I'll do some reporting. The only thing I'll guarantee you is an honest answer. If I can do it with less, I'll tell you. If I think I'll need more, I'll tell you that, too." I was adamant that I wouldn't weaken the newspaper with indiscriminate, thoughtless budget cuts.

Significantly, Smith and I agreed that I would manage the budget so that it would not exceed an unspecified percentage of the paper's revenues, generally around 12 percent to 13 percent, which was about the same level as the *Chicago Tribune*. How I achieved that level would be up to me. The process gave me more flexibility and the newsroom a stake in fixing the revenue drain that most papers faced at the time. We had a revenue problem that we were treating like a cost problem, which would only make the revenue problem worse. If revenues tanked, as they usually did during a recession, I was more vulnerable, but it was a gamble I was willing to take.

In point of fact, my budget deal with Smith was somewhat unusual in a newsroom. Traditionally, editors didn't concern themselves a great deal with revenues or finances; they were journalists, after all, people who were supposed to worry about the news regardless of financial consequence. But that attitude—that revenue was the realm of the business side of the paper—had developed when monopoly ad markets minted money and newspaper editors were driven to work in chauffeured cars. I had a budget of about $130 million, which sounds like a lot of money until you consider what it takes to cover everything from Hollywood and Washington to the war in Iraq (the Baghdad bureau alone cost me about $1.5 million a year). If I didn't want to cut the budget, I had to figure out a way to help *finance* our journalism. I couldn't just do it by slashing a budget or sitting tight and waiting for things to get better. Those days were over.

At heart, newspaper budgets are really paper and people. In Los Angeles, the newsroom cost ratio for people is about 80/20, or about $.80 of every dollar you spend pays the salary and benefits of the journalist writing or editing the news and $.20 covers expenses, things like travel, meals, notebooks, cameras, and overhead. Bean counters usually place the other major expenses—newsprint and ink—in a separate budget. A newspaper like the *Los Angeles Times* can spend $160 million to $170 million a year on ink and paper alone. In the Tribune's top-down budget process, accountants usually gave you the bad news in two messages. In one, they would order, say, $8 million or $10 million in newsprint savings, leaving editors to come up with recommendations to the publisher regarding which sections to slash or kill. In a second message, they'd squeeze your editorial spending, demanding something like a 5 percent cut in a $130 million budget, or $6.5 million. Do the math, and it's easy to see why hitting that target without getting rid of people is almost impossible. Assuming 80 percent of a $130 million budget is devoted to salary and benefits, you would have to cut $6.5 million out of the remaining $26 million if you didn't want to axe people. A 25 percent reduction in expense money would seriously diminish most newsrooms.

In our first budget dance, Hiller tried to hit me with a huge staff cut, but I objected in strong terms, actually storming out of the building after arguing that I needed a chance to rejuvenate sections that were losing money and to increase revenues in others. To his credit, Hiller backed off. I truly believed I could resolve the problems in the *Los Angeles Times* newsroom, but I also knew I wouldn't make any progress unless—and until—I won the respect and confidence of the staff. To do that, I needed Hiller's help, and he needed mine. But barbs inevitably developed that complicated our relationship and made me realize that I faced a far larger hurdle than I'd anticipated.

In early December, I walked into my office and noticed my schedule placed me in Hollywood for much of the day at a ceremony in which the *Los Angeles Times*, in honor of its 125th anniversary, would become the first newspaper to be awarded a star on the Hollywood Walk of Fame. "What is this?" I asked Polly Ross, my assistant. "Are you kidding? I'm not going. I've got better things to do with my time." But Ross reminded me that my newfound stature dictated otherwise. "You have to go," she said. "You are the editor. They would be insulted if you didn't show up."

To my surprise, one of the people who would take offense was Hiller. Later in the morning, Clayton from the metro desk came to see me, her eyes bulging in disbelief that the publisher's office had called the city desk to ask about our plans to cover the Walk of Fame ceremony. This was not something that a publisher at the *Los Angeles Times* would have done in the past, and Clayton was shocked by the suggestion we cover something so lacking in substance. I told Clayton not to worry; I would take care of it. I called the photo editor and told him to send a photographer up to Hollywood to take pictures at the event. "As far as a picture in the paper," I said, "judge it in the context of the day's news. If it doesn't measure up to the rest of the news, it doesn't measure up." Many of the pictures a photographer takes don't make it into the newspaper and I couldn't imagine that such an image would ever appear in the news columns of the *Los Angeles Times*. It simply wasn't newsworthy. It was a publicity stunt.

But Hiller saw things differently. When the *Times* limo pulled up at the Hollywood Roosevelt Hotel, Hiller stepped out, beaming. He was thrilled to be *Los Angeles Times* publisher when the paper got a star on the Hollywood Walk of Fame. Certainly, there had been a time when being awarded a star had been a big deal, but by late 2006, it didn't take much to get one. More than 2,000 stars dotted sidewalks in the neighborhood. Even Charlie Tuna had one! Stars were not ceremoniously handed out solely for a lifetime of achievement, either. Recipients forked over $25,000 for their pink terrazzo, five-point star rimmed in bronze.

As the *Times* entourage neared the sidewalk where our star was laid, Hiller met Johnny Grant, the honorary mayor of Hollywood who ran the star selection committee. Grant, an avuncular, glad-handing legend, shook hands with Hiller, sealing a union of kindred spirits. A delighted Hiller stepped to the lectern and praised Grant and some *Times* veterans who had shown up for the ceremony. Grant, who died months later, unveiled the star and more pictures were taken. Ed Begley, Jr., spoke at a lunch at the Roosevelt Hotel and then it was finally over. I got back to the office just before the 3:30 news meeting with my editors. No one mentioned the Walk of Fame, and I didn't bring it up.

As I was driving home, Hiller called me, wanting to know about coverage of the *Times* star in the Saturday paper. I told him that we had sent a photographer to cover the event, but that the picture didn't measure up to the news of the day and that we wouldn't run anything. A moment of silence passed uncomfortably. When Hiller finally responded, he was furious.

"They'll run negative stories about us all the time," Hiller barked, referring to the coverage allotted to his dismissal of Baquet, "but when something positive happens, no story." I tried to settle Hiller down, explaining that the event was the kind of public relations stunt we simply didn't cover: It wasn't news. When I pointed out that the newspaper had paid for the star, Hiller shot back, "What do you mean we paid for it?" I told him that I had heard we paid for the event, but that

I didn't have the details and would get back to him. "Well, I want a full and detailed report," he sputtered in frustration before hanging up.

The next Saturday afternoon, Hiller called me again, asking if I could run a photo of the event, or a story in the Sunday paper. I told him no, a story would be inappropriate, particularly given the circumstances of the award. I had subsequently learned that the deal to honor the paper with a star had been hatched when the head of the *Los Angeles Times* PR department met Johnny Grant at a party and suggested it. Twenty-five grand later, Grant agreed. "If you want something in the paper, you should run a house ad [an advertisement labeled as a *Times* ad and paid for by the paper]," I told Hiller. After more back and forth, an angry Hiller agreed, letting me know that he would take the space for the ad "out of the fucking newsroom budget." Within a week he ran a full-page house ad touting the paper's star.

The flap over the star exposed me to another side of Hiller for the first time, the one behind the smile. I felt bad for him. He obviously loved the klieg lights of Hollywood, and not to have a story in the paper about the glitzy event would have embarrassed him in front of his new Hollywood friends. But I was also concerned. As trivial as the Walk of Fame incident might seem, it made me realize the depth of Hiller's blind spots as a publisher. A major part of an editor's job is to educate the publisher. Lacking any true editorial experience, he honestly didn't seem to know where the publisher's job ended and the editor's began.

From my days in Chicago, I knew Hiller liked to intervene in stories, letting reporters and editors know what he liked and what he didn't. At first, Lipinski and I dismissed Hiller's meddlesome notes as naïveté, but they kept coming, and many were tinged with his own political bent. He often queried editors, seeking their views about the adequacy of *Chicago Tribune*'s and, later, the *Los Angeles Times'* stories, compared to accounts sent to him by conservative bloggers or political operatives. In his view, a publisher bore responsibility for the entire paper and should therefore weigh in on issues involving news coverage.

Hiller seemed oblivious to the impact that notes from the publisher would have on a reporter, particularly regarding political issues. Some staffers in Chicago appreciated his tendency to comment on their work; they felt he displayed more interest in them and their stories than former publishers. But in Los Angeles, no one appreciated his inter-ference. Publishers were supposed to stay out of the newsroom, and Hiller made many journalists feel uncomfortable.

There was also a significant difference between the two papers. At the *Tribune*, the editorial page reported to the editor. When Baquet became editor of the *Times*, the Tribune Company changed the report-ing relationship between the editor and the person who ran the editorial page. Under Carroll, the editorial and op-ed pages had been under the control of the editor, as it was in Chicago. Under Baquet, the editorial pages in the *Los Angeles Times* reported directly to the pub-lisher of the paper. There was nothing unusual about either system. Some papers put the editorial pages under the editor, and others under the publisher. I told Hiller that the arrangement in Los Angeles made him a more visible factor in the editorial page voice of the paper—something that was different from Chicago. Even if his intentions were benign, Hiller was treading on a minefield. Commenting on a news story could easily be seen by a reporter as an effort to align the story with the newspaper's editorial position.

I had warned Hiller about the difference in the structure of the two papers before we left Chicago and had suggested he curtail his notes and leave the newsroom to me. But he wouldn't stop his notes to the staff and even asked if the editorial board should be placed under me. I said no. It didn't help that many of his complaints about unfair headlines or stories revolved around conservative political issues or influential people in the community. I don't think he ever complained about stories written about liberals or poor people.

What's more, Hiller loved to interact with readers, showing them he cared about their views and often inviting them to deal directly with him. I hated to discourage anyone from talking to readers. In my mind, journalists hadn't done enough of that, particularly at the *Times*. I spent as much time as possible going to community forums where I would defend the paper against critics and convince readers I was in Los Angeles for the long haul, regardless of how long it would take to fix problems at their paper. I even encouraged them to come in and attend page-one meetings. But when readers and community leaders exchanged views with Hiller, he usually bypassed the reporter who'd written the story or the editor who had handled it and dealt with the complaining party himself—thereby angering staff and engendering resentment. When I suggested to Hiller that it was more effective for all concerned to refer readers to the staffers who'd been involved in the stories under scrutiny, he didn't listen. Instead, he started his own blog.

Tensions between editors and publishers were becoming increasingly common in American newsrooms. On the surface, newspaper finances in 2006 didn't seem that bad; the real estate boom that fueled the subprime mortgage crisis was in full swing, generating huge amounts of real estate classified ad revenue. But help wanted and automobile classified ads, a crucial component of newspaper revenue, were in a free fall, partially because of the Internet and partially because advertisers were aware of newspapers' declining circulations. Were the real estate market to soften—something that was only a matter of time—newspapers would be in real trouble.

In a near panic, publishers ordered marketing studies to help determine how they could reverse the slide. Civic-minded editors traditionally try to balance the needs of readers with their own agendas, providing stories about sports, money, and celebrities as well as reports on the environment, foreign news, and legislation. The marketing studies' results were music to a publisher's ears. Newspaper readers wanted local news about their communities, the surveys said, not lengthy expensive reports on the foibles of the Bush administration, the war in Iraq, or the political implications of some arms treaty. Of course, the answers to questions in these surveys depended a lot on how the question was asked and who was asking it. But it soon became pretty clear that things near and dear to the hearts of journalists—big, expensive foreign and national news bureaus that grappled with the weighty, significant subjects of the day—were the next targets for budget cutters. As accountants sharpened their knives, editors scrambled to protect their journalistic assets, while publishers felt the heat from stockholders and Wall Street. Tensions escalated sharply across the country as journalists and publishers squared off over which journalistic assets should be cut and which should be spared.

In Los Angeles, Hiller had inherited a gimmick to attract readers' attention when he took over from Johnson, in the form of a "guest editor" venture. In an effort to make the paper more relevant or entertaining to the local community, the weekly Sunday opinion section would be assigned to a famous non-journalist. The guest editor would select the stories, get writers, edit the copy, and give readers a perspective on his or her choices when the section was published in the biggest paper of the week. The *Times* editorial page editor, Andrés Martinez, who had been recruited by Hiller's predecessor, had selected an all-star team of news makers as guest editors, including celebrities such as Hollywood's Brian Grazer, the spike-haired producer of big hits like TV's *24*, and film's *American Gangster*, *A Beautiful Mind*, and *The Da Vinci Code*. I didn't see much harm in the idea, particularly since it involved the editorial board, which was out of my purview. Hiller loved it.

Problems soon surfaced in its execution, though. The newsroom was abuzz with gossip that editorial page editor Martinez had separated from his wife and was romantically involved with an attractive woman who worked for a public relations firm where Grazer was a client. I didn't know a lot about all of the personalities involved, but after thirty years as a journalist, I knew how this story would read:

> The editorial page editor of the *Los Angeles Times* relinquished the paper's Sunday Opinion Section to a big-time Hollywood producer represented by a PR firm where the editor's girlfriend works.

*LA Observed* would have a field day.

Hiller had sent me an e-mail saying he might need my counsel about something. Then Wolinsky dropped by my office to report on the newsroom gossip mill. "I know this isn't your area, but somebody's got to do something," Wolinsky said. Soon Nick Goldberg, Martinez's deputy, came into my office and implored me to intervene.

When I met with Hiller, I didn't have to raise the subject. He told me about Martinez and said he felt we could explain the situation in a note and publish the section. He asked me for my thoughts. I told him to kill it. Hiller was shocked. "You are the only one to suggest that," he said. I told Hiller I had been a journalist for thirty years and I felt strongly that we'd be crucified for publishing Grazer's section, with or without a note.

The discussion went on for quite a while and spilled into the next day as Hiller called others seeking their views, a lawyerly tactic but one that also spread the story. Martinez was furious with me, and the blogs had a great time with it. But Hiller seemed far more worried about how Grazer would react. In the end, Hiller listened to me. He killed the section and the guest editor's project. Martinez resigned, a baffled Grazer was miffed, but Hiller got positive reviews from most observers.

More significantly, the incident seemed to bolster my credibility with Hiller in our ongoing wrangling over the budget. He was honest and would listen, but was vulnerable to adopting the position of the last person to get his ear. I learned with Hiller that I had to make sure that I was the last in line. Hiller had originally sought a budget number from the newsroom that would have required me to chop seventy-five to eighty people from the staff in addition to numerous space and expense cuts that were wrong for the paper and that would undermine my credibility. I reminded him of the agreement that I had struck with Smith and I argued for a less ham-handed approach.

Cutting staff is a horrible exercise under any circumstances, but it is particularly hard in journalism because many readers and sources in the community establish a bond with the reporters who cover them. Every single item in a newspaper has a constituency, whether it's the bridge column, the comics, a star columnist, or sometimes even a secretary.

Just months after I arrived at the *Times*, I started preparing my senior editors for an imminent staff reduction. We crafted a list of people who should be canned for performance issues. That was easy. Then I announced an open-ended voluntary buyout in which anyone who wanted to leave would receive a week's pay for every six months of service up to a year's pay. We gave the staff a few weeks to think about their options, as my editors fanned out through the newsroom and advised people on the poor-performance list that they should agree to the buyout, lest they be fired and get nothing. The open-ended nature of the buyout was dangerous; people who you didn't want to leave might take it.

Accountants arrived at the number of jobs I needed to eliminate in a buyout by assigning an average salary to a job. If people with salaries higher than the average accepted the offer, I wouldn't have to eliminate as many jobs. In my case, fifty-seven people, some who I wanted to leave and many who I didn't, raised their hands, giving me far more in total salary than I needed to meet my goal. I convinced Hiller to let me use the excess dollars to hire back about twenty-five younger journalists who were cheaper than some who had left. The deal left me with a net reduction of only thirty-two journalists and allowed me to inject some fresh blood into the staff, which was always good for morale.

In keeping with my deal with Smith, I also began looking for opportunities to increase revenues at the *Times*. Scanning a Baquet memo about future plans, I noticed a proposal for a fashion news section for Los Angeles. All things being equal, I probably wouldn't have dedicated precious resources to coverage about Ferragamo and fedoras when rampant corruption and war plagued the nation and the city. But all things were not equal. Fashion, properly covered, was news to many people and reflected broader social trends. Plus the section could generate fresh revenue from new advertisers, money that would help me finance stories on budgets and battles. Working with colleagues in the advertising department, John Montorio and his editors had proposed a brilliant section called Image that offered full-color, sophisticated coverage on a national scale.

We convinced Hiller to authorize the section and to approve an additional eight to ten hires to generate news that would result in revenue. Over a nine-month stretch, Montorio's editors produced thirty-eight sections to rave editorial reviews. Image attracted new advertisers, and while it generated more than $5.5 million in new revenues, it made more than $2 million in profit to prop up the paper's struggling cash flow. In effect, I had paid for the Baghdad bureau with coverage of shops, shoes, and Chanel.

By accident as much as design, I had started to achieve my goal of combining revenue enhancements with modest cost cuts to stabilize the newsroom and meet the budget. Sean Reily, an editor and a budget ace, proposed that we go through the entire paper and select sections where we could replicate our experience with Image.

■

The *Los Angeles Times* that I inherited was an excellent newspaper that regularly won Pulitzer Prizes. Consistent with Puerner's philosophy that paid content was a winning strategy, Carroll and Baquet had built exceptionally strong foreign and national news coverage, a vibrant Washington bureau competitive on major stories, and a stable of investigative reporters who regularly rooted out corruption and neglect with huge multipart stories. Under Montorio, the paper also had a collection of excellent feature sections, many of which Reily began to assess to determine whether they had the revenue potential of Image. But the paper had always had trouble crafting a strategy to cover the huge, sprawling city it called home. Anyone reading the *Los Angeles Times* didn't really get a good sense or feel for this fascinating, diverse city and region. I was determined to correct that imbalance and told everyone that metro was my highest priority in new hires and budgeting.

But the controversies kept coming. "Editors here have always had to live with controversy," Reily told me one day. "But I don't think I've ever seen anything like what's happening with you." Controversies over the paper's content were raised left and right. When Frantz had a problem with a story about the Armenian genocide (the writer, of Armenian descent, had shown that he had an opinion on the issue and we had reassigned it to another writer), there was an uproar in the strong and impressively large Armenian community in Los Angeles. Unlike me, who had once run a newsroom under attack by the powerful Chicago Israeli community, Hiller had never been at the other end of a gun aimed by a special-interest group. And the Armenians knew how to attack: They flooded the company with complaints. At one point, my BlackBerry was immobilized by the number of e-mails I received from Armenians.

Meanwhile, the circle of investors hovering over Tribune Company in hopes of buying it became far more controversial when Chicago real estate billionaire Sam Zell joined its ranks. Then, just as I was telling the newsroom who had agreed to the buyout, Mike Oneal of the *Chicago Tribune* broke a story about huge bonuses being awarded to key executives in Chicago who had agreed to stay on until the company had been sold, making it appear as if managers like me were cutting budgets to finance huge bonuses. I was livid and drafted a memo to the staff announcing the buyouts but also addressing the bonuses, which I characterized as indefensible. The blogosphere had a field day, of course, and Hiller called early the next morning to say, "I just got off the phone with one pissed-off chairman."

Gradually, though, the newsroom started to settle down. Some staffers privately said I spent too much time in my office and that I wasn't as open and charismatic as Baquet. Unfortunately, that was true. I didn't make time in Los Angeles to demonstrate my journalistic skills as an editor. That was my fault. But the newsroom had changed for the better under me. There was more hope in the air. The staff had removed most of the pictures of Baquet and Chandler and was busy getting back to work. I started hiring some new staff members and replacing others and the first Image section debuted.

About six months after I had arrived, FitzSimons came to Los Angeles for a visit. Over breakfast, we engaged in ritual chitchat. But after a few minutes, FitzSimons' brow furrowed, and he pulled from his briefcase my original memo on the *Los Angeles Times*. "Well, Jim, it's been six months," he said, "and I'm not too impressed." He wondered why I hadn't done more, a sly reference to my failure to fire Wolinsky and others on my masthead, and why I criticized the bonuses in my statement about staff buyouts. "You didn't even know what those bonuses were about," FitzSimons erroneously chided me, noting that the tone of my memo implied that I had an inflated view of myself and my role. "The day of the imperial CEO is over, Jim, and so is the day of the imperial editor."

# 16

## Before the Fall

Not long after I had walked into the newsroom as editor of the *Los Angeles Times*, Todd Kaplan, a high-powered Merrill Lynch investment banker, placed a phone call to one of his longtime clients, Sam Zell, a billionaire deal junkie who had nicknamed himself "the grave dancer" for his ability to pick up distressed properties for a dime on the dollar. Zell had balked at bidding on Tribune Company when Wall Street started shopping the company around: The asking price was too high. But Kaplan, who was advising Tribune and had done dozens of deals with Zell, convinced him to take another look.

FitzSimons' $2 billion stock buyback effort had saddled Tribune Company with a lot of debt and had infuriated the Chandlers. In private, the Chandlers had hinted they might shop their stock around because they were at loggerheads with Tribune over the valuation and tax treatment of their family trusts. The Tribune's announcement that the company would launch the stock buyback was the last straw. Lawyer William Stinehart fired off his harsh letter, dramatically elevating the row by publicly accusing FitzSimons and the Tribune board of incompetence and dismal performance, and of blindly pursuing a deeply flawed synergy strategy.

At the time, Tribune's revenues were declining, largely due to soft advertising in Los Angeles: As the subprime mortgage fiasco began to unfold, real estate ads were diminishing, and Hollywood movie studios, too, were drawing back on advertising. In the face of a declining market, traditional advertisers were exploring what options existed for them online. But things were not as bad as the Chandlers' sky-is-falling letter implied. Despite some rough patches, Tribune Company posted robust operating profit margins, earning about $1 billion in 2006, or profits equivalent to 18.5 percent of its revenues, down from the 20 percent level the year before, but still an enviable margin.

In his letter, Stinehart outlined a strategy for going forward and exploring "strategic alternatives," which included: "breaking up and selling or disposing in tax-free spinoffs some or all of its newspaper properties and the possibility of an acquisition of Tribune as a whole at an attractive premium." The Chandlers' outrage put enormous pressure on the board to sell the company, but before Tribune could be sold, it had to unwind the Chandler trusts. Shortly thereafter, FitzSimons and the Chandlers struck a compromise, and the Tribune board created a "Special Committee" of directors led by William Osborn, a respected Chicago banker from the Northern Trust Company, the Tribune Company's bank. The special board was established to explore strategic options, the financial market euphemism for a "For Sale" sign. The acrimony with the Chandlers didn't end there, though. By virtue of their large stockholdings, the Chandlers were not on the Special Committee composed of outside directors, a ploy to deny them the opportunity to leak board proceedings.

On Wall Street, the same investment banks that had sung Tribune's praises for its earnings and had pressured the company to keep posting sky-high cash flow margins had hammered its stock to about half of its all-time high per share. Analysts complained of soft ad markets, competition from the Internet, and, of course, declining circulations. The present may be okay, market analysts at places like Merrill Lynch assessed, but the future was bleak. The Tribune's Special Committee hired Morgan Stanley as an adviser, while Tribune Company hired a collection of firms under the Citigroup banner and Merrill Lynch, their longtime investment banker. The two largest shareholders hired advisers, too. The Chandlers hired Tom Unterman's private equity firm, Rustic Canyon Partners; the McCormick Foundation hired the Blackstone Group. The race for solutions was on.

Overall, Tribune investment bankers reached out to thirty-six parties to gauge interest in the company, ranging from huge private equity investors like Madison Dearborn Partners in Chicago and the Carlyle Group to the Chandlers, Eli Broad, and Ronald Burkle, a Los Angeles billionaire and close friend of President Bill Clinton. As the potential buyers pored over Tribune's books, though, the thirty-one firms that voiced interest dropped out one by one, and, by the time I arrived as editor of the *Los Angeles Times*, only a handful remained.

Down in the ranks, everyone watched anxiously as the bankers put the company up for grabs. Through pension, profit-sharing, and discounted stock acquisition plans, Tribune employees owned 11 percent of Tribune stock, making them the third-largest share-holder. Employees like myself had bet retirement plans, college tuitions, and financial security on Tribune stock. Hiller soon asked me to go to the Sidley Austin offices in the Gas Building in downtown Los Angeles to meet with the Chandlers, who'd assembled a room full of young analysts with big binders, all wearing blue shirts and ties, and explain where I wanted to take the paper. The sameness of the group made them resemble a room full of robots. Unterman was leading the discussion, while Stinehart sat quietly, his bloodless eyes taking it all in.

■

Capitalism had built the American newspaper industry. Tycoons like Chandler, McCormick, and Cowles had made a lot of money off newspapers, and most of the capitalists were hardly angels. But they built something useful, a business that created wealth but also served a socially useful purpose and employed people. By early 2007, Wall Street had undergone a dramatic transformation. The investors and investment bankers circling Tribune were out to make a buck by creating fee-laden packages of loans that could be converted into securities and peddled to big pension funds, institutional investors, or hedge funds and make even more money. If they created jobs, they were inside jobs designed to enrich themselves through the huge fees their clients forked over in exchange for access to the hordes of cash sloshing around on global markets.

The Tribune Special Committee hired Morgan Stanley to the tune of an unusually high $10 million, a large fee that reflected the bank's inability to participate in the lucrative loans Tribune would need to fund the various schemes under consideration. Advising the committee on which loan to pick would put the firm in a conflict, particularly if it stood to profit from the deal it told the committee to select. The Special Committee approved the fee, which was enough to fund four to five years of Iraq war coverage for readers of both the *Times* and the *Tribune*. Yet a few months later, Morgan Stanley would try to muscle its way into the loan-packaging deal, provoking howls of protests from bankers at Citigroup, the Tribune's prime banker, and Merrill Lynch, or "Sam's bank," as one banker would refer to the firm. After Michael Costa, the Tribune's man at Merrill Lynch, challenged Morgan Stanley's math in its financing proposal, Crane Kenney, the company's general counsel, remarked, "Always said the banking intramurals were ugly, but this is probably the worst example I've seen. You are right to be upset," Kenney told Costa.

As each of the bankers lined up behind competing financing schemes created for a healthy company that had essentially created a fire sale, nerves frayed and tempers flared. At one point, the Chandlers considered selling the family's stock to the McCormick Foundation, but they could barely bring themselves to speak to the foundation, whose board included FitzSimons, Madigan, Hiller, and Smith, whom the Chandlers considered an extension of Tribune management.

And sure enough, before long, the idea of a sale degenerated into the insults that characterized relations between the California family and the boys from Chicago.

"We looked out and saw a ski slope," Stinehart later recalled. "Management looked at the ski slope as though it [were] a bunny hill you can traverse across by cost cutting and [by catching] the Internet chairlift and go to the top, but what the [Chandler] Trusts saw was a four-star black-diamond run headed straight downhill. Cost cutting gets you nowhere, and the chairlift's broken. Essentially there were two different versions of where the world was going, and we wanted off the ski slope." Morgan Stanley was concerned that the Chandlers were pushing yet another alternative scheme because it would generate a tax windfall for the family but not necessarily for everyone else.

Once Kaplan had convinced Zell to reconsider an investment in Tribune, the dynamics changed overnight. The mere thought of doing a deal with the legendary Zell made the investment bankers' mouths water. He had the ability to open doors. Zell had invested in everything from radio stations and cruise ships to trailer parks, not always successfully, but his calling card was his genius at real estate investments. Editors like myself, weary of FitzSimons and his penny-pinching ways, welcomed the idea of Zell, even though he was known as a financial buccaneer. He had just sold his Equity Office Properties real estate venture to the Blackstone Group for $39 billion, adding to his reputation as an investor with a Midas touch. Just as *Los Angeles Times* journalists once welcomed Willes because of his reputation as a financial wizard, we welcomed Zell as a savvy entrepreneur who might have some good ideas about getting Tribune back on track and succeeding at mission impossible: making Tribune shareholders *and* its journalists happy.

Despite my many years in Chicago, I didn't know Zell. He had a reputation for being secretive, crude, tough, and dismissive, but also incredibly loyal to trusted colleagues and widely admired for his unbelievable capitalistic instincts and addiction to deals. He loved to brag about how many people he'd made millionaires and always seemed to have someone with him. Yet he also seemed alone, even in a room full of people. Despite his high profile and billion-dollar deals, precious little had been written about him. A *Chicago Tribune* magazine article by Greg Burns that ran in the paper when I was managing editor was a rare exception. The lack of sound information on Zell made us all curious to find out with whom we'd be dealing.

While he was reporting the story, Burns had talked to many people who knew and praised Zell, but he also uncovered court files that showed how Zell, early in his career, had turned state's evidence and testified in a court case involving a tax-fraud scheme, a Caribbean bank, and a Nevada high-rise. His testimony had helped prosecutors win a conviction and a two-year prison term for one of his co-conspirators— his brother-in-law, Roger Baskes, who told Burns years later that he didn't bear a grudge.

Burns' piece closely examined Zell's remarkable career, including his sometimes acrimonious relationship with his father, a strict, demanding Polish Jew who came to America in 1941 to flee the Nazis and promptly shortened the family name from Zielonka to Zell. Zell declined Burns' request for an interview: "*This Is Your Life* is not my kind of thing," Zell told Burns in reference to a popular TV show from the 1950s, but even without his subject's participation, Burns nonetheless detailed his amazing rise from a University of Michigan–trained lawyer working for $58 a week to one of the globe's largest owners of real estate. Zell hated the piece and would complain about it for years. Few other reporters had the guts to do such a story on Zell, and few papers, other than the *Chicago Tribune*, had the backbone to run it. Now the company that owned the offending paper was being considered an investment opportunity by the man himself.

To put together a bid, Zell activated an "A" team at Equity Group Investments, his privately held company. Years before, Zell had instructed a colleague to go out and hire the smartest person he could find. The search led to the door of William Pate, a lawyer whose family had owned the *Madill Record*, a tiny weekly and pillar of the community that helped two generations of Pates land in the Oklahoma Press Hall of Fame.

While at law school at the University of Chicago, Pate rented out the basement of his Hyde Park building. It was there that he met Nils Larsen, a New Hampshire native and bearded environmentalist who was driving through and had spent the night on the couch of Pate's tenant. Pate and Larsen chatted and hit it off, particularly after Larsen told him he had quit his job as a Wall Street investment banker because he found the atmosphere stuffy. After Pate joined Zell's venture, the company hired Larsen, too. It was a good fit for bright young people who could bike to work in jeans and look the other way when a colleague had an occasional extramarital affair. Within thirteen years, Pate rose to become Zell's top investment officer, and Larsen became a managing director at Zell's investment arm. Together they put together a bid for Tribune.

The ingenious proposal that Zell, Pate, and Larsen crafted demonstrated that Zell indeed had a great eye for talent. A few years before, Zell had invested in a waste energy firm, Covanta, which he picked up out of bankruptcy court. A bank that submitted a competing offer for Covanta wanted to use an employee stock ownership plan, known as an ESOP, and a tax-advantaged S corporation to fund its bid. The tactic didn't work, but the idea stayed in Pate's mind. When he took a look at Tribune Company, he wondered if a similar scheme would work with a company that owned newspapers, assets that were close to his Oklahoma roots.

The offer that Equity Group built puzzled many of the investment bankers involved in the Tribune deal. Most of them had little knowledge about ESOPs, and hardly anyone had ever seen a scheme marrying an ESOP with an S corporation. Essentially, Zell proposed that Tribune borrow enough money to buy all of the stock owned by the Chandlers, the McCormick Trust, employees, and other shareholders and take the company private—or remove its stock from public markets—as an S corporation owned by a nonprofit ESOP that would be owned by Tribune employees and be exempt from federal income taxes. The idea would saddle the company with about $12 billion to $13 billion in debt, a staggering sum to mortals but not such a big deal to a real estate tycoon who loved to operate with other people's money. Indeed, after Zell got interested, Pate called Brit Bartter, a Zell contact at JPMorgan Chase, and informed him about the Tribune multibillion dollar deal to gauge the bank's interest in providing financing. A mere five days later, Bartter told Pate that JPMorgan Chase was "there for them on their big project."

Zell's proposal had some intriguing benefits, too. To repay the Tribune's debt, the new company could rely on the $1.3 billion that Tribune already generated each year in cash flow plus another $300 million to $500 million the company would no longer have to pay in income taxes by virtue of being owned by a nonprofit ESOP. Ditto for the $200 million to $300 million a year it had been paying to shareholders in dividends. The total level of debt could be cut by selling off assets that didn't contribute to cash flow—like the Chicago Cubs baseball team, which was valued in excess of $1 billion. And the new company wouldn't have to cough up the $60 million to $70 million a year it had paid to employee 401(k) plans because employees would receive benefits as owners, thanks to the ESOP categorization. Initially, Zell said he would personally invest $200 million in Tribune and that existing shareholders, including employees, would get around $30 a share for their stock, a price that would have been laughable even two years earlier but now had to be considered. Once the debt was repaid, everyone would be fat and happy.

The idea of an ESOP would probably have gone nowhere without Zell. Even with his backing, financial advisers like the Special Committee's Thomas Whayne of Morgan Stanley didn't know what to think: "What was novel was that it was an S-Corp. ESOP. That was the part that was truly unprecedented. I'd never seen that done. I subsequently became educated that it had been done for other private companies. But I'm still not aware that it had been done in other public companies." Some bankers involved in the deal were cool to the idea. Julie Persily of Citigroup's leveraged finance department, a unit that would have to eventually peddle the billion-dollar loans to other investors, said she had talked to Merrill Lynch about it: "I spoke to ML.

They are on board with this silly ESOP structure. I am unequivocally not on board. . . . But ML explained why they think it works. ML is Sam's bank. They'll do anything for him."

But Citigroup had never corralled Zell as a client despite its strong local Chicago banking ties to companies like Tribune. In reference to Zell, Persily said she was "in awe of him," and others at the bank noted that lending money to the Zell-backed ESOP could have its own benefits. Christina Mohr, a managing director in Citigroup's mergers and acquisitions wing, liked the ESOP idea and got an e-mail from Paul Ingrassia, one of the bank's managing directors, that suggested just how meaningful an "in" with Zell could be for business: "Christina. If we end up helping Sam, if appropriate, please let him know how important his relationship is to our [other operations] and real estate teams, and that we were consulted. We are trying to win a book position on his IPO of Equity International."

In the newsrooms, Tribune journalists, blissfully ignorant of the behind-the-scenes skirmishes, worried about whether we would restore an editor or two to a depleted news or copy desk rather than about the very real threat of how the company's heavy debt would trigger the need for drastic budget cuts. Even FitzSimons and Smith, who viewed budget cuts as a simple matter of fact, worried about employee reaction. But Zell was a rock star, a new face that appealed to news junkies in newsrooms. Everyone liked the idea that Zell had eclipsed FitzSimons.

Zell, too, started to get pumped as the deal developed the kind of rhythm that made his heart beat. When Costa, the Tribune's banker, expressed his disappointment to Pate that Zell's bid wouldn't command more than $30 a share, Zell upped the ante to $33 per share. Sweetening the pot didn't immediately win over big Tribune shareholders like the McCormick Foundation, which favored a "self-help plan," a leveraged buyout in which the company's management would line up the loans to buy the company and continue to run it as a private entity. Truth be told, Madigan and FitzSimons, like many in the Chicago business establishment, viewed Zell as a crude, uncouth maverick who was tolerated because of his billions.

The McCormick Foundation also raised a legitimate issue. Any plan would require approval by the Federal Communications Commission (FCC) because broadcast licenses would have to be transferred and Zell's initial offer would take nine months to close, a long time in which anything could happen to derail the deal. On this point, the Chandlers actually agreed with the boys from Chicago. But Zell had an answer: To minimize the risks to Tribune's existing shareholders, he would split the proposed deal into two phases. His deal called for acquiring 50 percent of the stock in May 2007 (thereby giving the company's shareholders a chance to cash in on half of their earnings soon), and the other 50 percent by December 2007 after the company got approval from the FCC.

Mohr recalled how FitzSimons and the Chicagoans were hot and cold on the two-phase ESOP deal: "It wasn't as if we all looked at Zell and said let's do it. We thought about it, pushed back among financing teams and adviser teams. This was something that had not been done on this scale. . . . People got up some mornings and were comfortable, other mornings people said they were uncomfortable with the risk. . . . It was live, dead, live, dead, dead, live."

At one point, the back and forth that plagued Tribune Company also frustrated Zell, who called Tribune General Counsel Kenney and demanded, "So do you think I'm some sort of schmuck?" When Kenney said, "No," Zell barked, "Well then, why are you treating me like one? Do you have anyone there who knows how to do a deal?" FitzSimons also got frantic phone calls, not from Zell but from Tribune's longtime New York lawyer, Marty Lipton of Watchell & Lipton, who had built the company's anti-takeover defenses: "Marty called me one morning and said, 'You know, I was tossing and turning all night, I couldn't sleep, and I think we really have to think about this very, very carefully given the scrutiny that it's going to receive down in Washington.'"

Tribune Company had already received terrible press when it misread the depth of the opposition to an earlier FCC rule change, one that it had pushed to ease the level of media concentration permitted under federal regulations. "The press," FitzSimons said, "loves board-room drama, and they love it even more when you have a media company involved."

FitzSimons had all but abandoned the Zell proposal until Osborn, who chaired the Special Committee, told him that he had called Zell and asked him to revive his bid. "Bill Osborn told me, 'Look, we need to fully explore this,'" FitzSimons said.

■

By March 2007, the intramural sniping among the bankers was in full swing. Morgan Stanley had quietly prepared a proposal that would have financed management's self-help scheme, while Merrill Lynch had swung its full support behind the Zell plan. Merrill Lynch advisers who had once questioned the Zell deal had learned more about the ESOP, liked the higher price Zell had offered, anticipated improved Tribune cash flows due to synergies, and had confidence in Zell's ability to do something he had implied to employees he would not do—impose deep cost cuts.

But Morgan Stanley's Whayne said that Costa and Kaplan became big fans of the Zell deal because "they would make a lot of money—more debt, more fees." Indeed, when Kaplan told Costa that Merrill could expect to earn $33 million to $35 million on fees from the Zell deal, Costa pushed back saying they should be "more aggressive." When Kaplan questioned what his colleague meant, Costa replied, "More money."

"The banks were climbing all over themselves to get into this deal," said Kenney, "so much that Merrill Lynch, who was the strategic adviser to Tribune, resigned as the strategic adviser because . . . if you're advising on the strategic alternatives, you can't also be playing in the financing role, and at one point, Merrill said, 'If we have to choose be-tween being the historic adviser to the company or participating in this financing, we will leave you at the altar [because] we want to go plan the financing because there's more fees.'"

In late March, Zell broke the logjam when he increased his bid to $34 a share and upped his personal investment to $315 million, part of an incredible deal in which the grave dancer would get a ten-year option to buy about 40 percent of the company for no more than $600 million. The Chandlers swung behind the Zell deal once they figured out that they could minimize their capital gains taxes. Even skeptics like Persily at Citigroup began to understand that the enhancements to the Tribune's cash flow enabled by Zell's unique structure made the finances of Zell's deal comparable to management's self-help plan, despite the higher debt levels. "That's how I got comfortable. At the end of the day, there wasn't that much difference between them," said Persily. At the last minute, Zell also cut into the deal another big player—Bank of America, an institution that had a track record with Zell and Tribune and one he had been secretly courting since early March. To make room for Bank of America's fees, he reduced the other banks' share of the take, particularly Citigroup, with whom he had no relations. The Zell team also tucked into its proposal a provision that would reward key Tribune managers with a hefty "success" bonus if the deal worked. The Tribune Special Committee, elated to have found a complete solution to its problems in a single deal, approved of Zell's deal with the company's board on April 1, 2007.

There was no end of whooping and backslapping among the investment banks that won the Tribune lottery. At JPMorgan Chase, Sanjay Jain, the firm's vice president, sent a note congratulating the bank's Tribune team, including Peter Cohen, the bank's Tribune client executive, pointing out that the bank's chairman, Jamie Dimon, who once worked in Chicago, had been watching the Tribune deal closely. Cohen, who had flown to Chicago from a ski vacation in Aspen, Colorado, responded: "Thx dude. Can you say ka-ching!" At Merrill Lynch, Costa and Mohr got several "way to go" messages, including one from an investment banking colleague who colored his note with a tinge of caution: "Guys—truly amazing financial engineering. Even more kudos after reading [about the details.] In terms of applicability, my biggest question is can you (and would anyone really want to) do this. . . . Would any management team or Board really want to tighten the screws this much if they weren't effectively forced into it and had no other options."

But Jieun (Jayna) Choi, an analyst at JPMorgan Chase, exposed, in a crude e-mail, the attitudes that then prevailed on Wall Street, where the banks had built a billion-dollar business collecting big fees for mega-loans that they made and quickly fobbed off on other investors:

> There is wide speculation that [Tribune] might have [taken on] so much debt that all of its assets aren't gonna cover the debt in case of (knock-knock) you know what. Well that's what we [the bank's Tribune team] are saying, too. But we're doing this 'cause it's enough to cover our bank debt. So, lesson learned from this deal: our (here I mean JPM's) business strategy for TRB, but probably not only limited to TRB is 'hit and run'—we'll s_uck the sponsor's a$$ as long as we can s_uck $$$ out of the (dying or dead?) client's pocket, and we really don't care as long as our a$$ is well-covered. Fxxk 2nd/private guys— they'll be swallowed by big a$$ banks like us, anyways."

For their work over six months that ended in June 2007, Tribune paid the investment bankers and advisers a total of $146.7 million. Add to that the $14.2 million in other fees related to phase one of the deal and you get to about $161 million, more than enough to fund a newsroom that would bring news to the citizens of Los Angeles for a year and employ more than nine hundred journalists.

By now, FitzSimons had climbed on the Zell bandwagon, too, saying the company had the kind of strong cash flows to help pay down the debt encumbered in the Zell deal and that it would "reengineer" its operations to create more efficiencies. In other words, more cuts, mainly in staffing. Zell praised the deal, although he was singing from a different hymnal. The way he saw it, Tribune's assets were worth

$16 billion, and it was only taking on $12 billion to $13 billion in loans, far more than enough to cover any investors who owned the debt. Tribune shareholders approved the deal, too. Nearly 65 percent of the company's shares outstanding voted, and 97.5 percent gave the deal a thumbs-up.

Even though anyone with an ounce of financial sense could see that the deal would generate inevitable cost cuts, I, and journalists like me, preferred to think otherwise. Hearing someone talk about a future that didn't rely solely on cost cuts was music to our ears. As I listened to the new boss, I foolishly believed that I had just gained a partner in trying to figure out the correct mix of revenues and budgetary discipline to finance journalism. Not too long after the first phase of the deal had closed, my phone rang and the soft voice on the other end of the line threw me. "This is Sam Zell. You wanted to talk to me?" Zell asked. I had called Zell's office after he'd given an interview to the *Chicago Tribune*, and I asked for equal treatment for the *Los Angeles Times*. Zell was polite and solicitous, telling me he was at Stanford University in northern California giving a speech, that he would be glad to talk to the *Los Angeles Times*, and that he would soon be heading my way to spend the weekend at his house in Malibu. To facilitate an interview, I naïvely offered to pick him up at the airport and drive him to his home, but he informed me his personal jet could easily deposit him near Malibu, one of Los Angeles' most coveted, affluent neighborhoods. He said he would get back to me shortly with plans.

About an hour after his call, my phone rang. Zell said he would fly into the Signature Air offices at the Los Angeles Airport, where he had lined up a private room. My reporters and I could talk to him over refreshments. "Does that sound good?" he asked. After I replied yes, his tone assumed the hard, blunt edge I would hear often in the coming months.

"I was going to invite all of you to come to my house in Malibu until you sent a fucking reporter up there and scared the shit out of my housekeeper," Zell barked. I was unaware that we had sent anyone anywhere near Zell's house and asked what he was talking about. "Some guy named Lopez," he responded. "Let me tell you something, you want to talk to me, call me and I'll talk. But you don't fuck with my employees. Got that?" I apologized if any of our reporters has scared anyone, and added that he must be referring to our columnist, Steve Lopez, who, I assured Zell, was a professional. I couldn't imagine him bullying anyone, particularly a housekeeper. I told Zell I would look into it and get back to him, but he hung up after telling me where we would meet early on a Friday afternoon. I asked Doug Frantz to find Lopez and learn what had happened.

A couple of days later, I watched as Zell's huge jet pulled up to the Signature Air hanger and a diminutive, balding, elfish-looking, sixty-five-year-old man with gray hair and a beard stepped off. He ranked number fifty-two on the *Forbes* list of the four hundred richest Americans and had a personal fortune estimated at $4.5 billion before the latest $39 billion sale of his real estate venture, but you never would have guessed it from his appearance. He wore his signature jeans, an open-collared striped shirt, and a rumpled blue jacket.

Zell may have known a lot about deals and finance, but it soon became clear he didn't know much about the newspaper game. Any columnist worth his salt loves anything that adds juice to a column, and Zell's reaction to a simple inquiry by Lopez had quickly elevated a spat over beach access in tony Malibu from a ho-hum column to an opportunity to publicly needle the new boss. I could see Lopez smiling as he gave his side of his story in his column, in which he affirmed his point of view to the new man in town:

> Zell lives a couple of hundred yards from the public beach in question. But since you have to go through gates to get to his place or to the surf, I thought it was only fair to ask if he knew anything about the dispute. So I rang the buzzer at his compound and a female voice answered on the intercom, saying he wasn't in. I asked where he could be reached, then left my name and phone number.

A half hour later an editor reached me on my cellphone. He said Zell had heard about my visit and wanted to know why some guy named Lopez was harassing his house staff. He said he makes himself directly available to those who need to talk to him and he didn't appreciate me upsetting the staff.

Wait a minute pal. I've harassed people before and this wasn't harassment.

And another thing, Your plan for buying this company makes me a co-owner, so let me be the first to inform you that you didn't buy another trailer park [a reference to a story we had run involving a trailer park owned by Zell's firm]. This is a newspaper, and it's our job to chase stories, even if it means knocking on the boss' door.

Frantz showed me the Lopez column, which concluded that Zell's property wasn't involved in the dispute, and I told him to run it. As I introduced the *Times* staffers present at the airport interview, I told Zell that Lopez had explained what had happened in a column the morning after the exchange with his housekeeper. He clearly hadn't read it, and I could see he didn't intend to. But as quickly as his temperature rose at the mention of Lopez's name, Zell reverted to his charming side, answering questions politely, smiling at reporters, particularly Sallie Hofmeister, then a deputy financial editor, who peppered him with queries about his plans. When she asked Zell what it was about FitzSimons that had impressed him, he dropped his bomb: "Did I ever say I was impressed with Dennis?" Zell shot back. "Did I ever say *anything* about Dennis? He is sincere. And I think he hopes the deal goes through."

# 17

## The Penguin Parable

On June 4, 2007, JPMorgan Chase and Merrill Lynch made a series of wire transfers of just over $7 billion to Tribune Company. Tribune used the money to buy back 126 million shares of Tribune stock at $34 each; pay Citicorp the $2.5 billion it had borrowed to fund the company's 2006 stock buyback scheme; pay $1.46 million to the Wall Street law firm that had advised the banks involved in the deal; and fork over $161 million to the investment bankers that financed Zell's acquisition of the company. The transfers and fees paid only for the first phase of Zell's debt-laden takeover of Tribune Company, but that was enough for now: The transfer rescued Tribune shareholders of all stripes, including employees like me. The deal was on.

Love him or hate him, we all owed the grave dancer a vote of thanks. Without Zell in the picture, short sellers and other Wall Street sharks probably would have driven the company's stock on the open market far below $20 per share. Investors who responded to Zell's tender offer tried to sell back 90 percent of Tribune's outstanding stock to the company, but the two-phase buyback had been structured so that Tribune would reacquire only half its shares during the first phase of the deal. So the company prorated the Zell offer and sopped up 52 percent of outstanding Tribune shares, leaving those still holding Tribune stock with the option to either sell them in the open market or hold them until phase two of Zell's $34 per share offer kicked in, probably six months down the road.

The fire sale on Wall Street had a bigger impact in Tribune corporate suites than in the company's newsrooms. *Tribune* journalists held stock in the company but not anywhere near the levels held by the people who had thrust the company into its mess. Many *Tribune* reporters and editors were just as interested in the comments that Zell had made at the airport as they were in the selling price of Tribune stock. Zell knew exactly what he was doing when he responded to Hofmeister's question about FitzSimons, and his answer fueled speculation that the Tribune CEO was doomed, which was fine with most journalists at the *Los Angeles Times* as well as at the *Chicago Tribune*.

FitzSimons had shown little respect for print journalists and newsroom leaders wedded to traditional journalistic values, but he was particularly hostile to editors who he felt had slighted him, like Wolinsky at the *Times*, a paper that FitzSimons really liked to disparage. Just after telling me over breakfast that he didn't think I'd accomplished much, FitzSimons came to a lunch with my top editors that Hiller had arranged. Hiller, who loved to attend gabfests, bowed out of this one, and I soon found out why. Midway through the lunch, FitzSimons asked everyone for their thoughts on the *Wall Street Journal*'s recent decision to place ads on page one of its paper. He knew the mere mention of the subject would cause indigestion around a table of editors who immediately attacked the idea. But he clearly enjoyed upsetting everyone, arguing that all papers would have to consider the appearance of ads on prominent page one. As he left the building to return to Chicago, he knew he had left me to deal with the fallout. "Sorry to do that," he said to me with a smile, as I walked with him toward an elevator. "But *I just had* to come out here and drop that bomb."

By then, the journalists in the newsroom of the *Los Angeles Times* had done what I asked of them on my first day: They had given me the opportunity to earn their respect, despite their skepticism about my ties to Tribune. And I had tried to live up to my word to make tough but fair decisions. Not everyone agreed with my approach, and some journalists probably agreed with FitzSimons. FitzSimons, after all, wasn't the only one urging me to dump Wolinsky and editors like him who adhered strongly to the values that had been championed by Otis Chandler. Some of the more Internet savvy journalists saw the Wolinskys of the world as "old school" *Times* stalwarts who fought change simply to preserve their positions of power and influence. There was a kernel of truth to that. Wolinsky probably would have benefited from a change. But removing Wolinsky was hardly a priority for me at the time.

Some in the newsroom compared me to Baquet and thought I came out wanting. Baquet had spent more time talking about stories, signaling that he cared deeply about quality journalism. And it's true, I didn't walk the floor enough. It wasn't as if I didn't care about good journalism, as anyone with whom I'd worked at the *Chicago Tribune* could attest. But I had to face head on some of the issues that Baquet had deferred. Days after I'd arrived in Los Angeles, I had a long dinner and cigars with Baquet. He forecasted what I'd face when I arrived—of the strengths and weaknesses on the staff, the changes he'd put off because he spent so much time wrangling over the budget. At one point, I told my assistant Polly Ross to set aside one hour a day for me to roam around the newsroom to talk to reporters and editors. But inevitably, she reassigned those sacred hours for more pressing items of the day. All too often I agreed because I knew Ross was one of the few people I could count on to watch my back. I should have done better.

I also knew that running a newsroom was no popularity contest. I deeply respected Baquet. But I was not going to get anywhere trying to be like him. I had to be my own person, make my own decisions, follow my guts, and live with my decisions. I actually dealt with many of the issues that Baquet and I had discussed, like the paper's Sunday magazine, which was losing $6 million a year. I cut the magazine staff, appointed a new editor, made it a monthly magazine instead of a weekly, renamed it the *Los Angeles Times Magazine*, and reoriented it to showcase profiles written by some of the paper's best writers. By the time I left, it was nearly in the black.

But the biggest change I made at the *Times* involved the relations between the printed newspaper and www.latimes.com. Both Baquet and Carroll agreed that they, like a lot of editors around the country, had failed to pay enough attention to the Internet as a medium for news. When I took over, relations between the paper and its online effort were awful. Many Internet journalists viewed print reporters at the *Times* as stodgy old coots who didn't get that the world had evolved to a new diet of news with more liberal standards. Journalists could no longer wait for the daily deadline to post a story; they had to do it now and be judged by how many people clicked on the story, not by how important it was deemed by some ivory-towered editor. Print journalists viewed their online brethren as a bunch of naïve kids unschooled in the basics of journalism and the standards that made the *Times* Otis Chandler's newspaper. Both sides ignored one another, and almost all stories had to run in the newspaper before they got posted online. I knew that things had to change.

Baquet had created a group of top-notch reporters and editors he dubbed the Spring Street Project to explore a way forward for the paper. I met with the group soon after I'd arrived, just as they were drafting a report that called for a vigorous renewal of time, effort, and money for the paper's floundering online efforts. Capitalizing on Baquet's report, I decided to launch an initiative to change the staff's thinking about www.latimes.com. I replaced the editor in charge of the newsroom's online efforts and scheduled a speech to announce some major changes to the staff. I told the journalists in the room some of the unpleasant truths I'd discovered in my initial months at our paper—about how journalists needed to get concerned about precipitous declines in ad revenue that paid their salaries; about the cold, defensive, bunker mentality I had encountered in an otherwise skilled newsroom; about the crucial need for a change in attitude. From that day forward, I said the *Times* would break news on the Internet twenty-four hours a day and explain or analyze it in the newspaper, a complete change in thinking.

I appointed Russ Stanton, a *Times* business editor who had displayed an interest in online news, as a special editor for innovation. Stanton would report directly to me. One of his first tasks would be to create a crash training program to turn every journalist in the newsroom into a savvy, multimedia journalist. I would be his first student. I launched a redesign of the print newspaper with a twist that made many in the room with memories of the Staples incident squirm. The redesign committee I created would be led by people schooled in the values of the newsroom but would also include people from our online efforts and from the circulation, marketing, advertising, and production departments at the paper. I decided to put the squabbling tribes in a room and make them agree on a path forward that would transform a great newspaper into an awesome, powerful storytelling machine in print and online. My challenge to them: Build me the kind of newspaper you would design if you were starting from scratch.

Frankly, my speech was long overdue. Editors rally journalists by confronting them with facts and challenging them to overcome obstacles, regardless of their height. I gave the newsroom some cold hard facts about revenues that helped pay for them and their journalism: In 2004, the *Los Angeles Times* had collected $102 million in print advertising from auto dealers. By 2007, that total would fall to around $55 million. "That's $47 million dollars gone," I said. "We've made some of that up online. In 2004, online auto classified ads totaled only $7 million. By 2007, digital auto ads would come in at $31 million, or an increase of $24 million. But," I told them, "notice what is happening here—we lost $47 million in print and only recovered $24 million online. For every $2 we lost in print, we are recouping only $1 online. The story is similar in other areas: Some categories such as real estate are doing well, but it is only a matter of time before it too goes south unless we build online readership faster while keeping our print readers."

I allowed that there were many reasons for the declines, some having to do with the way we practiced journalism, and some not. I continued, "But we can't hide from the fact that smart competitors like Google and craigslist are stealing readers and advertisers from us through innovative strategies that are undermining the business model we've relied on for decades." I told the staff we had to change and change now.

My speech, to my surprise, got a lot of national attention and a good reception in the editorial department, where I had started to pick up some support. It's always hard for anyone to judge how well they are doing in volatile situations like the one into which I had walked. Colleagues around the country with friends on the staff would occasionally call to tell me if they had heard good or bad things about me from their friends. Most of the time they were positive. One exchange made me feel particularly good; a metro reporter I encountered in the newsroom told me that he and his colleagues were once again talking about stories at news meetings, rather than their problems. I had started wrestling with the biggest challenge I faced—how to cover this large, sprawling, disjointed metropolis I now called home—when the first signs of trouble hit.

Newspapers and the Tribune Company had done precious little research and development despite the challenges they faced. I looked at what data we had, but I knew of its limits and that the real answers rested in insights developed by interactions with readers. So, I spent a lot of time trying to learn about the community during the sixteen months I was editor of the *Times*. I had time to attend functions at night since my wife had remained in Chicago and I was alone. Trying to commute back to Chicago proved tough, too, so I often remained in Los Angeles over the weekends. Sometimes I would bike or drive to a certain community to get a feel for Los Angeles and just walk around and talk to people, ask them questions about what they wanted and needed from a newspaper like the *Los Angeles Times*. But every chance I could, I also tried to meet with community groups such as Zocalo, a cultural forum that attracted many *Los Angeles Times* readers interested in cultural issues, to hone my instincts for the right mix of news for metro coverage.

Not too long after FitzSimons had dropped his bomb about front-page ads, I met Hiller at a meeting of community leaders in the Inland Empire, a vast, rapidly growing swath of suburban communities and towns east of Los Angeles. I had been told by numerous readers that *Times* editors seemed like nose-in-the-air types who didn't have a feel for the wide range of communities on which the paper had to report. I thought it wouldn't hurt to spend a little time with readers and leaders outside of the office. Like a lot of folks I met, the Inland Empire group told me that the *Times* lacked a strong presence in the community. They wanted coverage of state politics, the price of water, the economy, and trade issues related to the businesses that had located in the Inland Empire to be near rail and truck routes that linked the region to the Los Angeles port, a huge 7,500-acre international transportation hub twenty miles south of downtown Los Angeles. It handled more than 40 percent of the waterborne container traffic flowing into the United States.

Because California voters tend to pass initiatives that inhibit local government, community leaders like Greg Devereaux, the city manager of Ontario, told me that towns like his needed enhanced coverage from Sacramento and Washington and that they didn't "expect the *Times* to cover our local school board." I soon began thinking of a twofold metro strategy that was similar to Puerner's idea: Build a better local presence by beefing up and showcasing new bureaus strategically located throughout the region, and capitalize on the paper's ability to cover the big issues of the day through its seasoned journalists at national and international bureaus, particularly our correspondents in Sacramento, the state capitol.

But Puerner was Carroll's publisher; Hiller was mine and he didn't agree with me or Puerner. David Murphy, a *Chicago Tribune* advertising man dispatched to Los Angeles to revive the paper's sagging ad revenues, had Hiller's ear. He told him advertisers didn't like the weighty content in the *Times*. "The dogs don't like the dog food," he would often say. Murphy and others argued for zoned local sections with news tailored to specific towns, an expensive editorial proposition that would force me to divert resources to attempt something that was impossible—beating the locals at their own game. It was a strategy designed for advertisers, not readers, and one championed by FitzSimons. Some editors, particularly those allied with www.latimes.com, agreed with Murphy's local zoning initiatives, which also included more "innovative" ad positions in the pages of the paper. But others told me the *Times* had tried zoning and it hadn't worked. As I gave Hiller a ride back from the Inland Empire, he told me that the company's lackluster revenues were jeopardizing the Zell deal. Just before we reached downtown Los Angeles, he mentioned he'd all but decided to help resolve the problem by adopting some innovative ad positions, including one on page one of the newspaper.

I knew my reaction angered Hiller; his face got red and he grew silent when I told him that I not only opposed ads on page one, but that I didn't know if I wanted to be the editor who put them there. Over the ensuing weeks, I discussed front-page ads often, not only with Hiller but also with William Pate and Nils Larsen, Zell's top lieutenants who had responded positively to my invitation to come to the *Los Angeles Times* to learn about the biggest paper in the company.

Once his anger eased, Hiller actually tried to understand my thinking. I did—and still do—oppose ads on the front page of the newspaper. I told Hiller that every newspaper should have one page dedicated solely to the news and that it should be the front page, the place where knowledgeable, skilled editors steeped in the news select the most important, significant, and relevant news of the day for readers. An honest page one crafted by professionals would house news of death, sacrifice, heroics, and knotty decisions about complex policy decisions. At times, editors could punctuate the drama with lighter fare, something that was sheer fun to read. But commercial messages urging a reader to buy a Toyota Prius or a Prada purse had no place in that space; ads would rob the page of integrity, cheapen it, and chip away at its authority. To my mind, the dispute was about the values of the paper. About who we were, not about money.

Moreover, I told Hiller, Pate, and Larsen that front-page ads could endanger the paper's perceived value as an advertising medium. As an avid newspaper consumer, I knew Tiffany often ran its small ads on page two of the *New York Times*, the *Chicago Tribune*, and the *Los Angeles Times*, and I expected to see them there. I couldn't—and still don't—remember who advertises on page one of the *Wall Street Journal*. I pick up page one to get the news, not to see where I can get a good deal on a car. What will happen, I asked, if an advertiser buys an ad on page one of the *Los Angeles Times* and fails to get a good response because of readers like me? As I saw it, advertisers would be scratching their heads over why they bothered to purchase ad space on any page of the paper if they didn't receive the response they were after from the almighty page one.

I think I was more adamantly opposed to page one ads than my staff. As scuttlebutt about my disagreement with the publisher swept through the newsroom, some reporters and editors told me they sympathized with me but understood if I had to acquiesce. But I wasn't budging on this one. I told Hiller that he was the publisher and that, if he wanted to run ads on page one, that was his decision. But, I also told him, as the paper's editor, I felt an obligation to oppose him and, if questioned about the change in policy, to be publicly critical if he decided to diminish the front page of a paper I edited. I later learned that Hiller had decided against the ads, but FitzSimons forced his hand. When he announced his decision, I was publicly critical. I thought my comments were mild, but editors urged me to tone them down lest I come off as insubordinate. In the end, I merely said I disagreed with the decision and that I didn't think ads had a place on page one. The story announcing Hiller's decision, in which my opinion was stated, ran on the inside pages of the business section and prompted a sharp rebuke from FitzSimons, who said my comments "made a fool of [the] publisher." Hiller probably agreed, and, although he never said so, I think it marked a turning point in our relationship. In retrospect, I should not have criticized him publicly. It was unfair of me to do so.

Even after we started putting ads on the front page, Hiller, Murphy, and I continued to joust over timing and taste, but the controversy regarding my relations with them paled in comparison to the turmoil in the financial markets after the first phase of the deal had closed. I had naïvely thought things would start to improve once the deal was in place. On their visit, Pate and Larsen spent a day at the *Times* and impressed the staff with their positive comments about the paper. They echoed Zell's remarks that we couldn't cut our way to prosperity and showed far more sophisticated understanding of newsroom dynamics than did FitzSimons. At a dinner the night before I escorted them into the newsroom, when I mentioned FitzSimons' anger at my comments about passing out bonuses while I was cutting staff, Pate responded, "What did he expect you to say? You're an editor." But things didn't get better after phase one—they got worse.

■

One thing overshadowed all else as the company lumbered toward the close of phase two. The debt burden that Zell had piled on Tribune further dimmed the company's lights on Wall Street. The loans gave Zell the money he needed to buy half of the company's stock at $34 per share, but shareholders who couldn't sell all of their stock in the phase one tender offer soon saw the price drop as analysts and traders speculated that added debt and Tribune Company's failure to hit its financial targets would sink the company before Zell could close phase two. The Chandlers didn't help things. In phase one the family had sold close to 28 million shares of Tribune for nearly $1 billion. Once the first phase closed, the three Chandler directors promptly resigned from the Tribune board and sold the family's remaining 20 million shares for $31.19 each (about $625 million) in one huge sale to Goldman Sachs. Goldman quickly resold the shares to other investors for $31.50 each, which was $6.2 million more than Goldman had paid for the stock. The Chandler sale put downward pressure on Tribune stock that the company had not yet reacquired. Investors speculated that the Chandlers would have waited a few months to get

$34 a share if they'd had any faith in the success of the Zell deal. Their sale to Goldman made prospective investors assume that there was something amiss.

Jill Greenthal, a Blackstone Group banker advising the McCormick Trust, noted: "From what I heard, Goldman was way oversubscribed on the Chandler block. The stock has pretty consistently traded over $32 a share, so the arbs [short for arbitrage, a class of trader that tries to make big money on small price movements] all thought getting a chance to buy at $31.50 [from Goldman] was a way to make sure money.... Interesting logic ... will be interesting [to see what happens when] they all try to capture [or profit from] the spread [by selling the stock].... The fun never stops." Stinehart said the stewards of the family wealth had an absolute duty to dump the stock: "A quarter of the [Chandler Trust's] net worth was in this stock, and they had suspended paying dividends for six months."

Zell dismissed speculation that the deal wouldn't close as "shit happens." When the first phase closed, he recalled, "I thought the chances of getting the second stage closed were pretty high. As the months [passed], my belief in it materially decreased. One week the stock was trading at 27, the next week someone was taking 34. I tried to get everyone to listen to me [telling investors he intended to close phase two at $34 per share]. It was indicative of where the markets were at the time; panic was in the air." A report from Lehman Brothers, a firm whose bone-headed decisions would plunge it into bankruptcy just twelve months hence, speculated that Tribune stock would fall to anywhere from $3 to $10 per share if phase two of the deal didn't close. Other analysts started bad-mouthing the deal, too.

Although Zell and his lieutenants publicly voiced confidence in the transaction, they scrambled behind the scenes as the panic-induced pressure intensified and everyone looked for ways to keep the banks from pulling back on their commitment to fund phase two of the deal. Hiller asked that I squeeze expenses and stop filling open jobs to help lower the budget. Although I complied, I began to worry that we were reverting to the Tribune's ironclad controls where accountants, not editors, made crucial decisions on newsroom resources. But Chris Avetisian, an accountant on the business side, pleaded, "Just do this for me so we can get this deal closed and get these assholes in Chicago off our backs."

But the real problem wasn't in Chicago; it was in New York, on Wall Street, where speculation about Tribune's fate soon bit the hand of the investment banks that fed it. Although no one knew it at the time, the Tribune deal was a bellwether for the financial market meltdown that would bring the entire global economy to its knees in months. The same kind of greed, ego, and hubris that generated reckless lending and fat fees for bankers in the subprime market mess powered Zell's acquisition of Tribune. Davan Maharaj, a journalist I had promoted to business editor of the *Los Angeles Times*, started warning me in the summer of 2007 that a disaster loomed in the subprime mortgage market. Banks had made billions of dollars in mortgage loans to dubious borrowers, collected their loan origination fees, and promptly sold the loans to other investors so they didn't have to worry about getting their money back—a process called "syndication." In other words, repayment of the loan was now someone else's problem.

Tribune Company was hardly in a class with some schoolteacher in Temecula who had borrowed $1 million to buy an Inland Empire dream castle. FitzSimons had failed to hit the financial projections the company had made earlier in the year, and soft ad markets at papers where the real estate bubble was starting to burst (in California and Florida) knocked the company's 2007 operating profit off 40 percent. And the company wasn't generating the huge cash flows that it had racked up a few years earlier. But Tribune was still quite profitable; it earned $634 million in profit off revenues of just over $5 billion in 2007, a margin of 12.5 percent, hardly the kind of results that justified the doomsday forecasts on Wall Street.

Nevertheless, Tribune Company and FitzSimons faced a thorny problem: They needed more cash to generate the payments the company would have to make, not only on the $7 billion debt that Zell had just piled on Tribune's books, but also on the $4 billion to

$5 billion debt he intended to take on to fund phase two of the deal. The banks had an even bigger problem.

When JPMorgan Chase tried to syndicate the loans and resell them to big institutional investors like pension and mutual funds, it encountered resistance. Short sellers who profited when stock prices fell and analysts like Craig Huber of Lehman Brothers whose reports on Tribune were particularly negative bred pessimism about the Zell deal. In effect, the market started treating Tribune like the schoolteacher in Temecula: While the schoolteacher might be able to get a $1 million mortgage loan, there was no way he could repay it on a teacher's salary. One brokerage firm analysis suggested Tribune was more likely to default on its bonds than was Ford Motor Company, which had just reported a $12.6 billion loss. Banks soon became increasingly reluctant to extend loans in the second half of 2007—not just to Tribune but to all types of borrowers.

At JPMorgan Chase, no one was singing "ka-ching." When the bank initially started syndicating the Tribune loans, traders in the secondary syndication markets had priced them at their face value. In other words, big institutional investors would pay $1 billion for $1 billion worth of Tribune debt so they could collect the interest (just under 8 percent at the time) the company was paying on the deal. But the uneasiness of the markets had changed things, and by July 2007, Peter Cohen told his boss, the bank's chairman Jamie Dimon, that the syndication efforts had garnered only $3 billion worth of orders on $7.1 billion in loans.

Cohen suggested that Dimon call FitzSimons and Zell, who had joined the Tribune board when the deal had closed, to discuss deal "enhancements" that would help the bank "clear the market and set the right tone for the second step"—billions more in loans to the Tribune to enable it to purchase the rest of the stock. "There is tremendous deal fatigue . . . particularly on the Tribune side," Cohen told his boss, "and it would be reassuring for Dennis [FitzSimons] to hear from you. He values your advice and will have to discuss these changes to the deal with his board this weekend." One of the enhancements to get the loans off the books of the banks involved a price cut. The fees that they were being paid to work with Tribune would be largely wiped out by the loss, but at least they would not have the loans on their books.

To close phase one of the deal, the Tribune had secured a solvency opinion, or a certification from an independent outside expert that examines a company's finances to make sure that the additional debt won't break the borrower's financial back. Federal banking regulations prohibit banks from making loans to companies that are insolvent, and banks often required opinions from solvency experts that function like a financial good housekeeping seal of approval. Now the Tribune Company needed another solvency opinion to close phase two of the deal, and the second opinion became crucial, because many analysts started speculating that the additional debt in phase two would push the company over the edge.

Soon the panicked mood that dominated the markets prompted Wall Street to begin speculating about what would happen if Tribune Company couldn't get the solvency opinion it needed to finish phase two. It wasn't long before the markets for the company's stock, bonds, and debt went haywire. Tribune stock, which Zell had already committed to buy back at $34 per share, dropped to $25 by August, no doubt helped along by short sellers who profited from declining prices. The company's outstanding bonds took an even bigger hit, and the $3 billion or so in loans that had already been syndicated fell in value by as much as 10 percent, presenting banks with a huge problem.

If a bank that had just lent Tribune Company $1 billion tried to sell the loan to someone else, the investor, jittery about the market chaos infecting Wall Street, might pay only $900 million to take the loan off the bank's hands. Why? Because the speculation about the company raised fears that Tribune would be unable to repay the loan. The investor demanded a discount to compensate for the higher risk involved in the deal. That meant that the banker trying to syndicate or sell the loan faced a $100 million loss. Multiply that number by four for the $4 billion in loans still on the banks' books and you get $400 million in red ink, more than double the fees they had collected for making the loans in the first place.

Of course, the banks could always simply do what banks were set up to do: make a loan and profit on the difference between what it paid depositors for its funds and what it collected in interest from the party that borrowed the money. The Tribune, after all, was paying just under 8 percent interest to the banks for the loan at a time when banks had to pay far less to depositors or other sources of lendable money. But that would have been dreadfully old-fashioned in markets that had developed things like credit default swaps—insurance contracts that Wall Street banks and big investors bought and sold in a trillion-dollar market so they could gamble on the borrower's ability to repay loans. But holding onto the loan presented a problem for the JPMorgan Chases of the world, too. Keeping the loan on their books would force banks to increase their financial reserves, a practice that crimped banks' style and profits. Meanwhile, the premiums banks would have to pay for insurance protecting against a default by Tribune soared.

At JPMorgan Chase, one alarmed banker working on the case wrote her boss that the bank was "totally underwater" on the Zell deal and suggested that someone meet with Zell to see if he could help clear the way to get the debt on the books of an institutional investor. Jimmy Lee, a JPMorgan Chase vice chairman who had also played a major role in Rupert Murdoch's acquisition of the *Wall Street Journal*, soon sat down with Zell to explain what they were up against: "Met with Sam today and told him all of the issues around selling the remainder of his acquisition debt . . . i.e., it couldn't be done," Lee recalled. "To his credit, he said he would do what was necessary to help us. We discussed him selling more assets, improving the yield, etc. I also raised it would probably be helpful for him to be involved in the operations of the company [as the CEO] to the extent permitted, given the softness in the space and our need to have a strong story to sell."

Zell wasn't willing to raise interest rates, put in more money, or do anything that would change the economics of the deal, but shortly after the meeting with Lee, FitzSimons, who assumed he would resume his post as CEO once phase two closed, asked Zell what he was thinking for the future. Zell put him off, saying they'd discuss that later in September. Some of the bankers, meanwhile, started thinking about ways to renege on their commitment to fund phase two of the deal. JPMorgan Chase banker Darryl Jacobson asked if the bank could suggest to the firm slated to do the crucial solvency opinion that the phase-two debt might so encumber Tribune Company that it would be unable to refinance some existing debt and meet its future "obligations as they come due," a key hurdle Tribune would have to overcome to get its solvency certificate. But Dimon wasn't about to shaft a major customer like Zell: "That's like asking if the weather was bad. Yes, by that time, the weather was bad. [But when] we sign the binding commitment, it's a binding commitment. That's . . . why you have a bank." One Deutsche Bank analyst concluded that Zell had locked the banks into the deal so securely that they couldn't get off the hook even if they wanted to: "We believe that the Tribune going private transaction will [close]," the bank told its clients. "There may be some unhappy lenders in the end, but our understanding is that Zell/ESOP [has] secured financing via commitment letter, which essentially locks in financing to complete the deal. Our impression is that the agreements are pretty tight."

Zell's determination to buy Tribune puzzled some, who speculated that he did the deal to show up the blue bloods in the Chicago business establishment—the people who had always looked down their noses at the blunt, motorcycle riding, rough-neck billionaire. But Dimon disagreed: "Sam until very late in the game thought he was going to make a lot of money on this." Zell claimed that he hadn't invested in Tribune to turn a quick buck; he was betting on the long haul and would make a killing by holding on to Tribune for ten years, at which point he could sell out with a huge profit structured in a way to avoid a big tax bill. "We've never been flip artists," Zell explained, "we've held stuff forever. I still own a building I bought in 1966." The internal math on the deal put Zell's rate of return at 20–30 percent. When Tribune's stock dropped to $25 a share, he approached JPMorgan Chase to see if he could accelerate loans to buy the stock on the open market instead of forking over $34 per share a few months later. But the bank turned him down because the proposed changes would have weakened its status as a creditor if the whole deal went belly up.

As fall approached, the banks began to realize that divine intervention would be necessary to renege on their commitments, which they compared to paying a dollar for something that was only worth 92 cents. Analysts at the lead banks suddenly became quite interested in Tribune operations, firing off e-mails to Tribune, each other, and to Nils Larsen at Equity Group Investments (EGI) asking eleventh-hour due diligence questions about the pricing and volume of the company's top twenty-five advertisers and whether the interactive business could maintain a growth rate of 15 percent if Tribune cut online investment by 50 percent. Some of their questions exposed the banks' superficial knowledge of the company to which they had just lent billions of dollars. At the *Los Angeles Times*, Jack Klunder had started paring back junk circulation, a move that resulted in reports of declining circulation, prompting Yang Chen at Citicorp to wonder what was going on: "What factors are driving this trend? Who is gaining share in these markets? Other newspapers?"

As the stock bobbed around in value and a cloud of doubt loomed over the deal, the pressure on the banks and the company increased. Bankers figured the only way that they could ditch their obligation was if Tribune failed its solvency test.

Things got pretty sticky. At Tribune, the company's CFO, Don Grenesko, and his aide, Chandler Bigelow, had hired a Milwaukee-based company, Valuation Research Corporation (VRC), to conduct the required tests to demonstrate that Tribune would be solvent, even after it had borrowed all of the money needed for both phases of the deal. Grenesko and Bigelow authorized Tribune to pay VRC $1.5 million for its analysis—a head-turner since it was the highest fee VRC had ever charged for an opinion. The company had never done such a big complex deal and it had to turn around the opinion in a relatively short time-frame.

Not long after Tribune had hired VRC, Citicorp approached Houlihan Lokey Howard & Zukin, a competitor to VRC, and offered it $500,000 for a quick analysis of VRC's work, a sum that Scott Beiser at the firm deemed "chump change" for something that "smelled like divorce work." At one point, Tribune and Zell agreed to some changes in the terms of phase two after Rajesh Kapadia from JPMorgan Chase told Larsen: "We are still losing money.... [The Tribune board should want] a market-clearing deal not [one that] leaves a levered company with its underwriters stuffed." Meanwhile, Zell's company, EGI, contacted a solvency expert to analyze the analysts. They claimed that they were not trying to shoot down someone else's work but trying to get an education in solvency process.

Tribune's general counsel, Crane Kenney, dismissed all the claims about getting an education regarding solvency opinions. "I mean these are the most sophisticated bankers in the world who have done thousands of deals involving solvency opinions, and they say they needed a firm to understand how they work?" Kenney recalled. "The solvency opinion became this issue because the banks I think probably reviewed the credit agreement and said, 'This thing's ironclad. The only hope we have that we don't have to fund these loans that we no longer want to fund is that we can somehow ... take a shot at the solvency.' ... I think they were trying to get out of their obligations by trying to squeeze the solvency certificate."

In the end, though, no one wanted to anger Zell by screwing up his deal. Ben Buettell, one manager at Houlihan Lokey Howard & Zukin, admitted that Houlihan didn't want to be the one to blow the whistle on the deal. "If we end up where I think we all know we would end up with our analysis, we may be the ones to 'kill the deal' so to speak and not certain we want to be involved in that mess," Buettell noted.

■

The wheeling and dealing surrounding the deal would have made great theater in the newsrooms of Tribune papers, had it played out in public. But it all took place behind the scenes far from the eyes and ears of reporters and editors who, thanks to FitzSimons' delusions that he would still be CEO when the deal closed, were contending with other issues. FitzSimons had fallen under the spell of John Kotter, a Harvard Business School professor and consultant who had written a parable about penguins called *Our Iceberg Is Melting*. Kotter used the story to teach companies the ABCs of "transformative change," one of those programs that consultants create to justify their lofty fees, and FitzSimons decided that Tribune needed to change drastically to survive.

Soon journalists saw the company's senior management team running around with Kotter's book preparing for a series of transformative change meetings that FitzSimons mandated. *Our Iceberg Is Melting* is a simplistic story about NoNo, a penguin who resists change (aka the Journalist), and Fred and Alice, penguins who embraced change (everyone else). The book sent a strong message that dissent was bad, and anyone who went the way of NoNo would end up in the drink as the iceberg melted.

The Kotter initiative had about as much a chance of rescuing the company from Wall Street as FitzSimons had of surviving Zell. Nonetheless FitzSimons summoned everyone to Chicago to attend a lecture by Kotter, the big penguin himself. When I didn't show, FitzSimons was livid. I remained in Los Angeles to deal with some angry readers with whom Hiller had promised to meet but whom he must have forgotten about because he had gone to Chicago. I was driving to a meeting in Glendale when Caroline Thorpe, Hiller's secretary called to relay FitzSimons' and Hiller's extreme dismay that I wasn't at the penguin convention. Truthfully, I hadn't known the meeting was mandatory and had told Hiller I would not attend. But I knew the damage had been done.

Sure enough, my failure to show up would result in yet another visit by FitzSimons and more penguin meetings. On the surface, the whole exercise seemed innocent enough. Who, after all, could argue with a company examining the way it did things to determine if the status quo had become harmful? But in months of navel gazing, the Kotter project unleashed pent-up anger in the Tribune's management ranks, igniting a civil war within the company between journalists and the business side, precisely when we desperately needed to work together to address the problems that were dogging the industry. More often than not, the transformative change meetings devolved into acrimony, particularly at the *Los Angeles Times*, where journalists felt they had targets on their backs.

At one session on the first floor of the *Times* headquarters, managing editor John Arthur, a seasoned veteran, vigorously challenged the argument that news decisions should be affected by market rather than straight-up journalistic standards. But folks from ad sales and marketing pointed out that the *Times* had to change because "the consumer was now in charge." Reports generated by the penguin initiative were loaded with phrases like "Retool Everything" and "Change the Culture," implying that traditional journalistic standards had to go. There were meetings and pre-meetings and MBAs from marketing who asked questions like: "You said you want to improve local coverage. When should I benchmark that?" Hiller had hired a consultant to facilitate the evolving debate who kept saying everyone should "get on the bus," until I told her I didn't want to "get on a bus" that was heading off a cliff.

The acrimony in the ranks was nothing compared to what was playing out between Zell and FitzSimons. Soon after the grave dancer had joined the Tribune board, FitzSimons let him know who was in charge of the cemetery. By Zell's account, his instructions from FitzSimons were, "You are on the board, you sit in the board. You don't sit on any committees. You don't have anything to do with it until it is a real deal." Tensions flared again when both men went to Washington to lobby the FCC and key congressmen to support the transfer of broadcast licenses that they needed for their deal. When a reporter at the *Times*' Washington bureau asked Zell a provocative question regarding his views on "current management," he gave an extremely elusive reply. Afterwards, FitzSimons let Zell know he was dealing with someone who grew up in the same space as Joe Giaimo: "I told Sam in no uncertain terms," FitzSimons recalled "that that wasn't acceptable because while I was running this company, I was running this company, and I didn't need anybody undercutting me. It was a little bit more colorful than that." Even after FitzSimons knew he was out of the picture as the deal was about to close, he sat in Zell's office and refused to budge, telling him: "I'm not doing anything. I'm not giving you any power until it closes, and I don't think it's going to close. I'm not moving because I'm not moving. If it doesn't close, then I'm still CEO."

For all of Zell's in-your-face persona, FitzSimons couldn't goad him into a confrontation he didn't want. Behind the scenes, he had asked his trusted aide, Pate, to write a detailed plan outlining what the Zell team should do during the first hundred days after it had taken over Tribune. And one of Pate's strongest recommendations was to dump FitzSimons. Pate felt that FitzSimons wasn't taking the concerns about the solvency of the company seriously enough. In addition to getting rid of FitzSimons, Pate recommended that the company devise some plans on what it would do if the second phase didn't close.

But Zell didn't seem concerned with solvency issues. Zell had planned a major role at the company for Randy Michaels, a former shock jock he had met when he took over a Cincinnati radio company in the 1990s. He asked Michaels to come up with his hundred-day plan for what they should do with Tribune. The plans couldn't have been more different.

In his blueprint, Pate urged Zell to remove not only FitzSimons but numerous other members of his executive team who he criticized for rushing to close the deal, concerned only about the bonuses they'd receive. He recommended meeting with Jack Fuller about the idea of recruiting him to a new board, a move that would signal journalism's place in the pie. And he suggested sharply downsizing the centralized corporate staff at the Tower and delegating to executives involved in operations decision making and profit responsibility. He went so far as to suggest meeting with Burkle and Geffen to assess their interest in buying the *Los Angeles Times*. "If their interest is below $1.5 billion, then pass. The *Los Angeles Times* media group could be a real winner if separated from the Tower," said Pate.

Michaels had something else in mind. In nine pages of bullet points, he reflected a purge mentality with frank suggestions such as: "Identify change leaders and resisters within Tribune, promote and eliminate as appropriate." Michaels saw the biggest challenge as changing the culture of the place: "Begin the process of creating products focused on consumer interest and demand as opposed to some idea of what the citizens ought to know. It's not what they need; it's what they'll read, what they'll watch, what they'll click on, and what they want delivered to the deck of their cellphone." In his plan, Michaels disparaged Tribune newspapers as "staid, grandfatherly and dated" publications holding the company back, although he gave no hint of how he'd engineer change. He recommended identifying people in the company they could get to "drink the Kool-Aid." Finally, he suggested they should conduct a road show "to major business units aimed at resetting the culture. Meet, shake hands with, and answer the questions of as many team members as possible." Journalists and the Tribune took themselves too seriously for Michael's money. In his report, he said they should "have fun."

Although I didn't know about any plans for a road show, a preview came to Los Angeles after Pate called and said Zell had received a request for a meeting with a prominent group of Los Angeles citizens worried about what was going on at the paper, including the late Warren Christopher, the former Secretary of State and probably the only high-level member of the Los Angeles community that could rally the disparate political, commercial, and cultural factions of Los Angeles. "They said Dennis wouldn't come out and meet with them," Pate said, "but I don't see anything wrong with Sam coming out and meeting them, do you?" I agreed that a meeting would be fine.

Warren Christopher and his group had been quite supportive, urging me to stand by my statements that I would not let the paper deteriorate. They believed that a first-class city needed a first-class newspaper and that the *Los Angeles Times* should be on a par with papers out East. "We view you as someone who we hope will hold the line and maintain the paper's stature," Christopher told me. So I worked with Hiller on a plan to stage a lunch in a large room that was once Dorothy Chandler's personal apartment at the *Times*.

A few weeks later, Zell showed up at the *Times* for the lunch wearing his signature jeans and open-collared striped shirt. "I was going to wear a suit and tie," he told the guests, "but I decided not to because I wanted you to see me the way I am." About two dozen women and men sitting around the large U-shaped table seemed charmed at his open and folksy manner. Zell fielded polite yet pointed questions with blunt but respectful replies. The guests came from the world of politics, business, culture, and film, men and women of accomplishment who cared about their community and its newspaper.

Over dessert, when Christopher, the gray eminence, spoke, he diplomatically told Zell of the group's concerns about cuts at the newspaper, particularly rumors of cuts in the *Los Angeles Times* foreign bureaus: "You know, Sam, we view our community as the gateway to the Pacific and we think foreign coverage is quite important." Without missing a beat Zell shot back, "You know, Warren, I don't give a fuck what you think. What I give a fuck about is what David Hiller here thinks, because from now on he's in charge of this newspaper, not some bureaucrat in Chicago."

The room fell silent and all eyes turned to Christopher in his tailored blue suit, French cuff shirt, and tasteful tie, exactly the kind of wardrobe that Zell and his team disparaged. "Well, Sam," Christopher replied, "we appreciate your frankness."

I had scheduled a meeting in my office between Zell and several editors eager to bend his ear. Midway through the session, I asked Steve Lopez to come in to meet the new boss, and both handled the situation with grace and humor. As we walked to the Globe Lobby in the *Times* where Zell's driver was to pick him up, he grabbed my tie and said, "What's with this?" I replied that I wanted him to see me the way I came to work every day and that I was sure he would not want me to dress down just for him. He smiled, pulled out a cigarette, and left for the airport.

# 18

## Closing the Deal

Not long after Zell requested hundred-day plans from Pate and Michaels, Wolinsky walked into my office and shut the door, announcing that there was something he had to tell me. Hiller, Wolinsky said, had been inviting groups of people to tell him how they thought I was doing as an editor, and how well I related to the newsroom.

The news didn't come as a shock to me. A few days before, Davan Maharaj, the paper's business editor, had cryptically told me, "There are people who are supposed to be watching your back who are not watching your back." And several others had appeared in my office in recent days with similar reports, indicating that Hiller was also asking people what they thought of Russ Stanton, the editor I had placed in charge of the newsroom's Internet efforts and a favorite of both Hiller and FitzSimons. I knew Hiller and I knew how he operated; he'd often asked me about people in the same fashion. I knew that he and FitzSimons liked Stanton because he wasn't, well, like me.

I sat down and fired off an e-mail to Hiller letting him know that the reports had gotten back to me and that he was undermining me, feeding newsroom speculation that he was looking for an excuse to depose me. If that's what he wanted, he, of course, had every right to replace me. But I preferred to deal with him head-on. Hiller denied he had any such intentions. But I knew by now that the penguin initiatives championed by FitzSimons drove his almost frantic pleas for change for change's sake.

After I had failed to show up for his Chicago meeting, FitzSimons came to the *Los Angeles Times* for a party hosted for KTLA's anniversary. The Zell team had made it increasingly clear that FitzSimons would not be the CEO once the deal closed. Frantz, the managing editor appointed by Baquet, had decided to step down, and I had appointed two new managing editors, John Arthur and John Montorio. I set up a lunch for them to meet FitzSimons. The night before the four of us would sit down, FitzSimons sent me an odd journalism review article regarding how journalists laid off at Belo papers in Dallas had found new, rewarding paths in life. When one editor heard FitzSimons was coming to Los Angeles again, he quipped: "I guess he wants to piss on the fireplug one more time."

The next day FitzSimons and I both arrived early, and we had a "frank exchange of views." He recited his litany—he wasn't too impressed with me, thought that I'd betrayed Hiller, and I should have kept silent about bonuses. I'd heard this all before. But this time FitzSimons extended another jab, voicing his dismay at my tolerance for a newsroom that had videotaped my introductory speech and put it online before clearing it with me. "If someone had done that to me, I would've fired him," FitzSimons said. Given that almost everything I said in the newsroom was simultaneously published in *LA Observed*, the incident hadn't bothered me. Besides, I thought firing someone on my first day as editor for covering a story in my own newsroom wasn't a good idea. And then, of course, he attacked Wolinsky.

I told FitzSimons that my initial views about the *Times* had changed once I got to know the paper and the people better, particularly Wolinsky. "When I first got here," I told him, "I thought he would be someone that would be a problem for me, but he actually turned out to be a help." FitzSimons retorted that no one else shared my view of Wolinsky, an assertion that was patently untrue. "What is this with you and Leo?" I demanded. "He's a one of my deputies. Why are you, the CEO of this company, so obsessed with him? I'd think you'd have better things to do."

FitzSimons came right back, letting me know he thought my refusal to fire Wolinsky revealed my reluctance to make an unpopular decision and my ultimate desire to "play to the staff." "We go back a ways," Fitz-Simons said, "and I just wanted to come here and talk to you honestly." When at last Montorio showed up, things returned to civil ground, and we made our way through lunch. In the end, I think FitzSimons felt he owed me a thumb in the eye. Just before he left, I asked him if there was a hidden message in the journalism review article he'd sent me. He laughed and said, "No. I just wanted you to see that all of the news about layoffs isn't bad."

■

I knew FitzSimons had little affection for journalists like me, and, unquestionably, he had a tough job at a tough time. But I found his conduct over the next few months bizarre. Anyone could see FitzSimons wasn't Zell's choice to lead the company once the deal closed. Pate and Larsen had made it pretty clear that the Zell organization felt new leadership was needed. Yet FitzSimons plowed ahead with his penguin initiatives like a man possessed, and a dual narrative began rippling through Tribune ranks.

Hiller, Smith, FitzSimons, and Bob Gremillion, a FitzSimons minion selected to be the czar of transformative change, started laying the groundwork for a future that resembled the past—steep budget cuts and austerity, that debtor's two-step that would hit newsrooms hard. Frankly I don't think they had a clue about how to grow revenues, other than "think local" and nebulous projections about a better life on the Internet. Over drinks in the Intercontinental Hotel on one of my visits to Chicago, Lipinski and I discussed the fate of our papers. She told me that we were both targets of much hostility during a large, transformative change meeting because of our opposition to front-page ads.

But Lipinski and I got different messages from Zell, Pate, and Larsen, who continued to emphasize the need for enhanced revenues and parroted the line that only fools would rely solely on budget cuts to meet the challenges ahead. They had discussed selective cuts but also some investment to enhance our ability to generate revenues. At times, it seemed like the right hand wasn't talking to the left, and I began to wonder if the Zell team knew existing publishers were building budgets with fairly steep cuts baked into projected expenses. I could tell that Pate and Larsen had steeped themselves in the company's financial operations. At one point, Pate remarked to me that a mismatch between total ad inches and ad revenues suggested that "a lot of discounting is going on out here."

What neither of us knew was that both narratives were being driven by the increasingly tense behind-the-scenes skirmishes between the company and its lenders. In August, the lead banks—JPMorgan Chase, Citicorp, Merrill Lynch, and Bank of America—had sent the company a five-page due diligence letter seeking detailed information about Tribune's strategy, markets, and business lines, including the rationale for everything from its assumption about publishing revenues and expenses to adjustment to its projections since April, when the company had made forecasts for phase one of the deal.

The company responded about a month later with a five-year financial model that included some pessimistic projections, those "sky is falling" scenarios that Tribune managers included in the model but didn't endorse. The response triggered more back and forth between the company and the banks regarding the terms of the loans, the feasibility of revenue and cash flow assumptions, and testy questions about the Tribune's ability to impose the deep cuts that would be needed to repay the debt.

At one point, the banks tried to restructure the loans to make them a better deal for themselves, a tactic that would also make them more appealing to investors in the secondary syndication markets. But the

Tribune board rejected the proposal without offering any alternatives. "We are clearly dealing with an organization at all levels unable to come to a decision," said a frustrated Michael Costa, the Tribune adviser at Merrill Lynch, who questioned whether the bank should deal directly with the board. "We should also seek direct dialogue with the board since management seems incapable of driving a decision."

Subsequently, the banks issued yet another detailed list of questions framed by the solvency expert their lawyers had hired to analyze the adequacy of the Tribune Company's solvency expert, Valuation Research Corp. (VRC). By having their lawyers hire the expert, the banks draped a cloak of lawyer-client secrecy over their communications, suggesting they anticipated court action. But the tactic backfired. The tenor of the questions made Tribune general counsel Kenney fear the banks were trying to "spook" VRC. Soon a lawyer from another Tribune law firm joined the discussions—one retained by Tribune to litigate in case the banks tried to abandon their commitments.

Tribune Company even disagreed with its own experts. VRC did an analysis of Tribune Company's financial projections for October 2007 and concluded that many should be adjusted downward to reflect the deteriorating market conditions. But Tribune CFO Don Grenesko and Chandler Bigelow, a vice president in the financial department, countered with reports that argued management's more optimistic assumptions were reasonable.

As the competing arguments began filtering down into the ranks, a dual narrative evolved and the stakes for closing the deal grew, creating an almost electric tension in the Tower. Tribune Company finally agreed to some changes in the terms for the phase-two loans, but the banks balked at extending the credit since the loans would translate into immediate red ink, despite the huge fees they stood to make. Tribune managers, who would rake in big bonuses if the deal closed, factored into their projections the kind of budget cuts that made Lipinski and me nervous. Zell and his team continued to argue that Tribune couldn't cut its way to success and needed additional revenue so he could make the millions he saw in the deal. At one point, the banks sounded each other out and learned that a couple were leaning against funding the loans because they felt they could make the case that the loans would render Tribune Company insolvent.

As I watched from afar, I knew nothing about the behind-the-scenes skirmishes. But my gut told me that this deal offered me salvation and doom in one fell swoop. I owned Tribune stock and, like everyone else, I wanted to see the deal close. Employees of my rank had to own twice their salary in Tribune stock. I had a lot of my life savings tied up in the shares. But I also knew that a debt-laden company would force me to make some hard, personal decisions. I agreed with Zell, Pate, and Larsen; Tribune could not simply cut its way to the future. Over the past five years, I'd trimmed fat out of many newsroom budgets and had lived with tight financial controls imposed by the accountants. I'd become an adept budgetary surgeon. But my patient never got any better.

The Image fashion section we'd created in the *Los Angeles Times* showed that the paper was capable of generating new revenue. Many of the high-class advertisers that snapped up space in Image had never been in the *Times*. But to lure that kind of revenue, we had to invest in the newspaper, and I didn't know if Zell and his team were really that committed.

Hiller agreed with me philosophically. He took one look at the debt we faced and concluded that the *Los Angeles Times* would be better off being sold to a local investor like Eli Broad or David Geffen. On a practical level, though, Hiller was in a difficult position to effect change. FitzSimons and Wall Street wanted cuts at Tribune's biggest newspapers, and Zell had told Hiller that he—and he alone— would have profit-and-loss responsibility for the *Times* once the deal closed, a break from the past when financial control was centered in Tribune Tower. Hiller was under the gun, and, as we began fashioning a financial blueprint for 2008, I feared the newsroom was heading in one direction—down.

The same thing was happening at newspapers across the county. Everyone was trying to figure out if the changes in print advertising markets were cyclical, a result of hard times triggered by a softening economy, or structural, more fundamental changes spawned by alterations in American advertising and consumption patterns. No one really knew the answer, although I figured it was probably a combination of both and would affect all newspapers and journalists like me.

I wasn't too worried about my immediate fate. I had the ear of the Zell group. Pate and Larsen made it clear that they wanted me to remain in Los Angeles, and I had met in Chicago with Randy Michaels, a pudgy, smiling man who asked me a lot of questions and didn't volunteer much, other than to tell me: "You are in for one hell of a ride." But as someone who was trained to look beyond impressions for facts, I began to wonder whether I would be able to live up to the pledges I'd made when I had joined the staff of the *Los Angeles Times* the year before.

When I had agreed to become editor of the paper, I had said that I wouldn't take the job unless I felt that I could make things better. I knew at the time that I would have to make some budget cuts and probably lay off some journalists. But I vowed to myself and to the community of concerned readers that I would not preside over the destruction of one of America's greatest newspapers. At all costs, I had to protect the integrity of the institution I ran and, by extension, the news and pass on to my successor a better paper than the one I had inherited. If the credibility of the newspaper and the respect with which it was held in the community diminished on my watch, I failed my community, my craft, my staff, my newspaper, and its owner, even if the owner failed to appreciate the distinction.

Soon I began wrestling with two options. Some friends advised me that resisting cuts was foolhardy and naïve. If *you* don't cut the budget, *someone* else will, the logic went, so why should I be hoisted by my own petard? One day, Stanton walked into my office and told me, "Don't quit." Although he didn't know it at the time, I knew they had already talked to him about my job. The other option was to resist—draw that proverbial line in the sand and flush out the facts to see where everyone really stood.

One day I would take a morning walk on the beach and say to myself, "All right, the gutsy thing to do is make the cuts, figure out how to minimize their impact, and preserve as much of the paper as you can. That would be hard, but I could do it. It's easy to walk out, but what do you accomplish?" But the next day, I would wonder if I were just fooling myself to keep a nice salary, a home on the beach, and the heady perks that come as editor of a famous newspaper—a soiree at Helen Mirren's house, a seat at the Academy Awards, or an introduction at a dinner at which Angelina Jolie was also present. The *right* thing to do, I would tell myself, is fight back, hard, even if it meant getting fired—a daunting prospect since I was of an age that it would probably mean the end of my career as a working journalist. I had reassured the readers of the *Los Angeles Times* I was no short-timer and that I would stay as long as it took to resolve problems at the paper. I wasn't done.

I plumbed the depths of my psyche searching for the right answer. I consulted friends, took long walks, thought through my dilemma on bike rides the length of Malibu, the wind my only companion. One day, walking along the surf near my apartment, I decided that the answer didn't cower in the recesses of my mind, waiting for a moment of insight. The answer was in my gut. I needed to rely on the instincts that I had honed during every chapter of my life. Where I'd been, what I had learned, and what I'd become told me what to do. You cut a budget to save a "job." But you stand firm to honor a calling. If the editor of a newspaper didn't stand up for readers, who would? I had to resist, consequences be damned. The values I had learned at the *Des Moines Register* prevailed: Journalism first, profits second.

By late October, as the banks continued their struggle to weasel out of their loan obligations, a furious forest fire erupted in the mountains of Santa Barbara. Back in the newsroom, coverage of the story started normally: Print reporters swung into action, the online folks were slow on the uptake since they rarely worked weekends. But a day into the fires, things changed. Thanks to my online newsroom initiatives, the print and online staffs started working in tandem, providing jaw-dropping coverage. I was proud. I didn't have to do a thing; my editors took over. This was the kind of awesome, multimedia journalism the future demanded—videos; photos from professionals and readers alike; great writing; smart editing; crisp, active headlines; taped interviews of people fleeing their homes. A few weeks later, I had lunch with Phil Bennett, the managing editor of the *Washington Post*, who told me he had watched our fire coverage from afar and felt that we had crossed some kind of a line.

After weeks of headlines and dramatic coverage, Maharaj came into my office and suggested we have a newsroom celebration. "We've had so many going-away parties for people who leave," said Maharaj. "You've hired a lot of people. Why don't you have a party for the people who came here. It would be great for morale." I thought it a terrific idea and was quite surprised when Susan Denley, the newsroom human relations liaison, told me more than seventy journalists new to the *Times* had been hired since I had become editor. Even though the total newsroom staff, including the Internet, had settled at about 920, I had filled numerous openings and vacancies and had created some new slots for Image.

At the same time, Richard Boudreaux, the *Times* Middle East bureau chief, had scheduled a home leave for December, and foreign editor Marjorie Miller suggested I set up a lunch with Zell, since he had strong interests in the Middle East. I e-mailed Zell and he invited Marjorie, Boudreaux, and me to join him and his wife, Helen, to have lunch at Geoffrey's, a posh restaurant that overlooks the water just south of Malibu. We met on a delightfully warm Friday, ate fresh salads, and downed a couple bottles of white wine. Zell charmed us with his ambitious plans and witty stories, although he didn't tell us any specific plans for the paper. But he did allow that he couldn't wait to get the deal closed. "You will be surprised at what we can do," Zell told me. "You may end up with more people."

Encouraged by the lunch, I arrived back at the *Times* building just in time for the newcomers' party, told Hiller about my conversation with Zell, and prepared to make some remarks. As usual, he asked if he could talk to the staff after me, to which I agreed. When Hiller faced the assembled audience, he commented on the more casual look I had adopted for my lunch with Zell and said, cryptically, "I sure hope you didn't stab me in the back." When someone later asked me what Hiller's comment had been about, I admitted I didn't know. "I think he meant it as a joke," I said. But in my gut, I suspected otherwise.

During the fire coverage, I learned of an intriguing *Times* project in which two reporters had been scrutinizing how government officials fought fires. They discovered that the fire-retardant chemicals that airplanes dumped from above might do more harm than good. It was just the kind of story I loved, and I told the reporters to forge ahead and see if we could get something in the paper about it before the year's end. I wanted to personally edit the story to demonstrate I was first and foremost an editor. A year after I left the paper, the project won a Pulitzer Prize.

The California fires soon tapered off, but the sparks continued to fly on Wall Street as the calendar slipped into mid-December and the banks zeroed in on the adequacy of Tribune's solvency expert's work. A roadblock had developed when VRC, under pressure from the banks, asked if another $4 billion in phase-two loans would give the company a major problem in 2014, when some Tribune debt would have to be refinanced. How could a company so encumbered with loans get a bank to refinance its debt, particularly if the economy didn't improve? By that time, VRC's own analysts had cast doubt on the financial projections supplied by Grenesko and Bigelow, and had asked them if they could get Morgan Stanley, the Special Committee's financial adviser, to affirm that Tribune could get the loans refinanced in 2014, an opinion that no investment bank would ever deliver.

After much to and fro, Grenesko and Bigelow, who would be promoted to Tribune CFO once the deal went through, gave VRC an answer. Although Morgan Stanley wouldn't issue any kind of formal opinion, they said, the bank would supply Tribune with data about the ability of companies with similar debt ratios to refinance loans. The data gave VRC justification to agree that refinancing was a reasonable assumption.

But on December 19, lead banker JPMorgan Chase, where one officer ranked Tribune management as "B at best," broke the logjam by once again hauling out its big guns. Jimmy Lee, the company's savvy vice president who'd played key roles in almost every media deal over the past decade, spoke to Zell that morning and later reported back to colleagues:

> Just had a long talk with Sam. He could not have been any clearer and more confident that the company is solvent. No financial issues in year one, more cushion than maybe we realized in deal. His commitment [is] to help us sell the paper [or loans] with more yield or whatever when the time is right, his reputation being totally on the line. I also spoke with him on the core issues of governance. He becomes CEO tomorrow. Dennis gone tomorrow. Bring in long-time Zell lieutenants to run each major business line. Osborn and [Betsy] Holden stay on board. Everybody else goes. It was the kind of call we needed to proceed given our concerns, all critical issues getting settled to our satisfaction, of course. I told him we were totally counting on him to make this work. He said "I don't make commitments I can't keep."

Lee's boss, Dimon, later characterized the conversation as an entreaty from Lee to Zell to improve Tribune's deteriorating financial performance. "This is just saying, 'Hey partner, we've got this far, we need to give it everything you got.'" Zell said he knew the bank would fund his deal after the phone call: "I never heard the word *solvency* with him, I've never had any conversations about this whole solvency issue other than in the board meetings. This is Jimmy, and he truly believes, as I do, that banking is personal. He wanted to make sure that I was still there, and I was."

On December 20, 2007, at 12:02 p.m., the deal, at long last, closed. The FCC, thanks to lobbying by Zell, had approved of it. VRC ignored every pessimistic projection of its own analysts and accepted the financial rationale of the Tribune managers, who had fat bonuses riding on the deal. Grenesko and Bigelow based their broadcasting revenue projections on an election year, when income from political ads inflated the ad revenue outlook, a step that would push the company over the solvency line, but later come back to haunt it. The banks wire-transferred funds to Tribune, which disbursed about $4 billion to Computershare Trust Co., to buy back the remaining Tribune stock at $34 per share. The company terminated its registration at the U.S. Securities and Exchange Commission and requested its common stock be delisted at the New York Stock Exchange. As a public company, Tribune was no more. Zell now controlled its fate, along with his "partners" in the ESOP.

A lot was written at the time about how Zell shafted the Tribune employees. That's not completely true. Many existing Tribune employees had investments in Tribune stock through 401(k) plans. They still had jobs and got $34 a share for their stock, not what it once fetched but still far more than they would have garnered had the grave dancer not waltzed along. The company had ended its defined-benefits pension plan and had set aside enough money so that it actually was overfunded and carried benefits backed by the federal government. The big question was the future. In doing the deal, Zell had cut things so close to the wire that the Tribune ESOP, which now owned most of the company, had an extremely narrow band for success: If the company's performance was off just 2 percent from its plan, the ESOP would have no value for five years. Nonetheless, employees at Tribune newspapers were thrilled on December 20, 2007. FitzSimons' departure made Wolinsky smile; he'd survived him to fight another day. But FitzSimons had reason to be even happier. His salary, bonus, and the price of stock he'd acquired over the years totaled $41 million, not a staggering amount compared to some of the golden parachutes other CEOs corralled, but still a tidy sum. Many of his friends in the company did well, too, particularly in corporate headquarters and on the broadcasting side. John Reardon, president of Tribune Broadcasting, walked away with about $10 million in salary, bonus, and benefits. Some thirty-two managers and other key employees involved in the strategic review process leading up to the deal got $6.5 million in benefits under a bonus and phantom stock plan. Don Grenesko, the senior vice president and CFO who played a key role in engineering the deal, got $13.8 million in salary, bonus, and stock proceeds after the deal closed.

On Wall Street, the banks and their advisers collected another $122 million in fees and expenses, bringing their total take to around $283 million. "Ka-ching" was no longer in the air, though, for they had to quickly mark down the debt to its trading value and simply collect interest from Tribune, which paid just under 8 percent on the loans, until—and unless—they could peddle the debt to other institutional investors, which would probably generate a loss. Zell later said the banks had to mark down the debt on their books by $400 million.

Nevertheless, Zell was happy. He had gained control of some nice assets for relatively little money. Overall, he put $315 million into the deal, which would represent about 5.25 percent of his reported net worth of $6 billion at the time. That's like a $5,250 investment for someone worth $100,000. For his money, Zell acquired control of a company that owned the best collection of daily newspapers in America, thirteen titles, including a presence in the nation's three largest cities; twenty-six television stations; a one-third interest in the Food Network; the Chicago Cubs baseball team; and a range of other properties, including a near-monopoly of the media market in Chicago. He probably laid off some of his investment on others he brought into the deal, but he had a potential bonanza on his hands if he could make the deal work. The imputed rate of return that he had figured on the deal ranged from 25 percent to 35 percent, depending on how long the grave dancer hung on to his new toy.

Nils Larsen called me later in the day to say how happy he was that the deal had finally closed. "Now what we have to do is go out and hire the best talent we can get," Larsen said. And I soon sat down with Sean Reily, an editor with an eye for finance, and told him to start going through the paper, section by section, to determine if and how they contributed to our mission to be the voice of California and the West. Our goal was to see if we could redirect some of our energies into more opportunities like Image. My family joined me for Christmas in Manhattan Beach, where the sun was shining and it was 70 degrees. We had a marvelous Christmas. I liked California. I wanted to stay.

But after the holidays, things changed quickly. Reily came into my office for a session on the budget. Hiller had imposed a hiring freeze that would frustrate my plans, and Reily said his sources in finance predicted he would not back down on tight controls on the editorial department, including a mandate that spending in 2008 could not exceed the levels set in October 2007. This was the kind of Tribune top-down micromanagement that simply didn't work. I wrote Hiller a memo outlining how his so-called flat spending blueprint actually represented a fairly large cut to the editorial department.

"I am not saying my budget can't be cut," I wrote, "and that we can't save money." I had always come in under budget and reminded him that I had given back $2.5 million the year before when asked. My real problem was that we were reverting to a system in which I had to seek approval to hire even a lower-level employee, a process I considered a waste of time. "If you can't rely on me to make routine decisions, I question why I'm even here," I wrote. I asked for some time for Reily and me to submit a spending plan that would hit his targets without hurting the paper and provide me with some flexibility. "Just give me a number to hit," I said, "and let me—and not some accountant upstairs—figure out how to hit it." But Hiller turned me down flat.

Any newsroom is a gossip mill, and soon rumors flew that our disagreements over the budget meant my days were numbered. Stanton dropped by. Klunder dropped by, too, and I asked him where he thought the situation was going. He doubted Hiller would do anything to get rid of me and risk having the newsroom hate him anymore than it already did. A few days later, we had a budget meeting in which Hiller and I disagreed. Afterward, he invited me to his office for a chat. It was time for the line in the sand.

I told him that an editorial budget with a hiring freeze and tight controls would not work. "Well, what do you think is going to happen?" he asked. "This paper has to keep getting smaller and smaller. You see what is going on around you. Do you think we can get bigger?" I replied no, but said this was not a discussion about the budget but one about a failed process. "I'm not saying we can't cut," I said, "but we need to reinvest those funds in journalism." Hiller almost looked sick. I could see the anger rising. I had smoked out his true feelings. "The future." he said, "is in cutting back." I told him I totally disagreed. We talked about whether he needed another editor who saw the world his way. "This is nothing personal," I told him. "I like you. But I simply don't think the current course is the way to solve our problem. If you think you need another editor, you're the publisher and that's your choice." "Let's sleep on that over the weekend," Hiller advised.

I was in my office on Monday writing a memo that Hiller had sought summarizing my accomplishments over the past year when he stuck his head in and asked if I wanted to "grab a bite." I said I wanted to finish my memo first and send it to him, knowing full well what was about to happen at our lunch. We went to TRAXX, a restaurant in Union Station in downtown Los Angeles, and I thought this wouldn't be a bad place to get fired—there were lots of others coming and going. Hiller made small talk about how much he loved old train stations as we picked our way through our lunches. Eventually, he got to the point.

"I've thought this over, and I want to make a transition," he said. "Believe me, I've thought a lot about this. I just read your accomplishments memo, and you did a lot. I asked you to come out here, and we owe you a lot." I told him that I agreed. But I also understood that the editor served at the publisher's pleasure and that the two had to see eye to eye on things. We didn't. Hiller seemed quite uncomfortable, even clumsy, dealing with the subject.

Then, to my astonishment, Hiller said he wanted to hold off on any changes until he checked with Zell to see if he was going to sell the paper. "We all know that David Geffen is still around, and he might want us to stay here until it is sold. Geffen may even want a new publisher. . . . Sam will probably say, 'Hiller, you are nuts. I want to keep him [Jim O'Shea], not you. You have a pretty good relationship with Zell, don't you?"

# 19

## Zell Hell

Hiller set his glasses down and drummed his fingers on the table of the sixth-floor conference room where he held his senior team meeting. After Zell had taken over, Hiller rarely wore a tie, and this morning was no different—his crisp, white shirt was open at the collar. A week had passed since our lunch downtown at Union Station's TRAXX, and Hiller still hadn't told me if he had talked to Zell. And he was acting strangely. We didn't talk much, and when we did, it was awkward. On Hiller's desk was a couple of months' worth of my expense reports, amounting to thousands of dollars, which he hadn't approved.

At our lunch, Hiller had asked me if I would consider staying on at the paper in some "advisory" role, but I had categorically rejected the idea and urged him to act sooner rather than later before his decision leaked, which would only make a bad situation worse. When he floated the idea of discreetly searching for a new editor, I flat out refused. It would be an impossible task, given the high profile of the job in question. I could tell that the members of the paper's senior leadership team, a group comprising about a dozen people around the table, knew nothing of what was about to happen.

After listening to Elisa Ney, a marketing department MBA, babble on about a visit to another paper where they had dumped editors who opposed change, I wrote in my notebook: "I made the right decision. Now let's get this over with by January 31."

Polly Ross, my trusted assistant, suspected something was up when I began canceling appointments, including one she was trying to make with Maria Shriver, to discuss a possible profile in the *Los Angeles Times Magazine*. I knew the 2008 newsroom budget would have to be cut by at least $5 million. But I suspected that was just the start of the process and I didn't want to impose cuts that would kick in after I'd left. So I asked my managing editors and Wolinsky to make the cuts themselves. When the editors assembled in my office, though, they started to question me about my goals for the coming year. I showed them what to cut in five minutes. Cutting a budget was easy; I'd had lots of practice.

I had decided that I would make a statement to the staff and to the community once the news of my departure broke. I felt I had an obligation to explain what had happened and that I had not abandoned the newspaper, particularly given the initial speculation that Tribune had, in the words of former editorial page editor Andrés Martinez, "sent me to the provinces to quell a rebellion by the natives." Besides, I had given my word that I was there for the long haul; they deserved an explanation from me and not some baloney from the PR department. But no matter *how* the news broke, I knew this wasn't going to be pretty. I was the third editor in three years and the second to be fired by Hiller in less than a year and a half.

I told a few trusted friends what was about to happen, including Ann Marie Lipinski. Lipinski wanted to phone Bill Pate, with whom she'd been in regular contact during the negotiations leading up to the sale. But Pate was traveling in the Middle East, and I was wary of running to someone in the Zell camp at the first sign of trouble. I finally called Nils Larsen myself and told him what had happened. "Well, I'm not for that," he said. He wanted to take up the matter with Zell. But I told him that I had called because I didn't want him to be blindsided by the news, not because I was hoping for an appeal. I urged him to give Hiller his day in court. When Pate returned to the United States, he wrote to Lipinski asking her if things were OK. When she replied that everything was OK in Chicago but there were "storm clouds out West," Pate never responded.

When he assumed control, Zell had emphatically told everyone that the publishers and CEOs of individual papers would be responsible for their operations, not some bureaucrat in the Tribune Tower. I didn't hold high hopes that he would countermand the first major decision that Hiller had made, even if he wanted to. But I also figured that my situation would force everyone to show their hand. I contacted my lawyer, Marty Cohn, in Chicago and was contemplating when I would leave, when Hiller called and asked me to come to his office.

Even in the best of times, Hiller rarely revealed his true thoughts. He desperately wanted to be liked and usually adopted his inquisitive, lawyerly manner in uncomfortable situations, using questions to make his point rather than uttering an opinion. He was doubly uneasy in my presence that day, arousing my suspicion about how he would handle any compensation I was due, particularly since he had never raised the subject. As I sat down, he asked my advice on my successor. I gave him my recommendations (which he would ignore) and asked him to call my lawyer to arrange details of my departure.

I had always been up front with Hiller. I told him frankly that I was going to make a public statement when the news of my departure broke. As usual, he asked if I would provide him my remarks in advance and, as usual, I declined. I had no problem openly disclosing what I intended to say, but I would not allow Hiller or anyone else to censor the words I chose. I assured him I would not be critical of him personally, but would comment on my disagreement with the way the company allocated resources to its newspapers, an issue that I considered central to our disagreement and one I hoped Zell would change. Visibly nervous, Hiller pressed for exactly *what* I would say.

But I wouldn't agree to share my statement before I issued it. At that point, I hadn't yet drafted my remarks.

The next week was extremely uncomfortable. I had not told anyone at the *Times* about Hiller's decision, and I sat through meetings, responding to questions with comments or observations that I knew to be irrelevant. I hated it. The newsroom gossip mill cranked out rumors that Hiller and I had deep disagreements on the budget, the kind that had led to Baquet's dismissal. I dreaded the appearance of a story in *LA Observed*. Finally, I phoned my friend Howard Bragman, owner of Fifteen Minutes, a public relations company that specialized in crisis communications, and consulted him about what to do. By the Friday before the Martin Luther King, Jr., holiday, rumors had escalated into speculation that Hiller wanted to replace me with Stanton. Several journalists dropped by my office to ask if the rumors were true; others, like Aaron Curtiss, a friend of Stanton, walked by me in the hallway and avoided my gaze. Finally, I approached Hiller and told him we needed to do *something* before we had a leak.

Although he acted as if he was still considering who would be editor, I knew Hiller wanted to appoint Stanton because Stanton would commit to the sort of deep newsroom cuts that Hiller felt were needed. But Hiller feared the blowback from members of the editorial department who supported me or didn't like Stanton. We talked for an hour or two about the situation and discussed several scenarios. In closing, Hiller said he was traveling to Chicago for the long weekend and would announce a decision when he returned on Tuesday. As I left that afternoon, I advised Hiller to have a plan in place in case the news leaked over the weekend. He agreed that he would. Once again, I asked him to call my lawyer.

On Sunday morning, a reporter from the *Wall Street Journal* called me at home. The reporter wasn't a regular on the media beat, and I figured she must have been put on the story by an editor who had received a tip. She allowed that the *Journal* would not publish a paper on the Monday holiday, but that her editors intended to immediately put a small item about my impending dismissal on the Internet. From her questions, I could tell the paper had solid information. I told her I couldn't comment publicly. As soon as I hung up, I called Hiller in Chicago. Hiller assured me that he didn't intend to comment, either. "So," he said, "if you don't comment and I don't comment, no story." I explained that that was not the way it worked, and that the *Journal* would probably have something online soon. Moments later, my Black-Berry buzzed; a friend had sent me a link to the small story that the *Journal* ran on its webpage.

I refused to talk to any reporter before I talked to my staff, which I planned to do on Tuesday morning. When the *Wall Street Journal* reporter called me back, I talked to her on the condition that the story wouldn't run until Tuesday, a commitment the paper honored. I then told her how to contact Hiller and spent the rest of the weekend ducking a flood of calls from other media reporters hot on the trail, as I worked on finalizing the remarks I would make to the staff.

The coverage in Tuesday's papers was heavy; newsroom sources told me that Hiller, who had made some less than flattering comments about me, objected strongly to placing the story on page one of the *Times*, but finally relented and apologized when editors convinced him it would look worse if he didn't. I called the newsroom and arranged to deliver my remarks at 10 a.m. on Tuesday and half wondered whether I would be locked out of the parking garage when I drove into the city that morning.

I walked into the building through the ad department (where I got some nice words and hugs from some of the sales reps), told Ross to get some boxes so I could pack my belongings, and was preparing to make my remarks when Hiller strode into my office. "Well," he said, "when things start flying, they really fly, don't they?" I replied that I was about to address the newsroom and reiterated that I wouldn't criticize him. It was my intention, I told him, to leave the *Times* after my speech. Again, I urged him to call my lawyer. After Hiller left my office, I walked to the same spot where I had spoken some fifteen months before and bid farewell to a great staff that had given me my chance to earn its respect.

After confirming that I was leaving, I told the staff why:

> In discussions about current and future budgets, it became clear that Publisher David Hiller and I didn't share a common vision for the future of the *Los Angeles Times*. In fact, we were far apart. So David decided he wanted a new editor. Had we been able to agree on a way forward, I was ready to commit to stay longer. But we couldn't and we decided it would be better to make a change now. It was his decision and I accept it.

We had accomplished much in my tenure and, after, highlighting our successes, I thanked everyone, apologized for not spending more time in the trenches, and said it was time to move on. In closing, I addressed the issue at the core of the disagreements between Hiller and myself, the allocation of resources that relied too heavily on accounting acrobatics and marketing clichés and not enough on the creativity and resourcefulness of journalists, who were often wrongly dismissed as budgetary adolescents.

As I explained to the assembled crowd,

> The biggest challenge we face . . . is to overcome this pervasive culture of defeat, the psychology of surrender that accepts decline as inevitable. This mind-set plagues our business and threatens our newspapers and livelihoods. I believe that when Sam Zell understands how asinine the current budgetary system is, he will change it for the better because he is a smart businessman and understands the value of wise investment. A dollar's worth of investment is worth far more than a barrel of budget cuts.

I made it clear that I hadn't quit. I refused to embrace a strategy that we would survive long term by diminishing the newspaper, not the printed product, but the values it represents and the quality of its news reports. When I finished and headed back to my office, Wolinsky congratulated me on my speech, but warned me, as he put it, that it was "going to cost [me] some money." By noon, I had packed my car, shook many hands, and said goodbye to the *Los Angeles Times*. I had taken my stand, said my piece, and referred all other calls from journalists to my departing remarks.

The next morning I arose early to a clear sky, a bright sun, and a story in the *Los Angeles Times* quoting Zell saying that he backed Hiller's decision. No surprise there. I e-mailed Zell and said I understood his thinking and that I would be glad to discuss my views of the paper and industry with him. He wrote back thanking me: "I think you can understand that if I'm going to autonomate the business units, I also have to give them responsibility. I therefore support David in his decisions and will continue to do so in the future. Having said that, I'm going to miss you and I very much appreciate your offer to help; don't be shocked if I take you up on it." As I sat on my front porch drinking a cup of coffee and watching the waves of the Pacific crashing down on Manhattan Beach, I suddenly realized something frightening: For the first time since I'd been a teenager, I didn't have anywhere to go that day. I didn't have a job.

■

I had been a journalist my entire adult life and didn't want to do anything else. My daughter was still in school, and I had her tuition bills to pay; my son was working on his PhD and needed support from time to time. Thankfully, my wife still had her job, so I didn't have to worry about health insurance. I had just been fired in a headline-grabbing incident that announced to the world I was in my sixties. I truly didn't know if the paper would continue my salary; it canceled my free subscription the day after my remarks.

I decided to stay in Manhattan Beach until the weather in Chicago improved. By mid-February, I received an e-mail from Tribune Company. When I had agreed to become editor of the *Los Angeles Times*, I had secured a two-year contract outlining my salary and benefits, including a provision that guaranteed my pay if I were "terminated without cause." One of their attorneys informed me that the terms of my contract would be honored only if I signed a "mutual non-disparagement agreement" that would prohibit me from saying anything negative or create an unfavorable impression "in any manner whatsoever" about "Tribune Company, its parents, subsidiaries, predecessors, successors, affiliates, officers, directors, agents, shareholders, attorney and employees or any of them" from here to eternity.

I had traveled the globe as a reporter and followed events closely as an editor; I'd seen a world where powerful people muzzle those who speak out. I had seen how dictators or despots immediately seized the press when they took power. I'd seen it happen time and again, the world over. Even in places like Guatemala, where authoritarian governments barely tolerated the press, newspapermen like José Zamora at *el Periodico* risked their lives to publish, to maintain a free press, to amplify the voices of the dispossessed. I was hardly on a par with a dissident in Moscow, or Nelson Mandela, or Zamora, but I now had a lawyer for a company that sponsored an institute dedicated to honoring freedom of speech trying to silence me or force me to voluntarily surrender my right to speak out. Agreeing to don a muzzle violated everything for which I stood. Handily, the company also read my contract in a way that would deny me extra money due for dismissal without cause.

We were not talking about a lot of money. The difference between my reading of the contract and the company's was at most around $50,000. I didn't leave Tribune with a huge bonus and stock holdings, either. Journalists at Tribune Company were not paid nearly as much as those on the corporate side, and few walked away with bonuses and stock holdings anywhere near the levels of FitzSimons and his allies. I was happy about my choices; I'd made more money as a journalist than I ever dreamed I would, and was able to provide for my family. But I didn't have enough to live off the income from my savings. And there was no way I would sign a "non-disparagement" clause, and voluntarily give up a right that people literally died for. My lawyer assured me he thought all of the financial issues in the dispute could be settled by giving up just a little, but that the company felt strongly about the muzzle clause. "When I tell them you won't sign it, they get real cool and say that's a real problem," Cohn explained. "The guy I'm dealing with over there says this is way above him and someone at the very top is calling the shots." There was only one man at the top at Tribune now—Zell.

I soon learned that Zell had demanded that the Tribune human relations department give him my contract. Zell had also started the company road show that Randy Michaels had advocated in his memo and, as one colleague at the *Los Angeles Times* reported, "he's trashing you." In a question-and-answer session at the *Times*, Zell told his audience I had "pissed all over" the company where I had worked for nearly thirty years, "shit all over the place," embarrassing the company and him. I didn't see things that way, and, profanities aside, I thought he was saying some of the same things I had said—that the company needed to worry much more about revenues, still had a lot of cash, and had great assets, a message that contrasted sharply with propaganda perpetuated by bloggers who liked to portray the *Los Angeles Times* as broke and Tribune Company as a failed operation. In 2007, the *Times* generated nearly $200 million in cash flow, off a troubling amount from the $240 million the year before, but hardly the results of a paper that was "broke."

It was hard to set aside Zell's profanities, given his frequent use of sexual metaphors and foul language on his road show. In Los Angeles, Zell compared the *Times*, which had survived for 126 years, to an old man in need of Viagra who now had to "get it up." He peppered his public remarks with "fuck this" and "fuck that" and told employees he didn't care if they watched porn at their desks, as long as they produced, adding, "let me know if you find any good sites." He defended his decision to allow strip-club ads in the *Times* with the quip that it was "un-American not to like pussy," and admitted to one group of employees that perhaps he needed to "go to language class to de-fuck my language," but that he was too old.

The whole exercise seemed like a scene out of a juvenile locker room until Zell got to Florida, where he tacked a very public "fuck you" onto his response to a young Latina photographer who had challenged his views about public service journalism. His meeting with the staff of the *Orlando Sentinel* had been videotaped and posted on YouTube for the world to see. More significantly, Zell, who had encouraged people to challenge the status quo, displayed thin skin when he himself was challenged and abruptly rejected suggestions from journalists, whom he pointedly and repeatedly characterized as arrogant elitists.

By the time Zell and Michaels showed up at the Tribune's Washington bureau, media reporters were chronicling the tour, and the resulting leaks and publicity were ugly. He zeroed in on a story that had run in the *Los Angeles Times* during my tenure as editor as an example of the arrogance of the paper. The piece involved a controversy about Zell's attempt to jack up rents at a California trailer park owned by one of the companies in his fold. He told Doyle McManus, the *Times* bureau chief, that one of the reporters who challenged him was an "asshole" who should be gone by midnight and that the bureau should be downsized since the paper doesn't contribute as much money to the company as the *Chicago Tribune*. By the time the tour was done, it was clear that Zell's views of the future mirrored Michaels'.

Theatrics aside, Zell's performance revealed his fundamental misunderstanding of the business he now controlled. At a *Los Angeles Times* printing plant, Zell said newspapers were like any other business. "I am not a newspaper guy," he said. "I am a businessman and I know that all that matters is the bottom line because if we have a bottom line, we have a newspaper." While he's right to be concerned about a healthy bottom line, newspaper executives also must take into account their status as a public service business. Readers who care and remain loyal don't judge newspaper executives on profits alone. They look at integrity of the work, the quality of a news report, the journalists' ability to rise above the rabble of daily life and deliver facts in a credible, nonjudgmental format. Newspapers are also in the business of exposing the fallibility of others, so you had better be ready to place your own conduct under a microscope.

Zell's crude comments, his denunciation of journalists and journalism, and the stupidity of the industry's leadership got wide exposure in the media. In the lingo of the ad markets, he trashed "his brand" and came off as an uncouth clown. He destroyed whatever credibility he and the company had accrued in the months leading to the close of the deal. Roderick at *LA Observed* was understandably thrilled with Zell; he was a headline machine. But many others recoiled at a billionaire with a potty mouth and a megaphone. For my part, I was truly saddened by Zell. In his other business ventures, he had never encountered the obligations shouldered by those who lived by virtue of the First Amendment and the special role of journalism in society. In my dealings with Pate and Larsen, I felt they understood the unique nature of the businesses they had acquired. But Zell's conduct shattered the credibility of his entire organization.

I didn't have much time or inclination to dwell on Zell's antics. I still didn't know from one paycheck to the next when the company might sever my only source of income. My expense payments finally got approved, but the company stonewalled any inquiries about the terms of my contract. I contacted Larry Feldman, Wolinsky's lawyer in Los Angeles, who was itching to sue Tribune Company because he thought its layoff and buyout policies were blatantly ageist. Even he advised me to sign the non-disparagement agreement. "I've read your contract, and there's no question you would win in court," Feldman admitted. "But your legal fees in litigating this would probably exceed what they owe you." Even with this counsel, my gut refused. I wouldn't, couldn't, sign it.

Weeks after I'd been fired, Hiller finally named Stanton to succeed me. I had lunch with Stanton shortly thereafter and gave him some advice. He was confident they couldn't fire him but told me they had inserted something during the negotiations over his contract that he called "the O'Shea clause"—a non-disparagement agreement. He had signed it, and I wished him the best. He graciously attended a farewell party Kathy Kristof, by now a friend and one of the paper's top financial columnists, gave for me at her home, and, as I prepared to leave Manhattan Beach, Stanton and the *Times*, unintentionally I'm sure, did me a huge favor.

The paper ran an investigative story in March disclosing new information supporting rapper Tupak Shakur's claims that he had been assaulted by associates of music executive Sean Diddy Combs in a 1994 incident in New York. The new information in the story was a police report that was soon exposed as a fake by a blogger who had done a little journalistic legwork. Critics eviscerated the *Times*, which had to retract the story. I called Cohn and said we should call the Tribune lawyers and ask them if they really wanted the former editor of the *Los Angeles Times* filing a lawsuit against them at a time like this. Shortly thereafter, Tribune lawyers called Cohen and indicated they might be interested in settling our differences. The company didn't pay me all that I was owed, but I never signed the non-disparagement agreement. Soon I heard that Hiller and Stanton ordered cuts that would take newsroom staffing levels from around 920 journalists to the mid-600 range. Within weeks, rebels in the *Times* newsroom covertly unfurled a huge three-story banner on the side of the paper's downtown Los Angeles headquarters. In big, thick, red-and-black capital letters it read: "ZELL'S HELL."

■

Journalists in Los Angeles might have had it bad, but at least they were 1,000 miles away from Tribune Tower. As I returned to Chicago, I encountered editors and journalists who had Zell and Michaels breathing down their necks. Lipinski had honed her skills as a reporter in City Hall and developed the ability to instinctually pick up on subtle signs that something might be amiss. In April 2007, shortly after the company had agreed to the Zell deal, Lipinski's first doubts about Zell surfaced during her lunch with him in the small, private dining room in his real estate office across town. Initially, the lunch involved a good conversation about journalists and how they think. Zell proudly told Lipinski how many people he'd made millionaires, and she advised him to focus on more than wealth when talking to the newsroom: "I told him you need to know that's not enough. Ideally, we all want to make money and have great journalism, but making money without great journalism won't go well."

Midway through the lunch, the conversation turned sharply when Zell brought up the profile that Greg Burns had written about him for the *Chicago Tribune Sunday Magazine* in 2004. "He remembered everything about it," Lipinski recalled, and his complaints about the story elevated into a screed against journalists, sentiments that would be expressed with increasing frequency over time.

Not long after the deal closed, Lipinski suffered one of the first casualties caused by the new owners—George de Lama, my good friend and longtime deputy who had succeeded me in running the newsroom at the *Tribune*. Proud of his heritage as a Latino and loyal to the *Chicago Tribune*, de Lama decided to leave the paper in May 2008. He didn't like the way the new owners disparaged a journalistic heritage of which he was proud, but an incident on Zell's road trip convinced him to give notice.

While at the *South Florida Sun Sentinel* in Fort Lauderdale, Zell made remarks that stuck in de Lama's craw: "I remember what he said. He said, 'You know we own this baseball team and we've got this mother-fucking schmuck that makes $25 million a year to play outfield and he can't even speak English.'" Zell was referring to Alfonso Soriano of the Chicago Cubs, a Latino. Coming on the heels of his crude put-down of a Latina photographer in Orlando, de Lama thought the remark displayed a remarkably callous and ignorant view of the heritage of one of the *Tribune's* largest pool of potential readers. "I could almost hear my dad saying to me, are you going to take that?" de Lama remembered. As he saw it, Zell and his henchmen had greatly disrespected a company for which he had risked his life as a correspondent. He resigned without another job.

In New York, de Lama's cousin, Louie Sito, got a break when the judge overseeing the sentencing of Sito and eight others involved in the *Newsday* circulation scandal decided not to send any of them to jail, leveling fines and forfeitures of $115,000 for Sito to $15,000 for Garcia, who had ordered that *Hoy* circulation numbers be inflated.

Banar's probe had taken on all of the trappings of an investigation that no one really wanted—long delays in sentencing, turnover of the staff in the trenches, and a U.S. Attorney who wanted to be a federal judge, not exactly a good posture from which to attack the local newspaper. The investigation started when Roslynn Mauskopf was U.S. Attorney for the Eastern District of New York, but she was appointed a federal judge in late 2007. By the time Sito and the others had been sentenced nine months later, Banar and most of her team had also moved on to other jobs outside of the government.

"I remain dubious [that the higher-ups at Tribune Company] didn't know what was going on," Judge Weinstein, who had presided over the *Newsday* case, told me. "I thought it would be unfair to give jail time to [lower-ranking employees]." He sentenced Sito and the others to probation and community service in addition to the fines. When asked what in the papers and records of the case made him think the prosecution didn't go far enough, he smiled and said: "Eighty-seven years of life in New York City, working on the docks, being on the bench for 40 years. You know, you gain a certain amount of moxie."

Lipinski was sorry to see de Lama go, but she remained determined to see the paper through a historic election in which a black man from Chicago was running for president of the United States. A gutsy and strong editor, Lipinski had done some unpopular things. I had watched her fire Bob Greene, a nationally known *Tribune* columnist, because she felt he had abused his position at the paper. She came under incredible pressure to back off, but she wouldn't. She did what she thought was right. She had also displayed backbone by traveling to the Sudan to demand that one of her reporters, Paul Salopek, be released from prison for entering the country without a visa. Now she confronted a problem of a totally different nature, one she had never encountered at Tribune Company. Zell had placed his alter ego, Randy Michaels, in charge of day-to-day operations, and Lipinski had already found his conduct alarming and offensive.

Michaels, whose real name was Benjamin Homel, seemed to generate controversy wherever he went. One of his associates described him as a man who could take one look at a radio tower and recite its vital statistics. Michaels had a similar reputation for assessing women. Complaints of sexual harassment, crude jokes, and boorish behavior dogged Michaels wherever he went. Zell's organization, including Larson and Pate, seemed mesmerized by Michaels, though, and to be fair, he was not without talent. He was a brilliant radio engineer, had made millions in the media and had helped Zell turn the 1993 acquisition of an ailing radio company named Jacor into an industry juggernaut. He and Zell peddled the company to Clear Channel Communications just five years later for $4.4 billion, a price tag that netted Zell a $1 billion profit. Within Zell's Equity Group, Michaels was considered a creative force who could impose brutal cost cuts with the crack of a joke.

The hundred-day Tribune plan Michaels provided Zell was a remarkable document. In nine pages of single-spaced bullet points about what to do with a company that owned America's best collection of daily newspapers, Michaels never mentioned the word *journalism*. If anything, he ridiculed the values for which Tribune once stood and targeted anyone who doubted his vision. "Empower opinion leaders who buy into the new vision," the document said. "Eliminate negative resistance and counterproductive team members immediately. Hang the turf Gods publicly." Michaels set out to rewrite the employee handbook and strip it of any policies that he viewed as politically correct. "Eliminate most of the HR Department," he proposed. "Ratings, contributive circulation, revenue and expense control are the new politics." And he advocated short, entertaining news stories focused heavily on attracting ad dollars. "We live in a ADD [attention deficit disorder] world," he said, where news stories should be short and newspapers scannable. Tribune Company should emulate Matt Drudge and Fox News and discontinue stale sections like "Tempo" in the *Chicago Tribune*. "Tempo," he said, "is so sixties. How about a section called 'Strange'? What's wrong with a section that holds news up to a funhouse mirror: 'Knuckleheads in News'?"

To implement his policies, Michaels began searching for opinion leaders within Tribune ranks who could sign on to policies to close news bureaus, eliminate middle management, downsize the staff, and create a news report that gave readers what they—and not some editor—wanted. Although Michaels' plan contained strongly worded policies that treated "middle management" as a scourge to be scrubbed from the Tower, he didn't highlight the replacements he had in mind—a platoon of cronies he recruited from his days in the radio business. In all, in less than a year, Michaels hired into senior positions more than twenty former associates, ranging from Marc Chase, a senior vice president of programming at Clear Channel Communications whom Michaels placed in charge of Tribune Interactive despite his dearth of Internet experience, to John Phillips, a traffic reporter for Michaels in Cincinnati who took over as building manager of Tribune Tower. When Tribune, which once had a strict policy on nepotism, hired Phillips' fiancée, Kim Johnson, as a senior vice president for local sales, the press release jokingly described her as "a former waitress at Knockers—the Place for Hot Rocks and Cold Brews."

"They tried to purge from the building and the company anything about the company's legacy or history, all of the Colonel stuff," recalled Mary Jo Mandula, who managed Tribune Tower until she was replaced by Phillips. "They started trying to get rid of the [First Amendment] Museum right away. I think they screwed up because they were getting a lot of rent for the museum. . . . Randy . . . wanted to get rid of every-thing that had anything to do with what we were."

Michaels' most celebrated hire was Lee Abrams, a fifty-five-year-old white-haired radio industry hotshot who was named chief inno-vation officer at Tribune. Abrams became known for his frequent, rambling stream-of-consciousness memos that declared news the new rock and roll. To his credit, some of Abrams' observations—such as news organizations didn't do enough to promote their unique content—were on the mark. But his uneven, randomly punctuated and capitalized notes invited ridicule. He wrote, introducing himself to the company's staff:

> I start April 1st but I've been pretty engaged from afar. Thought I'd share some observations on TV, web and print. Small stuff, "think pieces" more than anything . . . not end alls, but when we re-think and maximize hundreds of little pieces within the framework of bigger pieces and it would be the part of the blueprint for something very powerful: NERVE TOUCHING. This is where you get people to stand up on their chair because you touch a nerve. One underused way is simply to play to passions.

Few knew what to think of Abrams. Lipinski had her doubts and didn't invite him to any meetings involving an impending redesign of the paper.

Abrams, Michaels, Zell, and his team loved to portray themselves as iconoclasts who wore blue jeans to work and ridiculed anyone in a necktie. Yet they succeeded in creating an intimidating atmosphere for anyone who didn't follow their dress code or their thinking. Shortly after he walked into Tribune Tower, Zell created a "Talk to Sam" e-mail box for employees to communicate directly with the boss. He told employees to "challenge authority" and speak out about the company's weaknesses. "Talk to Sam," of course, drew the inevitable sycophantic messages from people like Margaret Holt, who worked in the public editor's office of the *Chicago Tribune* and who had heard Zell go after "arrogant journalists." In her note to the big man, she suggested, "Ban—or sharply limit—journalism contest entries by Tribune newspapers. . . . This is heresy, of course, and would get me bounced from the fraternal order of journalistas if word leaked."

But Zell's "Talk to Sam" initiatives also courted notes from professionals like Jeff Coen, the *Chicago Tribune*'s solid, federal courts reporter who commended Zell for the shake-up he'd stirred. One of his more frequent correspondents was Jane Hirt, an editor at *Redeye*, the Tribune's youth paper, who suggested that the company could increase revenue with a "Second Life for Cats" feature wherein the feline pets of readers could "live out lives online, have alter egos, get married, get jobs, run businesses, etc." Of course, most of the correspondents didn't realize Zell was passing on their remarks to their bosses and they penned long rants complaining about career setbacks or rejection of their ideas by "arrogant newsroom leaders," ratting out their colleagues in an atmosphere that soon turned crude and ugly, particularly once they started steep layoffs.

Within six months of the close of the Tribune deal, the economy started to nose-dive in earnest, and Zell, in a near panic, began talking of a crisis. He had acquired big papers in Florida and California, two states hit particularly hard by the subprime mortgage debacle, and the company's cash flow suffered along with the rest of the industry. He had built a financial cushion into the deal in case projections fell short, but his cushion disappeared as the slump in the economy devoured spare cash, forcing him to order deep budget cuts and layoffs, a sharp contrast to his optimistic forecasts made just months before.

Tribune Tower had been a pretty buttoned-down place that Michaels promised to change so people could have some fun. He commissioned jukeboxes, pinball, and air hockey machines. Mandula couldn't believe the company was spending $40,000 to $50,000 on games when Tribune was laying off people, but she soon got a taste of the kind of morale-building exercises Michaels and his team intended to offset any bad news. While at the company's Freedom Center printing plant, Mandula received a call that a beer truck had shown up wanting to deliver twenty cases of beer:

> I didn't know what this was for so I checked it out and found out that Marc Chase had ordered it for Friday beer parties at Tribune Interactive. I told them not to deliver it yet because . . . we didn't have a liquor license

and parties had to be catered. Marc Chase went to Randy and told him I wouldn't let them have their beer. . . . Pretty soon he [Michaels] comes into my office, closes the door and starts screaming at me. He called me the "Queen of No." You say no to everything, to juke-boxes, to pinball machines, to parking spots for people and now to beer. You can easily be replaced. I asked him, "Are you done yet?" and then told him that I did get him his pinball machines and I did get them their beer. He actually apologized to me.

It was hard to believe she was talking to the top corporate officer at one of America's largest media companies. But the bizarre incidents continued, she recalled, "They wanted people in Tribune Interactive to come up with $1 million revenue ideas. So they told me they wanted me to get $1 million in cash so they could put it on the floor and people could roll around in it and get their picture taken. It was stupid, and a stunt. It was expensive, too. I had to get a Brinks truck to deliver it, get extra security."

The good times didn't roll for people with long and solid ties to the Tribune Company, though. They had reason to fear for their futures, unless, of course, they swore allegiance to Michaels and his cronies from Clear Channel, which Michaels had left after clashing with the family that controlled the company. Even Kern called Lipinski and said he was sick of the foul language and compared them to Brown-shirts, using words like "evil" and "stupid." But it didn't take long for Kern to realize he had already developed a policy that fit right into Michaels' playbook. The new boss embraced Kern's plans for a central-ized news desk that produced cookie-cutter foreign and national coverage for all Tribune papers with far fewer "journalists" than those Kern had counted as they ran around the nation and world covering stories for Tribune papers, particularly the *Los Angeles Times*. Kern's star soon began to rise and those Brownshirts seemed more like khaki. Bob Gremillion, the transformative change czar under

FitzSimons, began championing Kern's ideas, and both became fixtures of Michaels' team.

The antics spawned disbelief and guffaws on the blogs following the doings in the Tower, but they were not funny. Michaels created an atmosphere of fear. At one point, Michaels installed a sign in the lobby outside the *Chicago Tribune* newsroom headlined: "The Perils of Modern Journalism: Should Political Correctness Trump Accuracy." The line on the sign, "A customer is the most important visitor on our premises," was attributed to Mahatma Gandhi. To most people, the idea that Gandhi was into customer service was a stretch. The pep talk about the customer continued, "He is not dependent on us. We are dependent on him. He is not an interruption of our work. He is the purpose of it. He is not an outsider to our business. He is part of it. We are not doing him a favor by serving him. He is doing us a favor by giving us the opportunity to do so."

Of course, in a building full of journalists, someone quickly checked whether Gandhi had ever uttered these words and found experts who debunked the notion. When someone with a magic marker came along and put an (S) is front of every reference to "he," Michaels went into orbit. A huge blue banner was draped over the sign, relocated to the Tribune Tower lobby. It read: "This poster was defaced shortly after it was placed outside of the *Chicago Tribune* newsroom." As the bizarre become commonplace, Lipinski started wondering how long she could tolerate the situation.

■

Even before phase two of the deal closed, the banks had pressed Zell to sell assets, particularly the Chicago Cubs, a team then valued at $1 billion that didn't generate a lot of cash flow. The banks figured the sales proceeds could be used to reduce debt without hurting the cash stream needed to pay down the rest of the loans. Zell soon figured out a way to structure a deal in which he could maximize the price and get favorable tax treatment by selling the team to interested buyers, and Wrigley Field, its historic stadium, to the state, using tax-exempt bonds to finance the deal, creating a situation similar to that of U.S. Cellular Field, which the state had built for the Chicago White Sox.

His negotiators began some backroom dealings with representatives of Illinois Governor Rod Blagojevich, a controversial figure who at the time was being investigated for using state contracts to reap political donations. After another lunch in his office, Zell had told Lipinski that the *Tribune* should be tougher on Blagojevich. Unaware that Zell was in negotiations with the governor over the ballpark, she informed him that the paper had aggressively investigated the governor and that the editorial board had already called for his resignation. "Don't be a pussy," Zell responded. "You can always be harder on him." The paper didn't knuckle under to Zell's pressure, but when Lipinski later learned of the Zell negotiations, she became even more disenchanted with him. He eventually sold the Cubs for $900 million. But his dealings with Blagojevich cost him more than a red face. As one insider privy to the deal later told me, had Zell acted more quickly, he probably could have gotten one billion or more for the team: "He left $100 million or more on the table."

Lipinski is neither a prude nor Pollyanna, and she's no stranger to foul language. Anyone who has ever inhabited a newsroom knows the language can get raw. She had done layoffs before and had been informed by Scott Smith that she would have to do a new round soon. But in June 2008, Zell and his team forced Smith out. In July, it was Hiller's turn. Zell called him into his office in Chicago and said he was going to make a change in the leadership in Los Angeles. Both men had employment agreements that called for severance benefits of $12.4 million and $15.4 million, respectively, in salary, tax gross-ups, and stock options.

Bobby Gremillion had been named acting publisher in Chicago and met with Lipinski. Unbeknownst to him, she suspected her resignation was imminent but wanted to take responsibility for what she hoped would be a final round of layoff discussions so it didn't have to be the first thing her successor faced in assuming command of the newsroom. Gremillion told her what level of layoffs he required, then added that he needed two more things from her—to "let Lee Abrams on the floor" to redesign the paper and to work with Gerry Kern on his plans, both of which she had resisted. "I said, 'Look, Bobby, I have a lot to do today to get this layoff planning under way. How about we talk about the rest tomorrow?'" Lipinski met with her senior managers to deliver the grim layoff news and map out a plan for getting there. Early the next morning, she returned to Gremillion's office and told him she had decided to leave the paper. He spit out his coffee. "What?" She handed him a resignation letter. "But what will you do?" he asked. She said she didn't know but she couldn't stay. Later that day, she received a call from William Osborn, who was still on the Tribune board. He told her how sorry he was that she was leaving the paper but that he knew that things had become very difficult at the *Tribune*.

She also met with Michaels, who tried to pitch her to stay, promoting the virtues of what he claimed would be expanded news-gathering capacity as a result of closer working ties with WGN. Lipinski told him she was not resigning over resource issues and that she had come to see him to stress how untenable the culture had become, that conditions for women in particular were intolerable, and that her views were widely, if quietly, shared by others around the company who were exposed to the new class of managers. For a moment, Lipinski thought she had gotten through. Michaels said he had been eager to compel change at Tribune Company but was probably due for a course correction. "We've gone too far," he conceded. Lipinski talked about newsroom culture in particular, and how journalists were not choirboys, but that colorful language or stories had a purpose and were not told merely to threaten or insult. They discussed one story in particular—an Illinois congressman's affair with a teenage girl and the *Tribune's* unprecedented decision to publish a transcript of the federal government's recording of a sexually-explicit phone call. But the point was lost on Michaels. "Blow job? You put the word blow job in the paper? Excellent!" Lipinski left her resignation letter on his conference table. I attended her going-away party in the Billy Goat Tavern.

With Michaels' blessing, Kern was named editor of the *Chicago Tribune*. At long last, he'd gotten the job he so coveted. For his managing editor, he tapped Jane Hirt, the *Redeye* editor and proponent of a "Second Life for Cats." Much would be made in the ensuing months of the leadership of Tribune Company, as the *Chicago Tribune* turned a blind eye toward the raunchy conduct of Michaels and his team. Even Osborn and the board of Tribune Company were aware of Michaels' antics. For once, something had happened about which FitzSimons and I agreed. I decided life wasn't too bad after losing a job.

I figured the foul language and juvenile conduct in the newsroom would pass. I was far more concerned with what Michaels and company would do to the *Chicago Tribune*. At one going-away party in August, I saw Jim Kirk, then the *Tribune*'s associate managing editor for financial news, arguing, red-faced, with editors on his cellphone. When I asked what was wrong, he said he was trying to convince them to put the story of the Lehman Brothers bankruptcy, a blow on Wall Street that would trigger a collapse of the financial markets, on page one. "Jane wanted to know what it had to do with Chicago," Kirk explained. That day's paper led with a story about the Chicago Cubs.

By now, I had received a fellowship at the Joan Shorenstein Center on the Press, Politics and Public Policy at Harvard Kennedy School and was preparing to leave Chicago for Boston. Every day, the *Chicago Tribune* would land on my doorstep with an increasingly irrelevant front page. One day I picked it up and, in the same space on page one where *Tribune* reporters had published stories that transformed the global debate over the equity of the death penalty, I found a huge spread promoting a quest for the best cheeseburger in Chicago. Many great journalists and good friends remained at the *Chicago Tribune* laboring under rotten conditions. But as a reader, I simply could no longer pay them good money to endorse what they gave me in the paper. I canceled my subscription.

In December 2008, the Tribune Company filed for bankruptcy, claiming debts of $13 billion and assets of $7.6 billion. By then, the new owners had laid off more than 4,000 employees of Tribune

Company, including hundreds of journalists. In Los Angeles, just one year after I'd left, the newsroom was down by nearly 50 percent. The *Chicago Tribune* didn't escape the carnage, although the cuts were not as bad there since it wasn't as big as the *Los Angeles Times*. It had cut its newsroom and narrowed the space devoted to news to generate a positive cash flow only because it didn't have to pay its debts. Readership fell, too. Until the company filed for bankruptcy, Zell believed he would make a lot of money in the deal. By then, though, he had taken to calling his acquisition of Tribune, "The Deal From Hell." Zell had lost more money during his career as a maverick investor than he did in Tribune. But his reputation had taken a hit. In January 2009, I left Chicago and drove through snowstorms for Cambridge, Massachusetts, leaving "The Deal From Hell" and my life as a newspaperman on the shores of Lake Michigan. Or so I thought.

# Epilogue

I loved my time at the Joan Shorenstein Center on the Press, Politics and Public Policy. When I arrived in Cambridge, snow covered the Harvard campus. Barack Obama had just been inaugurated president of the United States. I walked to a local cycling store, bought a bike for transportation, and started my fellowship—a marvelous program that provided me with an office, a research assistant, a stipend, and Harvard's vast resources. The other fellows at the Shorenstein Center were Maralee Schwartz, a former editor at the *Washington Post*; Michael Traugott, a professor of communications from the University of Michigan; and Mitchell Stephens, a journalistic historian from New York University.

Shorenstein fellows spend a semester at Harvard writing a paper, speech, or contribution to a book about journalism. The luxury of the fellowship is ample time to think. Just as I started researching this book, I was asked to speak briefly at a lunch hosted by the Nieman fellows, a group of mid-career journalists who come to Harvard for a full academic year to expand their horizons. When the Nieman fellows stood up at the lunch to introduce themselves, it dawned on me how fortunate I'd been in my career. All of the Nieman fellows were exceptionally talented and accomplished people, like Kael Alford, an intrepid journalist who had risked her life in Iraq to take her gripping photographs. As they discussed their projects and what was next on their horizons, many of the Nieman fellows expressed fears about the future of journalism. They hoped, they told me, they would have a job or newspaper to return to when the fellowship ended.

The Nieman fellows' fears were real. By early 2009, hardly a day passed without a news headline about major media layoffs. As the economy slumped and the Internet devoured its ad revenues, even the *New York Times*, which had to that point resisted cutbacks, started buyouts and outright newsroom layoffs. Newspaper readership was in free fall as the recession deepened and managers continued to prune the junk circulation from their books. Retailers and customers watching declining circulation began questioning the true value of newspaper advertising. By relying too heavily on cost cuts to compensate for financial problems, the news industry had created an ongoing cycle of decline.

It began with the production process. You need printing plants, paper, ink, trucks, and gas to produce a paper and deliver it to a reader's doorstep in the morning. Those expenses—ones that are relatively fixed and hard to manipulate down if you want to stay in business—can account for 65 percent to 75 percent or more of the costs of producing a newspaper. By January 2009, newspaper managers faced an equally unbalanced revenue structure. Over time, publishers had, for a variety of reasons (including fear of losing readers), resisted raising the price of a daily newspaper. In effect, publishers conditioned Americans to get their news for far below the cost of production. Readers paid little for newspapers and they wanted it to stay that way. The economics were quite democratic; publishers delivered the news to everyone usually for less than a dollar. The media subsidized the cost of delivering the news with revenue from advertising purchased by businesses that wanted to put their commercial message in front of readers or viewers. At many big-city newspapers, advertising accounted for about 80 percent of the revenues. In their salad days, newspapers had a monopoly because no one else had access to their customers, and they could charge what they wanted for advertising. There were not many ways for companies to determine how many readers actually read their ads.

But the Internet had upended the media's traditional business model at newspapers and broadcast outlets. Suddenly, advertisers could appeal to potential customers much more cheaply by running commercial messages on their own websites, over e-mail, or through companies like Google. The rapidly growing Internet juggernaut based in Cupertino, California, attracted huge audiences by lifting newspaper and broadcast content for free off the Internet, telling advertisers they didn't have to pay for the low-cost ads adjacent to the content unless someone actually clicked on the message or bought something. Unlike news that relied on an intricate delivery system, Google delivered its information digitally, eliminating the expenses of a printing plant and truck. In effect, for every dollar advertisers paid a newspaper to run an ad, they could now get the same message on the Internet for a dime. And Google was collecting most of the dimes. Newspaper executives complained bitterly about Google, but there wasn't much they could do about the company.

Unless newspaper executives could find a solution, the decline would continue. Newspapers could cut their fixed costs only so much if they still wanted to deliver the newspaper to readers. Just as ad revenues began to plummet—partially because of the recession and partially because of the Googles of the world—newspapers balked at the kind of steep price increases needed to thrust their product onto stable financial footing, fearing a backlash of resistance from customers. Even worse, a new generation of younger readers accustomed to getting their news for free on the Internet didn't read newspapers. Traditional media companies tried to fight back by beefing up newspaper websites. But the websites had been starved by the industry's astonishing lack of research and development spending. Even if they were successful in improving their web presence, the monies papers got for advertising were far lower than they'd once been and the competition was much stronger. So, to lower costs, newspapers targeted their most valuable asset—the one thing that distinguished them from the others but also something they had devalued by pricing it so low: their journalism. Cuts to the heart of the industry created the kind of gloom-and-doom headlines that simply perpetuated the cycle of decline.

At the *Los Angeles Times*, Zell, Michaels, and their team imposed harsh newsroom cutbacks. They slashed the amount of space devoted to news and eliminated at least three hundred newsroom jobs, taking the staff down to fewer than six hundred journalists. One of those to go was Leo Wolinsky, who was let go in October 2008. *Times* editors masked some of the cuts with a relatively smart redesign of the paper and continued to invest what resources they could in their website. Thanks to the temporary respite of bankruptcy court, the *Times* no longer had to cough up much of the cash Tribune needed to repay the crushing debt Zell had piled onto the company. But the markets served by the *Los Angeles Times* had been hit particularly hard by the subprime mortgage mess, and ad revenues plunged.

In Chicago, Zell had turned his attention and his remaining billions to his other far-flung investments, admitting that his foray into newspapers had been a mistake. Not only was he out the $315 million he had invested in "The Deal From Hell," his reputation as a man with the Midas touch was in tatters as the company slogged through bankruptcy court. The company's creditors couldn't agree on a plan to reorganize Tribune—a necessary step for the business to emerge from bankruptcy and begin to repay its bank loans. Zell placed Tribune Company and the *Chicago Tribune* in the hands of Michaels, who implemented the steps he first laid out in his hundred-day plan for Tribune.

With Kern at the helm, Abrams was given access to the newsroom, which elevated his status in the newsroom and the industry. The paper cut its staff and the space allotted to news, while Abrams engineered a redesign of the paper at Michaels' behest. Kern closed the paper's foreign and national news bureaus and replaced them with his brand of cookie-cutter coverage that was centered in Chicago. Heavily promoted stories about fake food, taxi strikes, or American Girl's new digs replaced serious front-page national and foreign news at the *Chicago Tribune*. In line with Abrams and Michaels' formula for market-driven news, sports stories about the White Sox or the Chicago Cubs also got prominent play on page one. Before long, the *Chicago Tribune* began to resemble a splashy tabloid. The paper still contained serious news, but it was usually relegated to stripped-down wire reports on inside pages. Luckily for the *Los Angeles Times*, all Tribune papers started relying on the *Times'* national and foreign staffs for global coverage.

When one *Tribune* editor pitched a story on the city's troubled public housing program for page one, Hirt, Kern's managing editor, rejected it for not being in the paper's demographic, an editor at the meeting recounted. Representatives from the newspaper's marketing department started "helping" editors select news coverage, and a far more repressive atmosphere took root in the newsroom. Kirk, the paper's associate managing editor for financial news, saw a change soon after Lipinski stepped down when he objected to a company plan that he thought would damage a business columnist's credibility. Michaels summoned him into his office with Kern in tow, told him that he knew how to deal with "troublemakers," and warned Kirk "that he hadn't heard the last" from Michaels. Kirk left the paper soon thereafter.

Many decent, committed, and talented journalists remain on the staff of the *Chicago Tribune*, and they continue to pursue great journalism, particularly investigative series on local issues. Michael Oneal also continues the difficult job of covering the company's bankruptcy with skill and precision. The *Tribune* launched a crusade against people and politicians who used their political clout to get their kids—or friends' kids—into the University of Illinois. But the reporters didn't get the kind of leadership they deserved, and they still don't. The coverage of the University of Illinois lacked the context a good editor would have demanded to document the true scope of the problem, not just at the University of Illinois but in other states and at other schools. As a reader, I felt the paper's news judgment became sophomoric, parochial, and superficial. In January 2011, when Chicago's own President Obama gave a moving speech in Phoenix, Arizona, after congresswoman Gabrielle Giffords had been shot in the head by a disturbed young man, the *Chicago Tribune* barely mentioned the story on its front page. But at the end of the day, Michaels' conduct overshadowed the paper's dubious news judgment.

In my days at the *Chicago Tribune*, the Colonel's former office on the twenty-fourth floor was hallowed ground; the Colonel's massive Italian marble desk, his huge globe, and rare books all stood as symbols of the company's legacy and of his dedication to the First Amendment. When he became CEO, Madigan opened up the twenty-fourth floor for use as a company conference center, but most of the time, the offices were as quiet as a church sanctuary.

Michaels used the Colonel's office for a poker party. "We are in the office of the guy who ran the company from the 1920s to 1955," wrote John Phillips, the Cincinnati traffic reporter Michaels had installed as building manager of Tribune Tower, on Facebook. "We pretty well desecrated it with gambling, booze and cigars. Good thing we know the guy that runs the building," Phillips noted. His favorite trick in the poker room? Covering up the smoke detectors with Saran Wrap.

A terrace on the twenty-second floor of Tribune Tower became Michaels' coveted real estate. The space, with its expansive view of Lake Michigan, was big enough to host a small party. Michaels ordered picnic tables to be placed on the patio so he and his guests could enjoy the open area. But fresh air wasn't the only thing that Michaels enjoyed on the terrace. Michaels had been warned not to leave the french doors leading outside ajar, because an open door would trigger an alarm at the security office downstairs. One warm day in 2008, a Tribune Tower security guard noticed something had triggered the alarm and sent a colleague up to the twenty-second floor to investigate. Seeing the door open, the guard stepped out onto the terrace and later reported to his superiors that he had stumbled onto Michaels, standing with his arms extended as if on a cross, receiving fellatio from a young female *Tribune* employee. The guard abruptly returned to the security office. But Randy Michaels was now the man at the top of the Tower and he could do as he damn well pleased.

Michaels, who was married, compounded his boorish conduct at Tribune with open disregard toward Chicago Tribune journalists, so much so that one employee wrote anonymously to the company's board: "I feel compelled to report on some things that speak to the competency and qualifications of senior management at Tribune and the potential litigation risk they pose to an already fragile balance sheet." Michaels' dalliance with the young woman on the balcony was, the employee wrote, a lawsuit waiting to happen. When Zell took over in 2007, he had replaced everyone on the board except for Osborn and Betsy Holden, a former Kraft Foods executive. Zell became chairman and installed a new board composed of William Pate; Brian L. Greenspun, president and editor of the *Las Vegas Sun*; Jeffrey S. Berg, chairman and CEO of International Creative Management, a talent and literary agency in Los Angeles; Mark Shapiro, a former CEO of Six Flags Entertainment; and Frank Wood, CEO of Secret Communications, a Cincinnati venture capital company. Michaels was also named to the board later. But the investigation of his behavior and the rampant cronyism at Tribune Tower went nowhere. The author determined that at least one member of the board became aware of the substance of the letter and that the board authorized the Jenner & Block law firm to investigate the allegations. But the lawyers said no one had complained to the human relations department, an office that Michaels had belittled in his hundred-day plan. Instead the board and senior management at the company and the newspaper tolerated Michaels and the fraternity house atmosphere he brought to Tribune Tower for more than two years until David Carr, a media reporter at the *New York Times* exposed the lurid conduct and cronyism in a front-page story that shamed the board into seeking Michaels' resignation. He resigned on October 22, 2010. But many of the people he had placed in charge of the newspaper remain in their jobs and have collected more than $50 million in management bonuses.

Kern and the board publicly expressed dismay at the conduct exposed by Carr and ordered his reporters to cover the situation aggressively. But as Robert Feder, a Chicago columnist pointed out, "not one of them spoke up about what was going on inside their own company until the *New York Times* slapped it on its front page twelve days ago."

■

While I was at Harvard, I received reports of the off-putting atmosphere at the Tower from friends and former colleagues seeking recommendations for jobs in news organizations or, more frequently, jobs outside the industry. Midway through my fellowship, journalism jobs were disappearing all over the country, and the trend showed no signs of changing. I felt terrible for journalists who had to tolerate Michaels and his antics. But the *Tribune* and the *Times* were not the only victims of the economic carnage. I felt for several of the Nieman fellows I had befriended, including Dorothy Parvaz, a columnist and editorial writer at the *Seattle Post Intelligencer*. Soon after my talk, she had asked me to lunch to pick my brain about the future of journalism. I could see desperation in her eyes. She was smart, talented, dedicated, and committed to journalism, but suddenly she, like many other journalists I knew, faced something far worse than the prospect of losing a job. Critics of the so-called mainstream media, credible people and kooks alike, were saying what Parvaz, one of the best in her craft, had done for decades no longer had any value. She was like someone in the auto or steel industry whose plant had been shuttered. The pervasive mantra was "information is free." In the new paradigm, information could be gathered by ordinary citizens and bloggers working for free, not just by professional journalists. Parvaz's job had been outsourced to people who would work for little or nothing just to get a byline.

A professor at the Harvard Business School invited me to a workshop on the problems facing the newspaper industry. At the workshop, I suddenly realized the role that I had played in the crisis roiling the industry. In our quest to remain above the fray and deliver the news objectively, journalists had become so remote that our readers didn't appreciate the difference between reporting and simply gathering information. The seminar included some of the brightest students in America. Yet most of them clearly didn't understand what reporting, the backbone of journalism, was all about. One student offered that anyone could be a reporter—all he had to do was hold up an iPhone, record an event, and put it on the Internet. When the professor asked me to comment, I pointed out that if all I had ever done as a journalist was tell people what had happened at some event or meeting, I would never have given anyone the real story. Reporting involved digging through records, interviewing numerous sources, double-checking facts, and learning about deals cut behind the scenes. After the class, the professor thanked me for giving his students the perspective that journalists assumed everyone understood. My defense of our craft didn't help Parvaz, though. Before her fellowship ended, the *Seattle Post Intelligencer* folded its print edition to publish online. They offered Parvaz her job back at a far lower salary. She declined and moved to London.

At Harvard, I began wrestling with the question of how news organizations under duress would be able to sustain public service journalism, the kind of stories that exposed perilous conditions at King/Drew Hospital in Los Angeles or abuses of laws governing the death penalty in Illinois. In a research study, Thomas E. Patterson, a professor of government and the press at the Shorenstein Center, had documented how news organizations faced with shrinking audiences often turn to soft news or superficial negative reports that rely on dubious sources rather than careful investigative journalism. The result, particularly for young adults, was the kind of diminished interest in public affairs and news that I had witnessed at the business school. But Patterson's study was published in 2000 when newspapers were relatively healthy. Most newsrooms now faced steep cutbacks and had more to do as reporters and editors were called on to feed understaffed and underinvested websites trying to compensate for revenue drains. Public service journalism was hard and expensive work, and I wondered just how it would be done in the future and who would pay for it. In other words, while everyone offered their opinions and bloviated on the Internet for free, who was going to cover the courthouse?

Midway through my fellowship, I gave a talk at the *Harvard Crimson*, the student newspaper. Afterward, the *Crimson's* editor told me that he wanted to be just like me, to do just what I'd done. I, of course, questioned his sanity. After all, almost everyone I knew had been—or worried that they soon would be—laid off, as the business model that journalists had relied on for decades crumbled. But the young editor told me that my remarks to his staff showed how I had spent my life providing people with information they needed, that I had made a difference, something that he, too, wanted to do. I was humbled but also sad that idealistic young men and women who wanted to be journalists faced a much bleaker future than I had at their age.

A few weeks later, I went home to Chicago for the weekend and received a phone call from Peter Osnos, founder and editor-at-large of the house that published this book. I assumed he was checking on the progress of my work, but I was wrong. Osnos, who had a family retreat in Lakeside, Michigan, a small town across the lake from Chicago, and a group of neighbors alarmed at the decline of local media in Chicago wanted to start a public service news site online, and he asked if I could help. Osnos had two partners, Newton Minow, a former Tribune board member and leading civic figure in Chicago, and Martin (Mike) Koldyke, a businessman and education activist, both of whom were on the board of WTTW, the local public television station. Their plan was to piggyback on WTTW's nonprofit status and start a news organization that could legally accept tax-deductible donations. We didn't have any money, and we didn't really have a journalism plan laying out exactly what we would do with the funds we would raise to get us off the ground. Frankly, the last thing I wanted to do was run another news organization, particularly one that would compete against my old newspaper where I still had many friends. I also pointed out that I still owed him a book. But I told Osnos I would think about it and get back to him.

My career hadn't ended on the best note. Overall, though, I had had a great ride. The Tribune Company and the newspaper industry had been good to me. A scruffy kid from north St. Louis, I got the opportunity to see the world, tell stories, and run the newsrooms of two great newspapers. Perhaps it was time for some payback. I called

Osnos back and said I would be a catalyst by helping his group get something started. I told him I would work up to a year for no pay and that I would get him someone to run the effort long term, but that I didn't want to run another news organization.

Back at Harvard, I racked my brain about what to do. By now it was clear that the newspaper industry's problems were not about to go away. No matter what, the infrastructure of the newspaper couldn't ditch the significant expense of delivering its product to the doors of customers for far less than it cost. Many younger readers got their news on the Internet, where newspapers and a new breed of news aggregators offered it up for free in a desperate bid to win advertising dollars. Why would any rational person pay for a newspaper subscription when they could get the same thing online for free?

It doesn't take a genius to figure out the situation might not end well. Newspapers remain the backbone of the news. Although many newspaper staffs have been thinned, a dwindling core of journalists still file into courthouses, police stations, legislatures, and government agencies to report on the people's business. While news aggregators on the Internet boast snazzy websites and fresh content, if you peel back the surface, you'll find that most—if not all—of their content is based on a newspaper report. The Pew Research Center's Project for Excellence in Journalism did just that in a weeklong 2009 study on news in Baltimore, Maryland, generated by fifty-three news outlets that ranged from newspapers to bloggers and talk radio. The investigation winnowed the reports studied down to six major narrative threads that dominated the news, and tracked down the actual source for the six narratives. Even though the city had more news outlets than in previous years, eight of ten stories produced relied on information picked up from other sources. Indeed, 95 percent of the stories came from traditional media, mainly newspapers. The *Baltimore Sun*, a Tribune Company newspaper, accounted for nearly half of the stories. But over the last six years, the *Sun* has cut its newsroom by about 60 percent, a staggering reduction. And, the project discovered, the *Sun* produced 32 percent fewer stories on any subject than it had ten years earlier, in 1999. Few have grappled with the consequences of what will happen if this trend continues, or if the *Sun* and other newspapers like it can no longer afford to be the backbone of the news, which is not as far-fetched as some would like to believe.

I struggled to come up with an idea of what we should do with our proposed venture in Chicago. One night I went to bed thinking about the problem and woke up around 3 a.m. with a brainstorm: We should start a news cooperative dedicated to public service journalism that could be financed by contributions from readers. I had covered agricultural cooperatives early in my career at the *Des Moines Register*, and I suppose I summoned the idea from my journalistic subconscious. I got up, headed to the Internet, and began researching cooperatives. By the next morning, I had produced a memo for Osnos that became the foundation for the Chicago News Cooperative (CNC), where I am now editor.

As a journalist and someone who cares deeply about the future of my craft, I wish I could say I've figured out just where the news is headed. But I haven't, and neither has anyone else. We organized the CNC as a nonprofit that relies on tax-deductible donations. The idea was to raise enough money from foundations and individuals to start a website that would provide in-depth local coverage of civic and cultural institutions and fill in the gap created by cutbacks at struggling major media organizations in the city. With a website creating unique content, we would seek a small membership fee to join the coop, which would give access to our news reports and a voice in the news through interactive features. I figured if we could raise enough money to get 40,000 to 50,000 members over five years, or about one-half of 1 percent of the population of the Chicago metropolitan area, we would have enough money to create a self-sustaining news organization that could employ thirty to forty journalists to cover the city and provide true public service journalism created by skilled journalists and informed by readers.

Over the past year and a half, I've learned that achieving our goals is not as easy as it might sound. We've had some breaks. Editors at the *New York Times* got wind of our idea when the paper was exploring the possibility of setting up local partnerships to produce Chicago news for its Midwest edition. Impressed with our goals and the quality of the journalists we could attract to the CNC, the *Times* made a modest contribution to help us get started and signed a deal under which it would pay us to produce two pages of Chicago news for the *Times* twice a week. But the *Times'* financial contribution wasn't enough to get us off the ground until the MacArthur Foundation approved an expedited $500,000 grant. We started producing content for the *Times* in November 2009 and have been at it ever since.

We've also had some setbacks. When my fellowship ended and I was driving back to Chicago in July 2009, Osnos called to tell me that Minow had set up a meeting with a major foundation in Chicago to make a presentation for funding for the CNC. Minow was leaving town July 4 for the rest of the summer and wanted me to attend the presentation. I had to come up with a formal outline of our plans within a few days. From the road, I called a trusted, creative, and talented colleague from my days at the *Tribune*, Bill Parker, and asked for his help. He enlisted another *Tribune* colleague, Tony Majeri, and we all went to work on my idea and a presentation. I arrived in Chicago on a Friday and by the following Monday I found myself making my presentation to the McCormick Foundation and its newly minted CEO—David Hiller, who'd been hired by a board comprising Dennis FitzSimons, Scott Smith, Jim Dowdle, and John Madigan. The foundation denied our request.

Although I told Osnos the last thing I wanted to do was run another news organization, I remain the editor of the CNC. Over the last two years, I've had to learn lots of new things—about the world of fund-raising, about running a news organization with a far smaller staff, about the incredible allure and power of technology to resolve one problem and create another, and about a new economics that seems to create billionaires overnight.

Some of what I've learned gives me hope that the next generation will enjoy the same opportunities that I have enjoyed. When I first walked into the *Des Moines Register* in 1971, you had to be a multi-millionaire to buy the plants and equipment needed to start a newspaper. We did it at the CNC with little money. But some of what I've seen in the inexorable march of technology and economics makes me wonder what kind of world my children will inherit. Capitalism built the American newspaper industry, but it was the sort of capitalism embraced by men and women who wanted to build something that would endure, employ people, and make the founders rich by providing a vital service. I don't know that the kind of capitalism evolving in America holds the same promise. Many of today's capitalists seem more interested in creating companies with baked-in exit strategies designed to get their ventures up and running so they can be sold for billions to global investors far more interested in earning profits than serving the public. The citizens in a democracy need to base their decisions on good, solid information. The exit strategy for a democracy isn't exactly a pretty picture.

Reporting the news remains a struggle, not only for the CNC but also for many major media organizations. Unlike many other cities, Chicago still has two daily newspapers, the *Chicago Sun-Times* and the *Chicago Tribune*. The *Sun-Times* emerged from bankruptcy a little over a year ago, but it is still hanging on by a thread. The parent company of the *Tribune* and the *Los Angeles Times* is struggling to emerge from bankruptcy, but its plight has been complicated by controversy. In seeking an advantaged status as a creditor, one group owed money by Tribune alleged that its claims should take precedence over others because fraud played a hand in the Zell transaction. Bankruptcy Court Judge Kevin J. Carey appointed Kenneth N. Klee, a California law professor and bankruptcy expert, to examine the charges. Klee issued an expert opinion that concluded that a "fraudulent conveyance" charge could stick if the case went to court. Klee's investigation found that Donald Grenesko and Chandler Bigelow, Tribune's former and current chief financial officers, had provided information that suggested Tribune Company would be solvent after phase two of the Zell deal when, in fact, the opposite was true. Grenesko and Bigelow have denied the allegations. Klee's voluminous report exposes that almost every party involved in making sure the deal closed was rewarded with staggering fees and bonuses. His report has sparked litigation that also will make many lawyers rich. A cloud of doubt continues to loom over the Tribune Company, its newspapers and, most significantly, the employees who have already or might still lose their jobs. The bankruptcy even has spawned a raft of lawsuits against employees who had nothing to do with the details of the Zell deal, including Lipinski and me.

In many respects, the Tribune's plight is unique and far more complex than the dire situation that faces other newspapers and media organizations around the country and world. But in many ways, it also represents the stark reality of the battle facing those interested in the future of the news. Instead of pumping their energy and resources into building a new business model and creating a path to a successful future, newspapers remain institutions distracted by their fight to survive, shackled by declines in revenues, legal problems, new competitors, and, in the case of Tribune Company, diversion of resources into things that have nothing to do with providing the public with news. The company's professional fees in its bankruptcy case total $240 million and probably will top out at $300 million or more before it emerges from court, enough to run the combined *Los Angles Times* and *Chicago Tribune* newsrooms for more than a year.

When I speak to citizens in Chicago and elsewhere, people ask me: Will we still have newspapers? Of course, we will have newspapers. Newspapers today continue to create great journalism, too. But the great journalism that newspapers and broadcasters still produce often is episodic rather than the systematic examination of significant issues. Let's not kid ourselves, either. Newspapers and broadcast outlets will find it progressively harder to finance the delivery of high-quality news. We are moving into a world where someone wealthy enough to pay $2 a day and $6 on Sunday for the *New York Times* or $18,000 to $20,000 per year for a machine from Bloomberg News will get high-quality news, as good as or perhaps better than ever. Gone will be the days when everyone can get the same quality of news delivered to their doorsteps every day for a fraction of what it actually costs. And that is a fundamental change in our society, the implications of which we've not yet absorbed. The current practice of delivering news to readers far below its cost and relying on an advertising base that will continue to shrink is simply unsustainable. Someone has to find a new model based on new economics. Until then, newspapers will continue to shrink, become more expensive, have fewer subscribers, and be delivered less frequently, perhaps once or twice a week instead of every day.

Yet the need for quality journalism has never been greater. The Internet is flooding the world with raw information, demonstrating its awesome power to unleash democratic revolutions that topple dictators and despots. But raw information also incubates rumor, disinformation, and propaganda, which in turn breed chaos and ignorance that divide our world. We don't know yet what kind of governments will replace the autocratic regimes toppled by the information revolution spreading across the Middle East. The one thing we do know is that, for us to know what will happen, we need to get our information from good, solid reporting, the kind that sifts through rumor, innuendo, and distortion to create fact, context, and reason.

The real question we face is not whether we will still have newspapers; the real question is, will we still have journalism—not aggregated content gathered to foster ad sales—but hard-hitting, time-consuming investigative and analytical reporting about the major issues of the day?

I remain here at the CNC because I believe we must have that kind of journalism. So does Ann Marie Lipinski; she is one of the founding members of the CNC board. Good, solid journalism remains vital to Chicago, the nation, and the world. Throughout my career, I have seen a world without dogged reporting. Time and again, I've seen the press seized and silenced by soldiers marching in the clouds of dust stirred by the despot's boot. We cannot allow apathy and indifference to become the soldiers of silence in America. The answer is out there, perhaps in a fledgling operation like the CNC or one of dozens like it springing up across the land, or perhaps in the head of some entrepreneur. An audience for serious news is out there. It is smaller, more discerning, and willing to pay if the information is good and the reporting is solid. It is out there and when someone finds it, it will be one hell of a story. I know. After all, I'm still a reporter, I can feel that story—in my gut.

# ACKNOWLEDGMENTS

SO MANY PEOPLE helped with this book that it's hard to express my gratitude without inadvertently missing someone. So I apologize in advance if I failed to recognize anyone, and, if I did, it was an error of omission and not an intended slight. Several authors have written excellent books on the companies I covered in this book and the newspaper industry, including Richard Norton Smith, the late David Halberstam, Dennis McDougal, Charles M. Madigan, and the late A. J. Liebling. I borrowed material and insights from them and tried hard to appropriately recognize their fine work in the text and in notes. I am deeply indebted to Alex Jones and the Joan Shorenstein Center on the Press, Politics and Public Policy at Harvard University. Jones and the incredible staff at the Shorenstein Center threw me a lifeline when I needed one and provided the resources and encouragement to get this book off the ground. Special thanks should also go to my daughter, Bridget O'Shea, a dogged and determined researcher. This book never would have been completed without the help of Sharene Shariatzadeh of the Chicago News Cooperative, where I work. She calls herself my "handler" but in reality she was a crutch I leaned on time and again during a long journey. I owe everyone at the coop a debt of gratitude for the understanding they displayed when I was distracted by this project. The folks at PublicAffairs embraced my book and me with enthusiasm, particularly Peter Osnos, Susan Weinberg, and Morgen Van Vorst, an excellent editor with a sharp eye for a narrative. There are many people with whom I worked in the newspaper business who took the time to talk to me about their role in the saga, but I owe a special debt to my colleagues Ann Marie Lipinski, Bill Parker, and Leo Wolinsky. Because so much had been written about the *Times* before the *Tribune* acquired the paper, I decided to write the early chapters largely through the eyes of people who worked there, particularly Wolinsky, who shared with me the story of his incredible career at the paper. My agent, Larry Weissman, was a voice of enthusiasm and confidence. He helped me frame the story in its incarnation. Thanks, also, to Howard Bragman, who originally encouraged me to write the book. And, of course, my wife, Nancy, as always displayed incredible patience with me, the mess I made in the spare room and the hours I kept. And thanks so much to all of the journalists who made the *Des Moines Register*, the *Chicago Tribune*, and the *Los Angeles Times* such special places to work and grow.

# NOTES

## Introduction: The Merger

1     **In April 1999, John Madigan** Author's interview with John Madigan, Chicago, IL, winter 2008. The author interviewed Madigan after he had left the Tribune Company.

1     **hadn't flown to San Diego merely** "Aggressive plans unveiled as NAA publishers meet," by David Noack and Joe Nicholson, *Editor & Publisher*, May 1, 1999. The author got details of the meeting from this story and interviews with John Madigan, Chicago, IL, 2008; and Mark Willes, Salt Lake City, UT, 2010. In addition, he looked up weather reports to get details for the time of the meeting.

2     **He drove earnings into the stratosphere** 2003 Annual Report, Tribune Company, February 2004. The earnings data and computation of the stock value came from data in the company's annual report announcing Madigan's retirement.

2     **he had challenged David Hiller** Author's interviews with John Madigan, Chicago, IL, 2008; and David Hiller, Chicago, IL, winter 2008, and winter 2010.

3     **Sitting upstairs in his room** Author's interview with Mark Willes, Salt Lake City, UT, 2010. Willes' interview with the author was the first time that he discussed his experience as the chairman of Times Mirror since he left the job in 2000.

3     **At thirty-five, he'd been named** "Mark Willes, Ahead of the Times," by Edward L. Carter, *Marriott Alumni Magazine*, Brigham Young University, Summer 2001. Willes taught at Brigham Young, and the alumni magazine did a feature story on him.

3     **In 1998, advertisers had pumped** "Aggressive plans unveiled as NAA publishers meet," by David Noack and Joe Nicholson, *Editor & Publisher*, May 1, 1999. The discussion of ad revenues and the quotes from the NAA meeting came from this report.

4     **in the New Century Network** "New Century Network Announced," Press Release, April 1995. The author discussed the New Century Network with David

Hiller during interviews in Chicago, IL, winter 2008, and winter 2010; and Charles Brumback during interviews in Sarasota, FL, May 2010, and by telephone, 2008–2010.

5   **Craig Newmark, an ex-computer** Numerous news reports document that Newmark started craigslist as a site for his friends, and that after it became popular, he decided to organize it into a business.

5   **Using banks of computers, Sergey Brin and Larry Page** *Googled*, by Ken Auletta (New York: Penguin Press, 2009). Auletta's book is an excellent source of information on Google. The author also examined several articles about the early days of the start-up.

5   **Matt Drudge rooted through** "Hot links served up daily," by Joel Sappell, *Los Angeles Times*, August 4, 2007.

6   **boasting a combined daily circulation** "New Century Network Announced," Press Release, April 1995. The author discussed the New Century Network with David Hiller during interviews in Chicago, IL, winter 2008, and winter 2010; and Charles Brumback during interviews in Sarasota, FL, May 2010, and by telephone, 2008–2010. The author also interviewed James Cutie, a *New York Times* executive who was involved in the effort, by phone in February 2011 and Harry Chandler, a member of the Chandler family who was a member of the NCN board.

6   **For the design of the famous Tribune Tower,** Tribune Company Proxy Statement/Prospectus, May 5, 2000. The terms of the deal were announced in the document required of all public companies engaged in a merger by the Securities and Exchange Commission.

7   **The paper had won two Pulitzer Prizes** The Pulitzer Prizes, www.pulitzer.org. References to Pulitzer Prizes appear on the Pulitzer website.

7   **America Online, which injected $1.2 billion** Author's interviews with Charles Brumback, Sarasota, FL, May 2010; and Scott C. Smith, Chicago, IL, December 2010. Scott Smith brought the AOL investment proposition to the *Chicago Tribune*. Smith told the author he originally proposed that the Tribune invest $5 million in AOL. He thought about recommending that they double the initial investment to $10 million but backed off at the end.

7   **the Los Angeles Times had become widely respected,** *Privileged Son: Otis Chandler and the Rise and Fall of the L.A. Times Dynasty,* by Dennis McDougal (Cambridge: Perseus Publishing, 2001). The author relied heavily on MacDougal's book for the history of the *Los Angeles Times* and the Chandler family. MacDougal's book is an excellent, authoritative study of the family behind the *Times*. The narrative of *Privileged Son* ends as Tribune acquired Times Mirror.

8   **In its day, the Times' blatantly Republican** *The Powers That Be,* by David Halberstam (New York: Knopf, 1975).

8   **Though he didn't spell it out to Willes** Author's interview with John Madigan, Chicago, IL, winter 2008; and author's interview with Mark Willes, Salt Lake City, UT, 2010. In their respective interviews, both Madigan and Willes confirmed the details of their initial meeting and subsequent developments. As the author notes in the text, they disagreed on some details.

10 **When editors at other American papers** Author's telephone interview with Eugene Roberts, former editor of the *Philadelphia Inquirer* and managing editor of the *New York Times*, summer 2009. The author also personally heard complaints about the industry's use of the *Chicago Tribune* as a financial yardstick during his career at the paper.

## Chapter 1: Beginnings: Des Moines

15 **Gene Raffensperger swung around** Author's telephone interview with Gene Raffensperger, March 2009. The author relied on his memory of the encounter but had details corroborated by Raffensperger.

18 **A statewide paper, the *Register*** *Covering Iowa: The History of the Des Moines Register and Tribune Company, 1849–1985*, by William B. Friedricks (Ames: Iowa State University Press, 2000). The sign with the *Register's* promotion was present when the author joined the staff in 1971.

19 **By far, the most memorable character** Author relied on his memory for some details on Jimmy Larson as well as "Longtime Register news editor dies," by Ken Fuson, *Des Moines Register*, October 20, 2006.

19 **nearly 80 percent of Americans reported that** "Advancing Newspaper Media for the 21st Century," Newspaper Association of America, 2009. The author relied on data prepared by the NAA business analysis and research department, W.R. Simmons and Associates Research, Inc., and the A.C. Nielsen Company, for newspaper readership data.

21 **The *Register* was one of the last papers** "Cowles Family Publishing Legacy," by Herb Strentz. The papers, letters, and photos of the Cowles family are available for viewing at Drake University Cowles Library. The author relied on these papers for much of the history of the family in Iowa.

23 **They were people like Nick Kotz, whose exposé of** Details on Kotz, Mollenhoff, and others came from author's discussions over many years with numerous *Des Moines Register* reporters, including George Anthan.

24 **Jon Van, an Iowa native, who routinely** Author's interview with Jon Van, Chicago, IL, spring 2009. Van came into the newsroom every Saturday morning for years, took the phone, and followed up on leads provided by the state editor of the *Register*.

25 **Kruidenier beefed up the business operations** "Cowles Family Publishing Legacy," Drake University Cowles Library. David Kruidenier, Jr., was a grandson of Gardner Cowles, Sr.

## Chapter 2: Across the Street

28 **When, in 1931, Roy Howard of the Scripps Howard chain** *The Press*, by A. J. Liebling (New York: Ballantine Books, 1964). Liebling was the *New Yorker's* press critic in the 1960s and wrote extensively on the *Tribune* and The Colonel.

29 **and publisher Stan Cook and editor Clayton Kirkpatrick** Author's interview with Stanton R. Cook, Kenilworth, IL, fall 2009. Also, *Oral History*, by Robert Wiedrich, McCormick Foundation, December 1996. In the interview, Cook also disclosed, for the first time, details of the *Chicago Tribune's* infamous decision to publish an editorial calling for the resignation of Richard M. Nixon.

30 **Jimmy Breslin, the iconic, hard-drinking** "A 'Tabloid Guy' Calls It a Night After 41 Years with Murdoch," by Tim Arango, *New York Times*, September 29, 2008.

31 **George de Lama, one of the paper's first** Author's telephone interview with George de Lama, summer 2009. In fact, the metro editor was not taken to the 18th District Police Station, or arrested. Toolen was taken to Northwestern Memorial Hospital.

35 **Douglas Frantz recalled the ubiquitous** Conversation with Douglas Frantz. The author worked with Frantz at the *Chicago Tribune* and the *Los Angeles Times*. Frantz described the incident to the author when discussing the nature of Chicago.

36 **what Joseph Medill, the paper's patriarch,** *The Colonel, The Life and Legend of Robert R. McCormick*, by Richard Norton Smith (New York: Houghton Mifflin Company, 1997). The author relied on Smith's excellent biography for much of the Medill and McCormick history in the book. Some of the material on the Colonel came from the personal recollections of Kirkpatrick and others.

37 **In his will, he stipulated that** Comments of R. Bruce Dold, the current editorial page editor of the *Chicago Tribune*. Dold has repeated the story of Medill's will and the endorsement process in numerous places.

39 **The Midwest was America** The author relied on several passages in both Liebling's and Smith's books for the headlines and characterizations of the Colonel's political and cultural views and his linguistic preferences.

40 **Every Saturday evening at 9 p.m.** *The Press*, by A. J. Liebling (New York: Ballentine Books, 1964). The Colonel provided great material for Liebling's tongue-in-cheek humor.

## Chapter 3: Otis Chandler's Legacy

43 **Bleakwood Avenue runs through,** Author's interview with Leo Wolinsky, Los Angeles, CA, fall 2010; and by telephone, 2008–2010. The author interviewed Wolinsky several times over the course of researching and writing this book. In embarking on his research, the author knew that much had been written about the history of the *LA Times* but not much from someone who had actually worked at the paper for many years. The author decided to rely heavily on Wolinsky's history to provide a picture of the paper through the eyes of a credible, loyal employee.

44 **In the 1950s, S. J. Perelman** *Privileged Son: Otis Chandler and the Rise and Fall of the L.A. Times Dynasty*, by Dennis McDougal (Cambridge: Perseus Publishing, 2001). The author relied on McDougal's impressive book on the Chandler family and the *LA Times* for much of the history in this chapter. Some of the material was supplemented by personal recollections from his time as editor of the newspaper. The author also relied on "The Chandler Mystery," by David Margolick, *Vanity Fair*, September 1996, for some details of Otis Chandler's life and career.

44 **institution that dominated the California Republican party** *The Powers That Be*, by David Halberstam (New York: Knopf, 1975). The author also relied on Halberstam's book for history of the Chandlers, particularly the sections on the family's political leanings and for his reporting on Kyle Palmer, the political reporter and operative at the *LA Times*.

45 **But Frank Merriam, the Republican candidate favored** *The Campaign of the Century Upton Sinclair's E.P.I.C. Race for Governor of California and the Birth of Media Politics*, by Greg Mitchell (New York: Random House, 1992).

47 **"What is happening to us," the editorial asked** "Peril to Conservatives," signed editorial, Otis Chandler, *Los Angeles Times*, Sunday, March 12, 1961.

47 **"Otis is Zeus."** "The State of the American Newspaper: Down and Out in LA," by William Prochnau, *American Journalism Review*, January/February 2000.

48 **The *Los Angeles Times* circulates in an area** The author learned of details of the *Los Angeles Times* as editor of the newspaper from November 2006 to January 2008.

49 **"The way it was supposed to work," recalls Pete King** Author's phone interview of Peter King, summer 2010. King also wrote an excellent in-depth newspaper article about the *Los Angeles Times'* role in the civic affairs of Los Angeles for the newspaper's 125th Anniversary.

49 **about "knocking the *New York Times* off its perch."** The motive that King contradicted reportedly came from Otis Chandler on becoming publisher of the *LA Times*.

50 **Nowhere was the ability of the *Los Angeles Times*** *How Far Can a Piano Fly? And Other Tales From Column One in the Los Angeles Times*, An anthology of Column One stories with a forward by Patt Morrison (Los Angeles: Los Angeles Times Books, 2003). The anthology showcases some of the best writing in a newspaper by some of the *Times'* most gifted writers.

50 **At the top of the front page on March 12, 1961** *Los Angeles Times*, March 21, 1961.

## Chapter 4: Twilight

55 **For the U.S. newspaper industry,** "Advancing Newspaper Media for the 21st Century," Newspaper Association of America, 2009. The author relied on data prepared by the NAA business analysis and research department, W.R. Simmons and Associates Research, Inc., and the A.C. Nielsen Company, for newspaper readership data.

56 **as if they'd been tossed into a blender** Jack Fuller, who succeeded Squires as editor, first compared the newsroom under the Tennessee native to being thrown into a blender.

57 **Between 1970 and 1985, the number of women** U.S. Bureau of Labor Statistics. The data on the composition of the workforce came from U.S. government reports by the U.S. Department of Labor.

57 **In 1971, America had 1,425 evening newspapers** "Advancing Newspaper Media for the 21st Century," Newspaper Association of America, 2009. The author relied on data prepared by the NAA business analysis and research department, W.R. Simmons and Associates Research, Inc., and the A.C. Nielsen Company, for newspaper readership data.

58 **For much of the 1960s and 1970s** *Post Broadcast Democracy*, by Markus Prior (New York: Cambridge University Press, 2007). Prior's book is an excellent source

of material and analysis of the impact of cable TV on the nation's political activity. The author relied on Prior's analysis.

59 **Between 1960 and 1984, cable subscribers** Cable Statistics, 2009 Edition, National Cable and Telecommunications Association.

59 **For one thing, growth in Sunday** "Advancing Newspaper Media for the 21st Century," Newspaper Association of America, 2009. The author relied upon data prepared by the NAA business analysis and research department, W.R. Simmons and Associates Research, Inc., and the A.C. Nielsen Company, for newspaper readership data.

60 **Nowhere was this more evident than with Prescott Low** *The Collapse of the Great American Newspaper,* by Charles M. Madigan (Chicago: Ivan R. Dee, 2007). In his book, Madigan first reported on Low and unearthed a paper on the role of estate taxes on the decision to sell newspapers. The author also read the original paper and visited the *Patriot Ledger* offices in Quincy.

61 **Miller became the forerunner of what** *Confessions of an S.O.B.,* by Allen H. Neuharth (New York: Doubleday, 1989). The source for much of the material about Gannett, including the description of Neuharth by his second wife, came from Neuharth's entertaining autobiography. The author also relied on *Read All About It,* by James D. Squires (New York: Times Books, 1993).

61 **Gannett embarked on a trail blazed by** *Taking Stock Journalism and the Publicly-Traded Newspaper Company,* by Gilbert Cranberg, Randall Bezanson, and John Soloski (Ames: Iowa State University Press, 2001). This academic study is one of the few that ever looked at the implications of publicly held companies for journalism. Cranberg and his team interviewed many of Wall Street's top newspaper stock analysts and the quote cited came from an anonymous source in Cranberg's book.

63 **referring to their editorial departments as** "Upstairs and Down," by James Schermerhorn, *Editor & Publisher,* August 1909.

63 **To protect editorial departments from** "Tearing Down the 'Wall' in American Journalism," by Rodney D. Benson, *International Journal of the Humanities,* Paris, 2004. The author relied on the piece by Benson, a New York University professor, for background on the "wall."

64 **Hutchins Commission on the Freedom of the Press** Committee on the Freedom of the Press, 1947. The Hutchins Commission was chaired by Robert Hutchins, then president of the University of Chicago. It was formed in the midst of World War II by Henry Luce, publisher of *Time* and *Life* magazines, to inquire into the proper functions of the press in modern democracies. After studying the issue for four years, the commission issued its report that became a pivotal assertion of the media's role in a democratic society.

64 **Stan Cook, the chief executive officer** Author's interview with Stanton R. Cook. Kenilworth, IL, fall 2009. The author interviewed Cook in his home. Cook discussed the change in language policy during the interview, but the actual quote cited came from Kirkpatrick's message to readers in the *Chicago Tribune.*

66 **with analysts and institutional investors who** *Taking Stock Journalism and the Publicly-Traded Newspaper Company,* by Gilbert Cranberg, Randall Bezanson, and

John Soloski (Ames: Iowa State University Press, 2001). This academic study is one of the few that ever looked at the implications of publicly held companies for journalism. The author interviewed many of Wall Street's top newspaper stock analysts but the quote cited from the book was anonymous.

## Chapter 5: The New Order

69  **Charlie Brumback beamed with pride** Author's interview with José Moré, a *Chicago Tribune* photographer who attended the ceremony, Chicago, IL, winter 2010; and author's telephone interview with Robert Blau, a *Tribune* editor who also witnessed the spectacle in the newsroom, fall 2008. The cost of the project was confirmed by Al Gramzinski, a former Tribune Company building manager who supervised the construction of the stairway.

70  **In Florida, he had earned a reputation for** Author's interviews of Charles T. Brumback and *Oral History* of Brumback, by Robert Wiedrich, McCormick Foundation, 2000 and 2001. The author interviewed Brumback on several occasions, both by telephone from Chicago in 2008–2010 and at his home in Sarasota, FL, in May 2010. Much of the background and history of Brumback came from those sessions.

70  **Although he had graduated from** *Oral History* of Brumback by Robert Wiedrich, McCormick Foundation, 2000 and 2001.

71  **Brumback had received a powerful lesson** *Oral History* of Brumback by Robert Wiedrich, McCormick Foundation, 2000 and 2001.

75  **Squires understood how to play the game** *Read All About It*, by James D. Squires (New York: Times Books, 1993). Squires book contains a detailed account of his years with Brumback. The author also interviewed Squires by telephone, winter 2010.

75  **During the four years Brumback and Squires** *Read All About It*, by James D. Squires (New York: Times Books, 1993); and *Oral History* of Brumback, by Robert Wiedrich, McCormick Foundation, 2000 and 2001.

76  **When, in 1981, he named Brumback CEO** Author's interview with Stanton R. Cook, Kenilworth, IL, fall 2009.

78  **"He thought big," remembered Lisa Anderson** Author's telephone interview with Lisa Anderson, winter 2011.

79  **"I [became] a smoke and mirrors magician,"** *Read All About It*, by James D. Squires (New York: Times Books, 1993). In his book, Squires is quite candid about his bargain with Brumback and the implications for the newsroom he led.

82  **Squires didn't help himself with his** Author's telephone interview with James D. Squires, winter 2010. Squires also provided the author with a copy of the "Project Prosperity" report. His comments regarding his relationship with Madigan and his reaction to Brumback's comment came from this interview.

## Chapter 6: The Cereal Killer

85  **Leo Wolinsky stepped out** Author's interview with Leo Wolinsky, Los Angeles, CA, fall 2010; and by telephone, 2008–2010.

86    **the Chandler family had brought** Author's interview with Mark Willes, Salt Lake City, UT, 2010.

87    **They were, in Otis' words, a "pain in the ass."** *Privileged Son: Otis Chandler and the Rise and Fall of the L.A. Times Dynasty,* by Dennis McDougal (Cambridge: Perseus Publishing, 2001).

89    **Under Coffey's tenure, the** *Times* Author's interview with Leo Wolinsky, Los Angeles, CA, fall 2010; and by telephone, 2008–2010.

89    **Coffey, for a redesign that unfairly** *After Henry,* by Joan Didion (New York: Vintage, 1993). The book by Didion, a California native, contains a chapter on Los Angeles and the *Times* that discusses Coffey's tenure as editor as well as the newspaper's place in the civic, political, and cultural affairs of Los Angeles.

90    **Initially, Erburu found it relatively easy to** "Controlling stockholders and the disciplinary role of corporate payout policy: a study of the Times Mirror Company," by Harry DeAngelo, Linda DeAngelo, *Journal of Financial Economics,* 2000. The details of the dividend payout policy of Times Mirror Company and the Chandlers came from this academic study by professors at the Marshall School of Business, University of Southern California, Los Angeles.

92    **In Minneapolis at General Mills** Author's interview with Mark Willes, Salt Lake City, UT, 2010.

93    **as "Family Home Evening"—a time** "Mark Willes, Ahead of the Times," by Edward L. Carter, *Marriott Alumni Magazine,* summer 2001.

94    **When Willes arrived on the scene, Tim Rutten** "The State of the American Newspaper: Down and Out in LA," by William Prochnau, *American Journalism Review,* January/February 2000.

96    **The Chandlers who had brought Willes to the paper** Author's interview with Harry B. Chandler, Los Angeles, fall 2010. The author interviewed Chandler, who is Otis Chandler's son, and one of the few members of the family who will talk publicly about its affairs.

97    **Willes launched the first brand advertising** Author's interview with Leo Wolinsky, Los Angeles, CA, fall 2010; and by telephone, 2008–2010; and "Retreat Presentation," a detailed study of the *Los Angeles Times* readership and circulation. The study was done when Dean Baquet was editor of the paper in 2005 and 2006.

98    **He sold off Harry N. Abrams** *Privileged Son: Otis Chandler and the Rise and Fall of the L.A. Times Dynasty,* by Dennis McDougal (Cambridge: Perseus Publishing, 2001).

99    **revived the dividends the Chandlers had sought** "Controlling stockholders and the disciplinary role of corporate payout policy: a study of the Times Mirror Company," by Harry DeAngelo, Linda DeAngelo, *Journal of Financial Economics,* 2000. Details of the financial arrangements also came from the author's interview with Efrem (Skip) Zimbalist III, a former Times Mirror CFO, Los Angeles, CA, fall 2010, and by telephone, winter 2009.

101   **he infuriated the Chandlers by tapping** Author's interviews with Efrem (Skip) Zimbalist, III, Los Angeles, CA, fall 2010; and by telephone, winter 2009; and

Thomas Unterman, a Chandler family lawyer who manages the Chandler's money, Los Angeles, CA, fall 2010.

101 **Harry Chandler, Otis' son, had come to the** Author's interview with Harry B. Chandler, Los Angeles, CA, fall 2010.

## Chapter 7: His Seat on the Dais

105 **The white tour bus carrying** Author's interview with Tribune Company official who had accompanied Madigan on his trip. Participant spoke to the author in confidence.

105 **Almost fifty years earlier to the day, Jules Dubois** "Jules Dubois Dies in Bogata Hotel," *Sarasota Herald Tribune*, August 1966; and "The Press: Freedom Fighter," *Time*, April 1957. The details of Dubois' life came from these two articles and several others regarding his career with the *Tribune*.

106 **To anyone schooled in reading the tea leaves** Author's interview with Newton N. Minow, a former Tribune Company director, Chicago, IL, winter 2010.

106 **he concluded that the Tribune Company** *Oral History* of Brumback, by Robert Wiedrich, McCormick Foundation, 2000 and 2001.

107 **At one point, Brumback's mandate** *STRIKE, The Daily News War and the Future of American Labor*, by Richard Vigilante (New York: Simon and Schuster, 1994). Vigilante's book on the strike at the *Daily News* provided excellent details on the labor dispute.

108 **Meanwhile, Brumback openly expressed doubts** Author's telephone interview with Tim Jones, a former *Chicago Tribune* media reporter, fall 2009.

109 **His buttoned-down countenance obscured a** Author's interview with Donald Haider, a Northwestern University professor, Chicago, IL, 2009.

110 **After graduating from the University of Michigan** Author's interview with John Madigan, Chicago, IL, winter 2008.

110 **"The problem with being a private company, . . ."** Author's interview with Stanton R. Cook, Kenilworth, IL, fall 2009.

111 **Cook and Madigan shelved Kirkpatrick's journalistic** Author's interview with Anton (Tony) Majeri, Jr., Chicago, IL, 2009.

112 **By the time Cook stepped down as chairman of the company in 1993** Tribune Company, Proxy Statement, April 1994. Details of Cook and Madigan's stock holdings came from this document on file with the U.S. Securities and Exchange Commission.

115 **"All he ever cared about was his seat . . ."** Author's telephone interview with James D. Squires, winter 2010.

117 **Madigan expressed his frustration to** Author's telephone interview with Nicholas Horrock, winter 2010.

118 **"Charlie had a good idea but it wasn't the . . ."** Author's telephone interview with James Cutie, winter 2011.

118 **Within three years, NCN folded** "New Media Meltdown at New Century," by Jeanne Dugan, *BusinessWeek*, March 23, 1998.

119 **"He came before the board and told us that . . ."** Author's interview with Newton N. Minow, Chicago, IL, winter 2010.

120 **Madigan and Fuller also sharply increased** Tribune Company, 2003 Annual Report, February 2004. The details on the American Online transaction were confirmed in the author's interview with Scott C. Smith, Chicago, IL, December 2010.

### Chapter 8: Inside the Merger

123 **Once a year, the paper's editors** Author's interview with Leo Wolinsky, Los Angeles, CA, fall 2010, and by telephone, 2008–2010.

125 **He'd reported Madigan's approach to his board** Author's interview with Mark Willes, Salt Lake City, UT, 2010.

125 **Skip Zimbalist, who had just become the Times Mirror CFO** Author's interview with Efrem (Skip) Zimbalist III, Los Angeles, CA, fall 2010, and by telephone, winter 2009.

126 **"A fundamental premise of journalism"** "Trouble with the *LA Times*," News Hour with Jim Lehrer, December 1999. The quote came from a transcript of Weinstein's interview with Terence Smith regarding the Staples incident and other problems at the *Times*.

127 **"Mark Willes is just a symbol—and perhaps even a victim . . ."** "The Way We Live Now: 01-09-00: Word & Image; The Wall, Vindicated," by Max Frankel, *New York Times*, January 2000.

127 **Even Otis Chandler broke his silence** *Privileged Son: Otis Chandler and the Rise and Fall of the L.A. Times Dynasty*, by Dennis McDougal (Cambridge: Perseus Publishing, 2001).

128 **A native of Evanston, Illinois, Tom Unterman** Author's interviews with Thomas Unterman, Los Angeles, CA, fall 2010; and Jack Fuller, Chicago, IL, fall 2008 and winter 2009.

128 **"I told Tom we are not going to . . ."** Author's interview with Jack Fuller, Chicago, IL, fall 2008, and winter 2009; and with Efrem (Skip) Zimbalist, III, Los Angeles, CA, fall 2010; and by telephone, winter 2009.

129 **"We went there first and then they [the Chandlers] . . ."** Author's interview with John Madigan, Chicago, IL, winter 2008.

129 **His mentor, Ira Harris, considered him a strong** Author's telephone interview with Ira Harris, fall 2010.

130 **By March 2000, Madigan and the Chandlers** Tribune Company, Proxy Statement, May 2000. The details of the deal and the due diligence were outlined in the proxy report filed with the U.S. Securities and Exchange Commission.

132 **"Tom and everybody else were talking about . . ."** Author's interview with Mark Willes, Salt Lake City, UT, 2010.

132 **a severance package worth $64.5 million** The size of Willes' severance was originally computed by James Bates and Michael Hiltzek based on pubic records and figures that Willes provided to the two *Los Angeles Times* reporters. Several other reports said the figure could be higher, but Willes deferred some of his compensation and now is a substantial creditor in the Tribune Company bankruptcy.

133 **Tribune had acquired Times Mirror for $95 a share in cash and stock** Tribune Company, Proxy Statement, May 2000.

134 **The combined company's Internet audience** "The chicagotribune.com: Creating a Newspaper for The New Economy," by Professor Nina Ziv, Institute for Technology and Enterprise, Polytechnic University, New York, October 2000.

134 **On March 13, Hiller stood before** Author's interviews with David Hiller, Chicago, IL, winter 2008, and winter 2010.

## Chapter 9: Making News

135 **an extraordinary series called "Trial and Error"** "Prosecution on Trial in DuPage," by Maurice Possley and Ken Armstrong, *Chicago Tribune*, January 1999.

135 **But his sources in the legal community** Author's telephone interview with Ken Armstrong, former *Chicago Tribune* reporter, fall 2010.

137 **Three years later, in January 2003, late on a** Author's interview with Ann Marie Lipinski, Chicago, IL, winter 2010.

140 **The company made $650 million in profit on revenues of $5.3 billion the first year** Tribune Company, 2003 Annual Report, February 2004.

140 **country to report and write "Code Blue"** "Code Blue: Survival in the Sky," by John Crewdson, *Chicago Tribune*, July 1996.

141 **Organizations like Save the Children Federation** "The Miracle Merchants," by Lisa Anderson, *Chicago Tribune*, March 1998.

141 **Dr. Bob Arnot, the physician who regularly** Author's telephone conversation with Dr. Bob Arnot. Arnot called the author when he was deputy managing editor for news at the *Chicago Tribune* and the editor who supervised the Save the Children coverage.

## Chapter 10: A Changing Landscape

149 **Leo Wolinsky drove down the** Author's interview with Leo Wolinsky, Los Angeles, CA, fall 2010, and by telephone, 2008–2010.

150 **As editor of the *Baltimore Sun*, Carroll** Author's telephone interview with John Carroll, summer 2009.

150 **About three weeks before** In December 1999, David Willman of the *Los Angeles Times* wrote a two-part series reconstructing the Food and Drug Administration's fast-track approval process for the diabetes drug Rezulin and uncovered high-pressure lobbying, attempts to silence critics, and 33 deaths of people who had taken the medication.

151 **Carroll had been editor of the *Lexington* (Kentucky)** Author's telephone interview with John Carroll, summer 2009.

152 **All eyes fell upon the tall, lanky, unflappable** Author's interview with Leo Wolinsky, Los Angeles, CA, fall 2010, and by telephone, 2008–2010.

153 **In the business offices of the *Times*, Puerner shook** Author's telephone interview with John Puerner, winter 2010.

153 **Otis was happy about the change** Author's interview with Efrem (Skip) Zimbalist III, Los Angeles, CA, fall 2010, and by telephone, winter 2009. The substance of

the Chandlers' sentiment was also confirmed in the author's interview with John Madigan, Chicago, IL, winter 2008, and *Privileged Son: Otis Chandler and the Rise and Fall of the L.A. Times Dynasty*, by Dennis McDougal (Cambridge: Perseus Publishing, 2001).

154 **Dean P. Baquet was an unconventional** Author's telephone interview with Dean Baquet, winter 2010.

155 **One of his fondest New Orleans journalistic** Author's recollection of conversation with Dean Baquet. The quote was widely repeated and became standard fare in stories about Edwards. Other details on Baquet's career came from "Nothing but Fans," by Rachel Smolkin, *American Journalism Review*, August/September 2005.

157 **When two heavily armed gunmen wearing body** "Gunfire, Hostages and Terror, Suspect Slain, Ten Officers Injured in Heist Gone Awry," by Beth Schuster and Doug Smith, *Los Angeles Times*, March 1997.

158 **By 2003, Puerner had cut the** Author's telephone interview with John Puerner, winter 2010; and Tribune Company, 2003 Annual Report, February 2004.

158 **"For years, the newspaper industry had . . ."** Author's interview with David Hiller, Chicago, IL, winter 2008 and winter 2010.

160 **Much had been made over Carroll's zealous** The dispute over the similarities between the editor of the *Baltimore Sun* on Simon's show and John Carroll is well documented in various magazine and newspaper articles, such as "The Angriest Man in Television," by Mark Bowden, *Atlantic Magazine*, January/February 2008.

### Chapter 11: Market-Driven Journalism

163 **In July 1982, a tall, athletic** "Tribune's Chief Is Second to None," by Steve McClellan, *Broadcasting & Cable*, April 2003; and official Tribune Company biography for Dennis FitzSimons. The details of FitzSimons' early years at Tribune came from these sources and interviews with Tribune executives who knew him. FitzSimons confirmed the details in an interview with the author in Chicago, IL, winter 2010.

164 **In a profile of FitzSimons, *Los Angeles Times*, reporter** "Tribune CEO Is Expected to Keep His Cool in Fight; Dennis FitzSimons, who has been something of a mystery despite his job, faces public criticism," by Thomas S. Mulligan, *Los Angeles Times*, June 2006.

165 **Instead of acquiring programming, or shows** Author's telephone interview with Vinnie Malcolm, former manager of KTLA-TV in Los Angeles, a Tribune Company broadcast property, winter 2010.

165 **Within a year of arriving at Tribune** "Tribune's Chief Is Second to None," by Steve McClellan, *Broadcasting & Cable*, April 2003.

166 **Unlike Dowdle and Madigan, said Jim Kirk** Author's interview with Jim Kirk, former marketing and media columnist for the *Chicago Tribune*, winter 2011.

166 **WGN had been locked in a long feud** "Tribune's Chief Is Second to None," by Steve McClellan, *Broadcasting & Cable*, April 2003.

166 **Together, Dowdle and FitzSimons led** Tribune Company, 2003 Annual Report, February 2004.

167 **When TV syndication mogul Roger King** "Tribune's Chief Is Second to None," by Steve McClellan, *Broadcasting & Cable*, April 2003.

167 **When Barry Meyer, then head of Warner Bros. TV** "Tribune's Chief Is Second to None," by Steve McClellan, *Broadcasting & Cable*, April 2003.

168 **was a phenomenon known as "market-driven journalism,"** *Market Driven Journalism: Let the Citizen Beware?* by John H. McManus (London: Sage Publications, 1994).

169 **"Somewhere in the late 1960s . . ."** *Market Driven Journalism: Let the Citizen Beware?* by John H. McManus (London: Sage Publications, 1994).

171 **judged him by the yardstick most CEOs** Tribune Company, 2003 Annual Report, February 2004.

171 **"I'm always being accused of looking at everything through . . ."** Author's recollection of his first meeting with Dennis FitzSimons, Tribune Tower, 2000. The author reconstructed details of the meeting, partially from memory and partially from e-mails that the author had sent to others in Tribune Company documenting the meeting.

172 **"One of the issues that caused distress . . ."** Author's interview with David Hiller, Chicago, IL, winter 2008, and winter 2010.

173 **By 2001, Tribune owned twenty-three television stations** Tribune Company, 2003 Annual Report, February 2004.

175 **The average reader in Southern California** Author's interview with Leo Wolinsky, Los Angeles, CA, fall 2010, and by telephone, 2008–2010; and Wolinsky's "Retreat Presentation," a detailed study of the *Los Angeles Times* readership and circulation.

176 **"He [FitzSimons] wanted to edit the paper by referendum,"** Author's telephone interview with John Carroll, summer 2009.

178 **Geraldo Rivera, then a Fox News reporter** "War news from Rivera seems off the mark," by David Folkenflik, *Baltimore Sun*, December 2001. In the story, Rivera acknowledged that he never visited the "hallowed ground" where the battle took place.

### Chapter 12: Buy the Numbers

181 **a letter from a street-smart lawyer** Letter from Joseph O. Giaimo to Harold Foley of Utica, New York, dated September 7, 2000.

182 **The Colonel's *Tribune* had hired the likes** *The Colonel, The Life and Legend of Robert R. McCormick*, by Richard Norton Smith (New York: Houghton Mifflin Company, 1997).

182 **newsstands and even "toss a goon"** *The Colonel, The Life and Legend of Robert R. McCormick*, by Richard Norton Smith (New York: Houghton Mifflin Company, 1997).

182 **When Brumback took on the unions at the** *STRIKE, The Daily News War and the Future of American Labor*, by Richard Vigilante (New York: Simon and Schuster, 1994).

183 **Almost from the day that the Colonel's niece, Alicia** *The Colonel, The Life and Legend of Robert R. McCormick*, by Richard Norton Smith (New York: Houghton Mifflin Company, 1997).

183    **Tribune's only tabloid boasted the** Letter to advertisers from Patricia A. Burnagiel, vice president, advertising, *Newsday*, December 1, 2002. Also, attachment to advertising letter entitled, "For Some People, This is the Untold Circulation Story of the New York ADI." *Newsday/NY Newsday* is the largest newspaper in the NY ADI.

183    **From all appearances, Sito didn't** Author's interview with Louis Sito, Greeneville, SC, summer 2009.

184    **A federal prosecutor who investigated** Author's telephone interview with one of the prosecutors in the *Newsday* investigation who talked only on the condition of confidentiality.

185    **To make sure that *Newsday*'s circulation increased** *Crabhouse of Douglaston, Inc. et al.* vs. *Newsday, Inc.* et al., 4th Amended Class Action Complaint, U.S. District Court, Eastern District of New York, September 2006.

186    **Sito and his team also sold bulk subscriptions** Author's interview with Louis Sito, Greeneville, SC, summer 2009. After the *Newsday* scandal became public, the Audit Bureau of Circulations implemented a wide array of rule changes dealing with bulk circulation and many other problems that surfaced in the *Newsday* scandal.

186    **Although most people in the American** *Facts without Opinion, the First Fifty Years of the Audit Bureau of Circulations*, by Charles O. Bennett (Chicago: Audit Bureau of Circulations, 1965).

187    **In fact, under ABC rules, newspapers aren't** Audit Bureau of Circulations, Rule Changes and Board Activity from 2004–current, July 2008. The ABC revised its rules after the *Newsday* scandal became public.

188    **The next time you check into a hotel** Author's telephone interview with Jay Schiller, a former auditor for the Audit Bureau of Circulations, summer 2009, and winter 2010. The author had numerous conversations and e-mail exchanges with Schiller, who shared letters from hotel chains. Schiller also provided ABC audits of the circulation of *USA Today*.

188    **At *Newsday*, Sito engaged in far more sinister plots** Many details of the circulation scandal were first reported by Robert Kessler and James Madore, *Newsday* reporters who covered the scandal at their own paper. The alternative weekly, *Long Island Press*, aggressively covered the *Newsday* scandal.

189    **In March 1998, an arm of *Newsday*** Details of the March 1998, acquisition came from the author's interview with Louis Sito, Greeneville, SC, summer 2009, and the amended complaint. In addition, the author interviewed Michael Pouchie in Queens, NY, fall 2010, who told the author of the guns he was carrying when he entered the *Newsday* circulation facility.

189    **Ed Smith, a *Newsday* and *Hoy* circulation consultant** *United States of America* vs. *Ed Smith, Information*, U.S. District Court, Eastern District of New York, April 2006.

189    **Months before, Sito had noticed how** "Dismantling the Language Barrier," by Tim Porter, *American Journalism Review*, October/November 2003.

190    **During the first week *Hoy* was on the market** *Crabhouse of Douglaston, Inc. et al.* vs. *Newsday, Inc.* et al., 4th Amended Class Action Complaint, U.S. District Court, Eastern District of New York, September 2006. The details of the marketing cam-

paign and the exchanges at the holiday party came from the complaint and were reaffirmed in an interview with Michael Pouchie, Queens, NY, fall 2010.

191 **"When I got outside, there were like fourteen . . ."** Author's interview with Michael Pouchie, Queens, NY, fall 2010.

191 **Two days later when Pouchie showed up at Vreeburg's** Author's interview with Joseph O. Giaimo, Queens, NY, summer 2010.

191 **"Tell them we'll see 'em in court . . ."** Author's interview with Louis Sito, Greeneville, SC, summer 2009.

192 **"Look, they're dumping papers, they're dumping them . . ."** Author's interview with Joseph O. Giaimo, Queens, NY, summer 2010.

192 **at *Newsday* caught Timothy Knight off** Author's interview with Timothy Knight, Melville, NY, summer 2010.

193 **Elaine Banar, a hard-nosed federal prosecutor** Author's telephone interview with Elaine Banar, summer 2010.

194 **Fuller had selected a Cuban, Digby Solomon** Author's telephone interview with Digby Solomon, winter 2010.

195 **"He comes in and tells me that the story he told . . ."** Author's interview with Timothy Knight, Mellville, NY, summer 2010.

196 **"I called Banar from the airport to tell her I planned to travel . . ."** Author's interview with Joseph O. Giaimo, Queens, NY, summer 2010.

197 **A federal subpoena from the SEC soon demanded** Letter from Tribune lawyer Paul V. Gerlach to Susan E. Curtin, senior counsel, U.S. Securities and Exchange Commission, August 2004. The letter was in response to a subpoena and demands for information from the SEC regarding circulation and ad rates or revenue between Dennis FitzSimons, Jack Fuller, Donald Grenesko, David Hiller, Raymond Jansen, Louis Sito, Robert Brennan, Robert Garcia, and/or Robert Bergin.

197 **the auditors tried to clandestinely observe whether the sales** Many details of the circulation scandal were first reported by Robert Kessler and James Madore, *Newsday* reporters who covered the scandal at their own paper.

197 **There was more than a grain of truth to the "everybody does it"** Author's telephone interview with Elaine Banar, summer 2010.

197 **"But a lot of people aggressively pushed the limits . . ."** Author's interview with Jack Klunder, former director of circulation at the *Los Angeles Times*, fall 2010; and author's interview with Louis Sito, Greeneville, SC, summer 2009.

198 **By 2005, when the scandal was unfolding, ABC audits** ABC audits of 21 major metro daily newspapers from 2002 through 2008. In all, the author examined ABC audits of 21 major metropolitan daily newspapers—*Chicago Tribune, Washington Post, Boston Globe, Miami Herald, San Francisco Chronicle, Denver Post, Rocky Mountain News, Milwaukee Journal Sentinel, Los Angeles Times, Atlanta Journal-Constitution, Philadelphia Daily News, Dallas Morning News, St. Louis Post-Dispatch, Newsday, Florida Times-Union, Chicago Sun-Times, Houston Chronicle, The Commercial Appeal* (Memphis), *Las Vegas Review Journal, Sacramento Bee,* and *San Jose Mercury News.* The author calculated the total circulation and then deducted home delivery and mail and single-copy sales from the total to get the percentage of junk

circulation as a proportion of the total. In general, most of the papers fit the profile of the *Los Angeles Times*. *Times* junk circulation went from 7 percent of the total in 2002, before the *Newsday* scandal broke, to 24 percent in 2006. After the federal investigation of *Newsday's* fake circulation picked up steam, the percentage of circulation classified as junk started falling and settled at 9 percent of the total by 2008, as executives pruned the junk from their books. ABC also invoked some rule changes during that period, and advertisers objected to paying for dubious circulation. Not all papers reached as high a proportion of junk. The *Chicago Tribune* average peaked at 7 percent of the total in 2006, although the proportion was higher on days when advertising was heavier. Some papers, like the *Miami Herald* and the *Las Vegas Review Journal*, continued to post large proportions of junk numbers— 27 percent and 36 percent, respectively, in 2008. In general, though, the curve for all papers was strikingly similar.

199 **"I had written a memo about what I knew and gave it to . . ."** Author's telephone interview with Digby Solomon, winter 2010.

200 **Knight concluded that *Newsday* had overstated its circulation** Interview with Timothy Knight, corroborated by news releases that the company publicized announcing the results of its investigation.

## Chapter 13: Count Kern

201 **When the *Newsday* scandal broke** Author's interview with Jack Fuller, Chicago, IL, fall 2008, and winter 2009.

201 **Sito had openly disclosed bogus** Author's interview with Louis Sito, Greeneville, SC, summer 2009. The author also examined letters on *Hoy* letterhead, written by Sito.

201 **"In going over the papers and records of the case, I decided . . ."** Author's interview with U.S. District Court judge, Jack Weinstein.

202 **"The ABC guys were all paper folks."** Author's telephone interview with Elaine Banar, summer 2010.

203 **Fuller was incensed when** Author's interview with Jack Fuller, Chicago, IL, fall 2008, and winter 2009.

204 **Fuller announced his resignation** "Jack Fuller to retire as head of Tribune Publishing," by Tara Burghart, *AP Worldstream*, October 28, 2004.

205 **During Tyner's first editors' meeting** Author's interview with Ann Marie Lipinski, Chicago, IL, winter 2010.

208 **Kern was careful to couch his reports** "Hurricanes Katrina and Rita, Insights about Tribune's coverage of the big storms and implications for future national coverage," Tribune Publishing, October 2005. The 22-page report was prepared by Gerould Kern and concluded that Tribune papers should "strive to do more that is extraordinary and differentiating by doing less that is routine and commonly available." This was just one of numerous reports compiled by Kern.

210 **paid Sammy Sosa to swing a baseball bat** In fact, Sosa's annual salary with the Chicago Cubs in 2003–2004 was $16.8 million each year, far more than the Tribune saved in eliminating any kind of duplication.

211     **Wolinsky started to worry** Author's interview with Leo Wolinsky, Los Angeles, CA, fall 2010, and by telephone, 2008–2010.

211     **phone call he made to Chicago** Author's telephone interview with John Carroll, summer 2009.

212     **"There was just no way that you could out Long Beach . . ."** Author's telephone interview with John Puerner, winter 2010.

213     **Even industry stalwarts like Brumback** Author's interview with Charles Brumback, Sarasota, FL, May 2010, and by telephone, 2008–2010.

213     **"We were discounting deeply . . ."** Author's telephone interview with John Puerner, winter 2010.

213     **After Puerner's first year in the publisher's office** Audit Bureau of Circulations Report for the *Los Angeles Times*, 2005.

213     **Under Steven Lee, the marketing executive** Author's interview with Jeffrey Johnson, Los Angeles, CA, winter 2011.

214     **called "Ten for Ten"** Author's interview with David Murphy, Chicago, IL, summer 2008; and author's interview with Jack Klunder, Los Angeles, fall 2010. As the Tribune executive who assumed responsibility for the advertising and circulation at the *Los Angeles Times*, Murphy dealt directly with the fallout from the "Ten for Ten" program.

214     **Klunder had run the *Los Angeles Times*** Author's interview with Jack Klunder, Los Angeles, fall 2010.

215     **Carroll paid a visit to Norm Pearlstine** Author's telephone interview with John Carroll, summer 2009.

215     **David Geffen, who had made billions in Hollywood** Author's interview with Leo Wolinsky, Los Angeles, CA, fall 2010, and by telephone, 2008–2010.

216     **Carroll's departure, one writer happened to note** "John Carroll on Winning Pulitzers while Losing Circulation, and the Future of Corporate News Outlets," by Paul McLeary, *Columbia Journalism Review*, July 2005.

217     **By the time ABC auditors acted on Klunder's tip** Audit Bureau of Circulations Report for the *Los Angeles Times*, 2005.

## Chapter 14: Civil War

220     **Kern began compiling the raw material for** "Hurricanes Katrina and Rita, Insights about Tribune's coverage of the big storms and implications for future national coverage," Tribune Publishing, October 2005.

221     **Times employees had had it, and in a survey conducted by an** International Survey Research, LLC (ISR), Verbatim Comments of *Los Angeles Times* Editorial Department Respondents, March 2005. ISR was hired to do a statistical survey of the morale in the editorial department of the *Los Angeles Times*. Employees were also given the opportunities to supplement their answers to the survey with written comments. In all, 548 employees of the editorial department took advantage of the opportunity to comment on everything from the direction and goals of the company to the quality of their supervisors. Some of the comments were lengthy and harsh

regarding the leadership of the Tribune Company since it acquired the *Los Angeles Times*.

222 **The first dose came** The proxy said Tribune management began due diligence on March 10 and that the boards of the two companies approved the deal two days later on March 12. David Hiller said the Tribune due diligence team had scrutinized publicly available records on Times Mirror before March 10 and that the Matthew Bender tax problem was deemed an acceptable risk. Tom Unterman said he had informed Tribune Company how the Times Mirror tax department intended to handle the potential Bender tax liability. Author interviews with David Hiller, Chicago, winter 2010, and Tom Unterman, Los Angeles, fall 2010.

223 **However, about a year after the deal was closed** Author's interview with Thomas Unterman, Los Angeles, CA, fall 2010.

223 **To diversify the family's investment** Tribune Company, Proxy Statement, April 2007; and Tribune Company Form 10-K for fiscal year ended December 31, 2006.

223 **the Chandlers wanted to place valuations** Deposition of Dennis J. FitzSimons, Chicago, IL, June 25, 2010; and author's interviews with Scott C. Smith, Chicago, IL, December 2010, and David Hiller, Chicago, IL, winter 2008, and winter 2010.

223 **The dispute came to a head in May 2006** United States Bankruptcy Court, Report of Examiner, Kenneth M. Klee, Case Number 0813141. Deposition of Dennis J. FitzSimons, Chicago, IL, June 25, 2010. The contemporary history of the Tribune's financial problems were spelled out in detail in this voluminous report.

224 **But the move infuriated the Chandlers** United States Bankruptcy Court, Report of Examiner, Kenneth M. Klee, Case Number 0813141 and author's telephone interview with Thomas Unterman, March 2011.

224 **William Stinehart, who publicly filed a blistering eleven-page** Letter from William Stinehart, Jr., former director of Tribune/trustee of the Chandler Trusts to Tribune Company Board of Directors, June 13, 2006. The 11-page letter castigated Tribune managers, harshly criticizing them for lack of vision and strategic failures in running the company. The letter, in effect, put the company up for sale.

226 **Smith and FitzSimons summoned Johnson** Author's interview with Jeffrey Johnson, Los Angeles, CA, winter 2011.

227 **rumors emerged of a "suicide pact" between** "Baquet's Billionaire Boys Club," by Nikki Finke, Deadline Hollywood, *LA Weekly*, September 2006. Finke's widely read column reported on a suicide pact, but the three editors involved said there was no such thing and none resigned.

227 **"I didn't need Gerry Kern to make . . ."** Author's interview with Leo Wolinsky, Los Angeles, CA, fall 2010, and by telephone, 2008–2010.

### Chapter 15: Up Against a Saint and a Dead Man

231 **Baquet stood before the** "*Los Angeles Times* Editor Urges Others to Fight Cuts," by Katherine Q. Seelye, *New York Times*, October 2006.

233 **He seemed thrilled to see me** During his 15 months as editor of the *Los Angeles Times*, the author kept a diary in which he recorded key events and exchanges. Many

of the recollections and quotes from his time as editor came from this diary. The author usually recorded entries in the diary the same day that they occurred.

237 **"When people complained, I always . . ."** Author's recollection of conversation with John Madigan.

239 **In Baltimore, a wealthy hedge-fund investor** Letter from Bruce S. Sherman to Board of Directors, Knight Ridder, Inc., November 1, 2005. Bruce Sherman wrote to the board of directors on behalf of Private Capital Management, LP, Knight Ridder's largest shareholder. His letter triggered the sale of the company.

239 **including the *Minneapolis Star Tribune*** "Private Group Buys Start Tribune," by Matt McKinney, *Minneapolis Star Tribune*, December 27, 2006.

251 **a story about huge bonuses being** Author's memo to the staff of the *Los Angeles Times*, April 23, 2007.

252 **he said, "and I'm not too impressed."** Author's recollection of meeting with Dennis FitzSimons.

## Chapter 16: Before the Fall

253 **Not long after I had walked into** United States Bankruptcy Court, Report of Examiner, Kenneth M. Klee, Case Number 0813141.

253 **In private, the Chandlers had hinted they might** United States Bankruptcy Court, Report of Examiner, Kenneth M. Klee, Case Number 0813141; examiner's interview of William Stinehart, Jr., former director of Tribune/trustee of the Chandler Trusts, Los Angeles, June 28, 2010.

254 **Tribune Company posted robust 2006** United States Bankruptcy Court, Report of Examiner, Kenneth M. Klee, Case Number 0813141. The examiner's report contains extensive financial information on the Tribune Company, compiled from company reports as well as from company analysts and banks.

254 **In his letter, Stinehart outlined a** Letter from William Stinehart, Jr., former director of Tribune/trustee of Chandler Family Trusts to Tribune Company Board of Directors, June 13, 2006.

254 **The acrimony with the Chandlers didn't end** United States Bankruptcy Court, Report of Examiner, Kenneth M. Klee, Case Number 0813141.

255 **The Tribune's Special Committee hired Morgan Stanley** United States Bankruptcy Court, Report of Examiner, Kenneth M. Klee, Case Number 0813141.

255 **Overall, Tribune investment bankers** United States Bankruptcy Court, Report of Examiner, Kenneth M. Klee, Case Number 0813141.

255 **Tribune employees owned 11 percent of** United States Bankruptcy Court, Report of Examiner, Kenneth M. Klee, Case Number 0813141.

256 **to the tune of an unusually high $10 million, a large** United States Bankruptcy Court, Report of Examiner, Kenneth M. Klee, Case Number 0813141; and deposition of William A. Osborn, May 16, 2007.

256 **Morgan Stanley would try to muscle its way** United States Bankruptcy Court, Report of Examiner, Kenneth M. Klee, Case Number 0813141.

256   **"Always said the banking intramurals . . ."** United States Bankruptcy Court, Report of Examiner, Kenneth M. Klee, Case Number 0813141; and e-mail from Crane H. Kenney, general counsel, Tribune Company, to Michael R. Costa, former managing director, mergers and acquisitions, Merrill Lynch, February 24, 2007.

256   **At one point, the Chandlers considered selling** United States Bankruptcy Court, Report of Examiner, Kenneth M. Klee, Case Number 0813141; and examiner's interview of William Stinehart, Jr., former director of Tribune/trustee of the Chandler Trusts, Los Angeles, June 28, 2010; and deposition of Dennis J. FitzSimons, Chicago, IL, June 25, 2010.

257   **"We looked out and saw a ski slope,"** United States Bankruptcy Court, Report of Examiner, Kenneth M. Klee, Case Number 0813141; examiner's interview of William Stinehart, Jr., former director of Tribune/trustee of the Chandler Trusts, Los Angeles, June 28, 2010.

257   **The mere thought of doing a deal with** United States Bankruptcy Court, Report of Examiner, Kenneth M. Klee, Case Number 0813141; examiner's interview of Julie H. Persily, formerly with the Citigroup Leveraged Finance Department, New York, NY, July 8, 2010.

257   **He had just sold his Equity Office Properties** "Update—Zell Sells for $39 Billion," by Scott Reeves, *Forbes*, November 20, 2006.

258   **A *Chicago Tribune* magazine article** "Here's the Deal; How Sam Zell Beat a Tax-Fraud Rap and Rose to the Top of the Real Estate World," by Greg Burns, *Chicago Tribune*, July 25, 2004.

258   **To put together a bid, Zell activated an** Author's interview with confidential source from Equity Office Properties. The source spoke with author under the condition of anonymity.

259   **While at law school at the University of Chicago** Author's interview with confidential source from Equity Office Properties. The source spoke with author under the condition of anonymity.

259   **A few years before, Zell had invested in a waste** "Invest Like a Billionaire: Sam Zell," by Tatiana Serafin, Forbes.com, November 9, 2006. The author also learned of details of the ESOP and Covanta transaction from a confidential source at Equity Office Properties.

260   **A mere five days later, Bartter** United States Bankruptcy Court, Report of Examiner, Kenneth M. Klee, Case Number 0813141; examiner's interview of Brit Bartter, then vice chairman of investment banking group at JPMorgan Chase, Chicago, IL, June 16, 2010.

260   **Zell's proposal had some intriguing benefits, too.** United States Bankruptcy Court, Report of Examiner, Kenneth M. Klee, Case Number 0813141. Zell and others at Equity Office Properties spelled out the details of the proposal to the examiner.

260   **"What was novel was that it was an S-Corp. . . ."** United States Bankruptcy Court, Report of Examiner, Kenneth M. Klee, Case Number 0813141.

260   **Some bankers involved in the deal were cool to the idea.** United States Bankruptcy Court, Report of Examiner, Kenneth M. Klee, Case Number 0813141.

261   **Christina Mohr, a managing director in Citigroup's** United States Bankruptcy Court, Report of Examiner, Kenneth M. Klee, Case Number 0813141; e-mail from Paul Ingrassia, managing director, Citigroup, to Christina Mohr, February 20, 2007.

261   **When Costa, the Tribune's** United States Bankruptcy Court, Report of Examiner, Kenneth M. Klee, Case Number 0813141.

262   **Any plan would require approval by the Federal Communications Commission (FCC) because** United States Bankruptcy Court, Report of Examiner, Kenneth M. Klee, Case Number 0813141.

262   **But Zell had an answer** United States Bankruptcy Court, Report of Examiner, Kenneth M. Klee, Case Number 0813141.

262   **Mohr recalled how** United States Bankruptcy Court, Report of Examiner, Kenneth M. Klee, Case Number 0813141.

262   **Zell, who called Tribune General Counsel Kenney and demanded** Author's conversation with Crane Kenney in Los Angeles, 2007. The author noted the conversation in his diary.

262   **"Marty called me one morning and said . . ."** United States Bankruptcy Court, Report of Examiner, Kenneth M. Klee, Case Number 0813141; deposition of Dennis J. FitzSimons, Chicago, IL, June 25, 2010.

263   **the Zell proposal until Osborn** United States Bankruptcy Court, Report of Examiner, Kenneth M. Klee, Case Number 0813141; deposition of Dennis J. FitzSimons, Chicago, IL, June 25, 2010; and examiner's interview of Samuel H. Zell, Chicago, IL, June 14, 2010.

263   **But Morgan Stanley's Whayne** United States Bankruptcy Court, Report of Examiner, Kenneth M. Klee, Case Number 0813141; examiner's interview of Thomas Whayne, managing director, Morgan Stanley, New York, NY, June 11, 2010.

263   **Costa pushed back saying they should be "more aggressive."** United States Bankruptcy Court, Report of Examiner, Kenneth M. Klee, Case Number 0813141.

263   **"The banks were climbing . . ."** United States Bankruptcy Court, Report of Examiner, Kenneth M. Klee, Case Number 0813141; deposition of Crane H. Kenney, former General Counsel of Tribune, Chicago, IL, July 8, 2010.

264   **In late March, Zell broke** United States Bankruptcy Court, Report of Examiner, Kenneth M. Klee, Case Number 0813141.

264   **"That's how I got comfortable. At the end of the . . ."** United States Bankruptcy Court, Report of Examiner, Kenneth M. Klee, Case Number 0813141.

264   **At the last minute, Zell also cut** United States Bankruptcy Court, Report of Examiner, Kenneth M. Klee, Case Number 0813141.

264   **There was no end of whooping** United States Bankruptcy Court, Report of Examiner, Kenneth M. Klee, Case Number 0813141; e-mail from Sanjay Jain, vice president, JPMorgan Chase, to Peter Cohen, managing director, JPMorgan Chase, April 2, 2007.

264   **"Guys—truly amazing financial . . ."** United States Bankruptcy Court, Report of Examiner, Kenneth M. Klee, Case Number 0813141; Merrill Lynch inter-office e-mail from Chris Cormier to John Eidinger and Michael Costa, April 6, 2007.

265    **But Jieun (Jayna) Choi, an analyst at** United States Bankruptcy Court, Report of Examiner, Kenneth M. Klee, Case Number 0813141; JPMorgan Chase interoffice e-mail from Jieun (Jayna) Choi to Goh Silew Tan, April 5, 2007.

265    **For their work over six months** United States Bankruptcy Court, Report of Examiner, Kenneth M. Klee, Case Number 0813141. The author computed the fees from data disclosed in the examiner's report.

265    **By now, FitzSimons had climbed on** United States Bankruptcy Court, Report of Examiner, Kenneth M. Klee, Case Number 0813141; deposition of Dennis J. FitzSimons, Chicago, IL, June 25, 2010.

265    **The way he saw it, Tribune's assets** United States Bankruptcy Court, Report of Examiner, Kenneth M. Klee, Case Number 0813141; examiner's interview of Samuel H. Zell, Chicago, June 14, 2010.

267    **anything that adds juice to a column** "Public's beach is a beauty, but try to find it," by Steve Lopez, *Los Angeles Times*, April 6, 2007.

## Chapter 17: The Penguin Parable

269    **On June 4, 2007, JPMorgan Chase** United States Bankruptcy Court, Report of Examiner, Kenneth M. Klee, Case Number 0813141.

269    **have driven the company's stock** United States Bankruptcy Court, Report of Examiner, Kenneth M. Klee, Case Number 0813141. The report contained numerous estimates of what would happen if the deal had not closed, including one from Lehman Brothers that was particularly negative. That report suggested that the Tribune's stock could have fallen to below $10 per share.

272    **Both Baquet and Carroll agreed that** Author's telephone interview with John Carroll, summer 2009; and Dean Baquet, winter 2010.

272    **a report that called for a vigorous renewal of time** The Spring Street Project Report, *Los Angeles Times*, December 1, 2006. The report, which was initiated by Baquet, was an 11-page summary of the Spring Street Team's visits to other newspapers, web operations, research, and consulting offices including: Yahoo!, America Online, Technorati, and an interview with craigslist founder, Craig Newmark.

278    **The loans gave Zell the money he needed** United States Bankruptcy Court, Report of Examiner, Kenneth M. Klee, Case Number 0813141.

278    **The Chandlers didn't help things.** United States Bankruptcy Court, Report of Examiner, Kenneth M. Klee, Case Number 0813141.

279    **Jill Greenthal, a Blackstone Group** United States Bankruptcy Court, Report of Examiner, Kenneth M. Klee, Case Number 0813141; e-mail from Jill Greenthal, et al., to John Madigan, June 4, 2007.

279    **Zell dismissed speculation** United States Bankruptcy Court, Report of Examiner, Kenneth M. Klee, Case Number 0813141; transcript of lenders' meeting, April 26, 2007.

279    **"I thought the chances of getting the second ..."** United States Bankruptcy Court, Report of Examiner, Kenneth M. Klee, Case Number 0813141; examiner's interview of Samuel H. Zell, Chicago, IL, June 14, 2010.

279 **A report from Lehman Brothers** United States Bankruptcy Court, Report of Examiner, Kenneth M. Klee, Case Number 0813141.

280 **knocked the company's 2007 operating profit off 40 percent.** Tribune Company Form 10-K for fiscal year ended December 31, 2007.

281 **When JPMorgan Chase tried to syndicate** United States Bankruptcy Court, Report of Examiner, Kenneth M. Klee, Case Number 0813141. Series of interoffice e-mails at Merrill Lynch between Todd Kaplan and Victor Nesi that said the deal was not going well, May 10, 2007. Also, e-mail from Jeffrey A. Sell, former head of special credits group in the credit risk department of JPMorgan Chase, to Brian S. Sankey, May 12, 2007, that said the orders had fallen short.

281 **One brokerage firm analysis suggested Tribune** "Tribune Debt Default Risk Tops 50%, Swaps Show," by Tim Mullaney and Shannon D. Harrington, *Bloomberg Report*, July 20, 2007. The pessimistic forecast was done by CMA Datavision of London, England.

281 **Peter Cohen told his boss, the bank's chairman** United States Bankruptcy Court, Report of Examiner, Kenneth M. Klee, Case Number 0813141; JPMorgan Chase interoffice e-mail from Peter Cohen, managing director, to Jamie Dimon, chairman and CEO.

282 **To close phase one of the deal** United States Bankruptcy Court, Report of Examiner, Kenneth M. Klee, Case Number 0813141.

282 **The company's outstanding bonds took an even bigger hit and** "Tribune Debt Default Risk Tops 50%, Swaps Show," by Tim Mullaney and Shannon D. Harrington, *Bloomberg Report*, July 20, 2007.

283 **paying just under 8 percent interest** United States Bankruptcy Court, Report of Examiner, Kenneth M. Klee, Case Number 0813141.

283 **At JPMorgan Chase, one alarmed banker** United States Bankruptcy Court, Report of Examiner, Kenneth M. Klee, Case Number 0813141.

283 **Jimmy Lee, a JPMorgan Chase** United States Bankruptcy Court, Report of Examiner, Kenneth M. Klee, Case Number 0813141; JPMorgan Chase interoffice e-mail from James B. Lee, Jr., vice chairman, to Patricia Deans, analyst.

283 **FitzSimons, who assumed he would resume** United States Bankruptcy Court, Report of Examiner, Kenneth M. Klee, Case Number 0813141; deposition of Dennis J. FitzSimons, Chicago, IL, June 25, 2010.

284 **Darryl Jacobson asked if the bank could suggest** United States Bankruptcy Court, Report of Examiner, Kenneth M. Klee, Case Number 0813141; JPMorgan Chase Syndicated and Leverage Finance Group interoffice e-mail from Darryl Jacobson to Rajesh Kapadia, September 26, 2007.

284 **But Dimon wasn't about to shaft a major customer** United States Bankruptcy Court, Report of Examiner, Kenneth M. Klee, Case Number 0813141; JPMorgan Chase interoffice e-mail from Jamie Dimon to Darryl Jacobson, September 6, 2007.

284 **One Deutsche Bank analyst concluded** United States Bankruptcy Court, Report of Examiner, Kenneth M. Klee, Case Number 0813141.

284 **But Dimon disagreed: "Sam until very "** United States Bankruptcy Court, Report of Examiner, Kenneth M. Klee, Case Number 0813141; examiner's interview

of Jamie Dimon, chairman and CEO, JPMorgan Chase, New York, June 25, 2010.

284 **Zell claimed that he hadn't invested** United States Bankruptcy Court, Report of Examiner, Kenneth M. Klee, Case Number 0813141; examiner's interview of Samuel H. Zell, Chicago, IL, June 14, 2010.

284 **The internal math on the deal put Zell's rate of return** United States Bankruptcy Court, Report of Examiner, Kenneth M. Klee, Case Number 0813141.

284 **When Tribune's stock dropped to $25 a share,** United States Bankruptcy Court, Report of Examiner, Kenneth M. Klee, Case Number 0813141.

285 **Analysts at the lead banks suddenly became quite interested** United States Bankruptcy Court, Report of Examiner, Kenneth M. Klee, Case Number 0813141.

285 **prompting Yang Chen at Citicorp to** United States Bankruptcy Court, Report of Examiner, Kenneth M. Klee, Case Number 0813141.

285 **Things got pretty sticky. At Tribune, the** United States Bankruptcy Court, Report of Examiner, Kenneth M. Klee, Case Number 0813141.

285 **Not long after the Tribune had hired VRC, Citicorp** United States Bankruptcy Court, Report of Examiner, Kenneth M. Klee, Case Number 0813141.

286 **after Rajesh Kapadia from JPMorgan Chase told Larsen** United States Bankruptcy Court, Report of Examiner, Kenneth M. Klee, Case Number 0813141.

286 **Tribune's general counsel, Crane Kenney** United States Bankruptcy Court, Report of Examiner, Kenneth M. Klee, Case Number 0813141; deposition of Crane H. Kenney, former general counsel of Tribune, Chicago, IL, July 8, 2010.

286 **Ben Buettell, one manager at Houlihan Lokey Howard & Zukin** United States Bankruptcy Court, Report of Examiner, Kenneth M. Klee, Case Number 0813141; deposition of Ben Buettell, December 2, 2009.

287 **penguins called *Our Iceberg Is Melting*.** *Our Iceberg Is Melting*, by John Kotter (New York: St. Martin's Press, 2006).

288 **"You are on the board, you sit on the board...."** United States Bankruptcy Court, Report of Examiner, Kenneth M. Klee, Case Number 0813141; examiner's interview of Samuel H. Zell, Chicago, IL, June 14, 2010.

288 **Afterwards, FitzSimons let Zell know he was dealing with someone** United States Bankruptcy Court, Report of Examiner, Kenneth M. Klee, Case Number 0813141; deposition of Dennis J. FitzSimons, Chicago, IL, June 25, 2010.

289 **"I'm not doing anything. I'm not giving you any power ..."** United States Bankruptcy Court, Report of Examiner, Kenneth M. Klee, Case Number 0813141; examiner's interview of Samuel H. Zell, Chicago, June 14, 2010.

289 **Behind the scenes, he had asked his trusted aide** United States Bankruptcy Court, Report of Examiner, Kenneth M. Klee, Case Number 0813141; memorandum labeled, "Tower Strategy," to Sam Zell from Bill Pate, August 9, 2007.

289 **1990s. He asked Michaels to come up** United States Bankruptcy Court, Report of Examiner, Kenneth M. Klee, Case Number 0813141; e-mail from Randy Michaels to Sam Zell, August 20, 2007.

290 **"Begin the process of creating products focused on consumer . . ."** United States Bankruptcy Court, Report of Examiner, Kenneth M. Klee, Case Number 0813141; e-mail from Randy Michaels to Sam Zell, August 20, 2007.

290 **including the late Warren Christopher,** Author's recollection of luncheon. The author attended the lunch and took notes on the proceedings.

## Chapter 18: Closing the Deal

296 **In August, the lead banks—JPMorgan Chase** United States Bankruptcy Court, Report of Examiner, Kenneth M. Klee, Case Number 0813141.

296 **The response triggered more back and forth between** United States Bankruptcy Court, Report of Examiner, Kenneth M. Klee, Case Number 0813141.

297 **"We are clearly dealing with an organization at all . . ."** United States Bankruptcy Court, Report of Examiner, Kenneth M. Klee, Case Number 0813141; Merrill Lynch interoffice e-mail from Todd Kaplan to Michael Costa, November 7, 2007.

297 **By having their lawyers hire the expert, the banks draped a** United States Bankruptcy Court, Report of Examiner, Kenneth M. Klee, Case Number 0813141. Deposition of Crane H. Kenney, former general counsel of Tribune, Chicago, IL, July 8, 2010.

297 **But Tribune CFO Don Grenesko and Chandler Bigelow** United States Bankruptcy Court, Report of Examiner, Kenneth M. Klee, Case Number 0813141.

298 **At one point, the banks sounded each other out and learned that** United States Bankruptcy Court, Report of Examiner, Kenneth M. Klee, Case Number 0813141.

302 **VRC, under pressure** United States Bankruptcy Court, Report of Examiner, Kenneth M. Klee, Case Number 0813141.

302 **After much to and fro** United States Bankruptcy Court, Report of Examiner, Kenneth M. Klee, Case Number 0813141; Deposition of Nils Larsen, managing director, Equity Group International, July 7, 2010. Larsen told Bankruptcy Examiner Kenneth Klee that he didn't promise Bigelow the job of CFO but that he did suggest Bigelow had a good future with the new owners. "I'm sure that he would have gotten the sense from conversations with me that I thought that he was a valuable member of the team," Larsen said.

303 **"Just had a long talk with Sam. . . ."** United States Bankruptcy Court, Report of Examiner, Kenneth M. Klee, Case Number 0813141; JPMorgan Chase interoffice e-mail from James Lee to Jamie Dimon, December 19, 2007.

303 **Lee's boss, Dimon, later** United States Bankruptcy Court, Report of Examiner, Kenneth M. Klee, Case Number 0813141; examiner's interview of Jamie Dimon, chairman and CEO, JPMorgan Chase, New York, NY, June 25, 2010.

303 **Zell said he knew the bank** United States Bankruptcy Court, Report of Examiner, Kenneth M. Klee, Case Number 0813141.

304 **On December 20, 2007, at 12:02 p.m.** United States Bankruptcy Court, Report of Examiner, Kenneth M. Klee, Case Number 0813141.

304 **The banks wire-transferred funds to Tribune, which disbursed about** United States Bankruptcy Court, Report of Examiner, Kenneth M. Klee, Case Number 0813141.

304 **performance was off just 2 percent from its plan, the ESOP would have** United States Bankruptcy Court, Report of Examiner, Kenneth M. Klee, Case Number 0813141.

304 **But FitzSimons had reason to be even happier.** United States Bankruptcy Court, Report of Examiner, Kenneth M. Klee, Case Number 0813141, and news reports in the *Chicago Tribune* and other newspapers.

305 **Many of his friends in the company did well, too** United States Bankruptcy Court, Report of Examiner, Kenneth M. Klee, Case Number 0813141.

305 **On Wall Street, the banks and their advisers** United States Bankruptcy Court, Report of Examiner, Kenneth M. Klee, Case Number 0813141.

## Chapter 19: Zell Hell

315 **the *Los Angeles Times* quoting Zell saying** Zell e-mail to author, January, 23, 2008.

317 **In 2007, the *Times* generated nearly $200 million in cash flow, off** Tribune Company Form 10-K for fiscal year ended December 31, 2007 and author's recollection as recorded in his diary.

317 **Zell compared the *Times*, which had survived for 126 years** Video, "Sam Zell Visits the *Los Angeles Times*," February 7, 2008. Zell visited the *Los Angeles Times* printing facility, where he spoke with employees.

318 **The whole exercise seemed like a scene out of** Video, "Tribune Owner, Sam Zell, Says F#@k You" Visits *Orlando Sentinel*," January 31, 2008.

318 **By the time Zell and Michaels showed up** Tribune Company interoffice e-mail passed on to the author by anonymous sources, February 27, 2008.

320 **Lipinksi's first doubts about Zell surfaced during** Author's interview with Ann Marie Lipinski, Chicago, IL, winter 2010.

321 **Proud of his heritage as a Latino and loyal to** Author's telephone interview with George de Lama, summer 2009.

322 **but she remained determined to see the** Author's interview with Ann Marie Lipinski, Chicago, IL, winter 2010.

323 **Complaints of sexual harassment, crude jokes, and boorish behavior dogged Michaels** *Right of the Dial: The Rise of Clear Channel and the Fall of Commercial Radio*, by Alec Foge (New York: Faber and Faber, 2008).

323 **The hundred-day Tribune plan Michaels** United States Bankruptcy Court, Report of Examiner, Kenneth M. Klee, Case Number 0813141.

324 **In all, in less than a year, Michaels hired into senior positions** Author's telephone interview with Mary Jo Mandula, winter 2009. Mandula was the building manager at Tribune Tower.

324 **Michaels' most celebrated hire was Lee Abrams** "Lee Abrams Joins Tribune as CIO," *Arbitcast: All Things Satellite Radio*, March 11, 2008.

325 **"Talk to Sam" e-mail box for employees** Transcripts of TalktoSam Messages, December 2007–February 2008. Employees were unaware that Zell's e-mail messages were sent to their supervisors.

326 **forcing him to order deep budget cuts and layoffs** "Tribune Company Announces Hundreds of Job Cuts," Associated Press, February 13, 2008. Although Zell told Tribune employees that the company could not cut its way to prosperity, he began eliminating jobs and cutting the space for news soon after he took over.

326 **He commissioned jukeboxes, pinball** Author's interview with Mary Jo Mandula, winter 2009.

327 **Even Kern called Lipinski and said** Author's interview with Ann Marie Lipinski, Chicago, IL, winter 2010.

328 **"The Perils of Modern Journalism: Should Political . . ."** Author inspection of the sign after it had been removed from Tribune Tower.

329 **After another lunch in his office, Zell** Author's interview with Ann Marie Lipinski, Chicago, IL, winter 2010.

331 **In December 2008, the Tribune Company** "Tribune Company Files for Bankruptcy," by *Dealbook*, December 8, 2008.

## Epilogue

336 **In Chicago, Zell had turned his attention** "Sam Zell's Deal from Hell," by Emily Thornton, Michael Arndt, and Ronald Grover, *BusinessWeek*, July 30, 2008. In this and other pieces, Zell said his investment in Tribune Company was a mistake, one that he labeled "The Deal from Hell."

336 **Heavily promoted stories about fake food** The stories and promotions cited by the author appeared on page one of the *Chicago Tribune* on October 1 and October 8, 2008.

337 **When one Tribune editor pitched** Former Tribune associate managing editor for sports, Dan McGrath, was at the meeting in question and told the author about the decision, Chicago, IL, summer 2008.

338 **Michaels used the Colonel's office for a poker** "Poker Party 'desecrates' Tribune Tower Shrine," by Robert Feder, WBEZ 91.5, July 2, 2010. The piece by Feder included four pictures and a narrative of the event by John D. Phillips, the Tribune Tower manager appointed to his job by Michaels. Phillips posted the event on his Facebook page.

338 **A terrace on the twenty-second floor of Tribune Tower** The incident involving the sexual tryst between the secretary and Michaels was first reported in an anonymous letter to the Tribune Company board. The author confirmed the incident with Mary Jo Mandula, who managed the building and oversaw the security services that employed the guard who discovered Michaels and the young woman. The author also confirmed the incident with another high-ranking security official at Tribune Tower, although the official discussed the incident and asked that his name not be used. The alleged "investigation" of the incident by an outside law firm dismissed the allegation in the letter because no one had filed a complaint with the Tribune's human relations department, which Michaels had downsized. In his *New York Times* story of October 6, 2010, David Carr disclosed the incident but Michaels' name was withheld.

339 **"I feel compelled to report on some things . . ."** Anonymous letter to the Tribune board of directors outlining the sexual trysts and the hiring of numerous friends by Michaels. The letter, dated December 11, 2008, was signed "Concerned Employee." The author examined an e-mail that disclosed that a Tribune director was made aware of the substance of the letter. The author agreed to withhold details of the e-mail in return for examining it. The letter said that Michaels' conduct was widely known within the company and Tribune Tower. The employee's letter to the board contained numerous examples of Michaels' antics.

341 **Thomas E. Patterson, a professor of government** "Doing Well and Doing Good: How Soft News and Critical Journalism Are Shrinking the News Audience and Weakening Democracy—And What News Outlets Can Do About It," by Thomas E. Patterson, Joan Shorenstein Center on the Press, Politics and Public Policy, Cambridge, MA, December 2000.

343 **The Pew Research Center's Project for Excellence** "How News Happens—A Study of the News Ecosystem of Baltimore," January 11, 2010. The study by the Pew Center represents the only effort the author is aware of that attempts to document the true source of news in the age of the Internet.

343 **the Sun has cut its newsroom by about 60 percent** Author's interview with sources knowledgeable about staffing levels at the *Baltimore Sun*. In 2004, the *Baltimore Sun's* newsroom was composed of approximately 384 staffers, about two-thirds of whom, or 253, were members of the Washington-Baltimore Newspaper Guild, the bargaining unit for employees that were not management. By 2011 there were 98.

# INDEX

## A

ABC News, 142
Abrams, Lee, 324, 330, 336
Adams, John Quincy, 60
Advertising, newspaper
  business of, 72
  declining circulation and, 334
  *Los Angeles Times* campaign, 97
  monopoly control of, 28
  on page one, 270, 277
  strategies designed for, 276
Airlines, lack of emergency medical
    equipment on, 139
Alford, Kael, 334
American Express, 164
American Society of News Editors,
    154
America Online
  Brumback investment in, 7, 101,
    117–118
  Madigan sale of, 120–121
  Time Warner merger with, 102
Amin, Idi, 94
Andersen, Martin, 75
Anderson, Lisa, 78, 140, 142, 206, 220
Annenberg, Max, 182
Annenberg, Moe, 182
Anthan, George, 23
*Arizona Daily Star*, 4

*Arlington Heights Daily Herald* (suburban
    Chicago), 207
Armstrong, Ken, 135
Arnot, Bob, 141
Arthur, John, 47, 288, 295
Associated Advertising Club, 63
Associated Press (AP), 10, 209
Associated Press Managing Editors con-
    vention, 231
*Atlanta Journal and Constitution*, 169,
    198
Atorino, Edward, 224
Audit Bureau of Circulations (ABC)
  Brumback on, 213
  history of, 187–188
  newspaper connection to, 202
  purpose of, 82
  sales observations of, 197
  two percent list of, 217–218
  *See also* Circulation, newspaper
Avetisian, Chris, 280
Aviation Medical Assistance Act, 142

## B

Babcock, Susan, 102
Begley, Ed. Jr,. 243
Bailey, Charles, 33
Baker, Cissy, 170

Baker, Howard, 170
Ballin, Hugo, 43
Ballow, Robert, 107
*Baltimore Sun*, 133, 149, 160, 209,
    220–221, 343
Banar, Elaine, 193, 196, 199, 202, 322
Bank of America, 263, 296
Baquet, Dean P.
    AP Managing Editors convention
        speech (2006), 231
    as centralization foe, 225
    foreign and national news staff reduc-
        tions by, 221
    *Los Angeles Times* as national paper
        of the West, 159–160
    as *Los Angeles Times* managing editor,
        154, 216
    as New Orleans reporter, 155
    on "news hole" of *Los Angeles Times*,
        159
    O'Shea replacing, 228–229
Barry, Marion, 50
Bartter, Brit, 260
Baskes, Roger, 258
Batista, Fulgencio, 106
*Bayonet, The* (7th Infantry Division,
    U.S. Army), 18
Beck, Edward Scott, 123
Beck Awards, 123
Beiser, Scott, 286
Benchmark Company, 224
Bennett, Phil, 301
Berg, Jeffrey S., 339
Bernstein, Carl, 30
Bigelow, Chandler, 285, 297, 302, 304,
    346
Bilingual sections, of *Los Angeles Times*,
    97
Bingham family, 112
Black Journalists Association, 154
Blackstone Group, 255–256, 279
Blagojevich, Rod, 329
Blau, Robert, 136
Blogs
    *Deadline Hollywood*, 232
    of Hiller, 246

*LA Observed*, 221, 235, 248, 295,
    312, 319
    newsroom leaks to, 235–236
Bloomberg News, 347
Boudreaux, Richard, 301
Boyarsky, Bill, 52, 127
Bragman, Howard, 312
*Breeze, The*, 51
Brennan, Robert, 193–194, 197, 202,
    224
Breslin, Jimmy, 18, 30, 183
Brin, Sergey, 5
Brinkley, David, 59
Broad, Eli, 215, 226, 255, 298
Brown, Geoffrey, 147
Brown, Jeffrey, 143
Brown, Jerry, 53
Brown, Pat, 52
Brumback, Charles T.
    on ABC circulation numbers, 213
    accountant background of, 67, 69–83
    America Online investment by, 7,
        101, 117
    CLTV cable news channel started by,
        117
    on computerization, 78–79
    distribution changes by, 77–78
    on journalistic and business separa-
        tion, 73–75
    Madigan as successor to, 107–108
    New Century Network of, 4
    at *Orlando Sentinel*, 75–76
    productivity gains by, 79–81
    profit orientation of, 69–73
    Squires pressured by, 81–83
    on staffing levels, 76–77
    synergy demands of, 166
    Tribune Media Center and, 170
    Wall Street view of, 2
Budget deficits, in Reagan presidency, 55
Buettell, Ben, 286
Burkle, Ronald, 255, 289
Burns, Greg, 258, 321
Bush, George H. W., 81
Bush, George W., 177
Bush, Vannevar, 60

*Business Week* magazine, 94, 134, 171
Buyouts, employee, 249


C
Cable TV, 91, 117, 120
California Club, 129
Capital Cities Communications, 142
CareerBuilder.com, 158–159
Carey, Kevin J., 346
Carlyle Group, 255
Carr, David, 339
Carroll, John S.
    Baquet hiring by, 155
    "Editing by referendum" comment on
        FitzSimons, 176
    *Los Angeles Times* as national paper
        of the West, 159–160
    Montorio hiring by, 158
    negative view of synergy of, 205,
        208–209, 211
    newsroom understanding of, 151–152
    as Parks' replacement, 149
    Pulitzer Prize pursuit by, 160
    resignation of, 216
    *Tribune* hostility toward, 215
Carter, Jimmy, 30–31
Castro, Fidel, 105
Catledge, Turner, 45
Cauthorn, Robert, 4
CBS News, 105
Centralization of editorial decision
    making, 208. *See also* Synergy
Chandis Securities, 102
Chandler, Dorothy "Buff," 45, 290
Chandler, Harry, 44, 96, 99, 101–102
Chandler, Norman, 45
Chandler, Otis, 43–54
    family history, 43–45
    John Birch Society investigation of,
        46–47
    journalistic standards of, 47–48
    *Los Angeles Times* bureaus and,
        51–53
    *Los Angeles Times* controlled by, 8
    parents of, 45–46

    retirement of, 99–100
    staff reverence for, 87–88
    on Staples scandal, 127
    Wolinsky and, 48–51
Chandler, Philip, 45
Chandler family
    financial windfalls of, 99
    FitzSimons' tensions with,
        225–226
    Goldman Sachs stock buy from,
        278–279
    as local publishing monopoly, 21
    on merger, 125–126, 129–131
    Nixon and, 8
    special dividend scandal (1994),
        91–92
    stock sales by, 253–255
    super-voting status of Times Mirror
        stock of, 129–131
    Times Mirror Company stock of, 90,
        94–95
    Tribune Company and, 12
    unwinding of trusts by, 223–224
    Willes recruited by, 3, 89–92
    Willes' tension with, 99–101
    *See also Chicago Tribune*
Charity scam investigation, 157
Charles Schwab & Co., 5
Chase, Marc, 324, 326
Chen, Yang, 285
Chicago Bulls basketball team, 166
Chicago City Council corruption investi-
    gation, 155
Chicago Cubs baseball team, 166, 260,
    321, 328, 331
*Chicago Daily News*, 186
Chicago News Cooperative (CNC), 344,
    348
Chicago Online, 117
*Chicago Sun-Times*, 35, 79, 82, 107, 184,
    213, 346
*Chicago Theater of the Air*, 40
*Chicago Tribune*
    America Online investment by, 7,
        101, 117
    ethics policy of, 147–148

*Chicago Tribune (continued)*
foreign and national news coverage
of, 11
headquarters of, 6
history of, 28–29, 35–41
Jones, Bill, at, 27
junk circulation of, 198
Madigan as publisher of, 112–115
McCormick and Medill legacy to,
36–37, 41
newsroom of, 31–32
profit margins of, 139
Pulitzer Prizes of, 7, 155, 203, 207
Republican Party and, 7
Washington, D.C., bureau of, 55–57
*See also* Merger, of *Chicago Tribune*
and *Los Angeles Times*
*Chicago Tribune Sunday Magazine*, 321
Chicago White Sox baseball team, 166
Childreach, 141
Children International, 141, 142
Children's charities, investigation of,
140–142
*Chinatown* (film), 44
Choi, Jieun, 265
Christian Brothers, 17
Christian Children's Fund, 141
Christopher, Warren, 290–291
Ciccone, F. Richard, 170, 236
Circulation, newspaper
advertising declines due to, 246
of *Des Moines Register*, 19–20
maintaining, 86
monopoly control of, 28
*Newsday* and *Hoy* fraudulent inflation
of, 181–203
Willes' increases in, 97–99
Citigroup, 255–256, 260–261, 269, 285,
296
City News, 31–32
Classified Ad Federation, NAA, 5
Classified advertising
on Internet, 273
Internet effect on newspaper, 246
monopoly control of, 28
Monster.com effect on, 158

real estate decline of, 254
reductions in, 4
Classified Ventures, 128
Clayton, Janet, 236
Clear Channel Communications,
323–324, 327
*Cleveland News*, 28
Clinton, Bill, 142, 255
CLTV cable news channel, 117, 120
CNN, 170, 193
"Code Blue" (Crewdson), 140
Cody, Cardinal John, 35
Coen, Jeff, 325–326
Coffey, Shelby, III, 89
Cohn, Marty, 311, 320
Cohen, Peter, 263, 281
Collins, Gail, 183
Co-location, 208
Columbia University, 3, 155
Columbia University School of
Journalism, 30
Columbine High School, Littleton,
Colorado, 1
Column One feature, in *Los Angeles
Times*, 50
Combs, Sean Diddy, 320
Comics, in *Chicago Tribune*, 39
Communism, false accusations of, 46
Community leaders, newspapers as,
143
Computerization, 78–79
Computershare Trust Co., 304
Consolidation pressure, on newspapers,
102–103
Convergence of media, 6
Cook, Stan
Brumback as successor to, 66–67,
76
Kirkpatrick and, 29, 41, 64–65
Salomon Brothers and, 110
"Cops and Confessions" (Possley and
Mills), 136
Costa, Michael, 134, 256, 261, 263, 297
Cowles, Gardner, 21, 25
Cowles family, 21, 25–26. *See also Des
Moines Register*

Cox Enterprises, 91
craigslist.com, 5, 274
Crawford, Jan, 222
Credit default swaps, 283
Crewdson, John, 78, 140
Cronkite, Walter, 59
Cruzen, Nancy, 20
Culver Military Academy, 70
Cuomo, Mario, 107
Curie, James, 118
Curtiss, Aaron, 312
Czack, Richie, 194, 224

D
Daley, Richard, 134
*Dallas Morning News*, 213
Davis, Jack, 155
"Deal fatigue," 281
Death penalty cases, series on, in *Chicago
    Tribune*, 135–136
de Lama, George, 31–32, 56, 138, 201,
    321–322
Dellios, Hugh, 141
Denley, Susan, 301
Depreciation deductions, 99
*Des Moines Register*, 15–26
    circulation of, 19–20
    Cowles family as publishers of, 21,
        25–26
    *Des Moines Tribune* and, 57
    editing of, 22–25
    independence of, 20
    local stories in, 15–17
    newsroom of, 18–19, 22
    O'Shea, James at, 15, 30–31
    Pulitzer Prizes of, 18
    Raffensperger, Gene at, 15
    Zeleny hired from, 222
*Detroit Times*, 63
Devereaux, Greg, 275
Dewey, Thomas E., 37
Dimon, Jamie, 263, 281, 284, 303
Dinkins, David, 107
Discounted stock acquisition plans, of
    Tribune employees, 255

Distressed properties, Zell purchase of,
    253
Distribution, 72–73, 77–78. *See also*
    Circulation, newspaper
Distribution Systems of America (DSA),
    189
Dividends, Times Mirror Company,
    90–92, 94–95
Dole, Robert, 81
Donahue Paper Corp. of Canada, 107
"Do not call" list, 212
Dowdle, Jim, 109, 119, 163, 165–167,
    345
Dow Jones & Company, 61. *See also Wall
    Street Journal*
Downing, Kathryn, 86, 101, 126
Drudge, Matt, 5, 323
Drudge Report, 5
Dubois, Jules, 105
Duff & Phelps investment bankers, 110
Duplication of content, 208

E
"Editing by referendum," 176
Editor-reporter tension, 143
Edward, Edwin, 155
Eisenhower, Dwight D., 45
*el Periodico*, 316
*El Vocero de Puerto Rico* newspaper, 190
EPIC (End Poverty in California)
    platform, 45
Epton, Bernie, 35
Equity Group Investments (EGI), 258,
    285
Equity Office Properties, 257
Erburu, Robert, 88, 90–91
Erdoğan, Recep Tayyip, 178–179
ESOP (employee stock ownership
    plans), as funding instrument,
    259–261
Estate taxes, 26, 61. *See also* Chandler
    family
Ethics policy, at *Chicago Tribune*,
    147–148
Evening newspapers, decline of, 57–58

**F**
Facebook.com, 338
"Failure of the Death Penalty in Illinois"
    (Armstrong, Possley, and Mills),
    136
Family paper content, 208
Fax machine, 40
Feder, Robert, 339
Federal Aviation Administration (FAA),
    139, 142
Federal banking regulations, 282
Federal Communications Commission
    (FCC), 119, 165, 168, 262–263,
    304
Federal Reserve, 31
Federal Reserve Bank of Minneapolis, 3
Feldman, Larry, 149, 319
Field, Marshall, 35
Field family, 21
Fifteen Minutes public relations, 312
Financing schemes, for newspaper
    industry, 256
Finke, Nikki, 232
FitzSimons, Dennis J., 163–179
    cash needs in Zell deal and, 280–281
    centralization of editorial decision
        making and, 208
    Chandler family tensions with, 225
    control by, 215
    cost-cutting pressure on, 203
    as Dowdle's right-hand man,
        167–168
    golden parachute of, 304–305
    Internal Revenue Service challenges
        to, 222
    Kotter and, 287
    at KTLA party, 295
    market-driven journalism and,
        168–171, 174
    on McCormick Foundation board,
        345
    Newsday circulation fraud case and,
        197
    on page one ads, 270, 277
    refusal to meet with Turkish prime
        minister, 178–179
    Rumsfeld and, 178
    as Tribune Company CEO,
        171–174
    in WGN-TV advertising sales,
        163–164
    as WGN-TV head, 164–166
    on Zell proposal, 263–264
    Zell relationship with, 288–289
    zoned local sections, preference for,
        276
Flansburg, James, 25
Foley, Harold, 181, 189
Food and Drug Administration (FDA),
    150–151, 160
Ford, Gerald, 1
Ford, Henry, 37
Fordham University, 164
Fort Dodge Messenger, 20
Fox Broadcasting, 167
Fox News, 178, 323
Frankel, Max, 127
Frantz, Douglas, 35, 227, 234–235, 251,
    267
Fraudulent conveyance charge, 346
Freedom of Information Act, 140
Front Page, The (Hecht and MacArthur),
    18
FUDGE ABC software program, 181,
    189
Fuller, Jack
    background of, 112–113
    Carroll hired by, 149
    Newsday circulation fraud case and,
        192–193, 197
    News Values by, 128, 203
    resignation of, 201, 204–205
    Zell acquisition and, 289

**G**
"Gag Law," McCormick challenge to,
    38–39
Gannett, Frank, 61
Gannett Corporation, 6, 112, 133, 188
Gannett Newspaper Group, 61, 89
Garcia, Robert, 190, 224

Gartner, Michael, 25–26
Geffen, David, 215–216, 226–227, 236,
    289, 298, 308
Gehry, Frank, 48
General Mills, Inc., 3, 86–87
Giaimo, Joseph O., 182, 189, 191, 193,
    196, 200, 288
Gibson, Dunn & Crutcher law firm, 181
Giffords, Gabrielle, 338
Goldberg, Nick, 248
Goldman Sachs
    Chandler stock sale to, 278–279
    consolidation interests of, 102
    Times Mirror directors advised by,
        130–131
Google.com, 5, 274, 335
Graham, Katharine, 117
Graham, Philip, 41
Graham family, 21. *See also Washington
    Post*
Grant, Johnny, 243–244
Grazer, Brian, 247–248
Greeley, Horace, 37
Greene, Bob, 148, 322
Greenspun, Brian L., 339
Greenthal, Jill, 279
Greising, David, 171
Gremillion, Bob, 295, 327–329
Grenesko, Donald, 197, 285, 297, 302,
    304–305, 346
Grey Advertising, 164
Gridiron dinner, 117
Grumhaus, Hal, 65
Guggenheim, Harry, 183


H
Haider, Don, 109
Halberstam, David, 44–45
Hamill, Pete, 183
Harris, Ira, 110, 129
Harry N. Abrams publishing, 98
*Hartford Courant*, 133, 205
Harvard Business School, 287, 340
*Harvard Crimson* student newspaper, 341
Harvard University, 151, 333

Hearst, William Randolph, 3, 40, 94,
    115
Hecht, Ben, 18
Hiller, David
    background of, 236–238
    on Baquet speech at AP Managing
        Editors convention (2006),
        231–232
    blog of, 246
    as *Chicago Tribune* publisher, 199
    editorial pages reporting to, 245
    on FitzSimons as CEO, 172
    hiring freeze of, 306
    *Hoy* newspaper and, 194
    *Los Angeles Times* issues and,
        228–230, 298
    as McCormick Foundation CEO, 345
    *Newsday* circulation fraud case and,
        197
    O'Shea's firing and, 311–312, 314
    O'Shea's relationship with, 237–238,
        244–248, 277, 293
    staff cuts of, 240
    on strategically located news bureaus,
        275
    Times Mirror purchase idea of, 2,
        128, 134
    transformative change and, 287
    Zell deal cost cutting of, 279
    Zell's relationship with, 291
Hiltzik, Michael, 157
Hinckley, Gordon, 3
Hirt, Jane, 326, 331, 337
Hofmeister, Sallie, 268, 270
Hoge, James, 35, 107
Holden, Betsy, 303, 339
Hollywood Walk of Fame event,
    242–244
Holt, Margaret, 325
Homel, Benjamin, 323
Hood, Raymond, 6
Hoover, Herbert, 37
Hopper, Hedda, 39
Horrock, Nicholas, 78, 113, 117
Houlihan Lokey Howard & Zukin,
    285–286

*Houston Chronicle*, 198
Howard, Roy, 28
Howell, John, 6
*Hoy* LLC, fraudulent inflation of circula-
    tion numbers, 181–203
Huber, Craig, 281
Huntley, Chet, 59
Hurricane Katrina, 208, 219–220
Hussein, Saddam, 144
Hutchins Commission on the Freedom
    of the Press, 64


I
Ingrassia, Paul, 261
Inland Empire, 275–276
Insolvency, federal banking regulations
    and, 282
Inter American Press Association, 106
Interest rates in late 1970s, 31
Internal Revenue Service (IRS), 61, 196,
    222
International Creative Management,
    339
Internet
    *Chicago Tribune* content on, 118
    classified advertising affected by,
        246
    Classified Ventures and, 128
    Harry Chandler's interest in, 101
    LATimes.com 24-hour coverage on,
        273
    news industry response to, 4, 11
    newspaper impact of, 213
    print journalists vs., 272
    speed vs. accuracy on, 116
    traditional media business model
        and, 335
    Unterman view of, 132
Investment bankers. *See* Zell, Sam
Iraq
    Alford in, 334
    budget to cover, 204, 256
    Hussein victims in, 144
    local news vs. coverage of, 246
    war in, 177–178, 200

J
Jackson, Michael, 53
Jacobson, Darryl, 284
Jacor Radio, 323
Jain, Sanjay, 263
Jansen, Ray, 184–185, 191–192, 195,
    197, 199, 201
Jenner & Block law firm, 339
Joan Shorenstein Center on the Press,
    Politics and Public Policy at
    Harvard Kennedy School, 331,
    333, 341
John Birch Society, *LA Times* investiga-
    tion of, 46–47
Johnson, Jeffrey, 212, 216–217, 226,
    230
Johnson, Kim, 324
Johnson, Tom, 88–89
Jones, Bill, 27, 31
Jones, Tim, 108, 133
Jordan, Michael, 166
Journalism
    "anti-business," 26
    biased, unfair (McCormick), 37–39,
        65
    in Chicago, 28–29, 35. *See also*
        *Chicago Tribune*
    circulation declines and, 56–57, 199,
        274; *See also* Newspaper industry,
        decline of
    Columbia University School of
        Journalism, 30
    corporate, 62–67
    fundamental premise of, 126
    future of, 340–348
    "gods of," 116
    greed and business of, 4
    high standards in (Otis), 47–50,
        87–89
    Internet and, 335
    investigative, 30, 120–121
    Madigan distance from, 115–117
    Pew Research Center Project for
        Excellence in Journalism, 343
    market-driven, 79, 115, 168–171,
        174, 288, 300, 307, 337

meaningful, 209
politics and, 8
print vs. broadcast, 28–29
public service, 21, 341
Pulitzer Prize and. *See* Pulitzer Prize
Shorenstein Center at Harvard, 331, 333, 341
sloppy, 5, 146
tabloid, 35
University of Missouri School of Journalism, 15, 17
Washington, 29
"yellow," 18, 115
*See also Chicago Tribune; Des Moines Register; Los Angeles Times; New York Times; Orlando Sentinel;* and other named newspapers
Journalistic and business separation
Brumback on, 73–75
Erburu on, 88
Staples scandal and, 126–127
Willes on, 96–97
JPMorgan Chase, 260, 263–264, 269, 281, 283–284, 286, 296
"Junk" circulation, 198, 218, 334

K
Kamin, Blair, 207
Kapadia, Rajesh, 286
Kaplan, Todd, 253, 257, 263
Kaul, Donald, 24
Kellner, Jamie, 167–168
Kenney, Crane, 222, 256, 262, 286, 297
Kern, Gerould W.
centralized news desk idea of, 327–328, 330
as *Chicago Tribune* editor, 331, 336, 339
as *Chicago Tribune* metro editor, 207
at *Los Angeles Times*, 211
on natural disaster coverage, 220
staff reductions by, 212
synergy and, 208–210, 224
in Tribune Company, 207–208
Kessler, Robert E., 214

Kickbacks, 188–190
King, Pete, 49
King, Rodney, 49, 53
King, Roger, 167
King, Tom, 216
King & Ballow law firm, 107
King World Productions, 167
Kirk, Jim, 166, 331, 337
Kirkpatrick, Clayton, 29, 41, 46, 64–65
Klee, Kenneth N., 346
Kleiner Perkins, Inc., 118
Klunder, Jack
"junk" circulation reductions by, 285
as *Los Angeles Times* circulation manager, 214, 217–218
on *Newsday* circulation fraud, 197
Zell deal and, 306–307
Kneeland, Douglas, 56, 78
Knight, Frank, 71
Knight, Jack, 71–73
Knight, Timothy, 192, 194–196, 200
Knight Ridder Corp., 6
Knight Ridder Newspapers, 73, 133, 239
Koldyke, Martin (Mike), 342, 345
Kone, Korotoumou, 141, 142
Kotter, John, 287
Kotz, Nick, 23
Kraft Foods, 339
Kristof, Kathy, 51, 320
Kruidenier, David, 25–26
KTLA-TV, 165, 206, 294

L
Labor, organized, 107
Lance, Bert, 30
Landers, Ann, 39
*LA Observed* blog, 221, 235, 248, 295, 312, 319
*La Opinión* newspaper, 97
Lardner, Ring, 39
Larsen, Nils, 259, 276, 278, 285, 295–296, 306, 310
Larson, Jimmy, 19
*Las Vegas Sun*, 339
LATimes.com, 272

Laventhol, David, 89–90
Lawson, Victor, 186
Lee, Jimmy, 283, 303
Lee, Steven, 100, 213, 217–218
Legal publishing, 98, 101
Lehman Brothers, 281, 331
Leonard, Joe, 121, 136
Leveraged buyout, 261
Leveraged recapitalization (stock buy-
    back), 223–224, 253
*Lexington Herald-Leader* (Kentucky), 151
LexisNexis database, 135
Liebling, A. J., 6, 28, 34
*Life* magazine, 21, 25
Lincoln, Abraham, 37
Lipinski, Ann Marie
    Chicago News Cooperative (CNC)
        and, 348
    as *Chicago Tribune* deputy managing
        editor, 120–121
    as *Chicago Tribune* editor, 205
    ethics concerns of, 147
    FitzSimons and, 177
    front-page ad opposition of, 295–296
    merger and, 133
    O'Shea's alliance with, 137–139
    Pate and, 310
    Pulitzer Prize of, 155
    resignation of, 329–330
    Zell's meeting with, 320–321
Lipton, Marty, 262
Loan-packaging deals, 256
Local news, 175, 207–208, 275
Lombardo, Joey "The Clown," 146
*Long Beach Telegram*, 212
*Long Island Press*, 214
*Look* magazine, 21
Lopez, Steve, 226, 267, 291
*Los Angeles Daily Business Journal*, 127
*Los Angeles Times*
    advertising campaign of, 97
    bilingual sections of, 97
    correspondents of, 29
    history of, 43–47. *See also* Chandler
        family
    profit margins of, 140

    as publicly held corporation, 62
    Pulitzer Prizes of, 53, 215, 302
    Republican Party and, 45
    status of, 7–8
    *See also* Merger, of *Chicago Tribune*
        and *Los Angeles Times*
*Los Angeles Times Magazine*, 272, 310
*Louisville Courier-Journal*, 112
Low, Prescott, 60
Luce, Henry, 37


M
MacArthur, Charles, 18
MacArthur Foundation, 345
Madigan, John, 105–121
    advantages of, 109–111
    AOL investment sold by, 120–121
    as "bargain hunter," 119–120
    as Brumback successor, 107–108
    as *Chicago Tribune* publisher,
        112–115
    demeanor of, 106–107
    distance from journalism of, 115–117
    Fidel Castro and, 105
    on McCormick Foundation board,
        345
    Squires' view of, 82
    succession plan of, 171–173
    as Tribune Company CFO, 111–112
    Unterman's removal from board by,
        223
    Willes' meeting with, 1–3, 6, 8–9,
        103
    *See also* Merger, of *Chicago Tribune*
        and *Los Angeles Times*
*Madill Record* (Oklahoma), 258
Madison Dearborn Partners, 255
Madore, James, 214
Maharaj, Davan, 280, 293, 301
Majeri, Tony, 345
Mandula, Mary Jo, 324, 326
Market-driven journalism, 288, 337. *See
    also* FitzSimons, Dennis J.
Market-selection logic, 169
Marro, Tony, 183

Martinez, Andrés, 247–248, 310
Martin Luther King, Jr./Drew Medical
    Center investigation, 161
Marzullo, Vito, 146
Mastro, Randy M., 181
Matthew Bender Company, 98, 222
Maucker, Earl, 224
Mauskopf, Roslynn, 322
Maxwell, Robert, 107
McCarthy, Joseph, 29, 38
McClatchy publishing chain (Sacra-
    mento), 239
McCormick, Robert Rutherford
    conservatism of, 39
    "Gag Law" challenge of, 38
    legacy of, 2, 6, 21
    media acquisitions of, 40
    phobias of, 36–38
    *Tribune* structure and, 39–40
    *See also Chicago Tribune*
McCormick family, 35
McCormick Foundation, 255–256,
    261–262, 345
McCormick Trust, 41, 279
McCrohon, Max, 71
McDougal, Dennis, 87–88
McKinley, William, 44
McManus, Doyle, 318
McManus, John H., 169
McNiff, Leonard, 33
McNulty, Tim, 177
Medill, Joseph, 36
Medill family, 21
Merger, of *Chicago Tribune* and *Los
    Angeles Times*, 123–134
    Chandler family involvement in,
        125–126, 129–131
    independent directors and, 131–132
    industry reaction to, 133–134
    rumors of, 123–124
    Staples scandal, 126–129
    Willes surprised by, 124–125
Merriam, Frank, 45
Merrill Lynch
    due diligence requirements of,
        296–297

on ESOP as funding vehicle, 260–261
    merger brokered by, 129, 134
    on newspaper future, 254–255
    resignation as Tribune strategic
        adviser, 263
    as "Sam's bank," 256
    stock buyback funds from, 269
Meyer, Barry, 167–168
Meyer, Eugene, 41
Meyer, Rick, 154
Meyer family, 21
*Miami Herald*, 154, 198
Michaels, Randy
    behavior of, 338–339
    in charge of Tribune operations, 323
    cutbacks of, 336
    fearful atmosphere created at Tribune
        by, 328
    "fun" ideas of, 326
    Lipinski and, 330
    O'Shea meeting with, 299
    road show idea of, 317–318
    as "shock jock," 289
Miller, Marjorie, 301
Miller, Paul, 61
Mills, Steve, 136–137
*Minneapolis Star Tribune*, 239
Minow, Newton, 119, 342, 345
"Miracle Merchants, The" (Anderson),
    140
"Misery merchants," ambulance compa-
    nies as, 27
Mohr, Christina, 261, 263
Mollenhoff, Clark, 23
Monopoly control, in one-newspaper
    towns, 28–29
Monster.com, 158
Montorio, John, 158, 227, 250, 295
Moré, José, 141, 144
Morgan Stanley, 102, 255–256, 260, 263,
    302–303
*Morning Call* (Allentown, Pennsylvania),
    133
"Morning in America" (Reagan cam-
    paign), 55–56
Mosby, Inc., 98, 222

Moyers, Bill, 183
Mullen, Pat, 172–173
Mulligan, Tom, 164
Murdoch, Rupert, 36, 107, 283
Murphy, David, 275
Murphy, Tom, 142
Mutual Broadcasting System, 39

N
Nassau County (N.Y.) Sheriff's Office,
    196
National Academy of Recording Arts
    and Sciences, 157
National Basketball Association (NBA),
    166
*National Journal*, 98
National Public Radio, 11
NATO, 38
Natural disasters, coverage of, 219–220
Nepotism policies, 324
Neuharth, Allen, 61, 112
New Century Network (NCN), 4–5,
    118
New Deal, 37
Newmark, Craig, 5
*New Orleans States-Item*, 155
*Newport News* (Virginia), 133
News-aggregation websites, 5
Newscorp, 131
*Newsday*
    circulation investigation by, 214
    duplication of effort in, 209
    fraudulent inflation of circulation
        numbers, 181–203
    Laventhol as editor of, 89–90
    national and foreign staffs of, 221
    New York City edition attempts of,
        92, 174
    Patterson start of, 41, 91–92
    synergy with, 206
    on Times Mirror sale, 91–92
    as Tribune newspaper, 133
News literacy, 59
Newspaper Association of America
    (NAA), 1, 5, 103, 213

Newspaper industry, decline of, 55–67
    corporate takeover and, 61–67
    economic issues in, 56–57
    printing technology changes and,
        60–61
    television impact on, 58–59
    workforce dynamics and, 57–58
Newspaper in Education (NIE)
    programs, 198
Newspapers as community leaders, 143
Newsprint operations, 107
Newsroom leaks to blogs, 235–236
"News that readers value," 208
*News Values* (Fuller), 128, 203
New Trier Township High School, 109
*New York Daily News*, 40, 107
*New Yorker* magazine, 6, 28
*New York Evening World*, 28
*New York Newsday*, 92, 174
*New York Post*, 183
New York Stock Exchange, 304
*New York Times*
    Baquet hired away from, 154–155
    buyouts and layoffs at, 226, 334
    Chicago News Cooperative (CNC)
        and, 344–345
    on *Chicago Tribune* management
        conduct, 339–340
    *Los Angeles Times* vs., 45
    Montorio hired away from, 158
    New York Times Company, 131
    online news service of, 118
    as publicly held corporation, 62
    staff size of, 137
    Staples scandal and, 126–127
    stature of, 28
    website of, 134
    Zeleny hired by, 222
New York University, 333
Ney, Elisa, 310
Nieman fellows, 333–334
Nieman Foundation, Harvard University,
    151
Nixon, Richard M., 8, 109
Nondifferentiating content, 208
Non-disparagement clause, 316, 319

Northern Trust Company, 254
Northwestern University, 36, 109
"No shop" clause, in merger deal,
      130–131

O
Obama, Barack, 37, 333, 337
Ober, Eric, 105
Objective reporting, 29
Ochs family, 21. *See also New York Times*
O'Connor, John Joseph (Cardinal), 107
O'Connor, Flannery, 7, 142
Oklahoma Press Hall of Fame, 258
Oneal, Michael, 251, 337
*Oprah Winfrey Show*, 167
Orlacchio, Anthony, 189–190
*Orlando Sentinel*, 70–71, 75–76, 133,
      209, 220, 318
Osborne, Hank, 51
Osborn, William, 254, 263, 303, 330,
      339
O'Shea, James
   background of, 17
   Baquet replaced by, 228–229
   as *Chicago Tribune* foreign and
      national news editor, 113
   at *Chicago Tribune* Washington, D.C.,
      bureau, 55–57
   at *Des Moines Register*, 15–17, 30–31
   firing of, 311–312, 314
   foreign and national news staff
      reductions by, 221
   as *Los Angeles Times* editor, 233. *See
      also* O'Shea, James, at *Los Angeles
      Times*
   Michaels' meeting with, 299
O'Shea, James, at *Los Angeles Times*, 233
   controversies and, 250–252
   cost-cutting pressure on, 238–242,
      248–250
   difficulties as, 236–237
   Hiller's relationship with, 237–238,
      244–248, 277, 293
   Hollywood Walk of Fame event,
      242–244

newsroom leaks to bloggers, 235–236
   newsroom suspicions, 234–235
   public trust and, 238
Osnos, Peter, 342
Otis, Harrison Gray, 3, 43
*Our Iceberg Is Melting* (Kotter), 287

P
Page, Larry, 5
Page one ads, 270, 277
PageRank algorithm, 5
Paid-content strategy, 213
Palmer, Kyle, 45
Paper mills, 106–107
Parker, Bill, 345
Parks, Michael, 87, 96, 124, 149
Parsons College, 24
Parvaz, Dorothy, 340
Pate, William, 258–261, 276, 278, 289,
      295–296, 310, 339
*Patriot Ledger* (Quincy, Massachusetts),
      60
Patterson, Aaron, 137
Patterson, Alicia, 41, 183
Patterson, Eleanor "Cissy," 40
Patterson, Joseph, 40, 107
Patterson, Thomas E., 341
Patterson family, 21
Payola investigation, 157
Pearlstine, Norm, 215
"Penguin parable" (Kotter), 287, 294–295
Pension plans, of Tribune employees, 255
Perelman, S. J., 44
Persily, Julie, 260, 263
Pew Research Center Project for Excel-
      lence in Journalism, 343
*Philadelphia Inquirer*, 116
Philips, Chuck, 157
Phillips, John, 324, 338
Photocomposition process, 60
Possley, Maurice, 136
Pouchie, Michael, 189–190
*Powers That Be, The* (Halberstam), 44–45
Preferred stock, Times Mirror Company,
      91–92

Princeton University, 58, 70
Prior, Markus, 58
*Privileged Son* (McDougal), 88
Production, newspaper, 72
Profit margins, newspaper, 139
Profit-sharing plans, of Tribune employees, 255
"Project Prosperity" (Squires), 82
Prosecutorial misconduct, 135
PublicAffairs, 342
Public service institutions, newspapers as, 21
Puerner, John, 133, 151, 153, 155, 211–212
Pulitzer, Joseph, 28, 115
Pulitzer Prize Gold Medal, 161
Pulitzer Prizes
    Carroll's pursuit of, 160
    of *Chicago Tribune*, 7, 155, 203, 207
    of *Des Moines Register*, 18, 23
    of *Los Angeles Times*, 53, 215, 302
    of publicly held newspapers, 63
    of *Washington Post* for Watergate story, 30

R
Racketeering. *See* Circulation, newspaper
Radio industry payola investigation, 157
Raffensperger, Gene, 15, 19
"Reading by 9" children's program, in *Los Angeles Times*, 97
Reagan, Ronald, 31, 55, 164
Real estate advertising decline, 254
Reardon, John, 305
Recession of late 1970s, 31
*Redeye* newspaper for young people, 146–147, 326
Reily, Sean, 250, 306
Reinsdorf, Jerry, 166
Renaissance Communications, 166
Republican Party, 7, 36–37, 170
Reuben, Don, 35
Reynolds, Frank, 59
Rezulin diabetes drug investigation, 150, 160

Risser, James, 23, 31
Rivera, Geraldo, 167, 178
Roberts, Gene, 116
Roberts, Millard, 24
Roderick, Kevin, 221, 235, 319
Roosevelt, Eleanor, 38
Roosevelt, Franklin Delano, 37–38
Ross, Polly, 242, 271, 310
Royko, Mike, 31, 36
Rukeyser, Louis, 164
Rumsfeld, Donald, 109, 177–178, 233
Rustic Canyon Partners, 132, 255
Rutten, Tim, 94
Ryan, George, 136–137

S
Salomon, Bob, 111
Salomon Brothers, 110–112
Salopek, Paul, 144–145, 322
*San Jose Mercury News*, 198
Sarbanes-Oxley Act of 2002, 212
Save the Children Federation, 141, 142
Savings and loan scandal, 113
Schermerhorn, James, 63
Schiller, Jay, 188
Schlessinger, Laura, 1
Schlosberg, Richard T., III, 90–91, 95
Schwartz, Maralee, 333
Schwarzenegger, Arnold, 95, 236
S corporation, *Chicago Tribune* as, 259
Sears, Pete, 188
Sease, Cindy, 5
*Seattle Post Intelligencer*, 340–341
Secondary syndication markets, 296
Secret Communications, 339
Securities and Exchange Commission (SEC), 196–197, 304
"Securitizing" loans, 256
September 11, 2001, attacks, 139
Shah of Iran, 31
Shakur, Tupak, 320
Shapiro, Mark, 339
Shaw, David, 124, 127
Short sellers, 281

"Show doctors" (media consultants), 168

Shriver, Maria, 236, 310

Sidley Austin law firm, 129, 131, 134, 193, 202, 238, 255

Simon, David, 160

Simpson, O. J., 53

Sinclair, Upton, 45

Sito, Louis, 183–185, 189–191, 197, 201, 224, 322

Six Flags Entertainment, 339

Skadden & Arps, 192

Sloan, Allan, 91

Smith, Ed, 189, 224

Smith, Richard Norton, 37

Smith, Scott, 142, 177, 204, 225, 329, 345

Solomon, Digby, 194, 199

Solvency opinion, 282, 297, 346

Soriano, Alfonso, 321

South Florida Sun-Sentinel, 133, 209, 224, 321

Spears, Britney, 169

Springer, Jerry, 167

Spring Street Project, 272

Squires, Jim, 56, 71, 81–83, 112

St. John's Law School, 191

St. Louis Post Dispatch, 29

St. Louis Star, 28

Stanford University, 5, 45, 101, 266

Stanton, Russ, 273, 293, 299, 306, 312, 319

Staples scandal, 126–129, 236

Stephens, Mitchell, 333

Stern, David, 166

Stewart, Potter, 238

Stinehart, William, 224, 253–254, 279

Stock buyback, Times Mirror, 223–224, 253

Stone, W. Clement, 109

Strikes, newspaper, 107

Stumbo, Bella, 50

Subprime mortgage meltdown, 254, 280

Sulzberger, Arthur, 117

Sulzberger family, 21. See also New York Times

Sunday opinion section, Los Angeles Times, 247

Super-voting status, of Chandler stock, 129–131

Syndication, 280

Synergy, 166, 206–208

T

Taft, Robert, 45

Tax avoidance schemes, 99

Tax cuts, in Reagan presidency, 55

Teamsters Union, 76

Technology, newsroom, 80

Television
  newscasts, 29
  newspapers affected by, 57–59
  "vast wasteland" comment on, 119
  "watchdog" reports on, 170

"Ten for Ten" programs, 217

Thomas, Bill, 89

Thorpe, Caroline, 287

Time Inc., 215

Times Mirror Company, 1, 39, 89–90. See also Chandler family; Merger, of Chicago Tribune and Los Angeles Times

Times-Picayune (New Orleans), 155

Time Warner Corporation, 102

Toolen, Sean, 32

Transformative change, 287, 295, 327

Traugott, Michael, 333

"Trial and Error" series on death penalty cases, in Chicago Tribune, 135–136

Tribune Broadcasting. See FitzSimons, Dennis J.

Tribune Company, 1, 111–112, 280–281. See also Merger, of Chicago Tribune and Los Angeles Times

Tribune Interactive, 324

Twarowski, Chris, 214

Two percent list, of ABC, 217–218

Tyner, Howard, 120, 170–171, 205–206

**U**

Unions, 107
United Media Distributions, Inc.,
    189–190
United Nations, 37
University of Chicago, 259
University of Illinois, 337
University of Iowa, 62
University of Michigan, 109–110, 258,
    333
University of Missouri School of
    Journalism, 15, 17
University of Southern California
    (USC), 48
Unterman, Tom, 98–99, 128, 131–132,
    223, 255
U.S. Postal Service, 196
*USA Today,* 89, 134, 188

**V**

Valuation Research Corp. (VRC),
    285–286, 297
Van, Jon, 24
"Vast wasteland," television as, 119
Viacom International, 164
Volcker, Paul, 31
Vonnegut, Kurt, 31
Vreeburg, Elisabeth, 191

**W**

Wagner, Robert F., 191
Wall Street impact on newspaper
    industry, 256
*Wall Street Journal*
    on *Chicago Tribune* children's chari-
        ties investigation, 143
    Gartner hired from, 25
    Murdoch's acquisition of, 283
    O'Shea's firing in, 312
    page one ads in, 270, 277
    Pearlstine at, 215
    as publicly held corporation, 61
*Wall $treet Week* (Rukeyser), 164
Walsh, John, 142

Walt Disney Company, 78
Walt Disney Concert Hall, 48
Walter, John, 169
Ward, Arch, 39
Warner, Jack, 216
Warner Bros. TV, 167
Warner-Lambert, Inc., 150
Warren, Earl, 46
Warren, Jim, 170
Washington, Harold, 35
*Washington Post*
    Bennett at, 301
    Graham family's purchase of, 41
    layoffs at, 226
    as publicly held corporation, 62
    Pulitzer Prize for Watergate story, 30
    Schwartz at, 333
    stature of, 28
*Washington Times Herald,* 40
"Watchdog" reports, television, 170
Watchell & Lipton law firm, 262
Watergate scandal, 30, 65
Weinstein, Henry, 126
Weinstein, Jack, 201–202, 322
Weinstein, Moses "Mo," 191
Welch, Robert, 46
WGN, 38, 40, 120, 163–166, 330
Whayne, Thomas, 260, 263
Whistle blowers, 199
Willes, Mark Hinckley, 85–103
    assets sold by, 93–94
    as *BusinessWeek* "Manager to Watch
        in 1996," 94
    Chandler family recruitment of,
        89–92
    Chandler family tension with, 99–101
    circulation increases by, 97–99
    consolidation pressure and, 102–103
    consultant use by, 86
    job reductions by, 92–93, 100–101
    on journalistic and business separa-
        tion, 96–97
    Madigan's meeting with, 1–3, 6, 8–9,
        103
    political activities of, 95–96
    price reductions by, 93

Wolinsky's meeting with, 85–86
*See also* Merger, of *Chicago Tribune*
    and *Los Angeles Times*
Williams, Griff, 109
Williamson, Fred, 102
Willman, David, 150–151, 160
Winchell, Walter, 38
*Wire, The* (Simon), 160
Witt, Howard, 220
Wolinsky, Leo
    background of, 43, 47–48
    on Baquet, 156, 227
    budget cuts after Zell deal by, 310
    City County desk and, 52
    as city editor, 53
    firing of, 336
    Geffen's meeting with, 236
    Hiller's discussion with, 293
    Hiller's query about, 230
    journalistic standards of, 49–52
    Los Angeles knowledge of, 48–49
    *Los Angeles Times* career of, 8
    merger view of, 10, 123–124, 149, 152
    production knowledge of, 85
    on synergy issues, 211
    on Willes, 86, 98
    workplace changes and, 154
*Women's Wear Daily*, 78
Wood, Frank, 339
Wood, Henry, 32
Woodward, Bob, 30
World Vision U.S., 143
Wright, Jim, 81
WTTW public television, 342


Y
Yahoo.com, 101
"Yellow journalism," 18, 115

Z
Zamora, José, 316
Zeleny, Jeff, 222
Zell, Sam
    acquisition debt sale issues, 283–284
    background of, 257–258
    Chandler stock sale and, 279
    *Chicago Tribune* bid of, 258–259
    as *Chicago Tribune* investor, 251
    cost cuts required by, 266–267
    cutbacks of, 336
    ESOP use by, 259–261
    FCC approval and, 262–263
    FitzSimons' relationship with,
        288–289
    Hiller's relationship with, 291, 298
    investment banker interest in, 257,
        263–266
    Lipinski's meeting with, 320–321
    *Orlando Sentinel* visit of, 318
    plans of, 267–268
    profane language of, 317–319
    solvency opinion and, 346
    staff decisions of, 303
    "Talk to Sam" initiatives, 325–326
    as Tribune Company chairman, 339
    Tribune Company consideration by,
        253–254
    Tribune Company revenues and,
        276
Zimbalist, Efrem (Skip), III, 98, 125,
    131, 153
Zocalo cultural forum (Los Angeles),
    274
Zoned local sections, 275
Zoning strategy for local news, 207
Zuckerman, Mort, 108
Zyman, Sergio, 1

Award-winning journalist James O'Shea is former managing editor of the *Chicago Tribune* and past editor-in-chief of the *Los Angeles Times*, the nation's largest metropolitan daily. He is the founder and editor of the Chicago Newspaper Cooperative.

O'Shea has twice won both the Sigma Delta Chi Distinguished Service Award for Washington Correspondence and the Peter Lisagor Award from the organization's Chicago chapter. His honors also include the Associated Press Managing Editors' Public Service Award and the National Education Writers Award. Under his leadership, the *Tribune's* news staff received six Pulitzer Prizes. (Photo: José Moré)

PublicAffairs is a publishing house founded in 1997. It is a tribute to the standards, values, and flair of three persons who have served as mentors to countless reporters, writers, editors, and book people of all kinds, including me.

I. F. Stone, proprietor of *I. F. Stone's Weekly,* combined a commitment to the First Amendment with entrepreneurial zeal and reporting skill and became one of the great independent journalists in American history. At the age of eighty, Izzy published *The Trial of Socrates,* which was a national bestseller. He wrote the book after he taught himself ancient Greek.

Benjamin C. Bradlee was for nearly thirty years the charismatic editorial leader of *The Washington Post.* It was Ben who gave the *Post* the range and courage to pursue such historic issues as Watergate. He supported his reporters with a tenacity that made them fearless, and it is no accident that so many became authors of influential, best-selling books.

Robert L. Bernstein, the chief executive of Random House for more than a quarter century, guided one of the nation's premier publishing houses. Bob was personally responsible for many books of political dissent and argument that challenged tyranny around the globe. He is also the founder and was the longtime chair of Human Rights Watch, one of the most respected human rights organizations in the world.

· · ·

For fifty years, the banner of Public Affairs Press was carried by its owner Morris B. Schnapper, who published Gandhi, Nasser, Toynbee, Truman, and about 1,500 other authors. In 1983 Schnapper was described by *The Washington Post* as "a redoubtable gadfly." His legacy will endure in the books to come.

Peter Osnos, *Founder and Editor-at-Large*